A Pedagogy of Surprise

A Pedagogy of Surprise

Exploring Gifts, Wonder, and Gratitude in Curricular Settings

KEITH W. BROWN

Published by State University of New York Press, Albany

© 2025 State University of New York

All rights reserved

Printed in the United States of America

No part of this book may be used or reproduced in any manner whatsoever without written permission. No part of this book may be stored in a retrieval system or transmitted in any form or by any means including electronic, electrostatic, magnetic tape, mechanical, photocopying, recording, or otherwise without the prior permission in writing of the publisher.

Links to third-party websites are provided as a convenience and for informational purposes only. They do not constitute an endorsement or an approval of any of the products, services, or opinions of the organization, companies, or individuals. SUNY Press bears no responsibility for the accuracy, legality, or content of a URL, the external website, or for that of subsequent websites.

EU GPSR Authorised Representative:
Logos Europe, 9 rue Nicolas Poussin, 17000, La Rochelle, France
contact@logoseurope.eu

For information, contact State University of New York Press, Albany, NY
www.sunypress.edu

Library of Congress Cataloging-in-Publication Data

Name: Brown, Keith W., 1974– author.
Title: A pedagogy of surprise : exploring gifts, wonder, and gratitude in curricular settings / Keith Brown.
Description: Albany : State University of New York Press, [2025] | Includes bibliographical references and index.
Identifiers: LCCN 2024027045 | ISBN 9798855801248 (hardcover : alk. paper) | ISBN 9798855801262 (ebook) | ISBN 9798855801255 (pbk. : alk. paper)
Subjects: LCSH: Affective education. | Surprise. | Gifts—Philosophy. | Gratitude.
Classification: LCC LB1073 .B76 2025 | DDC 370.15/34—dc23/eng/20241106
LC record available at https://lccn.loc.gov/2024027045

Contents

Acknowledgments		vii
Introduction		1

Part I: Surprise

Chapter 1	Making Room for Surprise in the Classroom	21
Chapter 2	Teaching with Surprise	43
Chapter 3	The Four Pillars of Surprise	79

Part II: Gifts and Gratitude

Chapter 4	The Gift Paradigm	115
Chapter 5	Why Gratitude?	147
Chapter 6	The Tragic Side of Gratitude	169
Chapter 7	Four Gratitude-Based Metaphors	189

Part III: Applications in Teaching and the Classroom

Chapter 8	The Grateful Teacher: Exploring a Gifted Orientation in Classrooms	211

Chapter 9	Six "Gift Aporias": Core Conundrums in the Practice of Gratitude and the Gift in the Classroom	231
Chapter 10	Gift-Based Visualizations	253
References		283
Index		307

Acknowledgments

This book is dedicated to Venerable Master Sheng Yen as well as all the sangha and volunteers I have interacted with over the years at Dharma Drum Mountain Buddhist Association in Toronto, who have helped me on the path of learning meditation and the beautiful teachings of Chan Buddhism. I am also deeply inspired by my fellow meditation practitioners who have continued to inspire me on this journey.

Jack Miller, my doctoral thesis supervisor, has been the inspiration behind the current work. His presence not only inspired my doctoral thesis but continues to influence the way I think about education and how contemplation can be fostered in teachers to create long-term benefits, not only for classrooms but for teachers as well.

I am also deeply indebted to the following individuals who have played a crucial role in the thinking behind this manuscript: Kelli Nigh, Katherine Rehner, Heather Sykes, Jennifer Brant, Kathryn Broad, Kirby Mitchell, Janet Groen, Yishin Khoo, Suwimon Phaetthayanan, Jessie Chen, Yiran Zhang, Yukyung Kim-Cho, Selia Karsten, Tyler Walkland, Heesoon Bai, Patrick Finnessy, and Patricia Morgan.

To Mary Hess, whose Media Evangelism course and compassionate approaches to teaching have inspired me to explore the many ways in which teachers can envelop their classrooms with grace, prayer, and thankfulness.

Hue Pham, Hellen Zheng, and Lucy Guo—thank you for your continued kindness, friendship, and support in our shared spiritual practices.

Kelly Ann Zhang and Emma Lim for the continued dialogue, scholarship, and healing journeys of soul and mind.

Finally, I am thankful to my family and to Choujin (Judy) Wang for their kind love and support over the years.

Introduction

> A man is lost. He is confused about which way is north and which way south. He has a place he is trying to go but because of his confusion he can't get there. He feels disoriented and deeply uncomfortable. He has that sinking feeling of being lost, of not being in the place he wants and ought to be. But then he suddenly realizes there actually is no north or south—that these are just names people give to this way or that way, and that, no matter where he is, he is in fact here, where he has always been and will always be. Immediately, that man no longer has a feeling of being lost.
>
> —Norman Fischer, *When You Greet Me I Bow: Notes and Reflections from a Life in Zen*

Norman Fischer's remark about being lost dovetails with the main theme of this text: the enduring yet sometimes elusive power of surprise, gifts, and gratitude. If you've ever been lost, you are likely familiar with the sense of relief that comes over you when you find a familiar landmark that points you in the right direction. You may even have experienced the relief of finding a guide who will take you back to your true home. Similarly, the most pleasant surprises that teachers experience in their classrooms often arise from a sense of initial *derailment* or *disorientation*, in which the stated lesson does not always go according to plan and discrepancies emerge between the planning and delivery of curriculum (Dorovolomo et al., 2010). In fact, many teachers have experienced distinct moments in their careers in which being sidetracked from a lesson's stated purpose can lead to a more enriched and even much needed change in the direction of a class experience or learning path (Granziera et al., 2019; Palmer, 2017). Pre-service teachers often experience conflicts between attempting to plan a lesson in a linear fashion and factoring the uniqueness of the students' learning needs, which often cannot be known in advance of the lesson plan (Jensen & Rørbæk, 2022). Surprise can thus become an essential ingredient of the teaching path. In this text, I will suggest that teachers need to come well equipped with the means to not only cope with surprises but also tap into the unique strengths and opportunities that the emotion of surprise can offer to the classroom setting. This book will explore these potentials in greater detail, alongside the related themes of cultivating a sense of giftedness and gratitude toward classrooms and students.

Fischer is writing from a Zen Buddhist perspective. He relates how, in the context of his spiritual practice and tradition, the process of spiritual awakening is not found in the traditional ways of accumulating knowledge, seeking certain paths and refuting others. To the contrary, it can involve embracing the moment in which spiritual practitioners stop attaching to notions of where they should be or want to be in order to fully awaken to what is truly happening in the present moment. Here, notions of north and south, direction, and where one "ought" to go are relinquished in favor of a sense that one is truly at home where one *is*. In essence, thoughts about directions—which direction to travel, where one is going, or even where one is now in relation to the path—become irrelevant as one realizes that what they were looking for is here all along. To achieve this discovery, teachers must remain open to the possibilities that are presented and available within those moments. This is sometimes referred to as "being present," or cultivating a "bare awareness" (AnAlayo, 2019; Thera, 2008) in which one directly experiences moments using all the senses, rather than filtering an experience by way of memories or preconceived ideas.

Bringing a soft sense of compassion and kindness to this bare, non-judgmental awareness can deepen one's ability to non-reactively observe situations without rejecting difficult or challenging emotions (Nairn et al., 2019), which forms the cornerstones for the ability to "successfully regulate one's own emotions, thoughts, and behaviors in different situations" (McKown, 2019), a key principle of social-emotional learning (SEL). Research further suggests that the simple act of attending to the present moment with a sense of relaxed kindness (Binfet, 2022) can transform the way students and teachers alike approach learning (Whitehead et al., 2016). In addition, present moment awareness can stimulate the creativity needed to solve complex problems (Henriksen et al., 2020), which can, in turn, render classrooms more spontaneous and open to surprises (Munnich et al., 2019; Tiedens & Linton, 2001). One potential challenge to tapping into these surprises, however, is that teachers may lack the metaphorical grounding to trust, let alone reimagine, the classroom as a place where surprises can be transformative. In fact, as I shall argue throughout this text, teachers in today's classrooms are hemmed in by restrictive, exchange-based paradigms (Paricio, 2017) that oppose the notion that the classroom is a place of wonder, spontaneous learning, and constantly cycling gifts. For this reason, I have decided to write a book that explores the nature of surprise and the gift paradigm as it could potentially apply to educational settings.

Yet another important element of Fischer's quote is how feelings of loss often precede feelings of gratitude (Johnsen & Tømmeraas, 2022). That is, gratitude often arises when we thought we have irretrievably lost something, only to find it again in some other form, or through a process of internal reorientation. What, exactly, is the connection between gratitude and loss? Why, after all, would losing one's direction be followed by such an abrupt and life-changing moment as feeling at home? In this book, I would like to extend the analogy of the "lost individual" to suggest that perhaps the surprises of teaching are not too far away from a metaphor of being lost and found. For teachers to feel *surprised*, they may need to drop a lot of attachments to entrenched views about education that try to position learning as an outcomes-based process where one-size-fits-all, with few surprises. For teachers to feel *gifted*, they may need to let go of any clinging to the notion of the teacher as always being the giver, or someone lacking anything to truly receive in the way of gifts from their students. For teachers to feel *grateful*, they may need to drop deeply entrenched notions of teaching that privilege a standard template for how a classroom should go. Instead, they may need to learn to surrender to the classroom that is currently unfolding before their senses.

The purpose of this book is to suggest a preliminary roadmap for exploring how teachers can discover (or rediscover) the awe, wonder, and surprise that is already inherent to both being in a classroom and being a teacher.

Surprise, gifts, and gratitude are ideas that we don't often associate with education, particularly in the days of pen-and-paper tests, bell curves, and high-stakes admission to top schools. Recent studies suggest that teachers are spending a large percentage of time preparing their students for standardized tests, which restricts the possibility for authentic, spontaneous learning to happen in classrooms (Bausell & Glazier, 2018; Davis & Willson, 2015). Furthermore, the current test-centric climate of schooling appears to feed into the way education is often approached: simply as a form of vocational training performed in exchange for the guarantee of a paid profession. Henri Giroux (Giroux, 2014, 2020) has traced this recent turn in education back to an ideal that emphasizes profitability, prestige, and rankings over and above the ability to equip students to critically engage the social issues that could challenge social norms. Referring to the 2010 *Browne Review* to recommend changes to British higher education, Giroux identifies many key factors that tend to position higher education as a high-stakes, consumer-driven marketplace. Here, the notion of student choice takes precedence over learning itself, and institutions vie for each other for tuition fees and prestige:

> The report's guiding assumptions suggest that "student choice," a consumer model of pedagogy, an instrumentalist culture of auditing practices, and market-driven values are at the core of the new neoliberal university. Like most neoliberal models of education, higher education matters only to the extent that it promotes national prosperity and drives economic growth, innovation, and transformation. Tuition will be tripled in some cases. Numerous schools will be closed. Higher education will be effectively remade according to the dictates of a corporate culture. (Giroux, 2014, pp. 58–59)

Ironically, Giroux holds out hope that higher education can still expand students' ability to challenge existing social norms. He suggests, for example, that the university "is one of the few remaining institutions in which dissent, critical dialogue, and social problems can be critically engaged" (Giroux, 2014, p. 58). Yet in opposition to this hope are the entrenched views of the university that position students as paying customers (Bunce et al., 2017) or consumers who evaluate the "product" of teaching (Charteris & Smardon, 2019), while the schools themselves cater to an instrumentalist narrative of profitability and national growth (Blundell et al., 1999). Under such a climate, it is seldom admissible to allow for spontaneous interruptions or disruptions from the norm, as teachers carry out the business of preparing students for an individualistic marketplace predicated on competition and rankings. Yet without a sense of surprise, teaching and learning can easily be reduced to bland formulas in which teachers know the answers in advance and students in turn are simply expected to "get the right answers" to pass tests and be certified in their chosen profession.

In reality, all of professional life involves an engagement with the unknown and unexpected. At times, teachers themselves need to be prepared for situations that require responding without the requisite training to know just *how* to respond, or what Manen (2015) refers to as "pedagogical tact." This is especially the case when teachers are expected to teach in the most complex situations. How can surprise be encountered in a classroom that stresses predictability? Is surprise completely "unplanned," or can educators be trained or even encouraged to look for surprises in their students' work?

Surprise is intimately related to receiving gifts, and it can even enhance our memory and overall enjoyment of receiving a gift (Vanhamme et al., 2021). The capacity to be surprised is invoked whenever we receive a gift that was neither expected nor anticipated, when, for instance, someone gifts us without the intention of reward or exchange, or as an extension of the giver's heartfelt intentions (Belk & Coon, 1993). In contrast to receiving an expected credit or grade for performing a set task, surprising situations in classrooms can operate in ways similar to that of receiving a gift, by fostering a greater attentiveness to the unexpected or unfolding moment. Children from an early age are hardwired to pay greater attention to surprising or unexpected situations (Kagan, 2002), which suggests that surprise is connected to memory, retention of knowledge, and overall learning. More so, the capacity to feel gifted, like surprise itself, need not be linked to specifically desired objects. This capacity can, in fact, be rooted in a specific way of thinking and being in the world—one that remains open to gifts that are abundantly provided without the need for a reciprocal or obligatory exchange. Covey (2013) refers to an *abundance mindset* as one in which gifts are freely given precisely because one perceives that there is enough to go around, and, by extension, one person's gifts do not entail the deprivation of another's. In education, abundance may refer to the variety of talents, abilities, and experiences that both students and teachers alike can bring to the classroom. A *scarcity mindset*, by contrast, pits one student against another, invoking a "survival of the fittest" mentality that promotes a sense of mistrust in addition to the hoarding of classroom resources. Distinguishing between the two mindsets of scarcity and abundance, Steffen (2009) notes:

> An abundance mentality allows one to share freely, while a scarcity mentality may promote hoarding. People who are afraid of losing what they have do not enjoy it, and since they are unwilling or unable to share it with others, no one else gets

> to enjoy it either. In addition, people who have an attitude of scarcity view their life through the lens of loss and begin to see only the losses, not the wins. Their experiences provide proof that the world is a tough place and that each person needs to make it on his or her own. The scarcity mentality can lead to resentment, fear, anxiety, or anger. It also prevents creative approaches to problems. (p. 67)

By fostering surprise and shifting toward a gift paradigm in the classroom, teachers and students not only learn to enjoy the gifts of others but can also trust the plenitude of their own inherent gifts. Such an attitudinal shift toward a gifting dynamic can promote a more cooperative and less competitive and resentful interpersonal dynamic. In contrast, a scarcity mindset most certainly restricts creativity, by discouraging risk-taking and thereby limiting the possibilities for generating solutions to multilayered problems.

For a gift paradigm to be successfully implemented in classrooms, teachers must embrace a crucial paradox—namely, that to go beyond an exchange-based model of learning, a gift cannot have a calculated outcome in mind, such as a grade, a score, or a credit. Thinkers such as Jacques Derrida (Derrida & Kamuf, 1992; Hénaff, 2019) and Jean-Luc Marion (2020) have examined the ways in which "the given" defies conventions of economic exchange by arriving without expectation of calculated returns. Derrida contends that in order for a gift to escape the logic of exchange or "debt" and thus be considered as freely given, the giver must not be tied to a calculated act of giving with a specific return in mind. In fact, the receiver of the gift must not feel indebted to any giver. Malo (2012) succinctly notes that, according to Derrida's philosophy of the gift, "for a gift to exist, there must be no reciprocity, return, exchange, counter-gift, and above all no debt. Otherwise the gift cannot escape the economic cycle" (p. 151). This entails that gifting relationships do not require the compulsion to give back, the latter of which would count more as a form of exchange than as a true gift. Marion (2020) clarifies this point further when he remarks:

> This means positively: the gift can never again be envisaged within the system of exchange, the reciprocity of which connects giver and givee and freezes it in presence. In this so-called economy of the gift, it is literally givenness on which one economizes by totally transforming its gift into a subsisting being present in permanence, endowed with value (use and/or exchange) and

finality (utility, prestige, etc.), produced or destroyed by efficiency and calculation, caught in the grips of its causes—in short, into a common being. Such a common being can never appear as a gift, not because the concept of the gift would be contradictory but because this being in no way falls within the phenomenality of the gift. (pp. 81–82)

Marion contends that for a gift to truly be given, it must give itself "without a return on the investment, without awards received in return" (p. 83), a point he refers to as the *poverty* of the gift. For Marion, gifts challenge and even subvert the logic of exchange, first by exuding the possibility of gratuity and second by opposing a logic of return. That is, a gift must be given precisely on its own terms, without ulterior motive or expectation of exchange, or "without interest, therefore without motive, on the basis of itself and by itself" (p. 83). This idea positions the gift as diametrically opposed to something that could be reciprocated, thus symbolically pointing to a far more mysterious interconnection between the giver and receiver that is fundamentally unearned.

Yet another paradox of the given is that even when it is indelibly ours to own and keep, we must continually rediscover it in our lives by truly realizing what we already have, here in this moment. In other words, the given is both already here in this moment and continually being revealed or uncovered as a novel surprise. Physician and mindfulness teacher Jon Kabat-Zinn (2020) connects this capacity to feel blessed by the given with mindfulness in general when he notes how people can only become open to surprises when they drop what they *presume* to know about the present moment:

> The mindful attitude beginners mind provides the richness of present-moment experience [which] is the richness of life itself. Too often we let our thinking and our beliefs about what we "know" prevent us from seeing things as they really are. We tend to take the ordinary for granted and fail to grasp the extraordinariness of the ordinary. To see the richness of the present moment, we need to cultivate what has been called "beginners mind," a mind that is willing to see everything as if for the first time. (Kabat-Zinn, 2020, para. 1)

The ability to feel gifted hinges on the ability to continually discover what is freely given. This is a tricky paradox that challenges two extremes: on the one hand, taking everything around us for granted, and on the other, being overly attached to things that are simply not ours to begin with—that is, things that aren't *presented* to us but exist in a far-off future that may never arrive. If students and teachers alike can learn to enjoy the given moment of learning in the classroom instead of seeking faraway prizes or rewards, they would spend much more time engaged in the unfolding learning process itself. In a similar vein, if teachers were better able to behold what is given and a gift in their classrooms, they could actively train their minds to enjoy the revealed surprises in their classrooms.

Surprise, as I shall later argue in this book, is a state of mind that can be actively fostered much like any other mental or physical skill. The good news, then, is that one does not need to wait for the right moment or opportunity to cultivate a sense of surprise.

As I will elaborate in subsequent chapters, surprise is predicated on an active trust that the world is full of gifts that are waiting to be opened, seen, unpacked, and savored. Surprise, giftedness, and feeling grateful are all intimately related to a deep sense of trust in the unfolding perfection of moments.

Connection with Social-Emotional Learning Approaches

The chief aims of this book dovetail with many findings in the theory of social-emotional learning (SEL), a recent theoretical framework that suggests strong correlations between effective learning and training in emotional awareness. SEL has been defined as "an educational model for improving social-emotional competences of all students and a long-term education program connecting school, home, and community" (Kim et al., 2022, p. 1). SEL research has blossomed in recent years, stemming particularly from the observation that standardized testing all too often neglects the nuanced emotional aspects of learning, such as emotional regulation and communication skills, in favor of "zero tolerance policies" (Cervone & Cushman, 2017, p. 4) that serve to punish students whose learning styles don't accord with standardized testing. Hylen (2022) suggests that rather than simply imposing punishments for students who act out negative emotions such as anger, frustration, and anxiety, teachers attempt to foster both within themselves and their students a respect and tolerance for difficult and challenging emotional states. Notes Hylen (2022), "Being EQ mature is reflected by how comfortable we are with sharing our feelings and allowing others to do so as well" (p. 30). When feelings are beheld and fully accepted, teachers and students alike are able to respond more positively and constructively toward them, as opposed to trying to suppress or expel those emotions through passive or aggressive behaviors.

CASEL (https://www.casel.org) identifies five aspects of SEL, many of which are embedded within a holistic model of learning that stresses the value of emotions in both retention and processing of information. These are relationships skills, social awareness (which includes the ability to empathize with those who differ from our own cultural narratives and positionality), self-management (the ability to effectively regulate emotions, thoughts, and behaviors), self-awareness, and effective decision making (Rimm-Kaufman, 2020, xxi–xxii). SEL theorists have demonstrated through various studies that SEL can be built into the structure of any classroom through sufficient classroom planning, goals, and strategies (Rimm-Kaufman, 2021, xxviii–xxx). Some psychotherapists such as Nichols (2009) see social-emotional skills, such as active listening, as the result of prolonged practice, rather than being inborn or inherent to certain personality traits. As Nichols suggests, "*The ability to listen rests on how successfully we resist the impulse to react emotionally to the position of the other*" (p. 119), which opposes a commonplace view that listening is a passive trait than cannot be developed through effort or discipline. Rimm-Kaufman (2020) has also suggested that active listening requires not only the ability to reconstruct the meaning of what the speaker has said but also "involves social awareness in that students need to take the perspective of and empathize with others" (p. 22). Active listening is not a monolithic trait that some people have and others don't. In fact, from an SEL perspective, a quality such as good listening involves mobilizing a combination of skills, including self-awareness, empathy, receptiveness, and critical thinking. The good news is that all these qualities can be actively cultivated.

What makes this present book different from traditional SEL approaches is threefold.

First, unlike a typical SEL focus on students, this book aims to help teachers especially to develop their own SEL through the practices of cultivating surprise and actively seeking the hidden (or not so hidden) gifts in their classrooms and students. The premise of this book is that once teachers cultivate mindsets of surprise, discovery, and gratitude, these dispositions will eventually expand and color classroom dynamics through emotional contagion, "the primary mechanism through which emotions are shared" (Powell & Kusuma-Powell, 2010).

Second, rather than focusing on evaluative approaches to retooling classrooms with SEL-friendly cites of sharing and learning (McKown, 2019), this book aims to equip teachers with the ability to cognitively reframe their students and classrooms as gifts. Once teachers can reframe their students and classrooms through a gift-based mindset and metaphor, students too will reflect the teachers' curiosity and surprise, thereby fostering a greater sense of belonging and community in the classroom.

Third, a surprise-based pedagogy goes beyond simply "being present" to embracing the unknown future with a sense of hope and anticipation. Part of this involves training the mind to "disengage from the habit of compulsive thinking that pulls us into the past and future, and to root our attention in the present moment" (Nairn et al., 2019, p. 23). However, a surprise-based pedagogy extends the skill of "being present" toward delighting in the "still to come," or a sense of continually emerging and unfolding gifts. Using surprise-based pedagogy can help teachers become more attuned to the inherently unexpected nature of future events as well as the hidden surprises found in present experiences. This amplifies the uniqueness of each classroom experience, thereby preventing a sometimes monolithic or mundane sense of expectation and familiarity from enveloping the teacher's experience of their classrooms.

Some of the benefits of a surprise-based pedagogy and the gift also parallel some of the key goals embraced by SEL approaches to classroom management, namely,

- Fostering a sense of inclusiveness and belonging (Rimm-Kaufman, 2020, p. 5) by allowing teachers to find uniqueness in their students through an active and contemplative cultivation of surprise.

- Motivating students to achieve their best through a caring pedagogy that is grounded in heartfelt gratitude toward what students already bring to the classroom. When discussing the importance of care in fostering growth and learning in classrooms, Cervone and Cushman (2017) note, "Research backs up the educator's intuition and experience: students do their best for teachers who show they care" (p. 1).

- Enhancing the cultivation of emotional intelligence, specifically the ability to constructively use emotions to facilitate creative thought through a sustained reflection on novelty and discovery.

Mayer and Salovey (1997) define emotional intelligence as "the ability to access and/or generate feelings where they facilitate thought; the ability to understand emotion and emotional knowledge; and the ability to regulate emotions" (p. 10).

- Redefining the teacher's role as receiving and facilitating moments of surprise and discovery in the classroom, in which teachers "learn how to be participants rather than potentates in the classroom" (Cervone & Kushman, 2017, p. 62), and students, in turn, become teachers who share their experience and expertise. By positioning students as possessing gifts, teachers broaden their trust in the students' initiative and reposition teaching and learning as cyclic in nature—just as giving and receiving happens within reciprocal bonds of belonging and mutuality.

Rather than serving to replace SEL approaches, this book promises to enhance and, ultimately, complement the SEL literature through the lens of the gift economy, which goes beyond ideologies that typically position the students as "essentially good" (Rousseauian) or "essentially selfish" (Hobbesian), let alone the standard utilitarian or Malthusian belief that "children are perceived as either economic assets or liabilities" (Powell & Kusuma-Powell, 2010, p. 36). Through a gift-based view and philosophy, teachers will be able to cultivate a gap of *not knowing* who the student is or what she or he brings to the classroom situation. Furthermore, rather than being daunted or overwhelmed by the unknown, teachers will learn to develop the strong faith and curiosity to find out the surprises that are bound to lie within the student, only waiting to be revealed.

How This Book Originated

The theories and approaches outlined in this book stem from my doctoral thesis (Brown, 2022), which explored the effects of a gratitude visualization on how teachers assess their students' writing assignments. In this study, teachers were given a guided visualization, which I had prepared and delivered via mp3, that encouraged teachers to envision their students' writing as a gift. The teachers wrote reflections over a period of time in which they compared assessing their students' writing before and after the guided visualization.

Throughout this present book, I incorporate key findings from my doctoral thesis into the theories and ideas, suggesting how and why teachers were able to envision their students' contributions as gifts while also exploring key challenges to a gift orientation in the classroom.

Since I first joined a Chan Buddhist group in Toronto in 2006, I have developed a passion for using meditation to promote teacher well-being and development, having experienced the benefits of meditation in my own practices as a teacher and tutor. In 2013, I had the privilege of enrolling in the master's degree program in curriculum, teaching, and learning at University of Toronto's Ontario Institute for Studies in Education, where I later continued in the doctoral studies program, under the supervision of John P. (Jack) Miller. Jack Miller's tireless work in exploring the spiritual life of teachers under a holistic education paradigm has paved the way for this book. I am deeply thankful to Jack for the work he has done in teacher development and well-being.

Meditation, for me, has not only been a practice of calming the mind, as many would suggest, but has also provided me with insights into how suffering, stress, and vexations originate and can be alleviated through new insights into the mind. The meditations I have given teachers to explore are specific to core themes such as giftedness, gratitude, and loving kindness, all of which uplift a teacher's attunement to their own emotions as well as those of their students. I have written this book in the sincere hope that it will spark a curiosity for teachers to continue to explore the mind as a way to enhance their compassion (toward self and their students) as well as cultivate states of joy, even in the midst of the pressures that they face in today's classrooms. I certainly hope that this book will provide a starting point, or one of many chapters, in a teacher's personal journey through wellness, contemplation, meditation, and gratitude.

Structure of This Book

This book is divided into several interrelated chapters, which I will outline in detail in the following paragraphs. The chapters build on interlocking themes, which can roughly be categorized as surprise, giftedness, gratitude, and overall applications of these areas to the classroom.

Each of the chapters are grouped into three sections: "Surprise," "Gifts and Gratitude," and "Applications in Teaching and the Classroom."

Part I: Surprise

Chapter 1, "Making Room for Surprise in the Classroom," describes the current predicament in which many teachers find themselves, especially in modern Western educational settings. Looking closely at the recent applications of the marketing and "consumer-based" metaphors in classrooms, this chapter explores why the ideas of transmission and exchange often dominate current teacher-student relationships in North American educational settings, particularly tracing this view back to early twentieth-century ideas such as behaviorism and logical positivism. This chapter also shows how an educational system that focuses mainly on outcomes tends to suppress (or even exclude) a more organic way of being in the classroom that sees various elements of surprise, the unexpected, and everyday serendipitous moments. This chapter makes the case for a revision in the way teachers and students can interact in classrooms.

Chapter 2, "Teaching with Surprise," outlines the specific for a surprise-based pedagogy that stems from a greater sense of being gifted. Of particular importance in this chapter is the phenomenology of surprise, particularly detailing and unpacking such a phenomenology through the lens of Abraham Maslow's concept of the "peak experience" (Maslow, 1999) and Colin Wilson's "St. Neot's margin" experience (C. Wilson, 2016). This chapter outlines a few core elements of a surprise experience, with the support of current research on the psychology of surprise.

Chapter 3, "The Four Pillars of Surprise," takes a closer look at four elements that are central to surprise experiences—receptivity, empathy, discovery, and trust—especially as these elements pertain to surprise in education. After describing each of the four "pillars" and their theoretical framings, I lead the reader through a series of reflections, to do on their own or in groups, to foster a sense of how these elements of surprise can be applied to teaching situations and curricular settings. After reading about the four pillars, teachers will be more prepared to develop practices to cultivate surprise moments in the classroom. Throughout this chapter, I maintain key links between the theory of surprise I am proposing and real-world classrooms, exploring the relevance of the former to the latter.

Part II: Gifts and Gratitude

Chapter 4, "The Gift Paradigm," compares exchange- and gift-centered notions of education, with an emphasis on how they could be balanced and integrated in future curriculum. I suggest that shifting toward a gift model of education can allow for a greater sense of wonder and awe as well as an openness to surprise that cannot be reduced to something exchangeable, let alone easily quantified and predicted. As I suggest in this chapter, *giftedness* is not limited to exceptional circumstances or abilities. Instead, teachers can see gifts in practically every moment or situation, provided that they are able to cultivate a sense of receptiveness and acceptance of things as they are, even when they seem to go against the grain of the lesson plan.

Chapter 5, "Why Gratitude?," takes a deeper look at the relationship between gratitude and a surprise-based pedagogy. Drawing from research explored in my doctoral thesis on gratitude-based assessment practices (Brown, 2022), this chapter delves into the current educational research that centers around gratitude and its benefits to both teachers and students. Throughout this chapter, I explore different forms of gratitude in research and how they relate to the theme of giftedness introduced in the previous chapters, using current research to support new models of gratitude.

Chapter 6, "The Tragic Side of Gratitude," explores the connection between gratitude and tragedy. In this chapter, I attempt to answer the questions: Are feelings of gratitude and giftedness always about positive or pleasant experiences? How might a gift pedagogy expand to embrace the tragic elements of experience? Thus, I delve deeper into the question of whether gratitude always entails happiness and positive emotions, or, conversely, whether it can also embrace the sense of the tragic.

Chapter 7, "Four Gratitude-Based Metaphors," looks at four potential metaphorical framings through which gratitude, surprise, and giftedness can be cultivated through a revisioning of the classroom. This chapter is premised on the idea that in order for teachers to truly embody a gratitude orientation in their classrooms, they may need to experiment with different ways of relating to gratitude that stress concrete elements of giftedness, particularly through the exploration of key metaphors. By no means exhaustive, this chapter provides a small sample of potential metaphors that can be used to enhance the sense of giftedness and gratitude, particularly in classrooms. The core metaphors of tapestry, jewel net, fluid center, and holding space are explored respectively in this chapter.

PART III: APPLICATIONS IN TEACHING AND THE CLASSROOM

In chapter 8, "The Grateful Teacher: Exploring a Gifted Orientation in Classrooms," I examine some of the obstacles that may prevent teachers from seeing their classrooms as sources of surprise, gratitude, and gifts. In this chapter, I focus on what kinds of attitudes, both personal and systemic, might get in the way of fully appreciating gifts in the classroom or taking a gift-related approach.

In chapter 9, "Six 'Gift Aporias': Core Conundrums in the Practice of Gratitude and the Gift in the Classroom," I examine the unique and apparently insoluble paradoxes of a gift-based classroom, which I call "aporias." These paradoxes represent insoluble tensions that teachers navigate between a sense of giftedness and the pressures to teach according to current standards and market forces that impact education.

Chapter 10, "Gift-Based Visualizations" explores several practical visualizations that teachers can try in applying the principles of gratitude and gifts throughout the book itself. These visualizations can help ground teachers in a more felt sense of gratitude, wonder, and surprise than what could be accomplished through intellect or reflection alone. At the beginning of this chapter, I make the case for including visualization and relaxed meditation as an entry point to deeper feelings of giftedness encountered in the everyday.

How to Use This Book

The first few chapters of this book focus mostly on laying the theoretical foundation for a surprise-based pedagogy. Exercises will be interspersed both within and at the end of the chapters to give the reader a better sense of how the theories can be applied in educational settings. Readers are encouraged to have a notebook or scribble pad on hand to take notes as needed, draw images as they emerge, or actively engage in the reflections. The more you can stop and try the reflections, the more personalized you can make the learning itself. In chapter 10, you will have the opportunity to try out some guided meditations that explore gratitude, surprise, and gifts.

The exercises in this book consist of questions for discussion and questions for reflection. Questions for discussion are simple questions that intend to help the reader summarize key points made throughout the chapter, which could also become the focus of a book discussion group or tutorial. Questions for reflection, on the other hand, are more intended for personal reflection and review, as individual readers take time to quietly contemplate the concepts and how they can apply these to their practices as teachers, or even as learners.

While this book, like any of its kind, can be read in any order, it is best for the reader to start with the first four chapters to get a better understanding of the theories upon which subsequent sections will be based.

Special note on pronouns: Throughout this text, I have made efforts to use nonbinary ("they") or reference more than one gender (she or he) as opposed to a single gender. I have done so in the interests of ensuring that readers recognize that their preferred pronouns were properly and fairly represented throughout the text. I strongly believe that all genders deserve fair and honest representation, most especially in a text about teacher development and educating future generations of students to see the gifts that all of us bring into the world. On the other hand, please take note that texts from which I am quoting are referenced with their original gender pronouns, and no effort was made to correct these (including "*sic*" referencing), in the interests of keeping the original source text intact.

Questions for Discussion

1. What role might disorientation play in the learning and teaching cycle? Discuss an important time in your career, as a student or teacher, when you needed to experience disorientation, being lost, or lacking familiar reference points in order to make new connections with your learning.

2. When you hear the word "gifts," what associations, thoughts, or images come to mind? Are any of these images or associations connected with classrooms, schools, and other places of learning? How might learning be connected with the notion of gifts and giving? In what ways do you experience cognitive dissonance when trying to pair "gifts" with "education"?

Questions for Reflection

1. How trusting are you in the journey of teaching and learning? Consider a skill that took a long time for you to learn and was challenging to acquire (or are still trying to acquire to this day). Close your eyes and visualize what the experience of challenge and difficulty in learning the new skill felt like. You may even want to visualize the challenge through a drawing that represents the challenge either literally, metaphorically, or symbolically. After visualizing the experience, write a reflection on the following two points:

a. Were there times when you felt overwhelmed or discouraged and wanted to give up learning altogether? Write a reflection exploring what giving up felt like, and what reasons you had for wanting to give up.

   b. After reading the reflection you wrote in part *a*, consider how a trusting mindset would address the discouragement you experienced. Would being more trusting of your ability to learn the difficult skill or subject help you better learn or stay with the subject? What does trust look and feel like for you? What would it take for you to trust something you are not sure about or is unknown to you? Write a reflection exploring the possibilities of trusting what is unknown.

3. Think of a situation that accidentally helped you to overcome a challenge or solve a problem. This could be either an unplanned event or perhaps a planned downtime that allowed you to reframe a problem or challenge in a radically different way. Then reflect on the following:

   a. Did anything feel surprising or unusual when the solution came to mind? Was it a sudden "eureka" moment or a more gradual process of working out the problem? What kinds of processing or reflection did you engage in to arrive at the solution?

   b. Why might a detour from a standard or habitual process have been needed to arrive at the solution?

4. While many of our tastes in food, music, movies, and literature are seemingly inborn, others are acquired through a process of becoming exposed to a particular culture or body of work, often by accident or through a surprise encounter.

   a. Consider one particular taste that you acquired over the years as a result of a lucky accident, a conscious effort of cultivation, or a surprising, unexpected event. Describe the taste and how it grew into what it is today. You may even want to express this as a "chronology of taste" by drawing a timeline and noting the historical evolution of the taste you acquired.

      b. If possible, recollect when you were first exposed to that particular experience. Did you like it right away, or was it something you acquired gradually? To what extent did you need to give it time to grow on you?

5. After writing a reflection based on question 3, reflect on the following: To what extent are our current preferences hardwired? To what extent are they acquired through some kind of playful cultivation based on surprise, serendipity, and flow?

Part I
Surprise

Chapter 1

Making Room for Surprise in the Classroom

One of the more pervasive recent historical trends in North American schools has been to "standardize" testing and learning (Himelfarb, 2019; McNeil, 2000). A one-size-fits-all mentality pervades educational philosophies, wherein students' test results become the basis through which they move through the educational system in competition for position and top honors (Shindler, 2009; Daniels et al., 2020). What often results is a perception that a student's talents and abilities are exchangeable for another's, or can be quantified and compared with others within their cohort. From as early as kindergarten, children are often expected to complete tasks that are interchangeable with each other (Apple, 2018). Teachers, in turn, are often expected to show greater accountability (Cochran-Smith et al., 2018) for what's being learned in schools by preparing their students to succeed in standardized tests that are purported to measure a student's overall competencies, as compared with other students.

The ability to precisely measure learning outcomes is one of the most pervasive myths that arises from the recent trends in standardized testing, in which core competencies are reduced to scores on a test. But it's questionable whether a test can capture all forms of learning. Some studies have suggested that standardized tests force students to memorize facts instead of encouraging them to foster critical thinking skills (Krentler et al., 1994), while others point to how standardized tests reinforce inequities based on discrimination or socioeconomics (Camara & Schmidt, 1999; Grodsky et al., 2008). By focusing on preparing students to excel in predetermined competencies, teachers lack the time to teach innovatively and in accordance with their passions (Herman et al., 1994). These studies hardly support a model of student empowerment, let alone bolster the sense that tests accurately measure student potentials. Hylen (2022) refers to socio-emotional growth and student achievement as two competing claims that receive varying degrees of attention and support in classrooms, depending on how schools are evaluated. He thus notes how, even though schools tend to be judged only on "student achievement," "reliance on test scores and academic measurements alone do not represent a school's true impact on its students" (p. 9). And yet despite the emphasis on teaching for the sake of test scores, teachers still find themselves gravitating toward working with "students with social-emotional issues," even when they are "frustrated by the perceived lack of success they are having with students because of these traditional methods for measuring success and the pressure to produce high-scoring students" (p. 9). Hylen suggests that had teachers more time to devote to mentorship and addressing the emotional needs of students, their careers would be more fulfilling and invigorating.

Rather than allowing students to create assignments that are meaningful in themselves, standardized tests can pressure students to write according to predefined or preset standards of competency. Test taking has even been considered a "genre" unto itself (Hornof, 2008; Santman, 2002) whereby teachers invest as much time preparing students to handle the "features" of a test as they would, say, the classical genres of speech, poetry, and prose. This approach potentially straitjackets both students and teachers alike by forcing teachers to teach according to fixed models, instead of encouraging students to challenge these models or find new ways of expressing their ideas. Indeed, when we start to talk about standardized views of education, we are describing predetermined ideas of what constitutes good form and presentation. This trend moves away from the idea that learning might involve discovering new modes of expression or subverting existing genres. Standardized tests can thus encourage a numbing conformity to standard genres and modes of expression.

What is problematic about the notion that tests can measure learning? First, it fails to capture the recursive nature of learning. Learning has often been conceived as a cycle of feedback (Hanks, 2019) as opposed to a linear relationship that emphasizes the final evaluation over the process. By focusing more on results than on learning itself, teachers are pressured to prepare students for tests that "fix" or "determine" a student's future. There is little room in the curriculum for teachers to experiment or even change the pace of their teaching to match the students' needs. With looming pressures to prepare students for final tests, many students are not able to receive the help they need. The stress of teaching to the test leads to a neglect of nurturing connections, which becomes even more detrimental when students face discrimination and socioeconomic challenges outside the classroom. In their case study on Fenger High School, which is in one of the most violent neighborhoods in Chicago, Cervone and Cushman (2017) noted how the detrimental effects of "the unrelenting stress caused by extreme poverty, neglect, or abuse can weaken the architecture of the developing brain, with long term consequences for learning, behavior, and both physical and mental health" (p. 128). Without strong emotional rapport between teachers and their students, both cognitive neuroplasticity and the ability to adapt emotionally to new situations can be seriously compromised.

Standardized testing can also lead to depersonalization and a loss of the uniqueness that each student can bring to learning situations. The emphasis on teaching to the test can, indeed, prevent teachers from developing the social and emotional awareness to work with students of different races, ethnicities, and classes. As Rimm-Kaufman et al. (2023) have noted, "teachers do not automatically develop the skills needed to work with students who are different from them—an issue that plays out in unfortunate ways, such as low expectations and disproportionate disciplining of students of color or students with disabilities" (pp. 18–19). Classes are no longer catered to the needs of the individual student. In fact, there is simply little time (Stotsky, 2016), as teachers are strained to prepare their students for standardized tests. This also negatively impacts the relationship between student and teacher (Brady, 2008). With a heightened pressure to prepare students for high-stakes testing, teachers no longer feel as emotionally connected to their students and even find it difficult to find time to cater to students' needs, give meaningful feedback, and understand what is happening to students in their lived contexts.

Thus, even though in theory standardized testing is supposed to prepare students for the "real world," it paradoxically separates the student from places where they can exude their own personal knowledge and experiences. Some experimental schools, such as Springfield Renaissance School in Springfield, Massachusetts, are opposing this trend by allowing the students to define their own core values, thus centering on their own learning needs without the pressure to conform to supposedly objective learning goals. The students in this school identified seven character traits, namely "friendship, perseverance, responsibility, respect, self-discipline, cultural sensitivity, and courage" (p. 90) and used these traits as "reference points when assessing their own progress in family conferences and Passage Portfolios" (Cervone

& Cushman, 2017, p. 90). This approach empowers students to assess their learning using values that they define and that truly matter to them. Yet it also tends to be the exception rather than the rule, as many schools are still mandated to teach to the test instead of allowing students to define their learning trajectories themselves.

A second, equally troubling aspect of standardizing education is that it tends to feed into an acquisitive view of learning, which positions schools as repositories of uniform, standardized knowledge that all students are meant to passively absorb to be considered "fully educated." Erich Fromm (2013) suggests that this model of education most aligns with the view of knowledge as something that is owned rather than as a process of lived thinking. Western languages tend to refer to *having, acquiring*, or *absorbing* knowledge, all of which position knowledge as objects to be owned, similar to personal property, wealth, or prestige. Hence Fromm succinctly observes,

> Our education generally tries to train people to *have* knowledge as a possession, by and large commensurate with the amount of property or social prestige they are likely to have in later life. The minimum they receive is the amount they will need in order to function properly in their work. In addition they are each given a "luxury-knowledge package" to enhance their feeling of worth, with the size of each such package being in accord with the person's probable social prestige. The schools are the factories in which these overall knowledge packages are produced—although schools usually claim they mean to bring the students in touch with the highest achievements of the human mind. (Fromm, 2013, p. 36)

Fromm not only characterizes schools as "factories" where knowledge is accumulated but also suggests the ways in which acquisition of knowledge is reflective of a society focused more on prestige and position than on trusting one's own innate capacities to think and form insights, given an endless array of subjects.

Third, a standards-based model of education places teachers under intense pressures to churn out "test-ready" students. This view positions teaching as efficiency-based instead of focused on bringing out the unique skills and talents of students as individuals. Teachers indeed are often feeling hampered by educational systems that are no more than a series of standards. Outcome-based education (Spady, 1994) is highly regarded as a gold standard through which schools ensure that the same competency measures apply across different schools and teachers, thus purporting to provide more consistency in the quality of curricular design. However, teaching to fulfill measurable standards—sometimes referred to as "teaching to the test" (Popham 2001)—does not always accord with how teachers experience their classroom and evaluate their students' learning and progress. Some teachers experience conflicts between test standards and their own observations of student achievements (Frans et al., 2020), which challenges the view that tests can singularly sum up a student's performance (Popham, 2001). In one study of the relationship between teacher stress and standardized testing, Hughes (2006) has noted, among other stresses associated with teaching, a tendency to hold teachers accountable for how students perform on national tests:

> Teacher stress is a growing hazard in education, associated with problems of recruitment, health, and retention in the profession. It has become an increasingly stressful occupation characterized by an overload of responsibilities, poor career structure, and inadequate salary. Surveys and discussions reveal that reports of teacher stress are increasing, especially when correlated with the day-to-day activities and administration of modern schooling. These variables include disciplinary problems, lack of administrative support, decreased autonomy, excessive paperwork, intimidating inspection regimes, unrealistic deadlines, and accountability for student performance. (p. 24)

This passage pointedly illustrates the innumerable demands and pressures on teachers to prepare students for the global marketplace, sometimes to the point where teachers are feeling burnout and are leaving the profession altogether (Eva, 2022). Particularly noteworthy here is the added responsibility that teachers feel for their students' performance. Student performance is increasingly being gauged according to provincial tests for which teachers themselves have little or no input. It's no wonder that under these conditions teachers feel both increased pressures to fulfill state and provincial requirements and an accompanying decrease in a sense of personal autonomy.

Still other studies (Bausell & Glazier, 2018; Fuchsman et al., 2022) have noted an explicit connection between teacher attrition rates and standardized testing, emphasizing the relationships between standardized tests and factors such as "tenure decisions, provision of performance or merit pay, and influence on performance evaluations" (Ryan et al. 2017, p. 4). With the rise of high-stakes testing, teachers are more vulnerable than ever to stress and feeling overwhelmed by increasing demands on the profession itself, especially in ensuring personal accountability for students' test preparedness.

In parallel with the movement toward teacher accountability is a growing trend to regard student performance as objectively measurable using universally valid criteria (James, 2014). One advantage of standardized measurements is that criteria are purported to be valid across many different contexts, communicating to students what they need to improve (Pereira et al., 2018) and could thus promote greater transparency in the grading process (Boud, 2016). However, too much emphasis on discrete criteria can overlook the holistic nature of assessing student work (Joughin, 2008; Sadler, 2005) in which teachers are considered to assess the whole of a student's work before pinpointing specific criteria that are being met. Furthermore, an overreliance on criteria can condition some students to focus exclusively on meeting these criteria, rather than considering other, less discrete factors that affect the quality of complex work (Hendricks, 2013). From the teacher's perspective, however, teaching to the test leaves little room for teachers and students alike to explore complexity and mystery that characterize real-world problems. Notes Posner (2004),

> For real problems, the appropriate methods of attack are not immediately obvious and may well vary greatly from those that apply to problems that seem similar. In contrast, on a standardized test, where there is no time for subtlety or deep analysis, problems are by necessity formulaic. Could an education driven principally by standardized test scores leave students unable to understand such subtleties? For example, students in a classroom constitute a set of problems for a teacher that are superficially similar but at a deeper level radically different. Could the inability to appreciate these distinctions be another unintended consequence of teaching based on standardized tests? Consider that the pressure on teachers to "teach to the test" is more accurately described as pressure to "teach to the standardized test metrics" by which the teacher's performance is measured. Optimizing such metrics requires ignoring individual students in favour of statistical abstractions. (p. 751)

What's especially worth noting in this passage is the way standardized tests can overlook the complexity of real-life problems by presenting data as pregiven rather than as something to be discovered through research and, more often than not, a process of trial-and-error. In contrast to standardized tests, methods of approaching a problem in real life are often uncertain and involve many choices, variables, and possible outcomes. When variables are spelled out in the contexts of testing, there is little room for deep learning to take place. More importantly, however, the standardized test encourages teachers to overlook student individuality in favor of what Posner refers to above as "statistical abstractions." Objective and criteria-based teaching not only hold teachers accountable for fulfilling "measurable" objectives; they also leave very little room in the classroom for teachers to discover what is novel in their connections with students as individuals. Teachers might even begin to see their professional lives as a series of routines or tasks, given the many responsibilities they must undertake. Furthermore, teachers may even lose the sense that they are humans among other humans in relation to their students. Spontaneity in the classroom starts to disappear in the process.

The move toward standardized testing is but one of many ways in which teachers' working lives are becoming more regimented and routinized. Too much focus on efficiency in test preparation can cause teachers and students alike to lose the sense that learning itself is an unexpected and often unpredictable journey—something that, indeed, is altogether mysterious and not fully known or reduceable to a formula for success. Not only is learning itself an unplanned experience, but the paths of learning also vary from one student to the next (Romanelli et al., 2009). But as Schwartzman (2017) has noted, framing education as a consumable item has the additional drawback of not allowing students to practice reflective choice-making and personal initiative: "Instead of providing purity and precision to corrupt and capricious academe, the archetype of quantitatively driven, efficient education as a transaction between producers and consumers creates an atmosphere that can corrode educational quality. Not only does it foster a zero-sum competitiveness that enables the behaviors described in the preceding tale, but it also frames the process of education in ways that diminish the value of teaching and learning" (p. 335). Reducing learning to an efficient transaction of information flow between teacher and student has the deleterious effect of diminishing the real interchanges where learning is negotiated.

The idea that schools are designed to transmit knowledge and skills to prepare students to succeed in the marketplace is not a new one. In fact, I suggest that it is rooted in a notion of technical rationality (Kinsella, 2007; Blanco Ramirez, 2013) that dates back to the early twentieth century. Technical rationality is one way of looking at the goals of education that reduces education to training students to behave in socially desirable ways. Moreso, technical rationality is founded upon a behaviorist model of education, which favors observable outcomes over the internal, reflective processes attendant to learning. According to this view, the goal of education is not to encourage deeper reflection per se but to shape desirable social outcomes and behaviors. Technical rationality adopts many ideas from early industrialists such as Frederick Winslow Taylor, who suggested a model of the school that is predicated on improving efficiencies in factory contexts. Notes Watters (2021), "For schools, as for factories, scientific management meant the strict control of inputs and outputs; monitoring, analyzing, and planning all aspects of the job; setting standards so that workers were kept at the ideal pace on the ideal task. The key, for Taylor, was to conduct a time and motion study. For schools in particular, this meant adoption of many new procedures for measuring and accounting for what went on in the classroom" (p. 44). Under a technical rational view, all actions can be reduced to measurable inputs and standards that can be objectively isolated, studied, and replicated.

In addition to being heavily influenced by behaviorist psychology, technical rationality has its roots in logical positivism (Mayhall, 2003), an early twentieth-century European philosophical movement that attempted to explain how philosophical problems could be viewed as problems rooted in language. For logical positivists, any problem or dilemma that cannot be observed or proven through experiment is an error in language and therefore not based on real empirical evidence. This perspective opens the door to an elimination of speculative thinking or analysis that is not rooted in some kind of external behavior. One problem with trying to measure and quantify behaviors is that this approach does not account for the complexity with which professionals improvise on their knowledge and experience to create completely new behaviors. Donald Schon (1984) astutely observes how reflective practices do not offer an easy measurement of professional behaviors, as the latter often rely on improvisational and tacit learning that expands on existing technical knowledge. This is best illustrated in the way professionals such as teachers handle conflicting information within their chosen field:

> And if it is true, finally, that there are conflicting views of professional practice, it is also true that some practitioners do manage to make a thoughtful choice, or even a partial synthesis

from a babble of voices in their professions. Why, then, should leading professionals and educators find these phenomena so disturbing? Surely they are not unaware of the artful ways in which some practitioners deal competently with the indeterminacies and value conflicts of practice. It seems, rather, that they are disturbed because they have no satisfactory way of describing or accounting for the artful competence which practitioners sometimes reveal in what they do. They find it unsettling to be unable to make sense of these processes in terms of the model of professional knowledge which they have largely taken for granted. Complexity, instability, and uncertainty are not removed or resolved by applying specialized knowledge to well-defined tasks. If anything, the effective use of specialized knowledge depends on a prior restructuring of situations that are complex and uncertain. (pp. 18–19)

What is often missing from a technical rational perspective of education is the sense that thinking often abides in the mysterious and complex, or what Schon refers to as the "babble of voices." Conflicting perspectives require a tricky negotiation of perspectives, rather than simply a step-by-step analysis of predetermined actions. Furthermore, Schon points to the ways in which a lot of what educators know is neither explicitly spelled out in the form of a step-by-step procedure nor reduceable to explicit instruction or explanation.

With technical rationality comes the obsession with certainty, which often can only be established through a process of reasoning or repeated observation and measurement, two hallmarks of an empiricist or positivist way of knowing. Young (2013) roots the desire for explicit reasons for doing things to the Greek philosopher Plato's valorization of "knowing that" over "knowing how"—that is, being able to explain and potentially teach a process (*logos*) rather than simply knowing how to do it (*techne*) is, according to Plato, a hallmark of genuine knowing. Young suggests that this idea about what counts as knowledge is rooted in a desire to maximally control the environmental variables to create consistent outcomes that can lead to similar results over time:

> If we ask what links the unreliability and unteachability objections, the answer seems to be *control*: control of the natural and human environment. Since inspiration is fickle, the utterances

> of prophets and poets are unreliable. And even in the rare case where one of them is almost always right, their gift still cannot be communicated to others, which means that whatever control they facilitate is limited to their own time and place. What we need—whom we need to support and revere—is not prophecy and poetry but rather the sciences, at the apex of which stands philosophy. Only reason and scientific theory can produce a genuine *techne*, only reason can provide us with the "technology" to exert effective control over our environment. (Young, 2013, p. 7)

Young succinctly describes an idea that still pervades modern educational theories, namely that what counts as "teachable" knowledge is only that which can be explained using reason or, more precisely, the systematization of behavior into traceable steps that lead to the same universal outcomes. This reduction of "true" knowledge to that which can be measured and predicted has carried over into a view of learning that values the measurable over the uncertain. This approach even casts doubt on ways of knowing that cannot be put into words, let alone explicitly defined, including intuitive and contemplative forms of knowing (Ghadiali, 2021; Wright et al., 2023).

Although the trend toward technical rationality seems a fairly recent one historically, it's arguable that it is rooted in a more pervasive Newtonian model of the world (Capra & Luisi, 2014), one that suggests that the forces of nature are something to be manipulated and shaped to specific ends that are controlled by an overarching, disembodied rationality. Newton, in theorizing about the laws of gravity, heralded a long tradition of epistemology that stresses the separation of observer and observed, using a mechanical model of force and movement that haunts many disciplines, including education. Founded on early models of physical science, this perspective maintained that truth can only be attained through an objectively neutral observer who is distant enough from their subject of study to be able to quantitatively measure and establish repeatability in experiments. Fritjof Capra (2010) suggests that from the seventeenth to nineteenth century, European thought was pervaded with two trends: the first, to separate "matter" from "spirit," which is rooted in the Cartesian division between mind and body and "allowed scientists to treat matter as dead and completely separate . . . and to see the material world as a multitude of different objects assembled into a huge machine" (p. 22); the second, "the image of a monarchical God who ruled the world from above by imposing his divine law on it" (p. 22). Both ideas contribute to a picture of the external world that is distinct from our internal states, as well as a sense that learning must involve a disembodied, emotionless examination of objects in the world. It would not be a stretch to suggest that monarchical and disembodied qualities start creeping into the image of the all-knowing, adjudicating teacher in the classroom.

Discussion: A Desire-Based Curriculum

So far, this chapter has explored the ways in which Western curriculum often leaves little room for surprise, awe, or the unexpected. With the increased pressures of accountability and teaching to the test, teachers feel constrained by a curriculum that relies heavily on test-based measures of learning. In addition, they feel pressured to live up to a role that emphasizes their own content-based expertise over and above their capacity to connect with students. The sense of truly connecting with students gets lost as teachers feel pressured to pander to a specialized, narrow area of expertise while losing the sense of teaching as a craft unto itself. Schneider (2005) notes how this especially plays out in universities: "On the whole, faculty know that the academy rewards academic scholarships, not educational leadership, and that their contributions to the quality of general education are simply a form of pro bono enterprise. Faculty priorities follow the academic reward system. Faculty do spend time on the quality of their own individual courses. But on most campuses, they are neither expected to spend time on the quality of the collective general education curriculum nor rewarded for doing so" (p. 69). Paradoxically, teachers feel equally hemmed in by the pressure to be a caregiver in some contexts, while suppressing emotions in others. In her study of nurturance stress that teachers face when taking on caregiving roles to their students, Vanslyke-Briggs (2010) notes how, due to excessive historical expectations of women in patriarchal societies as "ultimate caregivers," female teachers in particular are faced with contradictory mandates to be all-caring toward their students while simultaneously suppressing emotion in favor of a distanced and dispassionate stance in relation to students: "There is a conflict in emotional states between what a woman's socialization expects and the expectations placed by a historically male administration when paired with the social understanding of distance between students and teachers. This creates a discord for the female teacher who has been socialized to be a nurturing quasi-mother, yet must remain distanced from emotional investment in her students" (p. 15).

Even when teachers are socialized to be caregivers through social and familial pressures, teacher training programs hardly prepare teachers for the tricky balance of self and other care that is needed to prevent burnout and nurturance stress. Quigley & Hall (2016) note how most teacher education programs "spend their time focusing on content-related strategies to help students achieve academic learning objectives and ignore the importance of preparing teachers to provide caring and nurturing environments for their students" (p. 181). Without a care-based pedagogy that emphasizes interpersonal relations, classrooms are filled with relational gaps that emphasize distance and duality, such as the gaps between student and teacher, knower and known, subject and object, thought and emotion, and so on. All these gaps can foster a tendency to portray learning as a process of acquiring things for individual enhancement alone, divorced from a sense of greater community and interconnection in the classroom. An acquisitive model of learning suggests that individuals must compete for knowledge as a commodity similar to a product (Kauppinen, 2014; Fromm, 2013), to the point of alienating or distancing parts of themselves that don't fit the mold of the knowledge they are seeking. Teachers similarly must suppress aspects of themselves that are at odds with a hierarchical and technical view of the classroom. While outcomes become more predictable through emotional distancing, this also ironically creates a sense of education as a process of striving to gain and fearing the repercussions of "not having." Marut (2014) articulates this as an accomplishment-based sense of selfhood, where people tend to measure their value by the skills they are thought to acquire:

> If we fully buy into an accomplishment-based understanding of selfhood, we'll be perpetually trying, and endlessly failing, to be *somebody enough*. When we wholly identify with one or another of the roles we play in the ongoing drama that is life, we may begin to suspect that no matter how successful we are—no matter how many promotions we win, how much money we accumulate, how much praise we receive—it will never be sufficient. If this is the gauge of self-approval, the bar will always be moving higher; there will always be more hoops to jump through and more rivers to cross, with no end in sight. (p. 13)

Marut's passage pointedly describes the pressure for an educational system that owns up to the demands of selfhood in modern Western society. If, as Marut suggests, an individual's sense of worth is based on the amount of money, praise, or promotions they receive, then it follows that educational systems must keep up with the needs of learners as acquisitive beings, whose sense of worth is based mainly upon what they perceive themselves to *have* instead of how they authentically experience themselves. Slote (2013) raises similar concerns that an overemphasis of rationality might often exalt a "Faustian" ideal of the achieving individual who is governed by "activity or activeness and autonomous control as opposed to being passive and/or receptive" (p. 3). This leads to an over-productive mode of being that pays little heed to the greater natural world, let alone the sustainability of an isolated, autonomous identity.

The pressures teachers face in classrooms today arise largely from a neoliberal push for standardization, coupled with the pressure to prepare to be competitive in a global market economy. The focus on an outcome-based education system can even affect parents, who project their success (or failure) narratives onto their children in the expectation that schools will shape children into the kinds of individuals they themselves aspired to be while growing up. Instead of focusing on the process of learning, an emphasis on what the child will become takes precedence. Psychotherapist Mark Epstein (2005) thus remarks,

> The intense pressure in our culture for individual attainment affects parents and children alike. All too often, at least in situations where children are not simply being ignored, from very early in life everyone worries about what will become of a child, about what (or who) he or she is going to be. There is little trust in the natural unfolding of the individual. The pressure is then from the beginning and is transmitted at all the landmarks of development, with parents who are insecure about their own achievements conditioning their children's approach to life. (p. 83)

Kohn (2005) has similarly maintained that exaggerating personal achievement at the expense of a child's unfolding identity can lead to many deleterious effects, such as an overemphasis on extrinsic reward, the sacrifice of depth of learning in favor of "scoring good grades," and the pressure to constantly live up to external demands at the expense of one's interests and passions. He particularly emphasizes how "competition makes self-esteem conditional and precarious" (p. 77) as well as the more frightening possibility that stressing high grades over the sheer enjoyment of an activity or process can erode a student's interest and motivation to do things for their own inherent good, pleasure, and worth: "Even a terrific story, or an exciting science project, quickly becomes less appealing when it's construed as something you have to get through to snag the A or 100 or gold star. The more a child is thinking about grades, the more likely it is that his or her natural curiosity about the world will start to evaporate" (p. 80). Both Kohn and Epstein emphasize how students can lose their inner identity in the anxiety to achieve, which often begins with parental anxieties to confirm their own self-esteem through their children. Kohn even surmises that this achievement orientation arises from the parents themselves being conditioned as children to focus only on grades, rather than learning and personal interest in a subject.

A combination of administrative pressure and a focus on individual success creates what I refer to as a *desire*-based curriculum, in which the teaching and learning moments of everyday life are sacrificed in favor of the expediency to prepare students for an imaginary future—one in which competition and individual self-assertion become the main priority. Part of what emerges from a desire-based curriculum is the sense that the goal of education is individual self-fulfillment, or what Taylor (1991) refers to as "justifying in the name of authenticity a concept of relationships as instrumental to individual self-fulfillment" (p. 22). What students might internalize from this experience is that (a) a good education guarantees a desirable outcome or future, such as a lucrative job or a happy career, and (b) education is an agonistic struggle or competition to achieve accolades necessary to compete in a "real" economic world. "More is better" might be an additional incidental attitude that is drilled into students schooled in this mentality. Clinical psychologist Timothy Miller (Miller, 1995) has reflected on how the drive for more shapes the current Western economic models, which pressure people by making them feel inadequate unless they consume and acquire more things. This attitude pervades a lot of our thinking and understanding in capitalist societies, where even knowledge and experiences are commodified. In the drive for More (capital *M* intended!), people truly believe that they do not have enough within themselves and are always focused outward in a push to acquire and achieve more things. Miller (1995) thus remarks, "It is hard for modern people to be sure that desire is insatiable. Advertising and popular culture constantly tell us that lasting contentment can be attained. Just get a better wardrobe, another degree, a faster PC, a more stylish car, a nicer body, or a more attractive romantic partner, and you will be home free" (p. 25). Miller goes on to maintain, as do many religious philosophies, how impossible it is for desires to be satiated, not only because "you will never possess many of the things you desire most deeply" but also because "it is inevitable that you will lose some of the good things you now possess, through misfortune, illness, old age, and death" (p. 26).

Technologies also reinforce a drive for More by creating a variety of different distractions, all of which reinforce the illusion of infinite power and choice while fostering the pervasive fear of missing out (FOMO) unless we respond immediately to our texts or instant messages (Underwood, 2015). Notes David Levy (2016), "Our devices have vastly extended our attentional choices, but the human attentional capacity remains unchanged . . . and so we must figure out how to make wise choices, and to figure out what constitutes a wise choice, so we can use our digital tools to their best advantage, and to ours" (p. 3). While online learning offers several logistical advantages to in-person classrooms that can make learning more convenient and efficient, its formats add to the sense that students don't need other students (let alone teachers) to succeed in school. In his study of solitude, David Vincent (2020) notes, "The launch of the smartphone in 2007, and its increasing use for asynchronous text-messaging rather than conversation, has created the emblematic figure of our times, silently hunched over a hand-held object, either in a separate space or mentally withdrawn from the immediate press of people" (p. 248). For Vincent, modern technologies promote individualism and an isolated identity through the affordance of allowing people to communicate at their own convenience and within the confines of their own physical and mental spaces. Miller (2018) similarly cautions that online messaging technologies, which incidentally have now become staples in the digital classroom, can make it altogether too easy for students to avoid the intimacy and challenges of interpersonal classroom dynamics, thereby promoting the student as isolated, autonomous, and disengaged from the messy worlds of negotiation and intimacy:

> Whatever the form of personal love, the physical presence of the other is crucial. Of course, Skyping can help us sustain communication, but if the discussion becomes difficult, it is too easy to sign off. When we are face to face, it is more difficult to walk away. The presence of the other person can help us work through difficulty. [Sherry] Turkle cites the research of Daniel Siegel who found that children need eye contact to develop the part of the brain that is involved in attachment. (p. 31)

For Miller, Skype or other forms of online communication can be greatly limited by the sense of ease through which participants can control the interaction whenever the situation becomes inconvenient or uncomfortable. "Signing out," both figuratively and literally, can entail easily and instantly leaving a shared virtual room without learning social skills such as patience, negotiation, or compromise. Inherent to online technology platforms is the prioritizing of personal ease over the needs of the whole classroom, a point that supports an individualistic and libertarian politics of the school. This also meshes with the research of Sherry Turkle, also referenced in Miller's work, who suggests that many modern innovations in online interactivity and robotics are intended to create substitutes for caregivers—minus the pain or difficulties of real person-to-person relationships. Turkle (2011), for instance, notes "how we are changed as technology offers us substitutes for connecting with each other face-to-face" (p. 11) and describes situations where young people forego the messiness of intimacy in favor of the substitute sense of connectedness found in online chatrooms. Moreso, lacking a sense of shared physical space through which people can communicate as a group can undermine the very concept of the classroom as a viable community of scholars that deserves guardianship and protection. Bob Samuels (2013) expands on this view by noting that even though distance education proves more convenient for many, it loses the nuanced texture of communication by making it too easy for students to succeed on their own, without the support of teams or groups:

> I worry that students are losing the ability to make eye contact and read body language, and that they are not being prepared to be effective citizens, workers, and family members. This disconnect from in-person communication also relates to a distance from the natural world, and a growing indifference to the destruction of our environment. In this alienation from nature and natural environments, people also lose the ability to distinguish between true and false representations. Since on the web, everything is a virtual image or simulation generated by digital code, we live in a state of constant indifference. (B. Samuels, 2013, para. 7)

Samuels relates disconnection to a growing alienation from the natural environment, which, he suggests, relates to an overreliance on technologies as surrogates for in-person communication.

In addition to having broader capabilities to engage and disengage at will, postsecondary students are faced with seemingly endless course offerings that promote the illusion of *infinite choice*, where students are often positioned as having a very broad array of different career paths from which to choose in the globalized marketplace. This is often coupled with the view that rationality can be used to accurately predict the future, which dovetails with the Enlightenment "assumption that perfection is possible" (Slote, 2013, p. 23), in contrast to "an accepting attitude toward the possibilities of our lives" (p. 23). While few people doubt the importance and benefits of choices in modern society, some have questioned whether having more choices leads to contentment and a generally good life. Guengerich (2020) writes,

> No matter how many options we face in a given moment, we can choose only one of them, a reality check that's especially consequential with things that matter most in life, such as spouses, children, careers, or homes. There may be an opportunity to choose differently in the future, but once we have made our choice in the present, we can't unmake it. The more options you have, the better the chance you will end up choosing the wrong one—or at least one that's inferior to an option you didn't choose. Inevitably, some of our decisions will not turn out as we intended. For this reason, we need to understand the meaning of our lives in a way that doesn't depend on everything working out for good. Sometimes it doesn't. (p. 23)

Guengerich raises an interesting possibility that optimizing career choices doesn't necessarily make for better decisions, let alone mitigate the potential (and inevitable) disappointments that attend making a less informed decision. This entails that education may need to prepare students for disappointed expectations, living with less than ideal outcomes, or having to work with the unanticipated outcomes of choices made. These skills or ways of seeing are not automatically guaranteed with training that prepares one for the working world. A curriculum that focuses on *the now* instead of an anticipated future may be one way of helping students acquire a feeling that what they have within them is sufficient; under this mentality, there is no need to rush to endlessly acquire. In addition, loosening the requirements to make perfect choices, given a range of many unknowns, can allow for a more surprise-based view of the future. As Slote (2013) aptly suggests,

"We shouldn't have plans for our future lives but rather should have or exemplify a more receptive attitude toward what our lives may or will bring us in the future" (p. 18). Having a calculating and narrow view of rational choice can sometimes make people "less receptive to what life *has* brought our way than it is desirable for us to be" (p. 18).

Finally, some have noted a tendency for modern Western cultures to exalt individual success without considering the possibility that success is based on the collective efforts and dedication of many. Instead of viewing success as the result of a shared vision that is greater than the self, social media tends to foster a cult of celebrity, which upholds the mythology that some are more special than others as well as the equally pervasive view that success is entirely the result of one's personal merit and efforts. The converse of this view is "an ideology whose most dangerous idea is that all problems are individual, that social problems do not exist" (Giroux, 2020), resulting in a tendency to focus more on the self and personal status as opposed to serving a greater community. Marut (2014), notes, "We're all en masse, and in pretty much the same ways, struggling to be unique individuals. This obsessive quest for distinctive identity drives us all equally, for we all believe that happiness and fulfillment will come through distinguishing ourselves, through being 'special.' Our contemporary culture of consumerism, materialism, narcissism, and the worship of fame encourages the idea that we will be happy only when we become exceptional" (xxv). A narrative of exceptionality certainly runs through most schools, as students compete for the highest honors and vie for the top grades. What's troubling is not the effort to do well, which is laudable, but instead the emphasis on select individuals as exceptional, rendering those individuals out of touch with the ways in which they are supported by fellow beings. Not all educational systems advocate this notion of exceptionality. As later chapters suggest, giftedness and exceptionality in Indigenous cultures refer more to the gifts that are shared across ancestry and communities. Indigenous scholars such as Jill Bevan-Brown (Bevan-Brown, 2009) have noted that gifts come not from the individual self's efforts but from a wider creation, which instills purpose in beings. People are not privileged with gifts so much as they are entrusted to use the gifts they have been uniquely given to the benefit of their communities.

What often happens with result-based, compartmentalized education is that students start to view school subjects as discrete "objects" that need to be tackled individually. Students move on from one subject to the next—and "passing" the subject can literally mean passing by or passing on, ready to move onto the next grade or subject. Taken in this way, students aren't encouraged to see the process of learning as a circular one, in which one's previous courses form the building blocks for the next and can be revisited and reviewed. Instead, to pass a course is to give permission for students never to have to revisit it again or even to revise their thinking about the subject itself. Once a subject is considered "learned," the possibility of revising or shifting one's understanding of it might be overlooked or altogether ignored.

It's perhaps fruitful to consider the ways in which one might reframe classroom learning from an orientation of *desiring an object* to one of *beholding an infinite subject*. That is, in lieu of seeing classrooms as places where discrete objects are mastered, learning might be seen from the perspective of an infinitely desiring student who is always learning and stands to learn when they revisit a subject many times. Mark Epstein (2005) has suggested that these two orientations represent masculine and feminine ways of approaching and engaging desire:

> The more commonly accepted form of desire, the one that is usually associated with masculine energy, is the familiar one of possession, acquisition and objectification. In this version of desire, the self actively tries to get its needs met by manipulating its environment, extracting what it requires from a world that is consistently objectified. But it is this version of desire that tends toward frustration and disappointment, that can never be entirely satisfied. The paradox of desire is that we are actually seeking another mode altogether, one that we have trouble imagining, or acknowledging . . . while desire's masculine energies are necessary, they are not, by themselves, sufficient. Desire, in its longing for completion, is ultimately in search of being. (pp. 131–132)

Epstein suggests that, contrary to an object-based orientation, people can relax "desire's fixed agenda" (p. 133) by shifting their orientation away from desiring an object and toward beholding and relaxing into an infinitely desiring subject. This entails many insights, among them the realization that desire is inexhaustible and can never be fully satiated. Like an itch that can never be fully scratched, desire for an object can only briefly be satiated, only to return in the form of yet another object to "possess." Instead of fixing one's gaze on a desired object, what would happen if the gaze were drawn inward toward the person who desires? Such an orientation would require a sense of renunciation, or what the Dalai Lama has referred to as "a weariness at the impossibility of desire's demands" (Epstein, 2005, p. 111). It also involves a contemplative respect and beholding for the desiring person as complete in their own right, not needing to be further completed through the conquering or objectifying of desire itself.

Although Epstein restricts his focus to personal relationships, I believe that his perspectives on desire could be applied to educational settings. Rather than focusing on classroom topics as discrete subjects to be mastered—which can involve an endless memorization of facts—what happens if the educational gaze shifts toward the student who is forever in a process of learning yet is already perfect in their desires to learn? What if, instead of seeing learning as the mastery of subjects like math, science, physics, and so on, students were to be viewed as always in the process of learning, relearning, revising, and revisioning their views based on what they have read and internalized? And what if, instead of seeing this process of revision as a sign of failure to learn, this actual revision is the sign of endless learning? Learning is not a credential that a person hangs on the wall so much as it is an ongoing journey subject to continual rereading, reinterpretation, and revision over time. Thus, an infinite view of learning might offer more opportunities for wonder, surprise, and tolerance for uncertainty and the unfinished educational journey.

In the midst of the standardization of the teacher role, is there room for teachers to cultivate attitudes of surprise, wonder, and gratitude in their daily practices in classrooms? The remainder of this book will suggest that only when there is a marked shift in orientation to a circle of gifting can teachers truly feel genuine surprise and wonder at their students' efforts and individuality. More importantly, the remainder of this book will seek to explore how teachers can balance the routine of their lives with a sense of novelty and surprise. The theoretical premise undergirding this effort is that a sense of surprise comes from the balance between attending to the details of moments and being able to pan out and actively create meaning through a reflection of things as totalities, in structures that interrelate. Teachers are best able to feel surprise when they are actively prepared, anticipating, and willing to discover the hidden and subtle meanings of their students' works and interactions.

In subsequent chapters of this book, I will firstly argue the need to incorporate surprise into a teacher's experiences of students and classrooms. By *surprise* I am referring to the act of spontaneously beholding and acknowledging what is given in a way that evokes novel discoveries and unexpected encounters. Secondly, this book will suggest that, contrary to popular belief, surprise is not accidental. Surprise can be evoked through a mindset of discovery and beholding the given as an unknown presence that is being forever revealed from moment to moment. I will suggest exercises throughout to explore how teachers can create surprise.

Questions for Discussion

1. In what ways have you felt the pressure to teach according to fixed standards?

2. How might preparing students for standardized tests have impacted your ability to meet an individual student's challenges? Reflect on times when the curriculum would not allow you to factor the diverse learning needs and interests of your classroom.

3. What kinds of surprises are you willing to accommodate into the classroom situation? What problems might arise when there is too much novelty in the classroom? How do you factor novelty into the classroom?

Questions for Reflection

1. Reflect on a situation in which you took an unexpected detour when setting out to teach or learn a specific subject or skill in a classroom setting.

    a. Describe the nature of the unexpected detour. Did it result in enriching the original topic you intended to study, or did it divert to a different interest or skill?

    b. What effect did the change in direction of teaching (or learning) have on you as an individual? On the class as a whole?

    c. How did this experience change the way you approach teaching and learning? Did it change your attitude toward the unexpected or sudden "diversions" that often take place in classrooms?

2. Imagine yourself entering the classroom, whether online or in person. Consider all the ways in which you value planning, "control" of the classroom flow, and other factors. On a sheet of paper, draw a chart with two columns: one called "within teacher's control" and "outside teacher's control." Under the first column, write down all the things that you consider within your influence or control. Under the second column, write down things that are more or less outside your control or influence as a teacher. Write quickly and without censoring or editing, capturing even the smallest details that are within or outside your control as a teacher.

    a. After you have filled the chart with as many points as possible, consider the following:

        i. How important do you feel your sense of being in control is to your well-being in the classroom? Your students' well-being? Write a reflection exploring the value and importance of being able to control specific factors in the classroom.

        ii. Imagine what it would be like to take one of the items in the list "within teacher's control" and relax the sense of control over that item. What would happen if you gradually loosened or eased the need or the impulse to control that one factor (e.g., students being punctual or submitting assignments on time, having a well-mapped class plan, knowing what to say when the class starts, etc.). Write a reflection exploring an area of control that you would like to try relaxing in your role as a teacher.

Chapter 2

Teaching with Surprise

The previous chapter outlined how teaching under strict standards and measures can sometimes take the surprise out of teaching and learning. Teachers who are pressured to "teach for the test," or who feel consigned to focus on preparing students for a competitive marketplace, may not leave room in their classrooms for elements of the spontaneous. Norman Jackson notes that along with the pressure to prepare students for prescribed tests, teachers find themselves having to stay within the rigid confines of "provider designed purposes and outcomes" that leave "no room for outcomes that are not anticipated or outcomes that learners individually recognize as being valuable to them" (Nygaard et al., 2010, xiii). In reality, more complex forms of learning require a great deal of unplanned and unstructured moments, as well as the courage to bear uncertainty, or what poet John Keats referred as "negative capability"—the capacity to be in "uncertainties, Mysteries, doubts, without any irritable reaching after fact & reason" (Keats & Rollins, 1958, pp. 193–194). One key point in this phrase is the notion of not attempting to explain away a complex situation into a single tangible concept but, alternately, to allow uncertainty to grow into wonderment. The key is thus to develop a tolerance for liminality (Conroy, 2004; Todd, 2014), or a transition space that leaves one disoriented by not yielding predefined answers or roles that prescribe a given direction. Paradoxically, inhabiting a liminal space often involves being comfortable with the feeling of being lost.

Students and teachers alike may sometimes need to rediscover that learning is not the result of following a predicable sequential path. For one, students all come to the classroom with unique backgrounds, cultures, and contexts, all of which can shape the ways in which they approach classrooms and assignments. Secondly, spontaneous and unplanned moments are a prerequisite for "deep learning," or what Smith and Colby (2007) refer to as "an intention to understand and impose meaning. Here, the student focuses on relationships between various aspects of the content, formulates hypotheses or beliefs about the structure of the problem or concept, and relates more to obtaining an intrinsic interest in learning and understanding" (p. 206). Deep learning does not automatically happen by a process of induction or sequentially putting elements in order. To the contrary, it involves a sustainable period of inquiry and investigation in which students are required to make a topic their own, especially through the effort to sift through and process many pieces of information. The goal here is not retention of knowledge per se but the intrinsic interest in learning and understanding, which entails a sustained emotional engagement in the subject matter. What emerges from deep learning is always a surprise, in the sense that it cannot be predicted ahead of time just what the students will learn from a particular topic, let alone how they will approach it. When students can passionately engage a subject or topic from a genuine interest and curiosity, teachers are more prone to feel surprised by the outcomes, particularly when their students have thoroughly engaged a topic in depth and thus reach their own unique conclusions.

In contrast to a behavioral or cognitive view of learning—which often sees learning as an outcome of predictable sequences—transformative and holistic views of learning often factor elements of the unexpected, uncertain, and unpredictable in the learning process. An example of transformative learning, or learning that leads to a change in the individual, is timeless learning, which Miller (2006) describes as learning that results in a more direct, immediate experience of the present. Miller emphasizes how timeless learning does not have a fixed schedule and can vary from person to person, which is somewhat akin to planting seeds in a garden: "Although timeless learning can be transformative, there is certainly no guarantee when, how, or under what conditions the transformation will occur. Some transformation can be incremented; other changes can be monumental" (Miller, 2006, p. 8).

Particularly in instances of creative endeavor, a learning outcome may not arrive as expected but may often take long periods of incubation (Gilhooly, 2016), frustration, and wrestling with conflicting observations and views. One example of complex or deep learning is the process of expressive or narrative writing (Peterson, 2008), in which students are asked to put together a story. In the beginning of this process, students may have a variety of choices to contend with when establishing character, plot, setting, and so on. Even young children need to negotiate the different ways in which the process of crafting a story unfolds. Donald Graves (1983) shares one delightful vignette in which a child is negotiating how to position a story and is actively reflecting on the story arc as he revises his drafts:

> There is a process to nine-year-old Brian's writing. It has all the elements of a craft. He gets ready, rehearses for his subject, "Gray Squirrels in New Hampshire," by reading, talking with friends and the teacher, and taking notes. But he does not impose his decisions on the material too quickly. Rather, he goes through many drafts; in this instance eight, to find out the truth about gray squirrels in New Hampshire. Brian puts his particular stamp on the material when he revises, selects what he thinks is the most important information, writes in the first person to strengthen his voice, cuts and pastes material to get the right organization. (pp. 6–7)

This passage suggests that even when first learning to write, the process of writing requires frequent deliberation, planning, and revisiting the same subject in different iterations, using new information gained from reflection and other information sources. This kind of learning cannot be replicated in a textbook, let alone formulated into a series of steps, since it requires processing large chunks of information and synthesizing them into newly gained insights and experiences. The process of creative writing, in this way, is a kind of unexpected surprise that cannot be reduced to a simple transmission of knowledge between teacher and learner. Hence, it's no wonder Graves cautions that teachers "lose out on the surprises children have for us because we don't let them write. Surprises come when children begin to control writing as a craft" (p. 3). He encourages teachers to view "the control of the craft as a long, painstaking process with energy supplied along the way through the joy of discovery" (p. 3).

For learning to even take place where creative thinking is involved, students need to be allowed to cultivate their unique passions and interests related to a subject, while teachers may sometimes need to skillfully connect the topic to something that genuinely concerns a student related to their special hobbies or cultural milieu. However, I want to also stress the importance of leaving a lesson slightly open to interpretation, completion, and even mystery or uncertainty, which, taken together, furnish curiosity. Learning requires curiosity, passion, and motivation (Litman, 2008; Singh & Manjaly, 2022), all of which position learning itself as an act of generosity, care, and love that cannot be reduced to instructions that everyone takes in the same moment and time. In fact, to foster a sense of curiosity in the classroom often requires the ability to furnish a sense of mystery or the unknown. Describing curiosity as a form of love that forms an essential part of learning, Miller (2018) relates the importance of leaving elements of mystery open for students to ponder, as opposed to sticking to neat or completed solutions at the end of each lesson:

> One method that always interests children is the use of stories. The sequence of the story and the plot carry the interest forward. The uncertainty of how a problem in the story will be resolved is usually the key to holding the students' interest. Growing up in the early days of television, there were many serials (e.g., *Don Winslow of the Navy*) that ran and each episode would conclude with some cliffhanger event that made me want to watch the next episode. (p. 55)

Even the act of choosing a topic of study can sometimes be a deep soul searching for students. When I was a university undergraduate in English literature, for example, topic choice was often entirely left to the student. I found myself occasionally puzzling over which topic I really would like to focus on, as well as how exactly to thematically approach the topic. Analyzing a work of literature has multiple entry points, which could include processes as complex as perspective-taking of different characters, examining narrative stance, and situating the novel within a specific historic or theoretical framework. These processes require moments of struggle and serendipity, as the topic is slowly solidified within one's mind. It's perhaps no wonder that, to this day, I sometimes see learning as a continually surprising series of decisions that can take us into many detours and diversions.

Surprise doesn't just apply to learning a topic; it can also apply to the art and practice of teaching. The question of how teachers can "keep curriculum fresh" hinges upon the deeper question of what makes work meaningful. Describing work from the perspective of his Buddhist spiritual practice, Richmond Lewis (1999) reflects on how, contrary to the modern workplace, with its focus on "competition, efficiency, technology, and profit," spiritual practice can be a lens through which "to focus on the part of our work that is beyond failure and success" (p. 19). Lewis reimagines the workplace as being a potential site for one's spiritual growth, in contrast with a market metaphor in modern education (Henig, 1995; Billingham, 2015) that positions schools as designed only to prepare students to be trained professionals.

How does this principle translate into teaching in the classroom? One way is to reimagine "success" and "failure" as relative concepts. Describing the notion of failure in work, he notes, "To say 'failure' is to make a judgment and a comparison. We put a label on our situation, fixing it in space and time, and measure it against some standard we have to set up for ourselves called success. This is not to say that failure is not real. It is. But its reality is tentative and relative. Many times we set ourselves up to fail by the limited or unrealistic way we define success" (Lewis, 1999, p. 102). Failure is often considered a sign of inadequacy in the teacher or student; that is, either the teacher failed to sufficiently prepare the student for an exam or assignment or the student failed to do their part in studying, concentration, or time management. But what if failure were reframed as an inevitable part of the learning cycle? When teachers are preparing students to succeed in tests or in their future careers, do they factor the need for students to explore, struggle, and wrestle with problems, drawing from multiple paths or learning to arrive at their own conclusions? Does "failure," however painful and disappointing it is bound to be, equate with "punishment"? Or can a thoughtful reflection on mistakes and failures be repositioned as a profound form of education? A more open perspective on the meaning of missteps and failures in education could invite teachers to see learning beyond the perspective of efficiency, numbers, and preparing students to achieve high standard results. In fact, it's viable to view failure as a necessary part of the learning process itself. Furthermore, failure might even be seen as part of a cycle that includes success. Learning could also be construed as the taking of many paths and detours, rather than one straight and narrow path that fits for everyone. Under this logic, formative assessment might be evaluated over and above an emphasis on summative evaluation (Brown et al., 2018).

Richmond Lewis's observations about the spirituality of work are not limited to a discussion of the relativity of success and failure. He redefines working life in general as a process of inner observation and development that transcends the job requirements themselves. That is, work is a form of spiritual or soulful reflection that takes a person into the roots of thought itself, rather than staying on the surfaces of tangible results and "products." Such an idea challenges and subverts the idea that work is intended only for the purposes of making a profit, driving up sales, or maximizing volumes on a product. It effectively recontextualizes work as an *inner* practice of the soul as much as it is an external practice of producing a needed service or product for others. E. F. Schumacher has similarly explored the nature of work from a Buddhist perspective. In his classic work *Small Is Beautiful* (1973), Schumacher has suggested the revision of working life so that humans do not serve machines, but rather machines serve human purposes. He distinguishes between two views of mechanization: one that "enhances a man's skill and power" and another that "turns the work of man over to a mechanised slave, leaving man in a position to have to serve the slave" (p. 58). For Schumacher, Buddhism positions work as an opportunity for a person to "overcome his ego-centeredness by joining with other people in a common task" (p. 58). Schumacher thus views work as an opportunity for mutual collaborations that create situations of spiritual uplift and ego diminishment, noting how this radically contrasts with and challenges the product-centered view of mass production. For both Schumacher and Lewis, work serves the spiritual purpose of refining a person's character by reducing a clinging to ego (or "having one's own way") in the process of working with others toward a shared goal.

The question of the meaning and value of work has significant impact to the educational profession. In fact, it's also a question that can undercut all professions in an age of accountability, micromanaging, and numbers. Yet it's important to note that work and life are not separate or unrelated compartments in a person's lived experience. Considering the amount of time that a person spends at work, it's no wonder that one's entire life and sense of meaning can be reflected in one's work, and vice versa. Matthew Fox (1994) articulates the role of work not as an isolated, measurable activity but as participation in a cosmic unfolding. He laments the modern malaise of unemployment, which, he suggests, adds to a "lack of cosmology," where cosmology refers to "awakening to the sense of the whole" (p. 59). Fox notes,

> Being without work means more than just being without a job, as critical a situation as that may prove to be for one's self-esteem and ability to pay the bills. Being without work means being without a place in the universe; it means *being cosmically homeless*. Being without good work means being a non-contributing citizen of the universe. It is like being in a circle dance but not dancing; when one person refuses to move in a circle the whole dance comes to a halt. (p. 61, italics mine)

As Fox's writings suggest, work is a calling not only to serve others but to participate in a cosmic unfolding, which establishes one's worth and importance within the community. Therefore, work at its most meaningful can never be reduced to something that is simply routine drudgery for the sake of payment or a promotion but must be viewed as an existential calling to purpose in relation to others.

So what is it about professional experience that can sometimes make it feel like it is nothing but a series of duties or checklists that need fulfilling? What are the pressures that might cause teachers to see teaching as a routine? An older conception of "vocation" (*vocere*) holds that the choice of vocation is a deeply personal one that is embedded in the sound of someone calling the other. Manen (1991) compares the notion of *vocere* to the calling of a child to a parent when he writes, "Being a parent means that one has a calling in life—a pedagogical calling. And similarly, being a child means being with someone who hears and heeds the 'calling' that gathers this child and this parent into connectedness, into oneness. The pedagogical calling is that which calls, summons us to listen to the child's needs. The term 'vocation' too carries the etymological meaning of calling (*vocare*). Wherein lies hearing the calling?" (pp. 25–26). Such a notion of vocation is voiced and personal; it comes from the circumstances in which a person is deeply embedded in the present moment. In Herman Hesse's novel *The Glass Bead Game* (Hesse, 1990), the main protagonist, Joseph Knecht, experiences a sense of vocation when a music master visits him and validates his eligibility to be admitted to an elite school. Notes the narrator, "There are many types and kinds of vocation, but the core of the experience is always the same: the soul is awakened by it, transformed or exalted, so that instead of dreams and presentiments from within a summons comes from without" (p. 58). In comparing vocation to a summons "from without," the narrator suggests a relational component of work that calls from outside of us summoning us into a profession. Yet those in demanding professions such as teaching may need to be periodically reminded that their profession is a deep calling into community. In fact, unless a teacher is reflective of teaching *as calling*, they are liable to forget the purpose and meaning of teaching. Instead, they might conceptualize teaching using the metaphor of a checklist or rubric. In contrast, the vision of the workplace as a calling is a summon for teachers to rediscover the inspiration and voices that called them to the profession in the first place. Perhaps more importantly, it repositions teaching as a gift that grants teachers the opportunity to connect and influence their students.

Surprise: A Thought Experiment for Teachers

What do we really mean by surprise as it plays out for a teacher? I would like to briefly sketch a scenario that could be used as a thought experiment to flesh out what I think surprise means in the classroom:

In the day-to-day grind of teaching, you may find yourself falling into routines as a way to manage the overall struggles of the classroom. This could include any number of things such as giving out assignments, marking tests, making announcements, delivering a lecture, disciplining a student, and so on. Now consider what would it be like if you were able to experience these events as if

a. *You are doing them for the first time*

b. *A student is seeing this task for the first time*

c. *This is the last time you will ever perform this task (due to an impending retirement or other opportunity)*

d. *The students you are teaching are all expected to become teachers in the future and regard you as their inspiration to teach*

e. *You have just recovered from an illness and are expected to make a full recovery*

f. *You are still learning how to perform the task you are teaching and need to follow the steps carefully to ensure you are correct*

g. *You regard each step in the process you are teaching as a work of art*

h. *You regard your role in the classroom as a sacred activity, worthy of the highest respect and care*

Jot down your responses to each scenario as you imagine them. Then rank the experiences in terms of highest imagined impact and lowest imagined impact.

From the foregoing thought experiment, readers may have gathered that even a slight shift in the sense of temporality of a classroom situation can foster a sense of breaking a familiar habit. A teacher who imagines that they are doing something for the last time, for instance, challenges the tendency to imagine teaching as a grind or a kind of psychic treadmill that stretches on indefinitely into the future. Coming into the classroom after a period of absence can similarly be disorienting yet relieving, especially when it marks an emergence from illness or isolation. And what if, indeed, teaching was regarded as something sacred and noble? These ideas challenge a commonplace understanding of teaching as the means to an end, such as a particular learning goal or occupation. Views of spatiality can also be challenged under these views. For example, elevating teaching to a sacred process or a work of art could change the view of how teaching occupies a particular space and time, especially by giving teaching a more esteemed place that situates it more firmly in a web of interconnected threads and stories.

Some teachers, including myself, may start to fall back into habitual ways of thinking, as a way of coping with the view that teaching is a series of tasks to be completed instead of as a moment that is worth enjoying in and of itself. According to this view, I had better don the mask of teacher as a way of coping with the multitude of times in which I have to perform a given task. On the other hand, when I imagine that something is happening or unfolding for the first or last time, something magically happens: my sense of the temporal starts to collapse, and I am able, at least briefly, to become more present with my actions and realize that there is only this *one* action that I need to attend to in any given moment. Alan Watts (1972) has aptly referred to this as the situation in which a task such as doing the dishes only involves doing *one dish at a time*:

> The art of washing dishes is that you only have to wash one at a time. If you're doing it day after day, you have in your mind's eye an enormous stack of filthy dishes which you have washed up in years past, and an enormous stack of filthy dishes which you will wash up in years future. But if you bring in your mind to the state of reality—which is, as I've pointed out to you, only now: this is where we are, there is only now—you only have to wash one dish. It's the only dish you'll ever have to wash. This one. You ignore all the rest. Because in reality there is no past and there is no future, there is just now. (para. 6)

One may characterize surprise as, for one, a slowing down, or disruption of the habitual sense of temporality, which often projects present (as well as past) actions into an indefinite future. What results from the habitual sense of temporality is often a vague sense of anxious projection into the future, as well as a vague *desacralizing* of the present. Moments, instead of being held uniquely as separate and special in themselves, are collapsed into a banal series of cascading tasks to be completed, which culminates in anxiety, malaise, and boredom.

So what happens when a person experiences a collapse in the sense of temporality so that there is only one moment, *this* moment, that needs to be attended to? Most of the above examples involve a subtle resacralizing[1] of the present, which is also a hallmark of the surprise experience. To "resacralize," in this context, is to restore a sacred or spiritual meaning to what may otherwise seem ordinary or mundane, particularly by reappraising its importance and uniqueness as an unfolding moment that will never appear again. Whether that resacralizing takes the form of reminding us that there is only *one* moment to fully attend to with all of our hearts, or there is at least one significant person who is profoundly impacted by our behavior as a teacher, the process of resacralization seems to involve the collapsing of temporal moments into this "eternal now."

Perhaps the real problem is not, then, that teaching lacks surprise but that, instead, teachers, like many professionals, are often under the spell of seeing their careers as a long and arduous path that is fragile and wrought with hazards, risks, and hidden or unexpected twists. As an alternative to dwelling on the eternal craft and process of being a teacher in the present moment, teachers may find themselves worrying about tomorrow's tasks or whether they will even "survive" or get through the following semester's tasks. All of these thoughts not only collectively contribute to anxiety but also make the teaching process appear to be a linear and indefinite line of familiar anxieties and fears. Lacking a sense of finitude, these tasks start to lose their eternal presence in the teacher's mind. As a result, the teacher often becomes consumed in the day-to-day anxieties of getting through another semester, let alone another day, of teaching.

Although the idea of being present has a significant impact on the experiences outlined in the previous thought experiment, other factors may also contribute to feelings of the unexpected or revisiting the classroom for the first time. Sudden shifts in how a teacher sees themselves as a continuous identity can often trigger experiences of surprise, wonder, or awe. For instance, knowing that our last day of work as a teacher may be today or tomorrow, our orientation toward teaching on that particular day would likely change dramatically—that is, away from thinking of the day as just another and toward realizing that each day is something to savor as though it could be our last. Yet another way that teachers may challenge their implicit or subconscious sense of identity is by changing their view of knowledge—away from the view of knowledge as a static body and toward something that dynamically changes as students and teachers alike

---

1. See Maslow (1993) for a discussion on desacralizing and resacralizing.

interact with the knowledge itself. Given that knowledge is bound to shift and evolve over time, does the teacher need to feel that they are a static "knower" who comes with predigested material that the students consume or even regurgitate? Better still, what kinds of knowing are available for teachers to impart to their students? Is the knowing itself something that is simply transmitted to students? Or can knowing also be embodied within the teacher's corporeality or even expressed passionately through the teacher's emotional investment in the topic itself? By challenging the framings through which knowledge is thought to be transmitted in classrooms, teachers can soften the need to come to a classroom fully loaded with information and prepared to upload it onto their students.

Finally, there is power in "presence," or the simple idea of teachers and students just showing up, in whatever ways they can. When I facilitate weekly meditation sessions at the University of Toronto, I often remind the attendees that their very decision to attend the session can have powerful and salutary benefits for the fellow meditation practitioners, regardless of their experience level or the intensity with which they engage meditation practice. The decision to physically be present with one's own body can have a powerful impact on sustaining the overall atmosphere and morale of the group meditation practice. I will even end the session by reminding the group to express gratitude both to themselves and to fellow participants for attending and adding to the energy of the meditation practice. Now it may seem a bit strange for someone to express gratitude toward *themselves*, and would that be necessary, one may wonder? However, if we contemplate deeply, we will find that even our decision to do something good for ourselves can be honored and given due respect, even if that decision may seem half-hearted or indecisive. In principle, there is always something that we can be thankful about when it comes to making decisions, even if the outcome did not turn out as planned. By truly appreciating the fact that I did one thing and not another, I am tapping into my own spontaneity and sense of flow, as well as my inner sense of contingency. And this loosens the sense of painful necessity and perfectionism that is often a source of suffering for many professionals, as when they subconsciously internalize an image of themselves that is an amalgamation of many "shoulds": being always knowledgeable, possessing all the answers, always being articulate and able to debate with students, and so on.

Is there anything that the examples in the above exercise have in common, aside from the fact that they are unusual or unexpected occurrences? Each of the examples outlined in the previous thought experiment suggests two major structural elements in the experience of surprise. One is the collapse of a diffuse existential anxiety through a shift from the view of time as succeeding moments that flow indefinitely into the future. This shift is accompanied by the clarity of knowing that this present moment is all that needs to be tended to, which releases the individual away from anxieties of a future that hasn't happened yet or a past that has already vanished. Surprise, whether it's pleasant or unpleasant, provides enough of a break from temporality that a person no longer feels chained to the future that seems to be a projection of the past. Secondly, surprise relieves the burden of a fixed, relatively solitary sense of self by reminding us that we are part of emerging moments, or *happenings*, that are not simply continuations of the past extending indefinitely into the future. In fact, if we can see each moment as something completely emergent and consisting of unfolding elements that are not discrete, unchanging "things," our experience of the classroom may change dramatically. Even our very own identities as teachers can start to seem contingent when we imagine that we are unfolding possibilities that are subject to change, as we witness when we become ill or when our daily teaching is interrupted by a strike or other unexpected occurrence.

To summarize these preliminary explorations of surprise, I would note the following:

- Surprise suspends the temporal by disrupting a taken-for-granted notion of causality that is thought to move sequentially (and inevitably) from past into future.

- Surprise can sometimes challenge or even subvert a self-identity that does not realistically reflect unfolding or contingent moments in time. This happens, for instance, when we come into the classroom expecting to have to be experts, only to find that the students have their own ideas and need only minimal prompting to spark a conversation.

- Surprise can take us away from a fixed identity and toward a more emergent sense of self that flows with other selves and *is carried* as much as it *carries*, that is, is interdependent with other selves.

- A surprising experience can remind us that all experiences are unique unto themselves and fundamentally don't compare to any other moments in time. At times, this can verge on "peak experiences," which have been described by Maslow (1993) as states where "there is an extreme narrowing of consciousness down to the particular percept, for example, the face or the painting, the child or the tree, etc. and in which the rest of the world is totally forgotten and in which the ego itself is totally forgotten" (p. 243). Such deep states of appreciation, while not always achievable within a bustling classroom, could at least in principle be applied to how a teacher perceives a student's unique contributions to a classroom.

A more specific case study and analysis of a surprise experience will be provided in the next two sections.

The Science of Surprise

In recent years, numerous studies have highlighted the unique features of surprise, attempting to delineate not only the characteristics of a surprise experience but also its overall evolutionary function and value. Munnich et al. (2019) suggest several areas in which research on surprise has blossomed, albeit sporadically and across different disciplines, with an emphasis on different levels of analyzing surprise as well as the causes and effects of surprise in learning. Tiedens and Linton (2001) have demonstrated that a sense of uncertainty generated by a surprising situation can provoke people to use more systematic approaches to learning, such as critical scrutiny of an event—as opposed to heuristic learning, which relies mainly on cues that provide shortcuts to assessing a situation. Other studies suggest that surprise motivates people to more critically examine information in the midst of uncertainty. In their studies of infants, Stahl and Feigenson (2015) found that infants are more inclined to seek information about an object and form hypotheses about its nature when the object behaves in an unexpected or unpredictable fashion, such as when an object doesn't fall after passing the edge of a table. These studies suggest that babies could potentially be hardwired to take greater notice of events that elicit surprise.

If surprise is "hardwired" at birth in response to the unexpected, can we then conclude that surprise is a basic emotion? One puzzle is trying to assess to what extent surprise is based on a primary emotion of an unexpected shock or a more retrospective appraisal of what cannot be explained cognitively (Munnich et al., 2019). To what extent is surprise purely emotional and therefore unreflective in nature, and where might surprise incorporate elements of thought, reflection, and retrospective awareness? Startle reflex (Asli & Flaten, 2012) is one example of a surprise response that does not appear to have a precognitive component, suggesting that surprise is one of the primary emotions, which are not cognitive or interpretive in nature (Damasio, 1999) and have a physiological basis. Many of us have, at some point, experienced increased heart rate and other fear responses long before we register what is causing the fear, such as when we automatically recoil upon seeing a rope in a dark room, thinking it is a snake. This suggests that surprise could be somatically induced, without requiring any prior awareness or higher-level cognitive processing.

In more recent years, however, psychologists have been embracing the roles that both interpretive stance and explanation (or lack thereof) play in determining the degree of surprise that people feel in response to events. These recent studies suggest that the sense of surprise is determined not only by prior assessments of the probability of events occurring but also by the sense that an outcome *contrasts* with another predicted or imagined outcome (Teigen & Keren, 2003). Wilson and Gilbert (2008) have found that when an initially surprising situation can be explained in subsequent encounters, it becomes more commonplace, habitual, and familiar, which causes surprise emotions to wear off or diminish in intensity. While some suggest that habituation is an innate mental process that happens simply through repeated exposure to the same event (Frederick & Loewenstein, 1999), others suggest that causal attributions can influence to what extent we can adjust to a surprising incident or experience. Wilson and Gilbert (2008) attribute these diminished feelings to the extent to which people can provide sufficient explanation for the events themselves: that is, when people are able to "transform them from extraordinary events that grab attention into ordinary events that do not" (p. 370). Wilson and Gilbert suggest a fourfold model of surprise that consists in (1) attending to a surprising or novel situation, (2) emotionally reacting to it, (3) attempting to "explain or emotionally understand" the event (p. 371), and (4) adapting to the event, which thereby diminishes the affective intensity of the initial event. The extent to which we feel surprise, according to this model, is based on a combination of the relevance of the event and the degree to which we can explain why an event happened. According to this model, a poorly understood experience is seen as most surprising when first encountered.

Wilson and Gilbert's analysis highlights the ways in which explanation mitigates and influences future iterations of the same experience or memory.

Other studies have explored how the structure of a story influences the role of scaffolding in *preparing* individuals to feel surprise. In some cases, surprise occurs due to a disruption of an expected schema that prescribes how events are supposed to unfold (Meyer et al., 1997; Gendolla & Koller, 2001). Grimes-Maguire and Keane (2005), for example, presented study participants with different versions of a story. One version contained predictable cues that would enable readers to reasonably predict an outcome—for instance, "The cup of coffee was balanced on the arm of the chair. Suddenly, Richard sneezed" (p. 833) predicts that the coffee will likely spill. Another version contained more neutral (i.e., vague or indeterminate) information that does not sufficiently predict an outcome. A third version of the story (unpredictable) contains no preparation of scaffolding details to allow the reader to predict what would happen. Still another variant of the study showed increased surprise when a detail that could possibly predict the surprise event changed to a completely unrelated or "undoing" event. The findings confirmed that participants "could in fact distinguish between the various levels of predictability depicted across the three story versions (as was evident in the different surprise ratings)" (p. 836). These studies suggest that a sense of surprise can be built into a story or lesson plan, either through the intentional, anticipatory buildup of suspenseful details or by subverting the reader's expectations altogether.

Surprise can enhance the emotions, positive or negative, that arise from an experience, thereby enhancing affective "valence" (Reisenzein, 1994; Lalla & Sheldon, 2021), or the degree to which objects or situations are experienced as pleasant or unpleasant. Mellers and McGraw (2004) rated college students' responses to incorrect answers on a spelling bee and found that the study participants had a stronger emotional reaction (negative or positive), which suggests that the sense of surprise magnifies emotions. Although many researchers have characterized surprise as an emotion with a powerful emotional valence, Drummond et al. (2013) suggest that surprise has a cognitive component that involves belief in the expected outcomes of an event. That is, surprise does not happen without an accompanying cognitive belief in what is expected to occur in a given situation. Foster and Keane (2019) describe several mitigating factors that influence whether or not we feel surprised by an event, including memory of similar experiences, knowledge at one's disposal that can be used to explain the surprising outcome, and the complexity of a situation that "acts to increase the cognitive work in explaining a surprising event," such as a task that "demands to find several rather than just one explanation" (p. 2). For Foster and Keane, the degree of surprise one experiences depends on the extent to which a situation can easily be explained, or what they refer to as "a metacognitive sense of the amount of cognitive work necessary to explain some target surprising event" (p. 3). Surprise therefore hinges to a large degree upon a cognitive assessment of how probable (or improbable) the surprising event is, depending on the explanatory factors at our disposal. Other researchers such as Valdesolo et al. (2017) have distinguished between surprise-based experiences that are unexpected but ultimately explainable—such as family members surprising us on our birthday—and more curiosity-based ones, which require epistemic processing to accommodate new information. Lorini and Castelfranchi (2006) suggest that varying levels of processing are involved when a person registers surprise, ranging from the "perceptual mismatch between what the agent *sees* and its sensory-motor expectations" (p. 1) to the more high-level thwarting of expectations that can arise from analogy, inferences, conventions, and a general theory of mind that undergirds beliefs about what should happen under the circumstances. The degree to which we feel surprised about something is mediated by our beliefs in what *should happen*, rather than being only related to a shocking stimulus.

One critical question we might ask at this juncture is, To what extent can surprise foster or enhance the classroom experience? Models of surprise that are cognitive in nature seem to suggest that building surprise into a lesson or case study can challenge students' abilities to make sense of complex or bewildering information, as well as develop tolerance for ambiguity and explore alternate perspectives that defy habitual ways of thinking and explaining the familiar. In an insightful study of the uses of narrative, Peter Brooks (2022) hypothesizes that characters in stories can be used to critically engage and experiment with voices that are different from our own. Surprise can play a key element in enriching the experience of narrative or fiction reading, as readers navigate perspectives and stories that are different from what they know. Notes Brooks,

> I would suggest that our love of fictional characters and our willingness to spend time with them and to let them seep into our everyday "real" lives, and also our reluctance to let go of them once our reading of the fiction is over, our continuing conversation about them, maybe with them, is largely as Proust describes it: a wish to travel from star to star through the vision provided by new sets of eyes, by new optical instruments. This is in the best of cases, in the novels we value most, not a passive or escapist process but one that has a cognitive and critical function. (Brooks, 2022, p. 89)

In keeping with Proust's theories of narrative, Brooks contends that the value of reading fiction is precisely to "unsettle our preconceptions and self-satisfactions," thereby aiding in "the extension of a single life and consciousness into multiple and diverse others" (p. 85).

Some studies indicate that surprise aids in the retention of information (Antony et al., 2023), which in turn suggests that the mind is hardwired to register unusual events or focus more on experiences that appear unexpected or out of the ordinary. Introducing more surprises into pedagogical situations can help students learn by offering opportunities to reflect on paradoxes and solve complex problems that are outside a particular logic or linearity. In chapter 7, I suggest that metaphorical learning, for example, operates on a principle of surprise by pairing together an image and an idea that don't necessarily go together at first glance. This helps deepen a learner's thinking process by stretching the learner's ability to extend a concept beyond its appearance. Many of the above studies suggest that surprising events can enhance both affective and cognitive components of experiences. In addition, dilemmas exposed through surprising or unexpected experiences can induce people toward a greater tolerance of paradox, which in turn enhances a sense of oneness with situations or nonduality (Loy, 2019). This in turn allows one to let go of both preconceptions and habitual thinking and thus to embrace a more grounded sense of gratitude that reprioritizes one's values and ways of thinking.

A potential drawback of recent studies in surprise is that they concentrate on surprise in the context of a process of explaining the unexplained—that is, the process of cognitive appraisal that turns an unfamiliar occurrence into an explainable or familiar one through a process of reasoning or problem-solving. Surprising events are thus characterized as situations that should be reasoned away or actively shaped into the context of existing cognitive frameworks. The tendency to view surprise as a cognitive process of readjusting one's beliefs in light of novel information essentially situates surprise in a transactional model of learning that stresses "solving a problem or pursuing some form of inquiry" (Miller, 2019, p. 14). An "integrated" model of surprise (Maguire et al., 2011) suggests that surprising events are prompted by an urgent need to integrate novel or unexpected information with existing cognitive schema that go against the novel event: "If you found your house keys were missing, and you had no way of explaining it, then you might experience a high level of surprise. However, if a plausible explanation subsequently emerged that allowed the anomaly to be resolved, such as realizing that you must have left the keys in the door, then the experience of surprise should subside" (p. 177). According to this view of surprise, interest in explaining a surprising event is sustained by the challenge of attempting to integrate the surprise into an existing schema, which thus increases interest in the surprising narrative. Conversely, too much unpredictability or missing information can lead to confusion and disengagement. This suggests an intimate relationship between surprise and the attempt to adjust previous knowledge to current experiences.

A more *transformative* model of surprise, on the other hand, might focus on using surprise as a turning point or teachable moment to behold or explore the mysterious or unknown. Hunter Brown (2019) has thus characterized the kind of surprise that comes from wondering "why things exist in the first place," which he refers to as the "peculiar gratuity" of experience in general:

> In the conventional approach, reason attends from the outset to causal dependence, and then from such dependence it goes in search for something that is not dependent. A point of departure in a powerful sense of strangeness, however, orients reason to inquire into what it might be about the world which causes such a reaction. Reason is preoccupied here not so much by a regress of causal dependence as by the intuition of a peculiar gratuity about the fact of existence. I use the term "gratuity" here to designate the apparent absence of causal antecedents sufficient to cause or explain a particular phenomenon, a connotation plainly evident in the choice of metaphorical language about miracle and gift. (pp. 25–26)

Brown orients his readers to the possibility of using reason differently than, say, trying to look for causes for things that can be seen in phenomena themselves. He turns, instead, to the question, Why is there anything at all? When we deeply probe into this question, we find that there is no satisfactory reason that can be found in reason itself. One can resort only to the language of miracles and gifts to truly fathom how anything can "be" rather than not exist at all. I believe that Hunter Brown is approaching a more cosmic and existential notion of surprise that is not predicated on novelty per se but on the ability to open the mind to wonder why anything exists at all, as well as to marvel at that possibility.

Two pedagogical benefits can emerge when surprise is used to promote transformative learning. The first is that it allows for greater tolerance of ambiguity and mystery—a skill that is definitely needed in interpersonal encounter and dialogue where answers are not clear-cut or easily analyzed into steps or processes. The second is that it fosters a deeper existential inquiry that can make the process of learning more personal and meaningful to the learner. With tolerance for mystery comes the capacity to behold paradoxical situations, thereby deepening one's view of a situation. Surprise thus relates to not only an unexpected event in itself but also my connection to the event and how my positionality changes or expands as a result of the surprising occurrence.

Finally, surprise can allow teachers themselves a space for transformative learning by allowing them to engage a more present moment awareness that is spontaneous and emergent—one that emphasizes the realization of inherent gifts in our experiences rather than only the acquisition and accommodation of new knowledge into existing cognitive frameworks. The subsequent section will explore an example of surprise as a transformative moment, thus forming a tentative model for the experience of surprise itself.

Toward a Phenomenology of Surprise

When I was a teenager, I stumbled upon a beaten copy of Colin Wilson's *The Outsider* (2016) at a used book sale close to where I lived. Feeling that the title and the simple yet auspicious black cover suited my teenage angst, I shelled out the three dollars for the book. Although I wasn't aware of it at the time, this book would have a significant influence on my life. Wilson was a British writer and philosopher who was concerned with, among other topics, peak experiences (Maslow, 1999; Tassone, 2019), which have been described as "transcendent moments of pure joy and elation" (Cherry, 2020) that involve "a heightened sense of wonder, awe, or ecstasy over an experience" (Privette, 2001). Wilson had a truly unique moment that can be defined as brief but life-affirming. The event starts rather inauspiciously, when Wilson is not in a particularly great mood, let alone eager to embark on an otherwise routine road trip: "One hot day in 1954, I was hitchhiking up the Great North Road in Peterborough, in a state of fatigue and 'life devaluation.' I didn't want to go to Peterborough—it was a boring duty call—and neither did I particularly want to return to London, where I was working in a dreary plastic factory and quarreling with my landlady. I felt so depressed that I did not even feel grateful when a truck finally stopped for me" (C. Wilson, 2016, pp. 327–328). What's notable in this passage is the overall feeling tone of anxiety—issues that float in Wilson's mind unresolved, such as a job he dislikes and a landlady with whom he frequently quarrels. Wilson initially experiences a mild sense of boredom and stress from a repetitive and despairing life. As a result, he reports not feeling any gratitude even for the generosity of a passing truck driver who decides to stop for him. However, he later faces the possibility of being late after two trucks that he hitches a ride on both, coincidentally, break down. It is then that Wilson experiences a kind of heightened state of consciousness, as he is faced with the possibility of the second truck's gearbox breaking down just as the first did: "A second truck stopped for me. Again, I felt no gratitude or relief. But after ten minutes or so, an absurd coincidence happened; there was an odd knocking noise from *his* gearbox too, and he said: 'It looks as if I'll have to drop you off at the next garage.' And for the first time that day I felt a positive emotion, a feeling of 'Oh *no!*' However, he drove on cautiously, and found that the noise stopped when he drove at less than twenty miles an hour" (p. 328). Upon realizing the possibility of not being on time, Wilson's senses became highly activated as though he were in a panic mode because he didn't think that the lorry he was riding on would make it to the destined location. Yet, curiously, Wilson describes this second experience as "a positive emotion," in opposition to the dreary and uneasy boredom he had experienced previously. Perhaps the second instance makes Wilson more attuned to the dire possibility of being late, yet it somehow makes him alert, which awakens him from the dull anxieties and thus starts to take on a heightened, excited feeling tone.

Suddenly, and seemingly by fluke, Wilson later realizes that he isn't going to be delayed after all and that his panic had proven to be unfounded. But what's most significant is how the possibility of being late puts Wilson in a highly activated state of attention. Not only does the situation strike him as novel, but it is also no longer something dreary and repetitive. The issue at hand suddenly matters to Wilson: "After half an hour of this—both of us listening with strained attention for the noise—he said: 'Well, I think we'll make it if we keep going at this speed.' And I suddenly felt an overwhelming sense of relief and delight" (p. 328).

Wilson notes that part of the reason for the relief and delight is that his focus had shifted entirely to listening intently to the sound of the gear box to discern whether he would be able to get a ride. He notes how an intense focus on the problem at hand led to a concentration that heightened both his senses and his ability to feel alive and exhilarated by the present, instead of being guided by habitual and vague anxieties related to mundane or routine occurrences. The sound of the gear box became a point of focus, whereby both passenger and driver were "listening with strained attention to the noise" (p. 328). Yet what is perhaps most remarkable is Wilson's insight that the experience was not an *additive* one, but instead seemed to have arisen from a reappraisal of his current situation. In fact, as he remarks, "And I caught myself feeling it, and noticed its absurdity. Nothing had been 'added' to me in the last half hour, nothing given. All that had happened was that I had been threatened with inconvenience, and the threat had been removed" (p. 328).

Two significant points arise in this passage. The first is that Wilson's sense of relief and delight does not come from a pleasurable experience added but more so from a sense of focus on a personally meaningful event that seems to have a stake in his journey—at least enough to raise Wilson out of what he calls "a childish 'spoiledness' that gets resentful and bored in the face of minor problems" (p. 328). In the moment that Wilson wonders whether the lorry will take him to his destination, his distracting and minor worries fizzle away. Wilson theorizes that discipline and effort were needed to overcome the painful boredom and distracted uneasiness he initially experiences, which requires "a certain *unconscious* discipline of the will" (p. 328). Wilson had to focus on the sound of the gears to allow his minor worries to dissolve. He later hints that the discipline of raising a sense of interest in the moment comes not from seeking some novel experience but more so from reevaluating the present in light of what's needed immediately, as opposed to the countless minor worries and anxieties about the future. Secondly, the experience hints at the value of *being surprised* or taken aback by an otherwise ordinary experience that defies his everyday expectations. That is, Wilson is pleasantly surprised (and relieved) by the fact that, contrary to his initial worries, he would not be late after all and the lorry would reach its destination fairly smoothly. Wilson's sense of surprise could be described as a sudden reappraisal of the ways he is unexpectedly supported by factors that are beyond his understanding, foresight, or control. At the same time, this experience also seemed to require a situation that solicited a mindful focus on what mattered the most in the moment—in this case, getting to a needed destination—as well as a clearing away from attachment to unnecessary or minor inconveniences or thoughts.

During his lifetime, Wilson became acquainted with Abraham Maslow, another thinker who was deeply interested in peak experiences, or transcendent, life-affirming moments that remind us of the fundamental joy of being. Both Wilson and Maslow agreed on the importance of peak experiences yet disagreed on the extent that peak experiences could be induced through some activity or agency (Wilson, 1985). While Maslow tended to think of peak experiences as often predicated on specific circumstances or surprises, Wilson became convinced in his own studies that peak experiences could be induced through a practice, discipline, or method. This latter possibility is good news for teachers because it suggests that surprise can become a part of a teacher's process of being and reflecting in the classroom rather than a random or happenstance experience that arrives simply out of the blue.

Most of us may not have had the luxury of getting ourselves into situations much like Wilson had encountered in his travels through Peterborough. However, both chapter 2 and chapter 3 of this book will explore two possibilities. First, surprise moments can be induced through a willful act of reprioritizing one's experiences, particularly through a process of suspending anxieties and run-of-the-mill hassles in the background, while bringing a sense of calm and grounding to the foreground. Second, surprise can be induced through a mindset and trust that there is always something novel to be discovered within what appears to be routine. Cultivating a discovery mindset is one way that this book attempts to help teachers cultivate surprise in the midst of their daily routines with their students.

Indeed, particularly in his later writings, Wilson has maintained that experiences of surprise, wonder, and a general sense of meaning can be actively cultivated, as long as the individual is prepared to look for meaning in the everyday, as opposed to taking the everyday ordinary perception as the sole reality. Referring to the phenomenological stance of epoche or "that method of 'standing back' and viewing things from a distance" (C. Wilson, 2016, p. 89), Wilson suggests that the combination of standing back to see things as a whole and the ability to *anticipate* new or novel connections are what characterize an attitude of creative surprise. Describing how poet Rupert Brooke was able to see wonder just from walking down a country road, he notes, "Brooke realized that he could bring on this feeling by looking at things in a certain way. And what was really happening when he did this was that he had somehow become aware that he could see more, become aware of more, *by looking at things as if they possessed hidden depths of meaning.* For it is true. He was becoming conscious of the intentional element in perception, that his 'seeing' was in itself a creative act" (p. 90, italics mine). Several key points emerge from this quotation and Wilson's analysis. First, it hints at how people can prime themselves to find meaning by being prepared to look for hidden meanings or signs in their experiences. Part of this act may involve trusting that whatever one experiences has a unique lesson or reason for being that can be appreciated and appraised in its own right, given sufficient attention and care. This is where Wilson notes that Brooke looks at things *as if* they possess depths of meaning; that is, seeing with intention to find meaning. This meshes with a cognitive view of memory as something that is pliable and open to new interpretations and meanings, as long as the mind is oriented toward care (whether for oneself or others) and not by a fight-or-flight response (Panksepp & Biven, 2012; Desmond, 2016). Second, Wilson's analysis suggests that, through faith in the hidden depths and surprises latent within situations or experiences, people can actively construct new connections using their imagination. Wilson contends that intention is a key element in the peak experience, and thus he views the act of seeing as a creative extension of imagination.

What characterizes the surprise experience that Colin Wilson relates? How might this unique experience of surprise inform our understanding of surprise experiences in general? I suggest that we can learn something about the nature of surprise in general by looking at the example of Colin Wilson's St. Neot's margin experience. I outline some key points below.

1. A Sudden Rupture in the Familiar and Habitual

Wilson's experience of potentially not getting to his destination puts him into a heightened alertness that he described as a sense of concentration but more broadly could be construed as a *sudden rupture* in the familiar or taken for granted, which often leads to a state of shock, excitement, or bafflement.

In a sense, the challenge of not getting to his meeting on time forces Wilson to let go of his previous certainties and engage more fully in the present to deal with the unfamiliar and unknown. This heightened awareness causes certain habitual or routine thinking and feeling tones to be less prevalent in Wilson's mind or to recede in the background altogether, creating a space for excitement, anticipation, and elation. Wilson observes that the boredom and repetition of the everyday start to recede. In order to feel alive, Wilson concludes, there needs to be a focus that consumes a person's being and hinges on fundamental existence and meaning. In these moments, the normal preoccupations related to purposes, goals, and tasks start to recede into the background and seem less important than before. A near-death experience (Lommel, 2010; Fox, 2003) could be one such example that increases a person's alertness to the present moment and subverts trivial matters that might, consciously or subconsciously, consume a person's awareness.

Alertness to the present is one of the hallmarks of mindfulness, which allows people to see surprises and potentialities in every moment rather than looking at new situations through the filters of previous memories or experiences. To see things anew means, for Moustakas (1994), to bracket assumptions about things that have been acquired through previous exposure and education in order to experience an everyday event as though for the first time. From this view, we can always see an experience in a more embodied and less conceptual way, which also makes the experience seem fresher in our minds. In many cases, experienced meditators have reported a loosening of conceptual boundaries between subject and object, as when the self no longer feels separated from the external surroundings. In one lucid description of the experience of unified mind, Susan Blackmore (1990) remarks,

> Imagine that I am walking one day through the woods and I stop by a large plane tree. There am I and there is the tree. As I look, I gradually stop perceiving the tree to be separate from me. Suddenly the tree and I are both similar, both just things standing there looking at each other. Then I am not so important anymore. There is me and there is the tree but each is as central as the other. . . . Gradually the sense of me looking at any of this dissolves. There is just a vast wood, and all the rest of the world, just as it is in the moment. There is no one looking at everything. In that moment everything seems to be just right, just as it is. Time seems not to be. (p. 66)

Blackmore suggests that even a simple act of looking at a tree without the conceptual filters of "subject" and "object" can enable the mind to stop jumping from thought to thought, which induces a lucidity, similar to what Wilson experienced while engaged with the problem of getting to his destination on time. Both Blackmore's and Wilson's experiences involve an expansion of awareness through a dropping away of attachment to a train of thoughts that tends to fragment our experiences and render us bored or de-energized.

2. An Awareness of Grace

Wilson's discovery of *getting to his destination after all* gives him a sudden feeling of being existentially gifted, which goes beyond the habitual mentality that defines our actions and behaviors as something to be earned. Once Wilson realizes that he will make it on time, he experiences "an overwhelming sense of relief and delight," which goes against his strong belief that he would not be able to make it through a combination of circumstances weighing against him. This has the effect of thwarting the calculating mind by suggesting that factors beyond one's control or foreknowledge could contribute in unexpected ways to one's well-being, a notion often described as grace (Brown, 2019) by many religious thinkers. Through a simple and unexpected act of grace, Wilson experiences a sudden release or relaxation that is no longer consumed by trying to control the future experience or outcome. Yet Wilson suggests that he didn't need to add anything to experience this natural sense of gratitude. To the contrary, the sense of being relieved of a highly inconvenient outcome seemed to take away Wilson's previous preoccupations, many of which contributed to a dissatisfaction with life that took the form of dull boredom or despair.

Once he realized that he was going to make his destination after all, Wilson develops the intuition that nothing more needs to be added to create feelings of satisfaction and contentment in life. This way of thinking suggests that perhaps, whether conscious of it or not, we are continually reaping the benefits of unearned grace and can feel those benefits simply by letting go of a seeking, grasping mindset. This can bring a person closer toward a sense of *already being* gifted before even achieving a coveted goal or reaching a destination; a point sometimes referred to as "being blessed" in religious traditions. The Indian philosopher Osho (2017) describes this sense of existential gratitude as the ability to behold gifts that may otherwise be taken for granted: "Existence gives you birth, gives you life, gives you love; it gives you everything that is invaluable, that you cannot pursue with money. Only those who are ready to give the whole credit of their lives to existence realize the beauty and the benediction; only those people are religious people. It is not a question of your doing. It is a question of your being absent, nondoing—letting things happen" (p. 112). It can be challenging for teachers and other professionals to give the "whole credit of their lives to existence," particularly when the process of professional education often emphasizes self-improvement and personal agency through knowledge and learning. However, perhaps the biggest takeaway is that existential gratitude allows for more space to let things happen spontaneously, as an alternative to insisting on being in control.

In addition, Wilson cultivates an intensity of relief and joy that, at least temporarily, allows him to see perfection in the present moment. How often are we as individuals able to see something good and uplifting in every moment, in spite of the fact that our future aspirations remain unmet or unfulfilled? This could be described as a sense of being gifted by existence itself. As Hanson (2013) succinctly notes, "I'm blown away by the fact that anything exists at all, that this universe is here with us in it. Talk about gifts!" (p. 64). Contrary to a view of gifts that requires a giver and receiver, existential or cosmic gratitude (Keltner & Haidt, 2003; Roberts, 2014; Steindl-Rast, 2004) emphasizes the givenness of being and experience as intrinsic gifts that are already inherent to being alive. Yet gratitude for being alive is not always easily accessible. For Wilson, the sense of being gifted with life comes with a sense of *relief*, or the lifting of a crisis situation that he experienced as threatening and alerting to all his senses. Thus, the existential gratitude that surfaces from this experience results from getting rid of extraneous worries and repetitive baggage that might otherwise prevent people from appreciating and enjoying the moment as a gift.

Existential gratitude, for many thinkers, involves cluing into the inherent giftedness that comes with being alive. Murphy-Shigematsu (2018) notes,

> There may be a universal sense that gratitude arises from both receiving help from others and focusing habitually on the positive aspects of life. If we take to heart this way of being, we find the sources of gratitude are infinite, and include such mundane events as waking up in the morning, or appreciating one's abilities, or seizing a chance to do meaningful work. The object of gratitude may be humans, nonhuman animals, nature, God, or the universe, or all of these—with gratitude being part of the wider life orientation toward noticing and appreciating the positive things in the world. (pp. 167–168)

What's significant about this passage is the way that the everyday, taken for granted, or given is elevated to the status of a miracle: something that could very well not exist yet does nonetheless exist. This may lead one to the question, Why this and not something else? Or, more crucially, what or who has allowed me to have this particular experience and not some other?

Existential gratitude does not have to refer to a specific giver but can be a more diffuse appreciation for life, having a body, or even breathing. Simple things that we might not even think about are elevated when we connect with how they uniquely furnish our present experience when they could just as well be absent. A sense of basic existential gratitude can extend not only to everyday objects but also to the body itself. Anyone who has experienced a temporary illness or setback, such as Wilson's on the lorry, might begin to recognize how certain kinds of limiting experiences might make a person more appreciative of what the body can do, as opposed to only focusing on acquiring, say, a longer life or a better figure or physique. Much talk about health focuses on the idealized body type or image; however, have we ever truly stopped to enjoy and contemplate the miracle that comes from simply having a body that functions? Even if the body does not function perfectly, thinkers such as Kabat-Zinn (2013) have emphasized that most of what we experience as a body does, in fact, function well enough, and we must not buy into the illusion of a body and mind that is perfectly "with it" and "together." In fact, there is much to be grateful for in the body's complex configuration of cells, tissues, and organs, all orchestrated together to somehow get the body from one place to the next.

Wilson is able to feel gifted by an otherwise mundane awareness that he would not be late—a realization that would otherwise have gone unnoticed or seem unremarkable unless there was a chance that he *could* be late. Gratitude opens the door to a deeply contingent and interdependent notion of life, which decenters the standard view of agency as based on linear patterns of cause and effect. Teachers similarly sometimes need to reorient themselves toward seeing the subtle ways in which their being and learning is supported by the various elements around them, just as Wilson was better able to appreciate the workings of the lorry in getting him to his preferred destination on time.

The concept of the gift economy (described in chapter 4) emphasizes the way in which we are mutually sustained through relationships of gifting that are neither contractual obligations nor predictable outcomes. Although this sense of being gifted by even the smallest things might make teachers feel more vulnerable to uncertain futures, it also can help teachers realize that they are not alone in the classroom and are not solely accountable for what happens within those four walls. This counteracts a tendency to view the teacher as the sole influencer of the classroom, a myth that undergirds the discourse of accountability in many of today's educational policies.

3. Yielding to the Unknown

It is intriguing to note that Wilson's experience allowed him to naturally reprioritize what feels most directly important, relevant, and meaningful in life by facing a situation that was beyond his cognitive or behavioral influence. Without the ability to see life events as gifts, it is very easy for people to succumb to subconsciously trying to control or influence a situation in their favor, particularly through anxious rumination, engaging in familiar rituals, or clinging to a vestige of knowledge or control. Although Wilson realizes that nothing he could do would change the situation, his sudden change of fortune allows him to appreciate something beneficent that is not fully known to him, much less controllable. This theme touches upon the difficulties that people experience in letting go of a sense of control, particularly in the face of threatened loss of meaning through death or another tragedy. In *The Year of Magical Thinking*, Joan Didion (2005) describes the many rituals that she performed after her husband's sudden and unexpected death, including her refusal to give away his shoes on account of her belief that he would return someday. Many thinkers have in a similar vein explored the role that illness (French, 1998) and death (Holecek, 2013) can play in helping people to inhabit the unknown in lieu of trying to cling to false beliefs about one's ability to control their life. By encouraging people to let go of this rather illusory sense of control, illness forces people to focus on the priorities that matter the most in life and thereby become more attuned to a fundamental sense of thankfulness for life. Jean Shinoda Bolen (2021) describes the often seismic shifts that can happen when a person faces severe illness and is forced into a position to reassess their relationships, priorities, and values:

> Illness, especially when death is a possibility, makes us acutely aware of how precious life is and how precious a particular life is. Priorities shift. We may see the truth of what matters, who matters, and what we have been doing with our lives and have to decide what to do—now that we know. Significant relationships are tested and either come through strengthened or fail. Pain and fear bring us to our knees in prayer. Our spiritual and religious convictions or lack of them are called into question. Illness is an ordeal for both body and soul and a time when healing of either or both can result. (pp. 6–7)

Shinoda Bolen stresses how illness can be a "descent into the underworld" or "the realm of depression when we are cut off from our feelings" (p. 16). However, she also emphasizes the preciousness of life and how illness can force people to let go of aspects of their life that are weighing them down, including the struggles to live up to impossible external standards such as beauty, perfect relationships, and success. Instead of worrying about trying to make life perfect and being consumed with all kinds of endless wants, a person in this stage returns to a more fundamental sense of being granted a truly unique opportunity to simply inhabit the moment. When an issue or problem reaches a state of urgency such that it begins to take center stage, people often find themselves having flow experiences (Csikszentmihalyi, 2008) with the problem itself, since a passionate urgency impels their whole mind and body to become fully engaged in solving the crisis. They become so absorbed with trying to address the problem that they even lose the sense of a self or time, which naturally causes the trivial to fall into the background and for a wholehearted feeling of presence and centeredness to arise.

However, the experience of wholeheartedly engaging with a mystery of great importance that is beyond one's knowledge or full control need not happen through an emergency or crisis. The process of being present without clinging to objects in mind is one way that people can cease the flow of endless narratives that decenter the mind and body. Miller (2006) suggests that even the decision to focus on one thing at a time can become a radical act of attention, which counteracts the tendency for people to use technologies as sources of endless distraction: "Videos, television shows, and much of our entertainment are based on the assumption of limited attention. We often feel the need to do two or three things at once because we become bored if we are simply doing one thing. If we become bored watching one show, we can use the remote to move through all the channels which can now number in the hundreds. The restless mind is constantly seeking to be entertained" (p. 36). The antidote to this endless distraction is for the mind to cultivate a bare awareness—that is, tapping into what is happening in the present moment, without attachments—or a compassionate attention that actively connects with a specific object of attention (McLeod, 2001). This experience sometimes requires, paradoxically, the ability to turn something that seems an obstacle at first into a subject of contemplation, which subsequently requires an intimate knowing that is not based on mere textbook learning or memorization. In her research on guided imagery, Belleruth Naparstek (1994) describes how we can only understand how to heal the body when we become more acquainted with how disease operates, what kinds of systems are mobilized to deal with illness, and how these can be sensorily imagined. She recommends an intimate kind of *knowing* the body that transcends the conceptual and thereby allows the mind to give direction to the body on how to deal with disease and bodily imbalance. Another example of intimate knowing can happen in meditation. Dzigar Kongtrul Rinpoche (2009) recommends a way of addressing pain that is based on intimate awareness, where the division between subject and object starts to become less distinct:

> You have to be able to sit with your experience and tolerate it, to learn to let things pass. Immediately jumping into practice to kill the pain doesn't work either, because of your desperation to remedy the pain. The pain doesn't even have time to blossom. By leaping into practice, you are too attached to the cessation of pain. Acting out of fear never works, and practice used dualistically, like water on fire, is not that effective. Summon up your courage to let the pain fade away by itself. To enhance that process, practice. (p. 67)

Another way of reprioritizing is to reflect on whether something is truly a need or simply a want. Chan Buddhist monk Master Sheng Yen's first adage is "Wants are many, needs are few" (Sheng Yen, 2009, p. 2). This adage points to the Buddhist idea that endless desires (and the self-attachment entailed) is the root of suffering. Reducing desires to focus on what matters the most is one important element of the peak experience that Wilson reports.

4. A Sense of Discovery and Adventure

What's subtle about Wilson's experience is the sense of adventure that it evoked. While potentially being late certainly evoked a sense of anxiety, it also led to a sense of being on a journey and, in retrospect, not really knowing where it would lead. Wilson reflects on being disoriented and how this momentary disorientation created a sense of novelty within him. Indeed, *not knowing* gave Wilson the sense of life being enshrouded in a mystery that has many potential outcomes. Instead of feeling trapped in the sense of repetition, the experience of being lost momentarily lifted that sense of repetition or sameness to embrace a sense of life as a potent force that is always moving toward something unexpected and new. Wilson, albeit briefly, experienced a sense of mystery that broke him out of the routine of thinking that his next experience would reflect all his previous ones.

Adventure can take the form of being transported into an unfamiliar place, but it can also involve cultivating curiosity for what otherwise seems familiar. Gilbert (2009) suggests that individuals who suffer from depression can foster an intentional attitude of discovery when they pretend to be "aliens" from another planet:

> Imagine that you come from a very different planet, maybe one where there is little light and the sky is dark, and you're visiting here. You are fascinated by everything that you see and sense; by

the sky and its ever-changing colour patterns, the smell and feel of the air, the sounds around you, the colours of the cars, the trees and the grass. Allow yourself to be amazed and fascinated by the greenness in the living plants and the shapes of leaves. The idea is to playfully begin to experience the world anew; to bring a freshness to our perceptions and senses. (pp. 137–138)

Imagining what it's like to see from another's eyes and thus explore a novel experience is not limited to a mindfulness practice but can encompass something as simple as reading fiction. According to transportation theory (Green, 2004), part of what makes empathy for characters in a novel possible is the lability of the mind in adopting narratives that have completely different parameters from the ones we are familiar with. The willingness to be transported into a new world is both a structure of the brain and something that needs to be cultivated through an openness to learn about other worlds and other peoples that are different from ours.

I have reason to suspect that a model of education that focuses on standardized testing does not easily allow for moments of discovery, adventure, or even mild curiosity to arise in teachers and students alike. First, too much competition for grades can narrow the focus to achievement. When getting the grade becomes the most important part of education, it leaves little room for the exploratory curiosity, which is sustained by "free play and solitude," both of which "require time" (Miller, 2018, p. 53). Miller further suggests that the ability to make room for curiosity in students can allow them to develop a sense of agency that enables the child to "ask questions and then pursue ways to find answers" (p. 54). While Miller here is referring to the cognitive and developmental benefits of cultivating curiosity, I would go further to suggest that curiosity has affective components as well, including the ability to cultivate patience with a question, to relax with the process rather than speeding hastily toward an answer or result, and an ability to tolerate uncertainty. Norman Jackson (Nygaard et al., 2010) suggests that for a curriculum to foster creativity, it must sufficiently prepare students to "encounter and learn to deal with situations that do not always result in success and which require resilience and persistence to overcome difficulties and meet the challenge" (xv) and deem successful those situations where students undertake "the process of taking risks and trying to achieve in such uncertain and difficult circumstances" (xv). When students are spending too much time determined to pass high-stakes exams, they miss the ability to remain with mystery and might also develop less tolerance for an uncertain outcome, including failure.

A tolerance of uncertainty is one of the hallmarks of creative thinking, where the thinker often has to endure periods of frustration (Patel et al., 2022) when there is no discernable answer or solution to a problem. While scientific discoveries seem to be neatly presented in textbooks, what is rarely depicted are the trial-and-error, missteps, dead ends, and constant revision of thought that go with actual scientific discoveries (Roberts, 1989). In fact, part of the meaning of discovery lies precisely in the way that we need to keep changing the way we think to accommodate new ways of thinking and being. Paradigm shifts are one example where a way of thinking gets upended by a completely new metaphor that is not predicated upon past experience.

I would also suggest that just as students can actively cultivate curiosity for their subjects and topics in school, so teachers also can enrich their curiosity for their students by cultivating forms of "appreciative inquiry" (Cooperrider & Whitney, 2010), which involves actively looking for hidden potentials even in the most difficult or challenging situations as well as a nonjudgmental appraisal of the contributions of the whole—that is, "looking for the positive and for points of connection" (Murphy-Shigematsu, 2018, p. 179). The process of appreciation may seem more time-consuming to implement for some teachers, requiring that they take more time to appreciate the contributions of each student as opposed to looking for and rewarding the "best" answer. However, looking for the positive in all contributions of a learning community is one way to foster more engagement and gratitude in educational settings.

5. Dissolving the Sense of Separation

One notable detail that is hardly discussed in Wilson's telling of the lorry experience is the relationship between himself and the lorry driver. When he first hitches a ride, Wilson is not feeling particularly grateful for the driver, much less the opportunity to go to a different city and experience a refreshing break from his routine. He notes, instead, "I felt so depressed that I did not even feel grateful when a truck finally stopped for me." Wilson is clearly preoccupied with his own worries and self-obsessions as the vignette opens, and he even notes how this induced a lack of gratitude for the driver's act of giving him a ride. When people are self-preoccupied, they tend to see others as background to their own misery: a truck driver is only an accessory to their own worries, and often merely functions as a secondary character who takes them from one destination to the next. Similarly, people in the modern world of conveniences may habitually relate to others according to the roles in which they serve in relation to the self. A uniformed clerk becomes "someone who will serve me," while a homeless person is seen as having no value in relation to my needs and wants. During his second truck ride, however, Wilson's narrative stance changes from "I" to "we," particularly when he notes, "After half an hour of this—both of us listening with strained attention for the noise—he said: 'Well, I think we'll make it if we keep going at this speed.'" The sound of the gearbox takes Wilson out of himself and into the shared world of another human being who, like himself, wants desperately for the truck to take them to their destination. At this point in the story, Wilson seems to relate more to the driver as a fellow human being, not simply as a functionary who is serving his own unique needs. This is an important point that I will explore in subsequent chapters: how moments of surprise can equalize the playing field between self and other by throwing one's traditional locus of inner control off kilter.

Surprise can sometimes thwart the culturally conditioned inner script that tells us we have full responsibility and agency over what happens to us (Metzinger, 2013). When we earn a highly coveted promotion in our workplace, we tend to think that it's through our efforts alone that it happened, rather than through the efforts of many working together toward a shared goal. What surprise can do is momentarily remind us of how interdependent we are with various factors—environmental, interpersonal, and social—that can only be seen as gifts because they cannot be earned by effort or talent alone.

While not necessarily typical of all surprise experiences, Wilson's St. Neot margin experience was chosen for this text because of the unique sense of "being lost then found" that echoes Norman Fischer's quote at the beginning of this book. In fact, it is the very process of discovering how one's deepest and truest aliveness was never lost in the first place that contributes to the blissful moment of truth: the unexpected sense of *being found* is what most seems to define Wilson's surprise experience and characterizes it as a process of undoing the grasping mind that sees itself as lost. More specifically, Wilson reports on a redemptive returning that leads him away from a sense of being forever lost and toward a sense of being already home in the universe—to being *closer* to his destination than he thought, thus relinquishing the burden and anxiety of having to return, yet not knowing *how* to return.

It is important to note that Wilson's sense of surprise operates on a sudden reversal of fortune or "turning back" from one extreme to another, which suggests a tension of opposites instead of attempting to transcend those opposites altogether. In other words, surprise does not suggest going to a permanent, blissful place, let alone denying the self in favor of a static heavenly state of mind. Similarly, teachers operate from specific positions of identity and authority in the classroom and do have a responsibility to fulfill their roles, which are bound to foster moments of creative tension, disunity, and discord. Teaching is, like most professions, an inherently complex balancing act of forces, many of which are beyond the teacher's foreknowledge or control. However, the discovery that there is much in the experience of a teacher that is fundamentally given prior to all the roles they adopt, is given in the classroom itself, and is inherently a *gifting* experience of being alive and present can be a turning point that allows teachers more room to breathe, feel, be present, and not attach to their idealized role of the teacher. That is, teachers can feel supported and sustained through the sense of grace that pervades every moment in the classroom and entails unexpected turns. Teaching can still be tough—there is a certainly a lot at stake for both teacher and student alike—but teachers need no longer be solely invested in the institutionalized image of the teacher as one who must know and extend care endlessly. All that is needed is that teachers be aware that each moment carries the possibility of the unexpected and is always a little bit beyond prediction. Each moment is surprising when it is seen with an attitude of anticipation, freshness, and discovery, and teachers need only choose to rest in this discovery to see their career as full of surprises. During the subsequent chapters of this book, I will make a theoretical case for the need for surprise in classrooms, as well as link the experience of surprise to a broader experience of giftedness: two intertwined ideas that form the theoretical framework of the first part of this book.

Questions for Discussion

1. What learning experience felt surprising to you? Think of a learning experience you had that contained unexpected surprises. Discuss what the surprise was and how the surprise enhanced or inhibited your learning of the subject.

2. Learners sometimes find that an experience becomes a source of learning only in hindsight, through repeated reflection on the experience. Take a moment to reflect on how an experience of something became a surprising source of self-knowledge or

insight at a later time. Can you think of why the experience yielded new insights later? Why might it have taken a while to learn something from the experience?

Questions for Reflection

1. Reflect on something that you do before or during the classroom that you consider an automatic, routine, or habitual exercise—for instance, greeting students when they come in the door, assigning quizzes, or marking assignments. Consider the possibility that there is a hidden treasure or surprise in this activity that you either didn't notice or didn't pay attention to. Attend to this same experience with a sense of relaxed and single-minded exclusion of all other thoughts, as though it were an urgent or fundamentally important matter that requires your full attention. Put aside all other projects or upcoming actions, and try to attend wholeheartedly to this one process.

   a. After doing this practice, write a short reflection describing the following:

      i. What did you feel when you did the exercise with full attention and in the present moment?

      ii. What surprises, if any, emerged from doing the exercise with full attention? Describe the surprises or unexpected twists or turns in the experience.

      iii. How did these sudden surprises shed new light on something that was done habitually before? How did these surprises perhaps change the way you look at this experience?

2. Have you ever had an experience similar to Wilson's St. Neot's margin? Describe a situation that contained an unexpected surprise that was accompanied with a sense of relief or even a peak experience. What happened? How was the situation similar to, or different from, Wilson's experience? From your own reflection, try to form a mental map of how you experience surprise and the unexpected or uncanny.

Chapter 3

The Four Pillars of Surprise

Chapter 2 explored key elements of surprise, using Colin Wilson's St. Neot's margin as a central case study for exploration. Surprise is often characterized as something that passively *happens* to a person, as when we read the expression "taken by surprise," or when it is seen as an interruption from an expected sequence of events (Noordewier et al., 2021). Surprise has even been characterized as contributing to tension and stress, as when uncertainty arises from a disruption in the expected (Huron, 2006), and it can even be associated with a negative reaction such as fear of the unknown. Luna and Renninger (2015) note how life events such as "death, illness, war, financial loss, relationship difficulties, and natural disasters are all the more devastating when they take us by surprise" (p. 44) and suggest that many surprises can force people to look for comfort and security rather than take greater risks.

Yet, as was suggested in chapter 2, surprises can be equally associated with feelings of relief as well as an expansion in the ability to see unique possibilities available in the present. Colin Wilson was convinced that there were ways to induce the sense of freshness and wonder through mental exercises that engage focus and awareness. Throughout his writings, he has explored the ways that the mind can emerge from the repetition of habitual thought to achieve the kinds of lucid experiences that can happen when surprised into a more awakened and appreciative state of being. What needs further elaboration, though, is how surprise can be induced within a classroom experience, as well as the affective elements that teachers can actively and individually cultivate to maximize feelings of surprise in classrooms.

What elements of surprise can teachers realistically experience and actively cultivate in classrooms? By analyzing surprise through the lenses of four discrete components that can potentially be enacted in the classroom, I hope that teachers can change their orientation toward surprise away from a passive "happening" and toward a process of searching and priming surprise, thereby actively seeking surprise in their classrooms instead of waiting for surprises to somehow magically appear.

In this chapter, I have constructed a fourfold model of surprise in the educational realm. Based on my research on teachers who practiced gratitude visualizations prior to assessing their students' writing (Brown, 2022), I contend that there are four major elements of a surprise experience.

The first is receptivity (Huntington, 2009), which relates to being *taken aback* by an event and allowing ourselves to fully receive it without the lenses of previous conceptual ideas or models. Receptivity can arise through willful suspension of the familiar or routine models through which we expect things or situations to unfold, as well as an openness to experiencing life anew.

A second quality is empathy (Bornstein et al., 2014; Matravers, 2017), an ability to see things from others' eyes and perspectives, which often follows from receptivity. When teachers suspend their habitual responses and ways of classifying their students, they often find themselves better able to connect with what students are really trying to convey through their presence, challenges, and expressions in the classroom.

A third element is discovery (Benson & Dresdow, 2003), which arises from a deliberate act of looking for "new finds" in what otherwise may appear to be routine or familiar. In this chapter, I suggest that the more teachers actively look for and expect novelty in their students' work, the more likely they will find something new in each student's contribution to the classroom. Discovery, like receptivity and empathy, also leads to a growing openness and vulnerability to the gifts that students bring to the present moment.

Finally, I will discuss the importance of trust—a growing insight into the way that situations around us come together in mysterious or indescribable ways to bring key insights and learning into fruition without our deliberate planning, thereby creating an expanding awareness full of meaning and interconnection. Unlike discovery and receptivity, trust allows teachers to stay grounded and centered in their sense of belonging to the whole, without becoming overly distracted or overwhelmed by the surprises they may experience or expect to find in their classrooms. Through trust, a teacher can maintain equanimity rather than becoming overly enmeshed in states of empathy or receptivity. Balancing an inward sense of trusting the gift of one's very own being and presence in the classroom can help counterbalance the outer-directed foci of discovery, receptivity, and empathy.

How might these pillars of surprise be enacted in the classroom? What do they look and feel like? Each subsection below will delve more deeply into the four pillars of surprise and how they can be applied to classroom situations. As you are reading each of the four pillars, you will find a reflection exercise at the very end of each section that will help to solidify the ideas presented, as well as bring them closer into the realm of your own teaching practice. Please take the time to engage each of these reflections before moving onto the next subsection. Doing so will enable you to better apply the theoretical ideas presented in this chapter, as well as have fun experimenting with them.

Cultivating Receptivity: Seeing the Familiar Anew

Receptivity refers to an ability to appreciate and receive what is unfolding in the moment, as opposed to actively trying to shape reality according to our wants and will (Slote, 2013). All too often, the qualities of yielding, passivity, and waiting have been given secondary status in classrooms, at least in comparison to so-called proactive qualities that we want to inculcate in students, such as taking initiative, being assertive, and pursuing predetermined goals. Western education has placed a high premium on the "active participant" who is always willing to be the first to answer questions in the classroom (Albertson, 2020). Yet a large part of what makes a classroom engaging and successful is the ability to fully accept a classroom as it is organically unfolding—not simply to shape the classroom through words, but to receive it with a sensitive and fresh awareness that is not encumbered by preconceived framings or the need to manipulate situations to foster a specific outcome. Learning requires a combination of both creative molding of source material for novel ends and a more receptive quality of not trying to exert oneself toward achieving a narrow end. Maslow (1993) refers to this quality as the removal of self-consciousness, or "dropping our efforts to influence, to impress, to please, to be lovable, to win applause," which thereby allows us to "devote ourselves, self-forgetfully, to the problem" (p. 63). Receptivity not only benefits problem-solving situations that might call for an expansion of consciousness but can also enrich our relationships. Educator David Hunt (2010) explains how one of the most important qualities in a friendship is the ability to surrender one's agendas and preconceptions to receive the sheer mystery of another human being. Here, he notes, "Friendship is mysterious and beyond your control, not only because it has a life of its own, but also because you cannot control other people's reaction. Honouring the Spirit of Friendship means letting go of any attempt to control the flow of friendship" (p. 168). While teachers are obviously responsible to a certain degree for controlling the direction and flow of their classrooms, at times it's possible for teachers to induce a sense of a greater receptivity, particularly through a guided meditation or a sense of focus, to receive and appreciate the classroom in a fresh and reinvigorating way. In these instances, the teacher can lose their sense of needing to be in control of all outcomes, yielding instead to the contingencies of the unfolding moment. Guided meditation (Gawain, 1982; Davenport, 2009; M. Samuels, 2013) has been known to sensitize people to otherwise taken-for-granted processes, such as the rhythms of the body, or even a particular sense, such as seeing or hearing. In the example of direct contemplation, all labels and conceptual framings are suspended in favor of simply being present with whatever we are sensing in the given moment. This can cause teachers to notice things around them that they would otherwise find routine or humdrum. Simply being primed for focus, passive awareness, and attention to small details can lead to a greater ability to be surprised by everyday occurrences.

Although the capacity to give and be generous are often lauded as growth-enhancing experiences (Ryan, 2018), we may fail to place an equal emphasis on the capacity to wholeheartedly *receive* an experience. How often do institutions give out awards for most wholeheartedly, thankfully received care or gifts? More often than not, the giver is considered more meritorious than the receiver of a gift or an experience, which in turn downplays the skill of receiving. One potential reason is that we are conditioned to the notion of constantly giving as a productive, generative force within a society. People may even associate receiving with "owing" someone else or being in debt, which leads to a tendency to downplay the receptive mode, or a sense of dependency on others that can, at times, threaten to undermine one's sense of identity (Siebert et al., 1999). As will be explained in chapter 5, the capacity to receive is a central hallmark of the capacity to feel genuine gratitude. Without the ability to stop and reflect deeply on what has been given to us throughout our lives, we may find ourselves unable to wholeheartedly enjoy the fruits of either our own or another's contributions to our lives. Charles Taylor (1991) and Thomas Moore (1996) have observed how a decline in ceremony and ritual in modern Western societies results in an impoverished sense of identity that lacks the ability to feel wholly appreciative or bound to the world around us. Matthew Fox (2016) has also remarked on the importance of ceremony as a form of continuity across generations, as individuals in communities are reminded that they depend on their elders, as well as the community as a whole, for all individual successes:

> Ancient peoples taught their children primarily through ceremonies. Ceremonies were intergenerational; the elders assisted the young. This working together of elders and youth is needed today on a grand scale. But one of the most serious problems we face is that we have had a loss of eldership, thanks to the breakdown of community and the destruction of indigenous communities. The older ones today, not having themselves undergone rites of passage and other transformative ceremonies, are in a bad place to be leading the young. (p. 136)

Fox here alludes to two intertwined issues: the erosion of a sense of community through the decline in ritual and a growing fragmentation of generations, whereby the young are often left in a position to learn for themselves, as opposed to having core knowledge or rites of passage passed down to them. Not only does the modern erosion of ceremony in Western culture deprive younger generations of the sense of giftedness or indebtedness that could be generated by participating in ceremonies where knowledge and responsibilities are passed down, but it also contributes to a fragmented, separated self. Even when this self reaches out to others in a spirit of generosity, there is still a deeply entrenched sense of "I" that remains separate from the community or previous generations. What seems like the valuing of altruistic giving in some societies may actually foster a covert sense of a separate self, as when we give credit to the self that gives rather than looking at the larger relationships that allow giving to take place. Indeed, what seems to be left out of the equation is the way in which receptiveness is a necessary adjunct to giving. Without the capacity to receive, the gift cannot be fully understood or appreciated, let alone fully reciprocated, in a spirit of gratitude and sharing.

In this section, I will explain how the capacity to receive what we've been gifted with is a skill that is just as essential as the ability to contribute according to one's capacities. In fact, I will go even further to suggest that receptivity is the most crucial quality needed to feeling a sense of connection to others.

An ontology that emphasizes discrete givers and receivers tends to privilege giving over receiving, seeing the former as more of a virtue than the latter. However, more thought and study have been given in recent years to the essential aspect of receptiveness as a precondition to all experience. One of the most significant shifts of twentieth-century philosophy has been the movement of phenomenology (Gallagher, 2012; Hycner, 1985), which stresses openness and receptivity as a cornerstone of experiential knowing. Phenomenology attempts not to *explain* an experience so much as to sufficiently describe it in a way that captures its felt essence and structures. This requires both a relentless search for the essence of a thing and paradoxically recognizing the impossibility of fully capturing the essence because it is always in the process of *being revealed*. Our experiences are thus not so much crafted from thoughts as they are derived from receiving something that is experienced as "given." According to this philosophy, the ability to receive is a key factor in breaking down prejudiced or unformulated ideas, to capture a more total and whole experience, or what Maslow (1993) refers to as the blurring between "figure and ground," where "relative importance becomes unimportant; all aspects equally important" (p. 250). What emerges from phenomenology is the ability to intensely and carefully experience a situation holistically, without the tendency to select only those aspects of an experience that benefit an assumed self. Engelland (2020) suggests that phenomenology straddles the boundaries between the search for "what is" and the awe and mystery of encounter—specifically of how we are able to experience anything to begin with, given the presupposed separation between observer and observed. Hence, Engelland remarks, "Phenomenology potently combines these two forces in philosophy, search for the elusive essence of things and wonder concerning the possibility of experiencing things. It renews Socrates's relentless inquiry into *what* things are. It renews the modern relentless inquiry into *how* things are experienced. Phenomenology's hybrid method holds these two counter movements in tension by applying them to each other. It asks, '*How* can we experience essences, and *what* is the essence of experience?'" (p. 11). To think "phenomenologically" could be one way of practicing seeing a situation as it is unfolding to the senses and one's being, as opposed to "categorically" through preformed concepts or preconceived associations that are attached to a given experience. This way of experiencing the world may also reverse a commonplace tendency to compartmentalize knowledge, thus allowing for a cross-disciplinary merging of distinct subject areas.

Mainstream schools in North America tend to treat knowing as a mastery of discrete subjects, such as mathematics, science, and other areas in which knowledge is rendered objectively. Biologist David Orr (1991) remarks, "In the modern curriculum we have fragmented the world into bits and pieces called disciplines and subdisciplines. As a result, after 12 or 16 or 20 years of education, most students graduate without any broad integrated sense of the unity of things" (p. 52). Without a unified, cross-relational map of school subjects, students can graduate without a distinct sense of belonging to the universe, thus reinforcing a separation of knower and known, whereby an isolated subject becomes the agent of mastering discrete objects of knowledge. What often results is an inability to appreciate the never-ending flow of being that gives rise to the thoughts themselves, which leads to clinging to specific thoughts and solidifying them into fixed "truths" or absolutes (Bohm, 1994). Heidegger was one Western philosopher of the twentieth century who deeply explored being that precedes the solidification of "knower" and "known" or "subject" and "object." Instead of seeing reality as something we acquire through a rational process of induction or deduction, Heidegger defines the source of thought as pre-intellectual being that is not mediated or bounded by a subject and object—that is, it exists prior to all categorization or "dividing" of experience that often happens subconsciously. Commenting on the nondualistic aspects of Heidegger's thinking and philosophy, Loy (2019) remarks,

> Heidegger says that the "openness" of the traversed region—the world of our surroundings, which each of us is most immediately "in"—is "not . . . created" in that it is prior to our dualistic understanding of an object presented to a subject. Heidegger challenges the notion that consciousness is the attribute of a discrete subject observing a nonconscious external world. That usual dualistic understanding is only one historically determined interpretation of the "open region." Here Heidegger goes beyond speculation about the nature of Being and for the first time tries to point directly to the presubjective ground that *is* Being. (p. 178)

The important point here is the clinging to specific *beings* and mistaking them as open, whereas it is the prereflective *Being* that is actually the living source of thought itself. Hence, Loy later remarks, "Just as men generally miss the openness of Being by clinging and trying to possess particular beings as if 'they were open in and of themselves' so thinkers tend to do the same with their own thoughts, thus missing that presubjective opening from which thoughts arise" (p. 179). This presubjective kind of being that Loy describes is not hemmed in by thinking, nor does it get altered by discriminating mind or any of the other ways that the mind is thought to be conditioned.

What does this mean for teachers? Why would a precognitive receptivity be such an important aspect of being in the classroom? One of the most humorous vignettes that Parker Palmer (2017) shares about teaching was how, as a younger teacher, he paid extreme attention to the student who was not attentive in his classroom. Referring humorously to the "student from hell," Palmer reflects on how, in his subconscious eagerness to get through to the one student who was not paying attention, he inadvertently ignored the rest of the class's needs and ended up reflecting negatively on his own self-image as a teacher: "For a long and anguished hour I aimed everything I had at this young man, trying desperately to awaken him from his dogmatic slumbers, but the harder I tried, the more he seemed to recede. Meanwhile, the other students became ciphers as my obsession with the Student from Hell made me oblivious to their needs. I learned that day what a black hole is: a place where the gravity is so intense that all traces of light disappear" (p. 44). Instead of seeing the classroom as an open field through which situations are constantly arising and perishing, Palmer's concentration on the "troubled student" transformed into an outright fixation that deflected from the flow of the moment itself. His experience was also twinged with self-consciousness, which, as many studies suggest (Baltzell, 2016; Weiskrantz, 2009), can blind people to the wide range of signals and information that they pick up unconsciously around them, forming broader pictures of the world. Palmer frequently alludes to the importance of spontaneity of learning, which he often describes as "teachable moments"—unplanned experiences that are not controlled by either teachers or students. However, in order to arrive at spontaneity, the complexity of the student, teacher, and classroom itself needs to be acknowledged, with all its paradoxes and tensions. To focus on one side of a situation or on a fixed, reified view of the teacher is to miss the wholeness of pedagogical moments. Palmer himself admits to how he often feels "tempted to protect my sense of self behind barricades of status or role, to withdraw myself from colleagues or students or ideas and from the collisions we will surely have" (p. 17).

Perhaps one way to describe the open awareness that characterizes receptivity is to compare the happenings of a movie to the screen on which the movie is being projected. While seeing the images in the movie could involve being drawn into dichotomous contrasts (good and evil, success and failure, attractive and unattractive, etc.), the screen upon which the movie is projected doesn't actually change due to the images that are being projected.

Hanson (2013) uses the evocative metaphor of the TV screen to describe the pleasure of pure awareness that is not attached or clinging to particular mental states or emotions when he remarks, "A TV screen is not changed by either the beautiful or the ugly images it shows. Similarly, awareness is never stained or damaged by what passes through it. This gives awareness an inherent quality of reliability and tranquility. Even if you are depressed or in great pain, you can find refuge and relief in the awareness that contains these, and any other difficult content of mind" (p. 89). Hanson suggests that simply tuning in to the inherent nature of awareness without looking for specific "positive" thoughts can be a peaceful and tranquil gifting experience.

A similar kind of awareness underpins the experience of sounds. Kabat-Zinn (2005) reflects on a time when, while meditating, he heard a loud sound outside. While he initially entertained the question of where the sound is coming from—such as from a garbage truck or a street sweeper—he later finds himself bombarded with a barrage of thoughts, including the conflict of wanting to be undisturbed yet lacking the "willpower" to achieve such a state of being. Instead of trying to find the source of sound, Kabat-Zinn discovers a pure awareness that is uncontaminated by the sound, or which simply receives all sounds in an accepting, enveloping way:

> Behind this play of my mind is pure sound. Hearing the sounds and not knowing "what" it is are both knowing. In this moment, can I simply rest in that knowing, the knowing that doesn't know and doesn't need to know, and is content because these sounds are already here in this moment? Things are already just like this right now. Can they be accepted as they are because anything else is going to lead to disliking, to frustration, to disturbance, to greater distraction? (p. 209)

Kabat-Zinn later refers to the "tranquility in the hearing and in the knowing underneath the sound" (pp. 209–210). While this might sound esoteric to some, the description nicely encapsulates an experience of pure awareness and acceptance that often happens in meditative states—one that contains all experiences without discrimination and allows one to *rest* in a knowing that is simply present with all that arises. To go back to Parker Palmer's example of the "student from hell," teachers can choose to rest in the present by tapping into an ever-present awareness that does not side with one thought or another but allows the paradoxes, tensions, and contradictions of life itself to enter the classroom without derailing the process of teaching and learning. The key is not to attach to one thought or the other, but instead to behold contradictions through recognizing the inherent awareness (the sense of "knowing" itself) that is *behind* all thought itself.

One of the applications of receptivity is humble inquiry, which, at times, can involve subverting the notion of being an authority on a given subject in favor of allowing the other to become an expert. Schein (2021) describes humble inquiry as a way of placing authority in the hands of the other:

> Humble Inquiry is an investment in that you are expending some of your *attention* up front, admitting your ignorance, and giving the other person some power. Your questions convey to the other person, "I am prepared to listen to you and am making myself vulnerable to you." You will get a return on your investment if what you learn is something that you did not know before. You will then appreciate that you have been told something new, and a positive relationship can begin to develop through successive cycles of asking and responding in which each of you is *receiving value through what you learn*. (p. 20)

What's most promising in this approach from an educational perspective is that it can position the teacher as a learner just like the student. But it also reveals how the teacher's value is not just found in how much knowledge they have to impart to students but also in their ability to foster the inner gifts of their students by placing themselves in the position of a humble learner. While this may seem scary at times in the sense of granting more power to the student, Schein suggests that in the end the return is expanded awareness as well as a deepened relationship with the student.

What's also significant are the deeper insights into a situation that can be obtained simply through an expanded awareness that is not based on the mental scaffolding of previous concepts. That is, to receive is to wholeheartedly embrace an experience as it authentically comes to the senses, rather than relying on previous concepts, hearsay, or culturally accepted ideas and narratives. Referring to the experience of the breath, which is often a hallmark of meditative practice, Fromm (1992) refers to how "awareness of breathing is something quite different from thinking about one's breathing. In fact, the two modes exclude each other" (p. 38). Furthermore, because receiving an experience such as breathing is not based on thinking *about* the experience itself, it does not try to compare the experience to another, let alone categorize it into positive or negative aspects. In fact, to receive is not to pick and choose between elements of an experience. Rather, it is simply to be open to the totality of a situation, regardless of our preferences, likes, or discriminations. Clark Moustakas (1994) refers to this receptivity as bracketing one's own preconceptions in favor of seeing the freshness of the current moment and not being presumptive in favor of a particular theory of an experience. One hallmark of phenomenological research that could become an attitude or stance in daily life is the willingness to suspend judgments and to simply take the given experience as an already integrated structural whole that is unfolding before our eyes.

Many spiritual thinkers have tied receptivity to the ability to wait. This waiting is somewhat different from the kind of waiting associated with anticipation, as when we are waiting in a supermarket line to pay for our groceries. Waiting does not refer to the expectation of a future good or reward, but more so it is a kind of openness to what is emerging in the present yet has not yet fully revealed itself. The French philosopher Simone Weil (2001) has described attention as a practice fundamental to all studies, not because of the content that is absorbed but how attention to school subjects can foster a single-minded attitude, similar to prayer, that can enhance students' spiritual capacities. She notes how, for students, the practice of attention needs to be applied "equally to all their tasks, with the idea that each one will help to form in them the habit of attention that is the substance of prayer" (p. 59). What's most fundamental to this form of attention, for Weil, is the ability to attend to the form without trying to grasp its meaning or understand it too quickly. She notes, "Our thoughts should be empty, waiting, not seeking anything, but ready to receive, in its naked truth, the object that is to penetrate it" (p. 62). For Weil, a learner needs the patience and faith to wait for a subject to reveal itself, instead of prematurely trying to grasp its essence using previously held knowledge and concepts. This requires a trusting kind of receptiveness to what is unfolding, without the need for quick and easy labeling.

Receptivity is also an important element to appreciating any form of art or literature. Oscar Wilde (1976) coined the term "artistic temperament" to refer to a quality of receptivity through which artists can create novelty in art. In addition to viewing the artist as receptive to new thoughts and ideas, Wilde also believes that an audience can be equally receptive to artistic work. Like one of his contemporaries, Emerson (1991), Wilde contends that the reader plays an active role in constructing the text of a work of art by properly seeing and thus receiving it. He contrasts the artistic temperament that is used to approach a work of art with an attitude of *exercising authority*, which involves imposing ideas or preconceived notions onto the work of art. He notes,

> If a man approaches a work of art with any desire to exercise authority over it and the artist, he approaches it in such a spirit that he cannot receive any artistic impression from it at all. The work of art is to dominate the spectator: the spectator is not to dominate the work of art. The spectator is to be receptive. He is to be the violin on which the master is to play. And the more completely he can suppress his own silly views, his own foolish prejudices, his own absurd ideas of what Art should be, or should not be, the more likely he is to understand and appreciate the work of art in question. (Wilde, 1976, p. 43)

What blocks receptivity? For Wilde, "any desire to exercise authority" over a work of art blocks the deeper meanings and qualities of that art from appearing to the mind. A person who is full of ideas and learning may tend to impose such ideas on the work itself, which makes it difficult to see or experience the newness of that experience or engage with it. In fact, for Wilde, having too many ideas about a work of art can truly block a person's ability to behold the special truths that emanate from it.

Receptivity is one value that, as Slote (2013) suggests, challenges the notion of equating enlightenment to standing over things and thus trying to control them in some way or another. Contrary to this view, Slote reasons that being receptive allows for a wider range of information and is aligned with an ethic of care. To be receptive is to tap into a more maternal way of thinking in which the aim is to nurture or to bring out the best that is deep within oneself in lieu of imposing a predefined structure. But at the same time, teachers should not try to uphold receptivity as yet another example of an ideal that needs to be strictly enforced. Part of receptivity also entails letting go of perfectionistic standards that teachers might hold toward themselves and their students. Spiritual practices such as Buddhism embrace the notion of accepting the imperfect, or even seeing "perfection" in imperfection. In describing the way meditation in the Buddhist tradition strives to transcend perfectionistic standards, Fabrice Midal (2017) notes,

> There is a certain danger in overemphasizing the calmness and serenity that the practice of meditation provides, making us

want to match up to this ideal. But the Way is not to try and be perfect, nor to measure up to some preexisting model, but instead to fully enter into a relationship with what is, including the shadows, the suffering, the accidents, and the misfortunes which make up the thread of all existence. True wisdom doesn't lie in being perfect but in being fully human. The way of the Buddha teaches us this. (p. 54)

A receptive attitude may encourage teachers to let go of the notion of a single perfection, opting instead to be open to relationships with *what is* and no longer feeling bounded by self-imposed beliefs of what is ideal.

What kinds of qualities can foster receptiveness? Mindfulness educator Patricia A. Jennings (2015) notes how the slowing down aspect of mindfulness can foster a sense of receptivity, as she learns to relate to time differently:

When I teach, it often feels like a constant flurry of activity, demands, and distractions. One student needs my help with problem-solving. Another needs me to help her stay on track. I have to monitor another's behavior while remembering the content I am teaching. This barrage of demands can create the illusion that there is no time to mindfully attend to what's going on and to listen to my students fully. When I bring mindful awareness to my teaching, time slows down. When my mind isn't distracted by a flood of thoughts about the past and future and I am present to what is happening now, I find I have more time than I realized, and I begin to notice the needs of my students. When I find myself becoming anxious because I think my class is chaotic, I can stop, calm down, and mindfully observe what is happening. In these moments, I often realize that the chaos is my mind and that the class is actually just fine. (pp. 10–11)

Among others, two insightful ideas emerge from this passage. The first is that the sense of distractedness can often foster a sense of accelerated time, as the mind attends to every detail of thought and experience rather than simply being aware and present in a nonattached manner to all the phenomena of the environment. The second is that when practicing having a present awareness, *time slows down*, and this essentially frees up the teacher's mind to tend to the needs of her students.

Reflection: Receiving the Gifts of Others

Reflect on your day-to-day practice as a teacher. In one column, take note of all "ideal" outcomes of a learning situation that you can think of. Imagine how you would like to feel, how the ideal classroom might look, and how students respond to your classroom, in the most ideal terms possible.

Then, in another column, take note of the "less than ideal" outcomes. In what way was your notion of learning and teaching disrupted?

In a third column, write down all the ways in which the less than ideal could be conceived of as a hidden gift. Here, you may want to imagine receiving both the ideal and less than ideal aspects of the class equally, like guests who have an equal part to play in a bustling classroom and have equal status as guests. In what ways might the less than ideal have enhanced the ideal, leading to an unexpected turn or change? After noting the details of each column, reflect on how your experience of less than ideal classroom outcomes may have changed.

Empathy

To cultivate feelings of surprise sometimes requires a suspension of the teacher's position as an all-knowing expert who oversees or manages the classroom affairs. To balance this approach, teachers must also be willing to see other perspectives that don't necessarily fall in line with their own. To cultivate empathy involves, at times, challenging a hierarchical notion of teaching that privileges the teacher's point of view over and above the students' views. Empathy, far from entailing enmeshment in another person's experience, involves what psychotherapist Carl Rogers refers to as an "as if" quality, which he succinctly describes as the ability "to sense the client's anger, fear, or confusion as if it were your own without your own anger, fear or confusion getting bound up in it" (Rogers, 2004, p. 284). Contrary to trying to *become* one's students, a healthy sense of empathy can allow teachers to safely try out different perspectives of their students while maintaining their sense of responsibility and role as a facilitator for the students' learning. Finally, empathy is a quality that can lead to gratitude, as teachers discover the ways that students bring unique stories and narratives into the collective learning of the classroom. Shared empathy can foster a sense of interdependence in a classroom setting, as the multiplicity of subjectivities in a classroom can provide an enriched opportunity for sharing and learning. This can lead to feelings of giftedness. As was discussed in chapter 2, I suggest that one of the unintended consequences of the surprise experience of Colin Wilson in St. Neot is that he begins to directly experience the situation without the filters of habit, familiarity, and the usual swirl of discursive thoughts that tend to separate "I" from the world. I interpret part of this experience to include, even for just a short moment, a sense of togetherness with the lorry driver. Perhaps there is even a sense that in spite of their differences in class, background, and occupation, they are traveling on the same road, sharing in the same anticipation and worry.

Empathy is an important element in how teachers are able to see the gifts in their students. What does empathy refer to? Philosopher Derek Matravers (2017) has succinctly defined empathy as *"using our imagination as a tool so as to adopt a different perspective in order to grasp how things appear (or feel) from there"* (pp. 1–2). What's potent about this definition is that rather than limiting the view of empathy to emotional contagion or "our 'catching' feelings from other people"—a view espoused by the British philosopher David Hume, among others—Matravers suggests that empathy is actively constructed through the imagination. And unlike sympathy, empathy involves a *feeling with* people, as well as the ability to wear people's shoes without a sense of condescension or othering. In contrast to pity, empathy allows the person empathizing to imagine a rich and complex view of another person—one that is not hindered through comparing my own state of being and having to someone else. Miller (2018) describes empathy as having "both affective and cognitive components" (p. 35), meaning that it can involve capacities "to feel what another person is experiencing or have some cognitive understanding of what is happening to another" (p. 35). While a lot of research has emphasized the role of mirror neurons in allowing people to *feel with* another person's situation, there are also certainly imaginative and distinctly cognitive aspects of empathy to consider. Classroom exercises such as those suggested on Anne Frank House's website[1] can encourage young students to mentally reconstruct the living conditions that Anne Frank must have faced during the Nazi occupation. This unique curriculum suggests the power of empathy as a form of mentally reconstructing events that happened in a distant historical past or even a different country or culture.

Contrary to some popular beliefs that empathy is merely "touchy feely," empathy extends beyond feeling to embrace how individuals respond to situations and suffering. It can even contain a cognitive component that is rooted in the effort to understand another individual. Henshon (2019)

---

1. https://www.annefrank.org/.

identifies three kinds of empathy that can be practiced in classroom situations, namely *cognitive* empathy, which entails "understanding another person's perspective or mental state"; *emotional* empathy, which means "the ability to feel another person's emotions"; and *compassionate* empathy, which entails "feeling for another person and taking action on his or her behalf" (p. 13). Henshon emphasizes how teachers should make the effort of compassionate empathy—that is to both "understand what our students are going through" and to "act on their behalf" (p. 13).

Why would empathy be an important element of surprise in the classroom? One reason is that an active cultivation of empathy can evoke new emotional connections with people that would otherwise go unnoticed. Fischer (2021) describes a six-week course he coordinates for Google called Search Inside Yourself, which is designed to help professionals develop emotional intelligence skills, including the capacity for empathy. One of the exercises he leads incorporates both mindfulness and empathy as tools in the practices of writing an email. Fischer instructs his participants to contemplate how it might feel to be the recipients of the emails they are about to send: "Instead of shooting off a hurried e-mail, and dealing with the consequences later, take an extra moment. Write the e-mail, then close your eyes and visualize the person who is going to receive it. Remember that he or she is alive, a feeling human being. Now go back and reread the e-mail, changing anything you now feel you want to change before sending" (p. 181). This practice, while seemingly simple in its design, effectively incorporates depth elements of empathy that can induce surprise. For instance, teachers who are about to give email feedback to their students might be surprised to imagine how their students might respond to the feedback. They might even discover new ways of seeing their students that might influence how they send feedback. But, perhaps most surprisingly, empathy is not necessarily limited to how the self imagines others to be. Hanson (2013) has designed a guided exercise that allows participants to explore their own positive qualities in a way analogous to seeing the strengths in a friend. He guides his readers to treat themselves as they would a friend by beholding the positive qualities within themselves:

> Consider a friend's positive qualities—perhaps honesty, likable quirks, and a warm heart. Would denying these qualities be a fair way to treat this friend? How would your friend benefit, instead, if you appreciated his or her positive qualities? Now turn it around: Can you see your own good qualities? It's a matter

of justice: You are telling the truth about yourself, much as you would tell the truth about a friend. Why would it be good to see good in your friend, but bad to see it in yourself? (p. 97)

When doing practices that induce surprise or gratitude, teachers may do well to heed Hanson's advice and consider their own unique contributions and strengths, instead of focusing exclusively on their students'. Hanson's suggestion reminds us that surprises can be found within our own actions, personality, and core sense of being if we are sufficiently attuned with and attentive to the qualities that make us unique and beneficent in the world.

An empathic approach encourages teachers to rethink how they deliver communication, while potentially discovering a new frame of reference from which to read their own feedback. Teachers in my study (Brown, 2022) found a deep connection between seeing gifts in their students and cultivating empathy, which seemed to be a natural result of being more open and attuned to the gifts in the students. This study found that for the teachers to feel gifted, they needed to focus less on the writing itself as an object and more so on the intentions behind the students—including their sincerity and efforts, which, they reflected, seemed to have enriched their appreciation of what the students created. Being able to imagine what the students were thinking and going through while constructing the assignment gave the teachers more appreciation when the students were struggling to communicate, not to mention seeing the student as a whole person who is uniquely shaped and influenced by their communities and families.

In addition, my research dovetails with recent studies on the effects of reading literature on cultivating a sense of empathy. Readers, according to transportation theory (Green, 2004), are effectively able to feel empathy through a cognitive construction of the world inhabited by the characters in a story or novel. While transportation theory entails that there are no limits to how readers can empathize with characters, it also suggests that readers tend to subconsciously empathize with people who they are most familiar with in terms of culture, gender, socioeconomics, and so on. Green's research suggests that simply being transported into the world of the narrative is not enough; sometimes readers need to make more conscious efforts to envision unfamiliar characters as worthy of empathy and care.

Finally, many holistic thinkers are associating empathy with deep contemplative states of knowing that may challenge a hierarchical model of teacher and student. However, the process of empathy requires not only a mirroring effect but also a cognitive reappraisal of the commonalities that link all beings collectively. Pearsall (2007) refers to this as "the awe of understanding" when he notes,

> My interviews indicate that the awe of understanding is almost always in reaction to nature or processes like a fuller awareness of *our own* senses, a strong emotion, giving birth, loss, illness, healing, dying suffering, loving and other manifestations of profound connection or disconnection from "something more." Based on what I've learned, true, thoughtful awe for another person also happens, but not because that person is perceived as somehow above us. Instead, the reverse seems true. Our awe of understanding derives from a deep and profound *sense of connection and sameness* with that person as being part of the same world and sharing our same struggle in that world. (pp. 212–213, italics mine)

Empathy, as Pearsall suggests, comes from moving beyond being awestruck by power and authority, whether it's from a teacher, a celebrity, or any other individual in power. Instead, the sense of awe may be coming from an ability to reflect on the similar journey of fellow sentient beings in this world, encompassing both the profound suffering of loss and the joys of creation and success. This may seem initially challenging when so many people can be drawn into the allure of status or even the air of the all-knowing teacher. However, being in awe of a shared struggle could be one way that teachers and students alike can cultivate greater empathy for their efforts.

Teachers in my study (Brown, 2022) often had to make great efforts to envision the effort of some students, particularly those who are deemed as not having placed enough due attention to the assignments they submitted. Some teachers in my study even felt shortchanged by the fact that they were making more efforts to empathize with students who did not make an "equivalent" effort when they handed in their assignments. This suggests that an altruistic empathy can sometimes be mixed with considerations of fairness and justice. On the other hand, some teachers in my study were able to better empathize with students because they challenged their own position of teacher as authority and were able to behold students as fellow human beings. One crucial aspect of empathy entails the ability to break the boundary between self and other so that there is no sense of separate "I" and "you."

Reflection on Empathy

Reflect on one student with whom you have experienced challenges or difficulties, particularly as it relates to completing an assignment. Write a reflection describing or outlining the difficulty: how it arose, what conflicts resulted in the difficulties, and any confusion that the student might have experienced while doing the assignment. Try to put yourself in the student's shoes. What was the student thinking in regard to the assignment? What might have put the student at a disadvantage in terms of understanding the assignment or fulfilling its requirements? Don't be afraid to use your imagination to create an "as if" reconstruction of the student's thoughts, as the goal of this exercise is not accuracy but rather the ability for the teacher to assume a different perspective.

After writing your paragraph, reflect: In what ways did the student's point of view seem to depart from yours when it comes to the assignment? What unexpected connections did you make with the student as you were practicing putting yourself in the student's shoes?

Discovery: Exploring a New Terrain

A surprise mindset reframes accidents or happenings that are not entirely within a person's control as possibilities for new horizons, knowledge, and growth. This yields to what I call a *discovery mindset*, in which teachers become more open to the unexpected learning opportunities of a sudden detour in a lesson plan. Although accidents can sometimes be viewed as catastrophic, it's notable that many famous scientific discoveries started out as accidents (Roberts, 1989; Maslow, 1993). That is, they can take the form of very sudden surprises that are not part of an original experiment. By analogy, teachers can embrace the accidental by allowing a lesson and its assessment to be more spontaneous and more unstructured so that students and teachers can negotiate the assessment process together (Bellugi, 2010). Accidents, like empathy, level off hierarchical leanings by suggesting that teacher and students alike are subject to uncertain turns that they need to work out together. This point challenges the view that a teacher can stand over and control their classrooms or exert a continual vigilance over students' performance. A skillful teacher can transform the shock of accidents into a meaningful discovery that can make it seem more like a gift that was planned by the universe as opposed to a mistake or misstep.

This ability can also extend to the process of writing a term paper or even this book, in which I have found myself frequently detouring from the original plan and taking risks to go in a different direction than what was originally expected. Unlike receptivity, discovery can be improvisational as it involves the willingness to detour from the norm of a classroom rubric or plan. Yet without a sense of centeredness and grounding in the teacher's inner sense of being and belonging, a discovery orientation may potentially derail or overwhelm a teacher. I therefore suggest that *trust* is a necessary counterbalance to being overwhelmed by the discovery mindset.

Discovery is related to exploring new ways of seeing and experiencing things and is often related to the ability to be surprised, which in turn relates to gifts. Dastur (2000) has written a great deal about the effect of surprise. She notes,

> The event in the strong sense of the word is therefore always a surprise, something which takes possession of us in an unforeseen manner, without warning, and which brings us towards an unanticipated future. The event, which arises in the becoming, constitutes something which is irremediably excessive in comparison to the usual representation of time as flow. It appears as something that dislocates time and gives a new form to it, something that puts the flow of time out of joint and changes its direction. (p. 182)

What characterizes surprise, according to Dastur, is the ability to be taken by the unexpected, which propels the subject toward the unanticipated result. Time becomes "out of joint" because the sense of continuity or the expected gets thrown out of joint. But how willing are teachers to be taken by the unexpected? To what extent do teachers allow themselves to be surprised or allow for the unknown in their classes?

While Dastur's quotation might suggest that surprise and discovery are unplanned or unpredictable events that happen without warning, other scholars contend that surprise can be planned or built into an activity. Surprise can be based on the elements of the unexpected found in situations and stories. Grimes-Maguire and Keane (2005) note, "Very few best-sellers describe the hero going to the office, working all day and then coming home and going to bed. Instead, writers often maintain a reader's interest with well-timed surprises; for instance, Raymond Chandler's murder discovery scenes often describe the dead body obliquely (e.g., a brown loafer protruding from the curtain), so that the reader's surprise at discovering the referent (i.e., that the shoe is attached to a corpse) mirrors the detective's surprise at discovering the body" (p. 833). Here, the authors suggest that surprise depends on well-timed and planned elements that are embedded in texts themselves. On the other hand, Grimes-Maguire and Keane also explore how surprise depends on how readers frame and represent texts. Thus, they further note,

> When presented with a story, readers do not just passively absorb what is on the page in front of them, but instead build up a rich representation of the depicted scenario. They make assumptions about the central characters, their goals and actions, and even form a mental picture of the location and time in which the story is set. This detailed representation is achieved by calling upon the wealth of background knowledge readers have about the world and is highly sensitive to the way in which the information is presented. We have also seen that, in turn, this representation strongly determines whether subsequent events will appear to be surprising or not, based on the degree to which they are supported by prior events in the discourse. (p. 837)

This may lead some to wonder: can surprise be similarly planned in curriculum events and situations? Yeo et al. (2018) see great potential here when they describe a study in which "surprise figured prominently in the experience of these faculty members as they engaged in the SoTL scholar's program. In a phenomenological frame, this surprise, for some, became the breach or rupture to their perception that allowed new ways of thinking about students and new ways of being in the classroom" (p. 26). Yeo et al. contend that surprise allows for a necessary rupture in habit and routine, which can allow for new information and knowledge opportunities for students.

Still another tenet of discovery-based learning is the idea that students should be able to learn for themselves through a process of inquiry that teaches students *how to think*, instead of replicating previously established knowledge and information. This requires that students actively construct knowledge through collaborative engagement, as opposed to passively absorbing information from teachers or textbooks. Describing an urban planning project, Gehry Nelson (2022) writes,

> To discourage students from engaging in replicative thinking, I wondered what would happen if I had them "back in" to learning what I was required to teach them. After trying out numerous ideas in my classroom, I thought about how a city's character is reflected in its location, its architecture, and the values of the people who live and work there. I thought about how parts of the city could be a metaphor for creative thinking and for all subject matter. What if I gave students a curriculum-based story about a city situated in a real place familiar to them, a story that asked them to imagine that city 100 years in the future? What if I had them build a rough model of their imagined City of the Future, shaped by their own Never-Before-Seen, roughly built solutions to subject-related, big topic dilemmas that they identified—*before* I taught them what others had done? (xxxiii)

Gehry Nelson paints an evocative metaphor of "backing in" to learning—meaning that concepts are discovered by the children before they are shown what others had done in the past. This gives students confidence in their own thinking rather than relying on the thoughts of others to arrive at their own conclusions. Finally, discovery-based learning is based on a constructivist view that portrays learning as placing the student in the position of an active explorer of knowledge, or, as Selwyn (2011) claims, "taking place best when it is problem-based and built upon the learner's previous experience and knowledge. In this sense, learning is rooted in processes of exploration, inquiry, interpretation and meaning-making" (p. 73). As we read about discovery-based learning, we may begin to wonder, What position do teachers have in relation to the role of explorer and *constructor* of knowledge? Are teachers simply serving to stand back and facilitate the role of students as pioneers of their own learning, or can teachers also adopt a discovery mode of viewing their students and their efforts? While a great deal of literature has been devoted to discovery-based learning for students, very few articles delve into the ways that teachers can also use a discovery mindset to see their students in a fresh and exhilarating way that can help them better appreciate their students' efforts.

Sadly, it appears that teachers are often stuck in a model of education in which they are seen as mere adjudicators of students' learning, rather than playing a part in the co-construction of student learning. That is, teachers are often considered "keepers of grades" (Blount, 1997), a title that suggests teachers judge their students' work from a place of cool neutrality instead of constructing student learning through a process of framing and representation of student work. But one can equally argue that teachers are just as much involved in the constructive framing of their student writing as artifacts of knowledge as the students are in terms of their construction of knowledge.

Furthermore, attitudes of discovery and a mindset of wanting to learn more and expecting to discover novelty in a student's work constitute ways in which a teacher can stay engaged with students, particularly when assessing the same assignment across many students triggers repetition or boredom.

REFLECTION ON DISCOVERY: THE EVOLVING CLASS PLAN

Take an old lesson plan that you have used in previous classes or semesters (this exercise works especially well if you have multiple drafts of the same lesson plan across a series of semesters, to see how this plan has changed over time. However, this is not absolutely necessary).

Try to discern or trace back the changes to the class rubric over time. How did the lesson plan change and evolve? Why exactly did it change? Was the lesson carved in stone from the very start, or were gradual tweaks made to streamline the plan or make it more accessible to certain students?

Then reflect on the reasons why the class plan did not stay the same over time. Write a short reflection explaining the ways in which even the simplest lesson plan or topic evolved according to the conditions and needs of both teacher and students. Appreciating and celebrating the novel ways in which the class design was innovated is one way of accepting that there is always something new to be learned and discovered from even the simplest lessons.

Trust: Surrender to the Journey

Trust entails a belief that people and situations are fundamentally positive if they are embraced fully, with a respect for their fundamental value and worth. Dunn and Schweitzer (2005) define trust as "the willingness to accept vulnerability based upon positive expectations about another's behavior" (p. 736), while other studies have similarly linked trust to the ability to be comfortable with vulnerability and free expression in group settings (Mayer et al., 1995). Physician Redford Williams (1991) has found correlations between heart disease and a tendency toward hostility and cynicism, which he traces back to a lack of trust in the goodness and helping behaviors of others. Some studies suggest that decisions involving uncertainty and ambiguity can trigger the amygdala, a part of the brain that is associated with a fearful response to perceived threats in the environment (Hsu et al., 2005). The good news is that when people are faced with decisions that involve less public scrutiny or evaluation, they appear more inclined to take risks and make mistakes without the fear of being judged for their decisions (Trautmann et al., 2008). This observation suggests that tolerance for ambiguity and surprise can be strengthened when people learn to reframe what are perceived mistakes as opportunities for growth, as well as cultivate the ability to put others at ease through an honest admission of our own mistakes or shortcomings. Perhaps most significantly, trust, like creativity, requires an openness to experience (Rogers, 2004), which "implies that an individual is willing to view experiences outside traditional categories, to consider new ideas, and to tolerate ambiguity if ambiguity exists" (Starko, 2010, p. 52).

What does it mean to *trust*? Why would trust be an important element of gratitude? Bowlby (1973) describes how in early infancy a trusting bond can form an important and essential aspect to how we function in the world and to what extent we flourish. For attachment theorists, trusting relationships mean that parents are neither too clinging to their children's safety nor too neglectful, to the point where a child feels safe to explore their environments in a spirit of play. Summarizing findings on how children respond to a "strange situation" in which children are deprived of familiar parental figures, Quinn and Mageo (2013) note, "Upon each of the mother's returns, a 'securely attached' infant seeks proximity or contact with the mother and then resumes exploration of the environment, evidenced by play with the toys that are available in the room. An 'insecurely attached' infant shows little or no tendency to approach mother on the mother's return (labeled *avoidant*) or, alternately, makes efforts to contact mother but also resists her (labeled *resistant*)" (p. 4). For infants, the ability to explore is predicated on a basic sense of trust and security, both within the child and in the parent. For the child, this might entail being able to safely explore the unknown with the knowledge that the parent is reliably present and the child is not overwhelmed with stimuli that she has to figure out on her own. Conversely, a lack of trust in the parent can cause a child to develop avoidant tendencies or even to shy away from exploration. Trust in one's experience is often built through one's formative relationships with caregivers and parents. Luna and Renninger (2015) thus note,

> Toddlers trot boldly into the unknown when they have a trusted parent close by. Kids with secure attachment to their parents

wander away in search of adventure. But for kids who can't rely on their parents, the playground is a minefield. They inch forward to explore then scuttle back and cling to their guardians. It seems illogical. Wouldn't the kids who are closest to their parents have the toughest time leaving them behind? But it's just the opposite. Trust is a psychological safety net that allows us to let go. (p. 47)

For the parent as well, a sense of trust is essential to allowing a child to make various discoveries, without anxiously clinging to the child or being overinvested in a child's safety. This has been likened to a mother who, while being present in a room, is not overly invested in her child's safety since she already knows that the child is safe and present. This *knowing* is quite different from always being watchful as though one were afraid of some hidden threat. An attitude of hypervigilance is the very opposite of trust, since it suggests a desire to control. Children who internalize a parent's sense of trust can feel more confident in their own abilities because they don't internalize the anxiety that their parents feel about them. On the other hand, trust does not entail a laissez-faire approach to parenting, where children are given absolute freedom to do as they please. Instead, trust entails the ability to set boundaries while allowing children the leeway to explore, play, and learn independently.

A deeper meaning of trust is that it entails a faith in life that is grounded in the acceptance of what is but also the belief that one's inner world and life is just as it should be. Carl Rogers (2004) has articulated the interesting paradox that the more a person can accept themselves as they are in all their complexity and diversity, the more open they are to change and becoming. What could explain this paradox? One possible explanation is that a person who authentically accepts the complex multiplicity of emotions has more energy and even humility to change, knowing that they are no longer protecting one area or *face* of their given being. It takes a lot of energy to suppress parts of ourselves that don't match with our idealized image of ourselves. This energy could be better invested in receiving the environment as it is and working fluidly and organically with situations and people, instead of being attached to a single, all-encompassing self. Rogers therefore suggests that authenticity is tied to an awareness of the many selves inhabiting a single consciousness, as opposed to a single monolithic self. That is, there is no dominant and authoritative sense of self; rather, awareness entails a balancing act between these multiple selves.

Still another form of trust arises from a contemplative awareness in which awareness no longer identifies with thoughts. When we ruminate on things that have happened in the past, we tend to view ourselves as existing within the thoughts themselves. We imagine that it is "myself" that is replaying the same experience that happened many years ago, so we create the image of an "I" that experiences the unfolding thought or is in the thought (e.g., "I am foolish because I behaved this way"). Once we begin to question the source of all these thoughts—What *is* this awareness that thinks?—we begin to create more space in which to realize that the thought is not "me." Adyashanti (2011) notes, "When you learn to separate the experience in these moments from the conclusions drawn by the mind, you begin to taste real freedom" (p. 106). That is, we begin to trust our more fundamental nature as present and unchanging when we are less identified with individual thoughts and simply identify with awareness as an ongoing process.

Trust is more fundamentally related to the ability to see the unfolding events in the classroom as natural and perfect in themselves. This is in accord with the Zen Buddhist principle of seeing that all causes and conditions are in their perfect place and have their own unique reasons for being present. In his seminal work *Zen Mind, Beginner's Mind*, Shunryu Suzuki (1994) cautions against trying to reject or transcend one's unique identity in favor of an idealized image of what the spiritual "should" resemble. Referring specifically to meditation practice, he urges practitioners to let go of a mindset of wanting "to achieve something" (p. 59) and suggests, instead, to conceptualize themselves as having their own unique and inherent gifts to contribute to the present moment:

> So try not to see something in particular; try not to achieve anything special. You already have everything in your own pure quality. If you understand this ultimate fact, there is no fear. There may be some difficulty, of course, but there is no fear. If people have difficulty without being aware of the difficulty, that is true difficulty . . . but if your effort is in the right direction, then there is no fear of losing anything. Even if it is in the wrong direction, if you are aware of that, you will not be deluded. There is nothing to lose. There is only the constant pure quality of right practice. (p. 61)

While "right practice" in this context refers mainly to sitting meditation practice, I would suggest that the attitude of Zen can be applied in different contexts, using a soft yet focused awareness to tend to one's present actions, without imposing the image of what one wants to achieve or is afraid to lose in the process. This requires a deep trust that we are not limited in any way by self-image but can, instead, trust the unfolding process of being in the world without the intermediary of a controlling ego or self.

How might a sense of trust unfold in the classroom? Miller (2000) has advocated bringing a teacher's *whole self* into the classroom as an antidote to compartmentalizing the self into different and separate parts. He describes a three-part model of the self, soul, and spirit, which he feels should all be equally nurtured and brought out in classroom settings. Of the three, soul is perhaps the most intermediary, in the sense that it bridges the concerns of spirit with the everyday concerns of the self, which requires a delicate balancing act of harmonizing different aspects of one's being: "It is through soul that we attempt to link our humanity with our divinity. If there is too much emphasis on spirit then we can lose touch with our humanity and daily life. On the other hand, an overemphasis on human self can let our lives become too narrowly focused on the mundane" (p. 24). Many of Miller's ideas thematically touch upon the concept of *yingyang* in Taoism (Wang, 2012), which emphasizes balance and harmonization. Taoism suggests an inner harmony in which good and bad are enfolded upon each other and there is a natural flow between the expected and unexpected, which is often most clearly reflected in nature. Miller (2018) notes, "We also see the rhythm of life in nature, as one moment we are being soaked in pouring rain and the next moment, we are feeling the warmth of the sun. Nature is constantly in transition. . . . Seeing change in nature can make it easier for us to accept change in our lives. Learning to accept change is part of making friends with ourselves" (p. 16). Teachers often find themselves navigating the balance between keeping a class focused on the materials that need to be covered and learning to accept the unpredictable. Parker Palmer (2017) has written about the teachable moment as one in which the unexpected turn in a classroom becomes the opportunity to introduce a novel form of learning that did not get factored in to the lesson plan itself.

Acceptance and trust can be cultivated actively in the classroom using meditation and reflection. In my study on gift visualization in teachers (Brown, 2022), the teachers found that meditating on the gifts that students bring to their assignments allowed them to accept the students' writing as their own inherent truth, instead of imposing a strict idea about what constitutes an acceptable assignment submission. In some instances, the teachers were able to accept and celebrate the authenticity of a student's writing, even if what they submitted did not fit the exact requirements of the assignment itself. When students detoured into their own personal lives, teachers who would initially approach these detours with skepticism were later able to suspend their disbelief or judgmental attitudes, which then allowed them to find unexpected connections between the writing submitted by the student and the assignment requirements. One example was a teacher whose student tried to define contemplation using video games as a metaphor. Although this teacher was initially leery of the comparison between video games and contemplation, he was later able to see that the comparison was not only warranted but relevant to his student's lived experience. A greater trust in the students' efforts to connect with the subject allowed teachers to feel more gifted by the unexpected aspects of the student's assignment.

Trust also plays a significant part of complexity theory, which Starkey (2012) argues is a balance between randomness and deterministic order. Notes Starkey,

> A complex system it not static, which adds to its unpredictability when faced with a change. A complex organization faces ongoing change in its structures, participants, parts, processes, and knowledge. In a schooling environment there are pupils (and their families) joining and leaving, staff changes, changing curriculum, resources updated, new content knowledge to teach, district or national policy changes, emerging knowledge from research and practitioner experience and many other changes, all of which contribute to the complexity of the context. (p. 6)

There are certainly a lot of changes that organizations need to cope with in the face of never-ending demands to adapt. Starkey notes that randomness and unpredictability are needed for organizations to cope with new changes. Thus, "it is through the apparent randomness and deterministic order that knowledge emerges, as ideas or innovations become part of organizational knowledge" (p. 7). On a more local level, teachers can shape their rubrics and assignments based on new input from their students, which reflects a much more dynamic approach to rubrics themselves.

REFLECTION ON TRUST

Reflect on a classroom situation that didn't go according to plan. Write down all the ways that the situation did not unfold as planned, from the perspective of a sense of failure and regret. Here, you could try to think of all the ways that an unexpected class plan became a failure, or a lesson failed in its main objective.

Then, in another column beside this, try to reframe the same situation from the perspective of trust. Ask yourself, in what way might this situation have unfolded for the best? What unexpected benefits arose from the experience of things not going as planned? What did you learn from it and how did it carry forward to future lesson plans?

When doing this exercise, try to contemplate aspects of the situation that either didn't turn out as planned or might have ended up improving over the long term. Examples might include when a class creates an unexpected variation in the lesson plan or brings new information about the students' interests and ways of learning. Why, in the end, might the experience have ended up being for the best?

Compare the two columns and contemplate the difference between a mindset based on failure and regret and one that is based on trust that things are for the best in all situations. With this exercise, it might be especially helpful to picture yourself as a camera that is panning out to embrace a wider view of things, seeing a greater and more long-term perspective on a challenging situation.

Discussion: How the Four Pillars of Surprise Work Together

Each exercise in this chapter has shown an element of surprise that can be practiced individually. However, it's important to emphasize that these elements work together to create an overall sense of surprise in the classroom. Each element complements the other while allowing for the sense of freshness needed to generate a genuine sense of surprise.

Of the four pillars discussed in this chapter, trust is the element of surprise that perhaps most helps teachers stay centered and ground themselves in a clear sense of their embodied presence, while cultivating a spacious openness to the classroom environment. Without the sense of a basic trust in their own ability to abide in present awareness, teachers may find surprises to be flooring, to say the least, particularly when they go against the course of a planned curriculum. As attachment theory suggests, the ability to be curious and discover the world in a spirit of adventure or play needs to be grounded in a secure confidence in one's being. Although this confidence often comes from secure parenting styles, it can also be actively cultivated by adults through a contemplative practice, such as meditation, that centers the awareness in the body and allows the mind to observe the passing of thoughts as impermanent and therefore not so overwhelming or vexing. Adyashanti (2011) roots this sense of trust in what he calls "aware" or "awake" spirit when he writes, "In order to find the end of struggle, we have to find a state of consciousness that's totally natural, that doesn't fight with the inner or outer environment. That's what I call 'aware spirit' or 'awake spirit.' It's an awake emptiness" (p. 90). He later suggests that an awakened state is founded on "a willingness to occupy this life, to occupy our incarnation, without grasping at it or identifying with it" (p. 165). When teachers no longer struggle with thoughts because they are grounded in a deeper sense of trust in fundamental awareness or reality, they are better able to mobilize those thoughts to create a harmonious classroom, rather than siding with one thought or the other. Instead of fighting or resisting a student's criticism of a lesson or resistance to an assignment, the teacher can gradually and nondefensively examine how that thought could be used to change the lesson, without interpreting the student's thought as a personal attack. Trust therefore serves as a foundation or a bedrock upon which surprises can be safely experienced.

With trust comes a greater ability to *receive* the gifts of the classroom. A teacher can start to drop their preconceptions about how a classroom should unfold, at what rate the students should learn, and how the students respond to the unfolding lesson plan. Receptivity expands the relaxed sense of trust into an ability to observe an unfolding process and fully accept the unknown, while beholding new surprises and events that are not foregrounded in a conceptual understanding. Just as a teacher can learn to stay grounded and embodied in their own sense of self and bodily awareness, so this sense of being grounded can also extend to an unfolding and complex environment such as a classroom. Here, the sense of stillness and acceptance gradually extends into a multilayered and changing environmental process that is genuinely experienced as surprising, without unsettling the teacher. Receptivity is quite simply an extended awareness of how situations around us are continually changing, yet it also allows us to welcome these changes in a spirit of openness.

Receptivity is often associated with a kind of precognitive state that even children naturally enjoy, especially considering that very young children lack the kinds of conditioning or mental filtering that classifies objects in terms of language or enculturation. However, receptivity in itself may not necessarily lead to a sense of surprise. As Maslow suggests, the capacity for people to be fully receptive to whatever is happening is akin to "the Taoist feeling of letting things happen rather than making them happen, and of being perfectly happy and accepting of this state of nonstriving, nonwishing, noninterfering, noncontrolling, nonwilling" (Maslow, 1993, p. 266). Though this state of receptivity is desirable in fostering a sense of equanimity and flow in classrooms, there is perhaps always the looming danger that such a state of contentment could lead to a lack of surprise, or even an unwillingness to be taken aback by something new. In order for receptivity to transform to surprise, then, teachers must cultivate the sense of anticipating surprises—that is, looking forward to something that is bound to surprise them in the future and allowing themselves to brace for a sense of the unfolding and unexpected, rather than simply abiding in what they receive in the present moment. This is where the teacher can utilize the discovery mindset: encountering a new situation as one of potency for surprises, while cultivating a sense of anticipation. In addition, discovery adds a more cognitive and reflective component to receptivity by encouraging teachers to actively select elements of the classroom experience that seem most surprising or noteworthy.

Finally, discovery can lead to new surprises, but eventually it must deepen to involve an expanded appreciation of students' efforts and uniqueness: that is, the givers behind the gifts. Ciaramicoli (Ciaramicoli & Ketcham, 2000) describes empathy as "an intelligent, deeply respectful exploration of what lies beneath the surface of our world" (p. 4), as well as "the inner force that allows us to adapt and change in response to our experiences" (p. 24) and, more prosaically, "a river that carries us along in its currents, gently guiding us into new territory and revealing the world itself as an unfolding mystery" (p. 24). These vivid descriptions suggest that empathy requires seeing beyond simple appearances as well as being able to connect with the deeper intentions and forces behind both everyday behaviors and creation as a whole. Without the empathic element of surprise and discovery, the sense of surprise does not eventually lead to a greater sense of connection, nor does it lead to a more unified vision of the classroom and students working toward larger goals. I suggest that empathy is the element of surprise that links the gifts to the givers—that is, it associates the gifts of the classrooms with students who bring in their unique contributions and subjectivities.

The following guided meditation will help solidify the practice of beholding surprise, using a four-step process that incorporates all the elements described above.

Choose a quiet spot and close your eyes while sitting comfortably. Allow your body to feel completely at ease by centering your awareness on each body part, from head to toe. Scanning the cranium, allow the muscles to gently relax, followed by the eyes, facial muscles, cheeks, and jaw . . . then scanning the whole body. Take a moment to marvel, appreciate, and trust that the body is already a miracle: from the way the cells work together to repair tissues and grow, to the way the neurons mobilize the body to perform a great many actions. Please take time to appreciate the body's abilities and trust that this present moment is all you need, without needing to reach outward for anything. Tell yourself that this moment is the best, and simply feel contented to be with your body and to trust that your mind can stay relaxed even in the most difficult moments of your classroom.

Now try opening your arms wide and bring your arms toward your chest, imagining that you are embracing the whole of your classroom: the challenges, the joys, the difficulties, and all the in-between moments. See yourself as embracing all these moments with a spirit of receiving the environment, in just the same way you were able to receive the sensations throughout your body. Allow yourself to receive everything without judgment, without clinging, and without rejection. Imagine that the environment itself is an extension of your body. Just as your arms are an integral part of you that equally deserve respect and care, so also the individual components of the environment naturally fit together in harmony. Receive all of these impressions evenly, with a balanced mind and heart.

After visualizing how you receive the classroom environment and embrace it evenly and equally, prepare yourself to be surprised. Recognize that each moment dissolves as soon as it appears, leaving a new moment to arise. Revel in the sense of novelty that each new moment will bring, and how endless possibilities can emanate from even a slight change in the conditions or even in the way you modulate your voice or manner. Be ready and prepared to be surprised and discover the new unfolding moment, as though a gift were being revealed to you each time.

Finally, reflect on the individuals in your classroom who are giving and receiving, including yourself. What are their dreams? What intentions do they have? What makes them happy? Reflect on their complex ideas, motivations, and intentions, knowing that their efforts are sincere ways of connecting with you, the classroom, or their fellow classmates on some level.

Questions for Discussion

1. Of the four pillars of surprise discussed in this chapter, which seems easiest to implement into a classroom situation, or at least more natural to you? Which seems the most challenging to implement?

2. For the pillar that seems most challenging for you, come up with three to four potential ways you can implement that pillar into your classroom or your attitude as a teacher.

Part II
Gifts and Gratitude

Chapter 4

The Gift Paradigm

The first part of this book was devoted to exploring how surprise can be actively fostered in classrooms, through a sense of receptiveness, trust, discovery, and empathy. This second section will explore the relationship between being surprised and cherishing the gifts that both students and teachers alike can bring to classrooms by actively cultivating attitudes of receptiveness, trust, discovery, and empathy. In order to articulate the connection between surprise and gifts, this chapter explores the difference between two etymologically similar yet somehow different terms, "the given" and "the gift," and how they have evolved in our daily life to sometimes mean different things. The underlying premise of this chapter is that a gift orientation shifts away from the notion of education as *exchange*, reenvisioning the classroom as one where gifts are given without expectation of return (Davies et al., 2010). In posing an alternative to an exchange paradigm, this chapter suggests ways that teachers can shift away from a mindset of fixed expectations toward one of appreciating what students can bring to the moment of a classroom—a shift that has been associated with greater resilience (Wilson, 2016b) and positive emotions such as joy (Fagley, 2018).

You may have recalled a time in your life when you were surprised with an unexpected gift, and how this may have come from a seemingly unknown place or for an unknown reason. What makes the gift special is precisely the fact that it comes seemingly unmediated, as if by grace or some other mysterious force. Yet one of the striking paradoxes of the gift is that it points to the thoughtful intentionality of a giver. A gift, in other words, cannot be so planned that it seems predicated upon the receiver's response, let alone the expectation of being given back in turn. At the same time, however, gifts don't just arise from out of nowhere. Somehow, at least in theory, feeling gifted often requires feeling a sense of beneficence in an individual, community, or the universe. Furthermore, the sense of being gifted goes beyond the term *given*. I have often heard the expression "the given" refer to something that is taken as obvious or for granted, as when we describe something as "a given." But gifts transcend givenness by pointing to something that is far more dynamic, contingent, and unfolding. Osteen (2010) has compared gifts to jazz improvisation, wherein both involve moments of risk, contingency, sociability, reciprocity, and excess. Notes Osteen, "Giving is pleasurable insofar as it is not egoistically motivated: liberation results from relinquishing considerations of personal benefit to affirm a commitment to caring for another person. In its most extreme expression, the gift threatens the sanctity of the rational, autonomous individual and his or her conscious self-interest. Giving and receiving gifts permits individuals to lose their autonomy" (p. 578). As with the nature of improvisation itself, gifts involve unplanned moments of openness that are often unexpected and thus could stretch, subvert, or challenge what is experientially possible within classrooms. Osteen also suggests that a gift metaphor challenges the view that all abilities or skills arise from a single individual's autonomous control. Moreso, the notion of improvisation brings with it a relaxing of order and autonomy in favor of more loose association of interlocking elements that weave in and out of the unfolding scene. Being contingent upon a variety of circumstances and emerging relations means that gifting moments cannot be calculated or anticipated in advance of a classroom situation, let alone engraved into a curriculum design. In opposition to being *taken as a given*, gifts suggest emergent possibilities that often feel surprising and unplanned.

As much as gifts may signify a blessing conferred from one being to another, they may also evoke feelings of precariousness and even dependency or vulnerability. Some cultures even find the concept of the gift to be burdensome, particularly when the receiver feels obliged to the giver due to a sense of indebtedness and structured reciprocity that underlies the gift (Giesler, 2006). In these circumstances, gifts are thought to demand reciprocity, or at the very least an expression of thanks. What the gift often points to, however, are delicate and fragile social balances, as when we notice that some are more gifted than others at different times in their lives. Gifts, in other words, are said to evoke a lack of symmetry. Gifts do not depend on a sense of "deservingness," nor are they automatically conferred upon us as a result of performing a certain modicum of work or effort. In fact, what makes the gift so special is that we do not know when it will arrive.

Furthermore, we often receive gifts in moments when we are least expecting a reward or a result, a point that roots the sense of gifting to a deeper notion of grace that goes beyond causality (Brown, 2019).

In this chapter, two major paradigms are explored that could be applied to educational contexts: the *exchange* paradigm and the *gift* paradigm. While these paradigms have been heavily explored in the areas of anthropology and sociology in recent decades (Cheal, 2016; Sherry, 1983), I want to shift the context of this chapter to an educational one. The central idea that undergirds this chapter is that education has been influenced by a greater way of thinking that emphasizes contractual relationships based on monetary exchange. This translates to a curriculum that stresses quantitative results over qualitative experiences and often overlooks the interrelational dynamics of learning, which can be best described, and even enhanced, using a gift paradigm. In this final section of this chapter, I suggest that gift economies feed into a cosmological sense of integral wholeness (O'Sullivan, 1999), which we are so badly in need of to counterbalance the modernist tendencies toward fragmentation in schools.

The Exchange Paradigm

Educational thinkers have long been exploring the "hidden curriculum" in education. Apple (2018) suggests that schools teach not only core subjects to prepare students to function in democratic society but also the necessary attitudes, dispositions, and orientations that help students to succeed in a capitalist world where some have more power and access to resources than others. He notes that, for some thinkers, the notion of an economic return on investment could appropriately apply to the culture of the school: "One measures input before students enter schools and then measures outputs along the way or when 'adults' enter the labor force. What actually goes on within the black box—what is taught, the concrete experience of children and teachers—is less important in this view than the more global and macroeconomic considerations of rate of return on investment, or, more radically, the reproduction of the division of labor" (p. 25). Some curriculum scholars have explored and challenged the factory model in education (Jacobs, 2014). According to the factory model, learning is subject to the same standards of efficiency, quality, measurability, and marketability that would apply to goods that are produced in a factory setting. Although people may liken the factory model to a technical-rational notion of teaching and learning, a more pervasive mentality underlies the factory metaphor, namely "an instrumental ideology that places efficiency, standardized technique, profit, increasing division and control of labor, and consensus at its very heart" (Apple, 2018, p. 143). Donald (2019) succinctly articulates how modern education dovetails with a need for trained workers who are capable of thriving in an economy where technical skills are supremely valued: "Public education was created in response to an economic need for more qualified workers to be properly prepared for work in the emerging marketplace and to take full advantage of growing commercial opportunities. Schools became places to prepare young people for this world of work, and the success of these preparations has been considered directly tied to the overall economic interests of the nation" (p. 108). The attitudes needed to be "successful" on the job, including submission to authority and rules, punctuality, and the ability to churn out large amounts of a quota or results, are instilled in students through even the simple ways in which students are asked to produce the same work. This is also revealed in the way students' seats are typically arranged in front of a teacher who oversees learning like a factory manager. The hidden curriculum suggests that schools are not isolated institutions but are, more so, shaped ideologically by the wider social currents and contexts that grant people differing levels of power.

In recent years, a more pervasive response to a neoliberal climate in education (Bocking, 2020) is that students position themselves as "paid customers." Budd (2017) identifies a trend in recent literature suggesting that "tuition fees frame a university degree as an 'investment in the self,' presupposing that learners behave as 'homo economicus,' primarily making decisions around university with a view to future employment" (p. 25). According to this view, students begin to see themselves as paid customers who expect grades in exchange for money and the privilege of going to a prestigious university or school. This view stems not only from a consumerist model but also from the growing tendency to view the individual as a competitor on a global marketplace. Rust and Kim (2021) have noted several trends toward positioning students as competitors stemming from globalization, including the tendency to globally rank universities, the designation of "world class" schools, and the attempt to set international standards that apply equally to schools around the world. Studies have suggested that students who are influenced by market metaphors in education feel more entitled to expect high grades in exchange for tuition fees (Reynolds, 2022) and even position themselves as in a bargaining position to appeal grades based on a sense of privilege. The "paying" student, in turn, sets up the teacher as a dispenser of grades, which can further diminish civility and morale as students expect to receive grades with no accompanying effort or engagement in learning (Knepp & Knepp, 2022). Instead of being perceived as a learning-based interaction, the teacher-student relationship becomes stilted and strained by the notion that students pay for the privilege of receiving grades. Furthermore, many teachers report feeling intimidated and afraid to give meaningful and authentic feedback because they fear the students' responses to the feedback. With online rating tools such as Rate My Professors (Liaw & Goh 2003; Stone, 2003), students are more empowered to evaluate teachers unfavorably, which puts the teacher in a vulnerable position when it comes to grading. Otto et al. (2008) note amusing yet scary anecdotal evidence that points to the deleterious consequences of students' leveraging public rating forums to denigrate their professors: "A professor mentioned that a student came to him for advising, and was not happy with the advice he received. At the end of the meeting, the student said, 'I'm gonna screw you on ratemyprofessor.' Sure enough, the next day there was a negative entry on the professor in ratemyprofessor.com" (p. 365). More to the point, it is numerical grading, not learning itself, that is positioned as something that stands to affect a student's future, not just within but outside the classroom. With high-stakes evaluation and an emphasis on ranking both inside and outside the classroom, students are pressuring teachers to grade them more favorably. Such an emphasis repositions the school as a marketplace where students and teachers alike negotiate for grades, as the standard currency for admission to the prestigious universities. Efficiency becomes a pervasive way of defining and limiting lifelong learning.

    The metaphor of the marketplace doesn't just negatively impact students. In the realm of higher education, teachers are pressured to play the part of grade administrators, as schools compete to attract the most promising students. Kirp (2005) refers to this broadly as "academic consumerism," wherein the universities vie to retain top students. This in turn shifts the goal of education away from developing students' minds and toward satisfying students as paid customers: "Today, sought-after applicants are treated like pampered consumers whose preferences must be *satisfied*, not as acolytes whose preferences are being *formed* in the process of being educated. In this rivalry, much more is at stake than bragging rights for trustees and alumni. Prestige brings tangible benefits, and in this winner-take-all world small differences in reputations have large consequences" (p. 116). Kirp goes on to state that attracting more "sought-after" (read: marketable) students in US universities entails the possibility of securing "the biggest gifts" (p.

116), which positions the university as a business. Along with the pressure to retain students comes a subtle shift away from fostering deep learning through immersion in multiple disciplines and toward catering to students' desires for high grades.

With the exchange paradigm, educators are more and more faced with the metaphor of student both as *customer* and *consumer* of education, which reduces education to little more than a market commodity. Gross and Hogler (2005) note,

> To attract, maintain, and increase enrollment, pedagogy can often become entertainment as faculty feels pressure to use techniques to overcome the short attention spans and the desire to be entertained as a method of learning. As with the purchase of a McDonald's product, students demand that professors be responsible for their learning (that is, their satisfaction) as opposed to being responsible for their own learning. The standard mode of learning, featuring the presentation and discussion of content, no longer suffices; in its place are multimedia performances (with the lights out so that they occur in the shadow of the classroom) and are nicely orchestrated packages of consumer goods. (p. 11–12)

The passivity of the consumer is what's most troubling about the marketplace metaphor—one that makes the whole project of education seem daunting, as teachers feel more pressured to entertain their students through an array of "pyrotechnic" entertainments designed to sustain diminishing student attention spans.

Halbesleben and Wheeler (2009) further give the example of a business student who embodies the student-as-consumer mentality and approach to education, noting,

> His job does not depend on his grade in the course as long as he passes. He attends class just enough to get the basic information. While he is there, he expects it to be reasonably entertaining to make it worth the time. He participates minimally in group projects because he feels they take up too much time and do not affect his grade significantly. He repeatedly asks the professor to post his or her class notes and slides on the Internet so that he can passively take in the lectures rather than take notes. He

has very low expectations for the course; he has paid his tuition and expects to be given a passing grade as a result. (p. 169)

Several key points emerge from this characterization. The first is the underlying belief that students are more concerned with extrinsic awards than with the intrinsic love of learning. Underlying this view is the notion of a contract mentality toward education, where mutual agreements are drawn up between teachers and students. According to the contract model of education, "Should the psychological contract be met, whereby each party fulfills his or her obligations toward the other party, one would expect positive individual and psychological outcomes" (p. 168). With the belief in an extrinsic value to education comes a more acute sensitivity to how effort is measured and compensated, in much the same way that a paid employee would be rewarded for performing a job efficiently. This can sometimes lead to students feeling entitled to the same attention or rewards as fellow students. More subtly, it also defines the student as existing in a distant transaction with the teacher: work is done for the sake of a grade, which subsequently becomes the ticket to future success. This places the student in the precarious position of having to compete with other students for top marks, which in turn adds extra pressure for students to achieve high grades in order to outdo their competition.

The Gift Paradigm

What is it about the gift that opposes—if not outright challenges—a notion of exchange in education? Some may suggest that gifts do not necessarily go against the idea of exchange, as some societies do consider the gift as something that requires reciprocation. Stauss (2023) has revealed how gifts are given with an underlying fear of the receiver's disappointment, which suggests that gifts are not necessarily spontaneous or given without consideration of others' reactions. Lanoue (2023) further suggests that gift economies rely on the exchange of social capital in much the same way that exchange economies might rely on monetary transactions: "It is today generally accepted that in many non-Western societies, reciprocity, whether direct or generalized, can be understood and measured in terms of investment in social and not economic capital. People invest in the well-being of others to help themselves, either for security, the acknowledgement of prestige, or simple survival. Conversely, people may invest in themselves the better to help others" (p. 48). However, this chapter suggests that a general paradigm of giftedness can challenge two major ways in which exchange can otherwise stultify interactions, particularly in classrooms. First, gifts are most often, and in most societies, predicated on spontaneity rather than a direct and preconditioned expectation of return. Instead of reducing the value of an experience to something that is intended to be paid in full later, gifts emphasize the free and unconditional motives of the giver. Second, gifts defy the taken-for-granted notion of education as a marketplace by reminding the receiver of the miraculous fragility and shifting nature of the present moment and its various conditions coming together to create reciprocal interactions. A gift is always a reminder of something given that may very well not have been given. In fact, even one's very being in this moment could have not been, or could have been something else for that matter. In contrast with the valorization of things "as they are" as though they were static entities, a gift-centered way of thinking focuses on the ways in which beings create endless provisions for each other, thereby fostering the grounds for an endless source of gratitude.

Many thinkers have attempted to challenge a recent historical trend that positions the self as an exchangeable and even disposable commodity. Gabriel Marcel (1962) is one philosopher who expressed his concern that the twentieth-century world was shifting away from a sacredness and toward modeling all relationships on exchange. He uses the example of the nursing profession to show how people have changed their perspectives on the health and serving professions:

> A quite characteristic example is furnished by the members of a hospital staff who, when they have completed their period of service during the course of a day, do not hesitate to "knock off," leaving the services which this or the other patient may be claiming of them completed. They owe nothing beyond what they have already given. As for what remains to be done, if it is not exactly up to the sick man to look after himself and clear things up, which would be nonsense, it is up to the hospital administration to do what is necessary; for their part, they wash their hands of it. (p. 196)

Marcel argues that reducing relationships to transactions results in a loss of an authentic responsibility that people might have toward one another. Hospital staff start to treat their patients as numbers or as jobs to be "knocked off" before an ending shift, rather than as people whose need for care extends beyond the fixed hours of a shift. A similar point could be made when professionals such as teachers view success only from the lens of the number of successful graduates who get jobs (Ali & Jalal, 2018) or the number of students who achieve top marks in the school system. Here, the success of both teachers and students is thought to be quantified in monetary terms, such as the presumed salary equivalent of a good grade. A sacred feeling of interconnection is thus replaced with a sense that obligations start and end with monetary transactions. As a Catholic philosopher, Marcel alludes to a different way of thinking in which Christians feel the givenness of their lives as being created and sustained by a creator. In place of a sense of personal agency is the sense of being placed into the world with sacred responsibilities for others. Marcel believes that service was valued in previous ages precisely because it entails "a kind of inwardness or, more precisely, not only a conscience but an effort on the part of that conscience at self-justification" (p. 193–194). Indigenous thinkers have gone further to suggest that the land itself is a place that generates a deep sense of responsibility and obligation (Atleo & Boron, 2022), which requires a cycle of gifting to express reciprocity for the land's bounty (Wolfstone, 2019). Simply being embedded within and part of the land means that one has a deep responsibility to preserve and protect its resources for all those who currently inhabit it as well as for future generations.

Reducing a learner to a quantifiable skill or achievement can reflect a problematic view of the scope of learning within a society. Whereas in previous times reason was considered to correspond with shared objective values, recent centuries have devalued reason to the status of a mere tool or, worse still, as having only an instrumental value to satisfy egoistic claims. Horkheimer (1974) suggests that this trend reflects a wider ideology that moves away from values and toward the manipulation of variables for consumerist ends. Horkheimer notes,

> The formalization of reason has made it safe from any serious attack on the part of metaphysics or philosophical theory, and this security seems to make it an extremely practical social instrument. At the same time, however, its neutrality means the wasting away of its real spirit, its relatedness to truth, once believed to be the same in science, art, and politics, and for all mankind. The death of speculative reason, at first religion's servant and later its foe, may prove catastrophic for religion itself. (p. 13)

According to Horkheimer, reason has become little more than a utilitarian instrument for human ends, as opposed to a way of discerning what is real or intrinsically worthwhile. Psychologist Aaron T. Beck (1991) has more pointedly warned that instrumental reason could lead to a view that does not meaningfully look at the human cost of doing things, thereby advocating an "end justifies the means" approach to engaging and governing populations. Referring to the dangers of *procedural thinking*, he notes, "Procedural thinking is typical of functionaries who fastidiously carry out the destructive assignments, apparently oblivious to their meaning or significance. These individuals can be so focused on what they are doing—a kind of tunnel vision—that they are able to blot out the fact that they are participating in an inhuman action. It seems likely that if they do think about it, they regard the victims as disposable" (p. 18). Charles Taylor (1991) has similarly suggested that an overemphasis on an instrumental view of reason tends to render things devoid of values, including the natural world itself, in contrast to previous periods in which humans were considered part of a greater chain of being yet not dominating it in any way:

> But at the same time as they restricted us, these orders gave meaning to the world and to the activities of social life. The things that surround us were not just potential raw materials or instruments for our projects, but they had the significance given them by their place in the chain of being. The eagle was not just another bird, but the king of the whole domain of animal life. By the same token, the rituals and norms of society had more than merely instrumental significance. The discrediting of these orders has been called the "disenchantment" of the world. With it, things lost some of their magic. (p. 3)

Other thinkers (O'Sullivan, 1999; Fox, 1990), have concurred that a more participatory, transpersonal cosmology might find us more enchanted with a world in which we inevitably participate. Heidegger (see chapter 2) has suggested a theory of the *given* (Bounds, 2018), which presupposes that there is a field of the known that exists in one's mind prior to even discerning difference or discriminating using reason. For Heidegger, knowing exists in a field wherein people find themselves immersed as co-participants. Thus, knowledge is deeply embedded in the way that people are *being in* the world, rather than through standing over the world as a neutral observer. To know, under this idea, is to participate in a field of experience with others. It's perhaps no wonder that knowledge, according to this perspective, is considered a gift—something that is given, as opposed to something acquired through conquest or through the isolation and manipulation of variables. Heidegger's participatory and ontological view of knowing starts to reposition learning itself as a gift, in the sense that is given within the life-worlds a person inhabits. Here, learning takes place in the midst of being in the world and is thus considered inseparable from everyday being.

Just what exactly is the *given*, and how does it differ from philosophies of exchange that often position people as buyers on the marketplace, or as having quantifiable talents and skills? Part of the challenge for teachers is to let go of the idea that their role is to control the student or shape them into an idealized self that is meant to compete in a homogenous global marketplace. Instead, they may start becoming empathically attuned with *givens* within a student's experience—the unique contributions that students bring to the classroom in the form of experiences, cultural capital, talents, and perspectives. The mindset of seeing gifts already existent within the classroom can offset a tendency to stifle the creative process in favor of a restrictive and assumed graduation window. Chetty (2010) suggests that postsecondary education may suffer from a mindset of trying to net as much dollar value from attracting (and graduating) as many students as possible, which makes it harder for students to learn the difficult and sometimes unpredictable creative process. She thus notes, "Within neoliberal contexts, where issues around funding are dominant and high student intake is encouraged, creativity is not seen as important. A key reason for the exclusion of principles of creativity is that it jeopardizes the monetary incentive, that is, the chances of students going quickly through the system and graduating within the minimum period. Much of the research training and research grants are geared toward these imperatives of funding, access, and graduating within the minimum period" (p. 140). A more gift-based paradigm in education could pose a challenge to a neoliberal mindset that places so much agency on the teacher as the controller and shaper of a learning experience, instead of seeing the learner as empowered to unfold their own unique learning experience. This also finds a parallel in challenging the stance of a teacher as a sole authority or a disseminator of knowledge.

One of the most intriguing motifs that could unpack the metaphor of giftedness in education is that of the seed or embryo that mysteriously contains yet simultaneously conceals its full potential. This seed contains everything that it needs to express its own uniqueness yet requires time and contingent conditions to properly unfold. To foster patience toward growth requires an attitude of both receiving and simultaneously nurturing something toward full growth: both the awareness of an already latent perfectionism and a sense of fragility and contingency that needs the protection of outside forces to grow and mature. Maria Montessori (1970) remarks, "The newborn child should be seen as a 'spiritual embryo'—a spirit enclosed in flesh in order to come into the world. Science, on the other hand, assumes that the new being comes with nothing. He is flesh but not spirit, for all that can be verified is the growth of tissues and organs that ultimately form a living whole. But this too is a mystery: is it possible that a complex, living body comes out of nothing?" (p. 29). Montessori contrasts the then prevailing scientific theories of behaviorism with a view of life as containing a rich universe within itself. She sees the child not as a blank slate to be filled with knowledge, but more so as a wonder that requires attentiveness on the part of the parent or teacher to be fully revealed. According to this view, children themselves are surprises waiting to unfold given the proper nurturance of parents, guardians, and teachers. The child contains a key to something larger than their own body, while also pointing to the eternal mystery of how life arrives in this historic moment in the first place. Given this view of the child, how could teachers and parents not feel surprised and awed by attentively observing the child's tendencies and instincts? This view also describes the parent and teacher as fellow explorers who, through a process of co-presence, can learn to discover the true character and destiny of the child. This is also echoed in James Hillman's idea of the "soul's code" (Hillman, 1996), which postulates all souls as coming into the body with an already existing plan and purpose. Drawing on the Platonic myth of Phaedrus and the "daemon" that contains a unique spiritual blueprint of a soul's unfolding purpose, Hillman adopts this idea to show how people are in the world having forgotten why they came but must—given the right people, conditions, and roots—find ways to fully embody their purpose. While not everyone can fulfill their destiny successfully, Hillman contextualizes the journey as meaningful precisely because there is an unfolding purpose. (More about the tragic impact of not fulfilling one's innermost gifts will be explored in chapter 6.)

In order to further the analogy of human giftedness, Montessori (1970) goes on to compare human growth to that of animals, using the analogy of machine vs. handcrafted goods to show that unlike mass-produced objects, humans are "worked by hand," and "each individual is different from the other, having his own distinctive created spirit, as if it were a natural work of art" (p. 32). Montessori shows how creation breathes into the human and endows human life with a unique incarnate spirit that cannot be duplicated in any other form. In one lengthy passage, she notes,

> The process by which the human personality is formed is the hidden work of incarnation. The helpless infant is an enigma. The only thing we know about him is that he could be anything but nobody knows what he will be or what he will do. His helpless body contains the most complex mechanism of any living creature, but it is distinctly his own. Man belongs to himself, and his special will furthers the work of incarnation. Musicians, singers, artists, athletes, tyrants, heroes, criminals, saints—all are born in the same way, but each carries within him the enigma of his own special development that motivates his unique activity in the world. (pp. 32–33)

The element of not knowing what a child is destined to become yet realizing their miraculous incarnation is one of the most crucial and inspiring aspects of the Montessori educational model. Montessori's theory of education suggests that instead of teaching students through direct instruction, teachers serve as receivers of their children. They are there to quietly observe the child and to understand the child, rather than to try to actively shape the child to be a certain way. By serving as a facilitator to the child's learning, the teacher changes their position to one of receiver rather than as an active creator of the child's thoughts and beliefs. Montessori has also described the sense of wonder that can be developed once teachers give up their tendencies to control children's destinies. Thus, Montessori's educational philosophy is predicated on a faith that children are naturally well-endowed to learn, given the proper environment and freedom to do so. Teachers, in turn, become gifted by the ability to observe children naturally learn and grow, given sufficient classroom preparation.

Finally, cosmologies of the gift can express the constant give and take of the universe, which often views giftedness as a shared energy that is continually moving through beings and reminding us of our deep interconnectedness. Swimme (1996) is one philosopher who has explored the notion of allurement as a natural way in which we are attracted to other things in the cosmos to develop our fullest potential. A cosmic vision of participatory unfolding allows us to envision gifts not as isolated elements but as the very things that mutually connect us.

Teacher: Giver or Receiver?

Nel Noddings (1986, 2010) is an educator who has focused on caring dynamics in the classroom. She has focused on the responsibilities of not only the caring but also the ones who are cared for. It's perhaps hard to believe that both the caring and cared for have *equal* positions to play in the classroom. For Noddings, caring is predicated on the relevance of care to the receiver as much as it is based on the giver's inclination to care. One of the interesting aspects of care is whether and to what extent the teacher as caregiver has become overemphasized in the classroom and thus overshadows the teacher's role as a receiver. Can teachers be overly positioned as caregivers without due emphasis on the cared-for aspects of the classroom and receiving students' behaviors? This is an important area to consider when looking at the role of the teacher in the classroom.

Noddings (2010) distinguishes between an ethic based on cultivating personal virtues and one that emphasizes care and empathy for others. She notes,

> Moral education in home and in schools often concentrates on the acquisition of virtues and/or moral reasoning. Both have something valuable to contribute to moral growth, but there is a fundamental difference in emphasis between these programs and programs aimed at increasing empathy. When we try to inculcate honesty, courage, obedience, or courtesy as personal virtues, attention is directed to the moral agent, the one who "possesses" the virtue. In contrast, when we try to promote empathy, attention is directed to others—to those who are affected by our actions. (p. 63–64)

Although caring is the basis for Nodding's ethical theory, it should be noted that teachers' caring overtures are not always based on the intention or willingness to meet others' needs. Noddings warns of the dangers that arise when teachers assume they are giving students the care they need without questioning the premises on which they base their understanding of care. Teachers who are overly attached to their ideas on what caring should be, without considering the student's true needs are not truly caring. Although they might believe that what they are doing is caring, they may be too invested in their own view of what counts as caring and, subsequently, may fail to consider what the student's moment-to-moment needs are. For this reason, caring has to preserve a proper interpersonal component. It needs to consider not only the caregivers' intentions and resources but also the investment and needs of the cared for. Perhaps for this reason, Noddings stresses a more balanced approach that does not privilege the desires of the caregiver over the needs and receptiveness of the cared for.

Teachers are often portrayed in the media as all-sacrificing givers, which overextends the giving side of the teacher role without giving due respect or attention to the ability to properly receive or respond to a student's unique gifts and contributions. It is the teacher, here, who is seen as the caregiver, whereas the student is positioned more as the receiver of the teacher's gifts. This ideology of the teacher as giver has, as Andrea O'Reilly has observed, a parallel in the patriarchal notion of female as an all-sacrificing mother, which dovetails with patriarchal notions of motherhood. Referring to "intensive mothering" as an ideology imposed on women that defines mothering as a form of sacrifice, O'Reilly (2006) notes,

> The ideology of intensive mothering dictates that: 1) children can only be properly cared for by the biological mother; 2) this mothering must be provided 24/7; 3) the mother must always put children's needs before their own; 4) mothers must turn to the experts for instruction; 5) the mother is fully satisfied, fulfilled, completed, and composed in motherhood; and finally, 6) mothers must lavish excessive amounts of time, energy, and money on the rearing of their children. Each demand is predicated on the eradication, or at very least, sublimation of a mother's own selfhood and in particular, her agency, autonomy, authenticity, and authority. (p. 43)

Llewellyn (2012), in a similar vein, suggests that the patriarchal notions typical of intensive mothering have also pervaded the role that women are expected to play in education, particularly as they are considered moral guardians for a democratic society. Part of this involves teachers mimicking an embodied respectability that focuses on impressions and appearances, as a means to reinforce traditional patriarchal attitudes toward gender and the family that are supposed to undergird an orderly, democratic society. Notes Llewellyn in her interview study of women teachers, "Women teachers had to negotiate respectable feminine appearances that wedded them to patriarchal values. Respectability was largely synonymous with restoring those lifestyle norms that had been shaken by the war. The paramount image teachers were expected to convey was that of a happy participant in the nuclear family. Interviews illustrate that women understood the imperative of this idealized model" (p. 90). Despite its "idealized" veneer, this ideology of respectability and sacrifice also constrains both mothers and teachers alike, giving them little room to express their authentic feelings for those under their care. Instead of responding to who the student is, teachers are responding from a demand to be all-giving and fulfill multiple roles including parent, administrator, counselor, and so on, in addition to the added burden of perpetuating a stereotype of a woman as a "moral guardian" of the family. The additional stresses and demands of teachers more recently dovetails with a high standard of excellence teachers place on themselves.

But what if the role of teacher were reversed, leading teachers to see themselves as the receivers of gifts rather than the sole providers of gifts? This would ease the burdens that teachers face when they are placed in the position of already knowing their students' needs. It also shifts away from a deficiency model that represents students as in need of help and learning whereby the teachers are the providers of that help and learning. It further positions teachers as receivers of the students' gifts, not necessarily having to correct or fix the students' mistakes or errors. This poses a radically different model and idea of the teacher than one traditionally held in Eurocentric education circles, in which teachers are often made responsible for a student's successes and failures outside of the classroom. Teachers, according to a Eurocentric model, take it upon themselves to be accountable for what happens to students when they leave the classroom. What sometimes results is a tendency to focus on a student's prestige within the social norm instead of the learning process. Llewellyn (2012) has maintained that a rationalist narrative tends to position teachers, particularly women, as "gatekeepers" of a democratic society, where the focus is on preparing citizens for academically or professionally recognized leadership roles that are privileged above other roles, such as nurturing or caregiving. Teachers in her study reported internalizing a sense of failure when their former students did not attain academic or professional prestige, attributing their lack of success to their inability to sufficiently prepare their students. Notes Llewelyn,

> Through stories of their former pupils, women teachers demonstrated that they had, in fact, produced leaders for their communities. Despite teaching in vocational and general as well as academic streams, few spoke of any students other than their university-bound. Furthermore, the interviewees rarely discussed

> classes as a whole, or students that they had personally helped from "slipping through the cracks" of the system. The women did not discuss failures in their classes, even when directly questioned. It was almost as if their memories of the most successful students ultimately kept the women from "slipping through the cracks" of educational "democracy" themselves. If their interviews are a reliable guide to their feelings, their relationship to star graduates was what made these teachers feel successful. (p. 58)

Notable here is the outward-facing stance of the women interviewees. Rather than introspecting on how they cared for their challenged students, the teachers construct narratives that position the teacher as nurturing a public success, particularly in the form of prestigious graduates or "rising" leaders, which is thought to uphold democracy. There is little emphasis in these interviews on the capacity to appreciate students intrinsically for their individual talents and difficulties.

Although Nodding's philosophical ethic focuses on caring, it's apt to describe it also as one of equal parts giving and receiving. For caring to be effective, there needs to be a receiver who is appreciating the gifts of the giver. This is why a sophisticated model of gifting would be an integral complement to Nodding's philosophy of caring. This model, or "gift" ethic, places equal emphasis on the ability to recognize and receive gifts as it does on the intention and desire to provide them. In addition, a gift ethic in education would not pigeonhole teachers as the ones giving and students as the ones receiving. Instead, an ethic of reciprocity pervades the gifting relationship, which will be further explored in the subsequent sections of this chapter.

The Gift Economy in the Classroom

Feminist scholars (Kailo, 2002; Shadmi, 2021) have suggested that exchange models of education dovetail with a patriarchal worldview. The patriarchal model has tended to monetize certain kinds of services and commodities while suppressing the contributions of nonmonetized work, including domestic labor and child-rearing. This creates a picture of an economy that privileges some kinds of work while absenting or devaluing other kinds of nonmonetized work traditionally held by women in many cultures, such as domestic labor and caregiving. Further, exchange models render work not recognized by an economic system invisible. Gifts, according to this view, are seen as little more than gratuities given on special occasions and are thus set in contrast to goods that are somehow earned, that is, recognized as commodities that can be exchanged in a marketplace.

When effort is measured solely by its monetary value, the invisible, nonmonetized efforts are not recognized or valued. Genevieve Vaughan notes how the domestic economy "has a logic of its own, which is different from the quid pro quo exchange" (Shadmi, 2021, p. 89) and is "based on giving in order to satisfy needs. It is transitive, and it confers value onto the receiver by implication" (p. 89). Unlike an exchange economy, in which goods are exchanged based on a predetermined monetary value, the gift economy gives according to need and extends to multiple community stakeholders. Thus, Vaughan notes how the gift economy is a form of relational ethics, which is modeled on reciprocity, in contrast to a fixed exchange. Commenting on the Indigenous concept of the gift economy as established by Marcel Mauss, Vaughan (2013) remarks how giving and receiving constitute a "positive and inclusive interaction" that "connects the interactors and establishes a relationship" (p. 89).

Vandevelde (2000) provides a succinct definition of the gift economy as follows:

> Market exchange is founded on a very strict notion of equality and on an immediate reciprocity. Rights and duties of the parties concerned are scrupulously fixed in advance, and in the event of one of the contractants not keeping his engagements, the aggrieved party can press charges in court. On the other hand, the reciprocity required by the logic of the gift is not strict, not immediate and unintentional. One who would immediately return the gift he received, would in doing so indicate that he is incapable of receiving: such is the case of Timon of Athens in Shakespeare's play. Every gift incites a countergift, but only at the appropriate juncture: some period of time must have elapsed, not in order to mask the interest calculation as the "objective truth of the gift" as Bourdieu suggests, but rather as a sign of accepting to enter into relation with the donator. (p. 2)

Several significant points emerge from this passage. First, the gift is not based on mere calculated exchange. Instead, reciprocity tends to be a more spontaneous relation geared toward symbolically maintaining a relation between donor and receiver. That is, the actual content of the gift and its "exchange value" are secondary to the relationship that giving itself represents. Second, a certain unspecified time must elapse between giving and receiving a gift. This is an important point that turns on the way gifts need to evoke some element of the unpredictable, thus reflecting a nonobligatory relationship that is freely chosen between the giver and recipient. What's tricky here is that reciprocity does not necessarily let the receiver off the hook when it comes to returning a gift. Instead, it demands that the receiver appreciate the chosen intention of the giver through a sense of indebtedness to the relationship that is not necessarily tied to a single predictable payment or gesture. One can think of this as a general bond between the giver and receiver rather than a specific transaction owed to the giver. Both giver and receiver must somehow engage in this interplay with a maximum sense of authenticity and faith in the other, lest the act of giving and receiving devolve into a kind of routinized gesture.

What do gift economies do? How might gift economies disrupt a taken-for-granted view that everything can be bought and sold, or that all human value can be fixed into quantifiable transactions? Gift economies acknowledge the *mutual indebtedness* that individuals have toward each other in their relationships. It's perhaps not a surprise that this is an ecosystemic worldview that connects human beings with the natural world. This account sees the earth as the prime giver of all benefits that people experience. To be indebted to the earth naturally entails being stewards of the earth (Suzuki, 2022), that is, accepting "responsibility to protect and care for the life of planet Earth and all of its inhabitants" (Noddings, 2012, p. 123) instead of claiming exclusive ownership of the earth's resources. Thinking in terms of the gift economy also requires a sense of balance and harmony: without a sense of indebtedness to the earth, people will consume more than they give back. According to theories of Indigenous gifts (Mauss, 1990), a spirit of *hau* is found within the gift, and that spirit needs to be returned in a perpetual cycle. The spirit of the gift is an important element of ritual in gifting. But this is not the same as exchange economy, which is founded on a contract theory of humanity. Anthropocentrism emerges when humans see themselves exclusively as the sole arbiters of value and exchange, whereas other natural elements are viewed as mere commodities or resources. This puts humans in an overly privileged position rather than seeing themselves as parts in a whole. With exchange economy, the starting point is the individual, and exchange guarantees that individuals maintain mutual autonomy, which cuts them off from the natural world. With the gift economy, on the other hand, a more cosmic and ecosystemic worldview allows people to ground themselves in a sense of wholeness, as fellow sharers of gifts.

The Role of the Gift Economy in Education

What are the implications of this view for teachers? Are there differences in exchange and gift economies that dynamically unfold in classrooms? Exchange economies in classrooms suggest that students are in the classroom to receive grades in exchange for effort; efforts, therefore, become quantified in accordance with a standard rubric or set of expectations that are preset. Students under this model are considered consumers in education, often expecting grades so that they can attend prestigious schools in return for "purchasing" an education. Students demand certain kinds of grades and therefore expect to play the role of negotiators with teachers in the attainment of a satisfactory grade. Teachers in turn are often intimidated into taking on the role of a dispenser of grades while feeling straitjacketed to teach according to standards and rubrics.

Is the rubric more of a fixed window into learning, or can it be dynamically negotiated between teachers and students? Some researchers (Cirio, 2019) have been exploring the idea that rubrics are more like invitations than concrete templates upon which students create work. According to the former view, a rubric is a co-created process that changes from one semester to the next. On the other hand, many educators and schools still abide by the philosophy that rubrics are *objective* measures that do not change from one context to the other. A neoliberal model of education tends to collapse the cultural contexts in which students situate themselves, learn, and grow in favor of an illusory neutrality in which all people are positioned as co-competitors on a global marketplace. Kohn (1999) laments the fact that students are often viewed as competitors for grades in the classroom. He even suggests that when students are conditioned through the punishment and reward of achieving grades, they tend to lose the intrinsic motivation to learn a subject for its own sake. Furthermore, with the transition into adolescence, students are pushed into more high-stakes situations in which they must use grades as the tokens through which they apply to and receive admittance into universities and programs. Students sometimes see themselves as numbers. Minkel (2014) notes a troubling tendency even among elementary school students to identify themselves with a grade or a numeric value:

> A friend teaching at a middle school in New York recently overheard two 5th graders talking as they left the building.
> "Are you a 2 or a 3?"
> "I'm a 2. What are you?"
> The child didn't say, "I got a 2 on a rubric for this test prep prompt we did today." He said, "I'm a 2." This student's identity has become fused with a test score.
> When students see themselves and their learning as numbers, what have we given them? What have we taken away? (Minkel, 2014, para. 1–9)

What's more, the effect of a grading dynamic in exchange theories reaches beyond student populations. Bell curves are one restrictive example in which teachers are pressured to grade according to an overall average. Teachers even feel reluctant to allow students to resubmit their work for fear that they will inflate the bell curve. Inflated marking reflects badly on teachers among the administration, giving the teachers the reputation of being soft markers or giving "easy A's" to the students. But this practice of bell curving deflects from the role of assessment itself, which is to foster *learning*. When grades are being used only as forms of behavior reinforcement, teachers and students alike lose the meaning of grades to engage learning instead of as a final summative appraisal. Beatty (2004) in particular has noted how the metaphor of grading as *market exchange* tends to reduce grades to a scant commodity—one designed to give recruiters and administrators an easy way to gauge eligibility for scarce positions:

> In order for As to be meaningful designators of excellence, their supply must be carefully rationed. Professors and academic programs protect the value of the grading currency by normalizing the grades—"grading on the curve"—to make sure that only a small percentage of students receive the top grade. Even if all students have done excellent work, grading on the curve requires that some portion receive the grades at the lower end of the tail. (p. 189)

Exchange views tend to see students as autonomous individuals, not part of a collective whole but entirely working toward their own ends. According to this view, the sense of responsibility is limited to what students can do for themselves and does not extend to the care of the classroom itself. Students become owners of their own knowledge as opposed to stewards of a greater totality that has its own intrinsic value and worth.

Some thinkers have stressed the role of personal responsibility as a way of grounding human beings in a sense of their own culpability as opposed to a reified destiny or fate. However, Charles Taylor has noted that a narrow emphasis on personal responsibility and "finding one's own voice" has tended to overlook the role that communities and rituals play in initiation into adulthood and identity. In *The Malaise of Modernity* (Taylor, 1991), he remarks on the contributions that others must make to the shaping of one's identity:

> We are expected to develop our own opinions, outlook, stances to things, to a considerable degree through solitary reflection. But this is not how things work with important issues, such as the definition of our identity. We define this always in dialogue with, sometimes in struggle against, the identities our significant others want to recognize in us. And even when we outgrow some of the latter—our parents, for instance—and they disappear from our lives, the conversation with them continues with us as long as we live. (p. 33)

Taylor suggests that the notion of a self-made and *self-chosen* identity often overlooks the shared horizons through which identities are made possible or sustainable, including the fact that identity itself is often predicated on a sense of recognition and value sanctioned within a society or community. Specific instances of identity "uniqueness" need to be recognized before they can even qualify as significant parts of one's identity. Yet, in spite of the socially constructed nature of identity, the myth of the self-made identity still pervades modern life and often lends credence to a commonsense idea that students must rely exclusively on their own initiatives, efforts, and goal setting to achieve meaning and purpose in their educational paths. This opens the door for blaming students when they don't measure up to curriculum standards, instead of looking at the broader systemic issues that could lead students with differing socioeconomic backgrounds to fare better than others in schools. The recent push toward student self-assessment (Taras & Wong, 2023) has also positioned students as adjudicators of their own learning, which dovetails with a notion of autonomy that is peculiar to modernity. This impoverishes both the view of responsibility, by narrowing responsibility to the self, and the view of learning, which characterizes students as achieving only personal learning goals.

In contrast to an exchange view of autonomy, a gift paradigm suggests that individuals come into the world as part of greater collective energies. According to this view, individuals are born to give and receive gifts, whether from nature, from one's ancestors, or from society. While biologists have recently been exploring the role that morphic resonance (Sheldrake, 2009) plays in shaping life toward a greater energy, this collective energy and spirit is an important aspect of what philosopher Christopher Bache has called "the living classroom." Bache (2008) hypothesized that there is a collective energy or spirit that accumulates in a classroom, containing and storing the learning that takes place across different semesters. This is an intriguing theory of the classroom, if not simply because of its analogies to the spirit of the gift in Mauss. Just as Mauss observed the *hau* as a spirit that must cycle back to a collective whole to be reused again, Bache's living classroom theory suggests that students contribute to and grow a classroom's spirit, just as one would cultivate a garden. The implications are that the students are not just bringing their own agendas into the classroom but are feeding both present and future learning within the classroom.

Finally, the gift paradigm stresses a nonhierarchical relationship between teachers and students. Rather than positioning the teacher as a dispenser of knowledge, the teacher and student alike learn from each other in a recursive circle. There is no privileging of one learner over the other because there is an inherent belief in the gifts (e.g., of knowledge and experience) that all students bring to the same table.

Students as "Gifted"

The notion of giftedness is not a new one in education, as the label "gifted" has been used to describe students who are exceptional or have skills that make them highly valued within the societies in which they are schooled. Sternberg et al. (2011) have proposed a pentagonal theory of giftedness that positions students as being gifted on the basis of (1) excellence in a particular skill or ability relative to their peers; (2) rarity (not everyone has the gift); (3) productivity, or seeing the gift as part of a whole; (4) demonstrability, or the ability to measurably see a gift through specific concrete actions and goals; and (5) value, or having an intrinsic worth that is not necessarily tied to test results or IQ scores. Some of the assumptions that are implicit to this model might be identified as follows:

> The label of "gifted" functions to distinguish the "exceptional" from the "average," which thus defines giftedness as a (potentially or actually) *quantifiable* ability or behavior that can be measured relative to others.

> Giftedness exists within *specific individuals*, much like a psychological "trait" (Costa & McCrae, 1991) that is relatively fixed within a person over time and does not fluctuate with external conditions (unlike "states" of mind, which do in fact fluctuate over time).

> Specific criteria can be used to identify traits. As the authors note, "Criterion-based measurement (in which measures are based on performance relative to some external standard, regardless of how other students perform) helps us avoid confounding excellence with rarity" (Sternberg et al. 2011, p. 9).

> Gifts are inherently *scarce*, meaning that it would be absurd (according to the authors) to insist on *everyone* being gifted, when in fact the function of a gifted label is precisely to identify those who are exceptional relative to others.

These assumptions about giftedness often seem to coincide with a Western model of education, which emphasizes individualism and individual achievement over the achievement of groups or communities.

What could be problematic about these assumptions? One potential drawback is that this view overlooks or underplays the role that environment, custom, and cultural difference can play in how giftedness is identified. Csikszentmihalyi (1996; Csikszentmihalyi & Robinson, 1991) has suggested the role that cultures play in identifying someone as "gifted," meaning that the label often entails a sense of some ability being in demand by a society or community at a certain time. As Sternberg et al. (2011) note, according to Csikszentmihalyi,

> Giftedness is not a personal trait but rather an interaction between an individual and the environment. Someone who has the innate

talent to be an exceptional writer will not become one in a preliterate society, and someone who could be an exceptional musician will not be in a society that has a religious prohibition against music, as do some societies today. Csikszentmihalyi also suggests that talent cannot be a stable trait, because people's capacity for action changes over the course of their life span as the cultural demands for performance change. (p. 28)

Two interesting points are noteworthy about Csikszentmihalyi's view of giftedness. First, for Csikszentmihalyi, gifts are not fixed and stable qualities but are more akin to relational qualities enacted between a giver who happens to have a socially esteemed ability in a given period of time and a receiver who appreciates and derives benefit from that ability. Perhaps one way of expressing this view is that gifts are not nouns so much as they are verbs or performances that occur in contextually rich moments of time. Gifts are not, according to Csikszentmihalyi, static in nature—people's gifts can change over time as they age or shift in their priorities. A talent or ability that was cultivated at an early age might be lost as a person's interest or time to devote to the talent decline with age. Second, the notion of acknowledging something as a gift (or someone as "gifted") is predicated on the needs of a society, which are bound to change over time. Examples might include trends in music. Where a person might be talented and skillful in using a particular instrument, that gift may fall into disuse as the fashion in music styles change. Csikszentmihalyi's observations are especially interesting because they hint at the socially constructed and mediated notion of gifts and giftedness. An ability cannot be recognized as a gift unless a society or a receiver grants value to the gift itself. Csikszentmihalyi hints at the role that teachers may play in fostering and recognizing gifts, since it is often the teacher who is said to discover a student's unique skills and talents, even before they themselves reckon it to be a gift.

A more incisive critique of Western, individualist notions of the gift could come from Indigenous views of giftedness. The Navajo theory of giftedness, as Phillipson and McCann (2007) articulate it, is as follows:

> People are each endowed [by the Holy People, the deities] from prebirth with a gift, and at birth it is the responsibility of the parents, grandparents, extended family and kinfolk to identify and cultivate this unique gift, ability and talent . . . giftedness is thus not only an individual existential experience but rather a complete, communal experience similar to the "whole being

greater than the sum of its parts." The Dine' epistemic conceptualisation, identification, and cultivation of giftedness are deeply embedded in the spiritual world. It is not just an academic construct but is accorded the utmost profundity in respect, reverence, and observance. (p. 160)

The first interesting aspect of this account of giftedness is how it claims people as each endowed with a gift from prebirth. What this means is that gifts, according to the Navajo view, are unique to each individual and abundant, meaning that they exist in all individuals. The second implication is that parents, teachers, and guardians have a special responsibility to identify and bring out these gifts that are unique to individuals. That is, giftedness is a *communal responsibility* that does not just lie with an individual or a single teacher but takes an entire group to summon or draw out. Third, the element of the sacred prefigures into the Navajo account of giftedness. Gifts come from the Spirit rather than being a genetic or intellectual trait that can be measured. This locates gifts as part of a great mystery that is beyond rationality and demands a special kind of reverence.

Bevan-Brown (2009) expands on the model of Indigenous giftedness when she describes how the Maori cultural notion of giftedness emphasizes the importance of character traits that benefit whole communities, not just personal advancement or ambition. Hence she remarks, "A second notable difference relates to the importance placed on intangible 'qualities' mainly in the affective, interpersonal and intrapersonal domains. These areas of giftedness are given top priority and include qualities such as: love, caring and sensitivity to others; courage; bravery; hospitality; familiness; industriousness; determination; patience, honesty, integrity, open mindedness, humility, serenity, reliability, selflessness, moral courage, humour and strength of character" (p. 12). Bevan-Brown goes on to suggest that gifts are valued only insofar as they are used in an active way to help the community in some way.

Summary and Discussion: Gifts as Relationships—Not Things

Classrooms today are often predicated on an idea of *exchange*. Students, according to this view, compete for grades and positions in the university. Schools are seen as designed to transition students to the marketplace, which analogously refers to the student as a paid customer in the business of teaching and learning. Teachers, as a result, are often expected to disseminate the kinds of knowledge and information that are expected to help students survive and thrive in the workplace. Standardized education is designed to "teach to the test," which essentially means that teachers have little time for spontaneous moments of learning since they are pressured to prepare students to pass tests and thus ensure students' academic future. Schools are often seen as little more than transitions to adulthood, and places where marks are bargained and negotiated. This leads to a sense of pressure on teachers as well as future burnout and job dissatisfaction for many. The classroom becomes a place of predicted drills, where even the bell curve encourages teachers to numerically compare their students as opposed to seeing them as unique individuals.

A *gift* model of education sees students not as numbers but as individuals who have unique spirits to bring into the classroom. The Indigenous model of education tends to emphasize the spiritual uniqueness of each student, which cannot be reduced to a grade or a predicted outcome. Anderson et al. (2017) summarize this view as follows:

> It is an immutable law that all growth proceeds from within, from the unseen. A child is not constructed from her disparate parts but is rather *brought into being*, emerging from what ultimately appears to be a vanishing point. In the same way, learning proceeds from within the child, which corresponds to the sense of wonder emphasized in inquiry-based learning. Wonder is innate and sacred and cannot be imposed from without. While all beings are sacred, children are especially so because they are closer to their spiritual source than adults. As different children are given different gifts, they are drawn in wonder to the world in unique ways; they bring their unique gifts with them on their learning journey. (p. 58)

This quote reveals several unique characteristics of a gift paradigm of education. First, it is based on a notion of sacred mystery. According to the many Indigenous models of education, children are coming from a sacred source of being. As Anderson et al. (2017) suggest, "Everything is always coming *into being* from a spiritual source. In a way, this is obvious; the origin of all things is unseen, beyond even the most microscopic forms, and ultimately beyond space and time. The origin of all things is a Great Mystery" (p. 58). With mystery, teachers are not trying to drill knowledge into students but are positioned as *receivers of gifts* that are an abundant source of surprise, mystery, awe, and wonder. In other words, to behold students as sacred sources of knowledge shifts teachers from a position of trying to control the outcome of a classroom situation to a position of yielding and allowing themselves to discover the innate gifts in children. The idea of student as *gift* reverberates in the writings of diverse educational thinkers such as Montessori and Waldorf. Montessori in particular writes about how the child comes into the world from a long spiritual journey and has specific goals that need to be fulfilled in the human lifetime. She stresses the need for teachers to recognize and foster the gifts that each student brings into the world, which requires an intuitive ability to discover this specialness within each child.

One final note, which could serve as a caveat in this chapter, is that this model of gifting constitutes an attempt to steer away from a view of giftedness that situates gifts *within* the self. Charles Taylor (1991) has referred to the problems that can arise when an emphasis on finding one's authentic identity or self leads to an overall estrangement from political and social commitments, as well as an overemphasis on the uniqueness of the self over and above commonalties. I have suggested throughout this chapter that an alternative way is to view giftedness as a form of interconnection or relationship. As Taylor suggests, what is of value to a person is often determined by how their value is spread to the society or community as well as the ways in which a person's giftedness reflects mutually shared goods and values. This goes against a model of education that sometimes stresses competencies that appear isolated from the real world.

Challenging the Western approach to giftedness is a model that stresses not individual competencies but acts of sharing with others. Indigenous views of the gift are more concerned with gifting itself as a kind of relationship or form of connection, rather than a prized object that only certain individuals possess. This hints at the possibility that being gifted does not require an object that we designate as a gift, but, in fact, can be a state of mind or, better still, interconnection that teachers can cultivate in a wide variety of situations with their students. In chapter 5, we will explore different aspects of gratitude as well as major orientations of gratitude that could prove of value in the classroom.

Finally, cultivating a gift paradigm in the classroom can shift both teachers and students toward a cosmological vision of planetary interbeing (Griffin, 1988; O'Sullivan, 1999) in which all beings have a unique value and belonging within a complex and fully integrated whole. O'Sullivan (1999) envisions such a cosmology as grounded in the "re-enchantment of the natural world," in which "the location of the human world as a participant world in the deep creative unfolding processes of the universe opens our horizons to the revelatory mysteries of nature" (p. 96). Rather than being mere observers who classify, label, and control the natural world, humans are positioned as fellow participants in an unfolding universe that is not known in advance of its revealing. This kind universe reenvisions humans as fellow travelers, participants, and receivers of gifts that are granted through grace, rather than guaranteed through a transactional exchange. To summarize a cosmological vision of the gift:

- In contrast to a fragmented view of the world as constituents or "parts" to be analyzed and commodified, cosmologies help people reenvision the universe as an integrated whole where all parts equally play a role and thus contain gifts that are highly valued to other beings.

- Cosmologies invoke the notion of *enchantment*, or the ability to appreciate the marvelous unfolding of interconnected events, thereby delighting in mystery and allurement rather than seeing these encounters as sources of fear or entrapment.

- A cosmological vision emphasizes the participatory notion of learning. We discover newness in each moment because each moment is a completely new set of conditions. By being participants, we displace the notion of "seeing in advance" of what is unfolding, thereby cultivating an epistemic humility in realizing that all views are inherently partial and subject to change and new conditions that make them never fully known or revealed.

As I will articulate in subsequent chapters, this vision strikes a fine balance between beholding the unique contributions of teachers and students alike and maintaining the harmony between gifts. Too much exaltation of uniqueness can lead to a disconnected romanticism or, worse still, a laissez-faire approach to teaching, which can lead to disconnection or moral relativism, summed up by the expression "to each their own." Too much of a collectivist approach can obscure what each student brings to the table, and might lead to a depersonalized or authoritarian approach. The alternative is to trust that each gift contributes to a totality, as long as students are given breadth and are entrusted to share their gifts. Perhaps O'Sullivan (1999) articulates the tension between individual self-development and community when he remarks, "To become oneself as a person or community is to become distinct, unique in different ways from all that exists in the present and all that has existed in the past or that will exist in the future. This means that what a person brings to any relationship can be given by no one else in the universe" (p. 223).

Questions for Discussion

1. What kinds of gifts do you experience in your classrooms? How have these gifts informed the classroom or enhanced the learning process?

2. Is it possible to compare student's assignments to gifts? What are the benefits of using the gift as a metaphor to describe the contributions of students? In what way might the metaphor seem to be a stretch or a challenge to you as a teacher?

3. Name one memorable gift that you received, tangible or intangible, from one of your students.

4. In this chapter, there are several examples of intangible qualities that can be considered as gifts, citing Bevan-Brown (2009). Compare these notions of gifts to your understanding of what giftedness looks and feels like in a classroom. Then reflect on how you might acknowledge intangible gifts or make them more visible in your classrooms. How might you encourage students to display the more intangible interpersonal qualities that Bevan-Brown outlines?

Questions for Reflection

1. Consider the classroom settings in which you teach. Write down activities that feel like receiving gifts and give you a sense of giftedness. Then write down activities that feel more like obligations that are done in exchange. Compare the two lists. Overall, what relationships do you feel most prevail: gifted relationships or exchange-based ones?

2. Using the list you created in question 1, consider one of the practices you consider to be more obligatory. Try to find ways to reframe it as a gifting experience. You may want to write a personal affirmation about the activity, draw a picture, or find other ways to create a new relationship with the activity in question.

3. Finally, reflect on question 2: What did it take to turn an exchange into a grateful experience?

Chapter 5

Why Gratitude?

When we hear the words "be grateful," what comes to mind? Is the feeling of gratitude perhaps a begrudging one or an open, expansive one? Does the thought of being grateful bring to mind an authentic joy of being gifted, or does it conjure the heavy responsibilities that are owed to others in return for their generosity? What sometimes comes to mind when we think of gratitude is a sense of debt toward others.

Some people remember, as children, growing up and being told to be grateful for all the things on their plate, even if the food was not their favorite. Furthermore, the statement "You should be grateful" often conjures up a sense of guilt; after all, why *aren't* we more grateful for the things that have freely been given to us? In this respect, gratitude is sometimes thought to be little more than an obligation toward others, and, on top of that, one that stems from a deep sense of indebtedness. In addition, when gratitude is grafted onto an already existing ethos that stresses independence and self-reliance, it often seems disempowering. To be grateful can at times appear as a veiled attempt to diminish one's hard-won autonomy, by giving credit to others instead of only crediting one's own efforts. Part of the challenge of acknowledging the benefits of gratitude lies in realizing that gratitude is neither an obligation nor an attempt at sacrificing the self and sense of achievement in favor of others. Since nobody really wants to be in debt in the first place, why would gratitude be a beneficial emotion that teachers can turn to in their classrooms?

In fact, while some thinkers might associate gratitude with indebtedness, others take a sunnier view, suggesting that gratitude is "a life orientation towards noticing and appreciating the positive in life" (Wood et al., 2010,

p. 891). According to this perspective, gratitude requires a genuine sense of being supported by the world around us, or what Emmons (2013a) refers to as acknowledging "the ways in which our lives are supported and sustained by others—close or distant, living or deceased, familiar or unknown to us" (p. 4). Here, Emmons focuses on ways in which gratitude stresses belonging and support, which has a different ring from feeling guilty or obligated for others' help. In contrast, a gratitude that stems from a mindset of individualism is often grudgingly provided, since someone who strongly values their autonomy may be afraid to admit their dependence on others or might even associate gratitude with weakness. Contrariwise, genuine gratitude requires a receptive appreciation of what is given, as well as one that is not tied to guilt, obligation, or sacrifice. A simple acknowledgment of interdependence suggests that one needn't do everything by oneself. A grateful person may also begin to acknowledge the role that others play in their own successes, thus countering the commonplace tendency to value one's own autonomy over and above the help provided by others on the path to success (Algoe & Haidt, 2009).

In order for gratitude to arise, one needs to cultivate a receptive attitude that counters the notion of an exchange. That is, if people see themselves as independent and not coexisting with others, they will tend to lose the sense that all beings are mutually depending on each other in a natural way. This tends to counter the view of instrumentalism, which suggests that we benefit others only for the sake of personal benefit—a view that is often found in social contract theories. As noted in chapter 4, the twentieth-century Catholic philosopher Gabriel Marcel (1962) suggests that, far from being a mutual exchange, working life is often conceptualized more as contractual labor that is designed to achieve quantifiable outcomes. People in caring professions might even fall into the trap of seeing their careers as primarily conducted for the sake of money. Referring to the nursing profession, Marcel notes,

> On the one hand, the male or female nurse in question is assimilating himself or herself to a machine which has to produce a definite output over a definite period. On the other hand, we should notice that—by a paradox that demands all our attention—this habit of regarding oneself as a machine, which might seem a degrading one, has as its other side a kind of pretention: a pretentious idea of oneself based on the idea of contract. I owe only what I am paid for—when I have carried out the

stipulations of my contract, I am my own master, nobody has the right to make any claim on me. (p. 196–197)

What happens when people start to see helping professions as a means for attaining a salary, rather than a deepfelt spiritual calling that is meant to serve others? Similarly, what can happen if, instead of viewing vocation as a calling to give and receive, people might start to see themselves only as machines serving preset roles? One unfortunate consequence is that professionals could prioritize the final result over the passion and purpose to work, which is often focused on benefiting and serving others. Another result is a calculating approach to work, in which professionals no longer claim responsibility beyond the scope of monetary reward. Gratitude is one emotion that might inspire people to go beyond the mere job description and embrace work as a calling to serve other beings or to cultivating a wider sense of interconnectedness.

As noted in chapter 4, gratitude entails a revisioning of the world that no longer sees all things as monetary exchange, but rather as freely given elements. That is, contrary to treating individual effort as an exchangeable good on a marketplace, many cultural understandings of gifts reveal a sacred interconnection that underlies them. Mauss (1990) articulates the way gifts in the Maori culture that he observed are invested with the soul of the giver and thereby must return it to its original source:

> What imposes obligation in the present received and exchanged, is the fact that the thing received is not inactive. Even when it has been abandoned by the giver, it still possesses something of him. Through it the giver has a hold over the beneficiary just as, being its owner, through it he has a hold over the thief. This is because the taonga [treasured possession] is animated by the hau [vital essence] of its forest, its native heath and soil. It is truly "native": the hau follows after anyone possessing the thing. . . . In reality, it is the hau that wishes to return to its birthplace, to the sanctuary of the forest and the clan, and to the owner. (p. 15)

Gifts, according to this view, are not distinct objects that are owned exclusively by one person but are more so endowed with a spirit that points back to an original source. Granting unique spiritual properties to a gift could be one way of reminding us that true gifts point to a wider orientation toward the universe—one in which spirit pervades all things and cannot be confined to a specific coveted object. Although this view originates in Maori culture, it can also translate into different spiritualities. In examining Muslim scriptures, Karen Armstrong (2022) notes how the Qu'ran contains many passages that exhort people to look upon nature as evidence of the generosity of the creator. She suggests that "instead of frightening themselves with images of hell," Muslims protect themselves against selfishness and greed through the ability to "meditate on the ayat of God's generosity in the natural world and, with gratitude, aspire to his benevolence" (p. 110). Armstrong points to the importance of developing an aesthetic that allows for an extensive gratitude—one that envisions the vastness and beauty of gifts that are freely and mysteriously granted to all beings, particularly the natural world. Speaking from a Buddhist perspective, Chan Buddhist Master Sheng Yen (2013) comments on how appreciating the natural world can similarly allow people to see that there is a vastness of phenomena freely available to all beings, one that is not bounded by a single room hemmed in by four walls:

> Within the confines of your own home you may feel you are the master, but if many others live there, the sense of being in your own space begins to diminish. When you go into the country, the expanse of sky and the earth form one big universal house and you can feel very small. At the same time, in that great open space you would feel that all nature is yours, and even with other people there, you still feel a sense of spaciousness. Therefore, after a period of staying indoors, people should go outside and experience, on the one hand, the smallness of themselves, and on the other, the largeness of themselves. (p. 33)

Experiencing the "smallness" of the self, far from diminishing one's experiences, is one way of seeing the awe-inspiring things that are granted simply in our belonging to a vast universe, which includes the natural world as well as all the beauty that exists just outside our window. Sheng Yen even suggests that the sense of covetousness that might arise from being in a confined space starts to lose its edge when we are out in the natural world, especially when there is so much available to be shared. These kinds of aesthetic experiences can make people more inclined to feel grateful, which also counters a mindset that sees things as scarce resources needing to be possessed and guarded against the intrusion of other beings.

Many studies have pointed to the transformative benefits of gratitude in classrooms, particularly when teachers choose to adopt gratitude practices, such as the simple yet life-transforming practice of keeping a gratitude journal. Teacher Owen Griffith (2016) has applied gratitude practices as a ritual practice in his teaching and has gradually extended these practices to his middle school classrooms. According to Griffith, gratitude helps teachers not only to feel an enhanced sense of being gifted by positive aspects of their classrooms but also to see the positive in otherwise difficult classroom situations. Griffith started keeping a gratitude journal after experiencing stresses in his classroom. After a bumpy start in which he needed to grow accustomed to a different way of seeing his everyday experiences, Griffith later experienced changes in his perceptions about the challenges he faced at work:

> As I kept writing this simple gratitude activity, some of the subtle incremental changes became more pronounced. I found myself reflecting on the good things that happened to me. What surprised me even more, when life was challenging, I would find something positive inside any negative situation. For example, when I had to stay late and work some overtime, I was immediately resentful. But when I took a breath and wrote a quick gratitude list, I became grateful that I had a job and that I would receive some overtime pay on my next paycheck. (xxi)

Griffith's example illustrates how gratitude practice can foster both appreciation of the good things one has experienced and the ability to grow through challenges. This positions gratitude not simply as an emotional state that happens passively when one receives a pleasant gift, but as a way of cognitively reframing difficult situations so that they can be viewed as worthy of gratitude.

Even a cursory glance at different understandings of gratitude and gifts can reveal multiple aspects and dimensions to gratitude. How might a gratitude orientation enhance or, conversely, challenge the ways teachers relate to their students? The following sections explore existing research and theories on the key aspects of gratitude in classrooms, with some examples of their implications for teachers' cultivation of gratitude.

Four Characteristics of Gratitude

Although gratitude can be potentially viewed from multiple angles or standpoints, there are a few key characteristics that could be used to explore gratitude in some detail. The following sections explore defining components of gratitude.

Receptivity

As noted in chapters 3 and 4, it's commonplace in many cultures to consider generosity as a virtue that is actively cultivated, while undervaluing the equally important skill of learning to receive. Most spiritual traditions place great importance on actively cultivating the ability to give, such as when monotheistic religions emphasize the importance of imitating the creator being, and Buddhism considers dana (generosity) to be one of the six paramitas that leads to wisdom. In fact, many people might take it for granted that they are able to receive things thankfully; after all, is it not easier to receive than it is to give? However, others are starting to acknowledge the importance of learning to fully appreciate and acknowledge gifts received. In one passage emphasizing the importance of accepting gifts, Nouwen (2020) notes,

> A gift only becomes a gift when it is received; and nothing we have to give—wealth, talents, competence, or just beauty—will ever be recognized as true gifts until someone is open to accept them. This all suggests that if we want others to grow—that is, to discover their potential and capacities, to experience that they have something to live and work for—we should first of all be able to recognize their gifts and be willing to receive them. For we only become fully human when we are received and accepted. (para. 1)

Nel Noddings (1986) has, in a similar vein, described the need for teachers to feel acknowledged by their students as a way of supporting their continued practice. If teachers don't receive feedback from their students, they don't have a realistic sense of whether the students are benefiting and learning from the subjects taught. This can lead to a loss of motivation, as when a teacher interprets a lack of student response as a failure to sufficiently care for the student: "In situations where the student rarely responds, is negative, denies the effort at caring, the teacher's caring quite predictably deteriorates to 'cares and burdens.' She becomes the needy target of her own caring. In such cases, we should supply special support to maintain the teacher as one-caring" (p. 191). The notion of the teacher as being on the receiving end of students as givers may sometimes appear to run against the image of the teacher as having infinite amounts of energy to give to support a classroom. However, both Nouwen and Noddings suggest that giving and receiving are two inseparable sides of the same coin. Without a proper reception of a gift, the giver lacks the knowledge or the context to know whether the gift really benefited the receiver. This also affirms the possibility that giving could be misdirected, as when a teacher's intention to help a student backfires by lacking the correct level of challenge to engage the student. For true giftedness to occur, both giver and receiver need to be attentive to the gift itself.

With receiving comes the accompanying attitude of being open and receptive to the gifts that are found in all experiences from moment to moment, which suggests the interconnection of things in an expanding circle of gifts. Guengerich (2020) describes a widening circle of gratitude for the gifts that sustain a person's life, which runs counter to the tendency to conceive of the self as exclusively giving or providing: "We begin with this inescapable reality: We are contingent creatures. We depend on our environment for everything we need. We depend on the largess of the natural world for our very existence, and we depend on the people around us for the quality of our ongoing lives" (p. 60). Guengerich describes receptiveness as an "abiding sense of joy" (p. 61) that isn't necessarily fixed to any given object or gift. For Guengerich, the role of gifts and gratitude is not to contract the self into a constellation of desires but, contrariwise, to situate oneself as someone in a state of dependence on nature and community. Yet far from encouraging passivity, the attitude of enjoying the gifts of others can lead to the cultivation of specific virtues that stem from an insight into our interdependence. Philosopher Alisdair MacIntyre has coined the term "dependent rational animals" (MacIntyre, 1999) to refer to the fact that in spite of the capacity to reason, human beings are forever dependent on others for their survival and thus continually reminded of their creatureliness. He notes that healthy maturity, far from implying a total repudiation of dependence, strikes a delicate yet necessary balance between self-reliance and acknowledging the needs of others. Guided by the theories of D. W. Winnicott, MacIntrye describes how well-adjusted children manage to "achieve the kind of independence that is able to acknowledge truthfully and realistically its dependences and attachments" (p. 85). The idea that human beings possess rationality and can potentially distance themselves from emotions does not entail that they are immune to disease, disability, environmental problems, or the basic necessities to keep their bodies alive. By debunking the common misconception that rationality gives humans ultimate control over their fates and destinies, MacIntyre allows greater room for exploring and valuing the Thomistic virtues of dependency, including faith, hope, and charity. These kinds of qualities can allow for a more socially engaged ethic that focuses on equity and social justice, ensuring that all can equally enjoy and have access to the gifts of society.

Wholeheartedness

Gratitude and gift giving are often studied as parts of ritual practices through which societies cohere (Zhou & Dong, 2023) and social or class status is affirmed (Hanson, 2015). Because gratitude is often considered a social "glue," it's common to view gratitude as a ritual that might not lack genuine feeling. That is, we sometimes might view gifts more as obligations than as heartfelt, spontaneous gestures. From a sociological perspective, gratitude may be described as the behaviors that preserve the continuity of gifts across generations and may therefore be considered a social grace or ritual rather than a feeling. Yet part of what distinguishes gratitude from "indebtedness" is the way that it comes from a heartfelt interpersonal exchange, as opposed to a sense of obligation or "paying back." The authentic feeling of thankfulness is essential to preventing gratitude from becoming an obligatory or compulsive ritual of thanking, sometimes referred to as "gratitude fatigue" (Emmons, 2013a). In their study of perceptions about receivers of gifts, Kong and Belkin (2019) distinguish between "controlled" motivation, which "arises when individuals are compelled to act in a certain way due to a sense of pressure" and "autonomous motivation," which arises when "individuals can voluntarily act with a sense of choice or wanting to do so" (p. 827). Although their study is limited to demonstrating how expressing thanks improves prosocial bonds and resource sharing between givers and receivers, it also suggests that gratitude is valued as an expression of underlying goodwill, as opposed to obligation.

While gratitude is most celebrated and enjoyed when it is truly heartfelt, research on the sustainability of teachers' heartfelt gratitude is problematic at best. Howells (2012) relates the challenges that teachers face when they were asked to intentionally partake in gratitude practices toward their students.

In some instances, the teachers felt pressured to *feel* grateful toward students and failed to see the importance of gratitude as an action rather than as a feeling state: "'It's hard to keep it up,' 'It's hard to be grateful all the time,' 'I often don't feel in the mood to the grateful.' Gratitude was a 'thing' to be 'applied' or something to 'be' or 'do'—'all the time,' and this was unattainable for them. I shared with them my own difficulties concerning my inability to be grateful all the time" (p. 46). Howells attempts to mitigate this dilemma by suggesting that teachers show gratitude *to* students through active behaviors, instead of waiting for moments when they feel grateful *for* specific things that students do. However, it can be difficult for teachers to cultivate a desire to make gratitude a daily practice in their classrooms, unless an authentic feeling of gratefulness is generated. Expressions of gratitude are not necessarily accompanied by *feelings* of gratitude, which entails that there is sometimes a question of which of these to prioritize and which comes first. While Howells suggests that an expression of gratitude can sometimes be followed by feelings of gratitude, it's not always the case that people feel gratitude through its mere expression. But it's important that gratitude have a genuine emotional source rather than being something that is performed by rote.

RECIPROCATION

Gratitude has also been positioned as a form of "moral affect" (McCullough et al., 2001), one that can induce prosocial behaviors such as reciprocity, kindness, and social graces. Unlike other forms of positive affect, such as joy and happiness, gratitude can inspire an intention to act for others, in the interest of long-term mutual benefit. Desteno et al. (2014) have shown that gratitude can reduce financial stresses and improve frustration tolerance by shifting one's orientation toward socially beneficial actions, which plays a part in "inhibiting decisions favoring immediate gratification" (p. 1263). Indigenous educators also link gratitude to a sense of heartfelt interdependence on other beings, particularly by stressing the importance of community as a source of self-awareness and recognition of the contributions of all beings. Cajete (2015) links the practice of gratitude with a sense of community and interconnection when he notes,

> Community is the context in which the American Indian person comes to know the nature of relationship, responsibility, and participation in the lifeways of one's people. Community is

> also the context in which the "affective" dimension of education unfolds. It is the "place" where one comes to know what it is to be related. It is the place of sharing life through everyday acts, through song, dance, story, and celebration. It is the place of teaching, learning, making art, and sharing thoughts, feelings, joy, and grief. It is the place for feeling and being "connected." (p. 366)

Prosocial, relational aspects of gratitude practices can enhance teachers' awareness of the social, interconnected nature of classrooms and assessment of students (Huot, 2002). Shay's (2005) study of how engineering students were assessed for their final year projects in a South African university illustrates how assessment is not a single event controlled by one assessing person, but it is the result of "different positions that assessors occupy in relation to the topic, the research project and the students" (p. 670). Shay recommends that assessment be positioned in the context of communities of practice as opposed to an isolated event that resides within a teacher's mind. Gratitude practices could extend the mutual dialogue of assessment by inspiring students and teachers alike to engage in relationships of thanking, appreciation, and acknowledgment. Recent research by Fredrickson (2004, 2013) also confirms the ability for gratitude to broaden and build prosocial dispositions, as does Hanson (2013), who suggests that feelings of gratitude can induce cycles of mutually reinforcing positive moods: "Feelings grow moods. For example, repeatedly taking in feelings of gladness and gratitude will tend to develop a mood of contentment. In turn, moods grow feelings. A basic sense of contentment with life fosters feelings of thankfulness and joy" (p. 81). By creating a baseline of thankfulness that prompts people to be more mindful of opportunities to give back, gratitude encourages an outward-facing orientation that builds confidence and positive social relationships. In this regard, gratitude supports a constellation of positive social emotions, ranging from generosity to patience, deep listening, and resilience.

One potential challenge to be addressed in future research is whether or not the prosocial qualities of gratitude depend on specific reciprocation from students. Noddings (1986) suggests that teachers need a cyclic feedback of support. The downside of gratitude practice is that it might create expectations in teachers that students reciprocate their expressions of gratitude. Howells (2012) echoes this concern when she describes the power dynamics that could ensue in a classroom if teachers practice gratitude under the expectation that students reciprocate through a mirroring response:

> The dimensions of gratitude that involve reciprocity can take an ugly turn if teachers make their students beholden to them in some way. Perhaps unknowingly a teacher may manipulate the dynamics of a giving and receiving situation so that students give back in the teacher's currency—of what they value and look for rather than what the students are wanting and able to give. Unhealthy relations stemming from the power of the teacher over the student can diminish the purity of the intention. (p. 57)

Howells references the work of Patricia White (1999), who has suggested that teachers can mitigate this tension by perceiving the relationship between teacher and student as one of mutual goodwill as opposed to an obligatory exchange. Howells remarks, "Teachers may express gratitude to their students as they become increasingly aware of everything they have received from them—without a planned exchange in mind" (p. 58).

ASYMMETRY

Gratitude and gift giving are often positioned as parts of ritual practices through which societies cohere (Visser, 2008) and social or class status is affirmed (Hanson, 2015). Yet what distinguishes gratitude from "indebtedness" is that it comes from a heartfelt sense of surprise (Ortony et al., 1988) and involves asymmetrical patterns of giving and receiving (Galea, 2006), as opposed to a two-way exchange (Buck, 2004). The authentic feeling of surprise and wonder is thought to be essential to preventing gratitude from becoming an obligatory, automatic, or compulsive ritual of thanking. Yet this sense of surprise often does not arise through intentional reflection alone. Howells (2012) remarks how the teachers in her study expressed difficulties when they were asked to intentionally practice gratitude as a continuous emotional orientation toward their students. Many expressed the belief that "gratitude was a 'thing' to be 'applied' or something to 'be' or 'do'—'all the time,' and this was unattainable for them" (p. 46). If lacking heartfelt feelings of gratitude, teachers may not have intrinsic desire to express thankfulness to their students or, worse still, may approach gratitude as a form of emotional labor (Hochschild, 2003).

One promising way of tapping into the asymmetric possibilities of gratitude is to explore the way teacher-student relationships could be modeled as maternal relationships. Maternal pedagogies offer a radically fresh perspective on what gifts could be by examining the ways in which mothering gifts children, as well as how this gifting can analogously extend to teacher-student encounters. One pioneer in maternal thinking, Sara Ruddick (1995), has articulated maternal thought as being based on protection, nurturance, and training. Vaughan and Estola (2007) note the unique position in which mothering challenges traditional notions of gifts as inevitable forms of exchange when they are named as such: "Mothers commonly do a great deal of gift giving, which is unrecognized. In fact, mothering can be seen as a mode of distribution (presently confined to the 'private sphere') in which goods are given directly to needs" (p. 248). Vaughan (2013) has written extensively about the way that gifts form image schemas in early childhood, characterizing early ideas of the gift as "an intercorporeal schema derived from mothering and being mothered, giving and receiving, which I call the image schema of the gift. This schema, abstracted in early childhood from the experience of being nurtured, includes the other from the beginning as giver and receiver of nurturing" (p. 57). In both passages, one finds the positioning of gifts as asymmetrical by necessity, meaning that they go beyond the logic of utility and exchange to embrace meeting the specific needs of others. Just as mothers unconditionally give attention and meet the needs of their children, so teachers could also model mothering relationships, with an emphasis on a maternal ethic of "attentive love, an ethics of care, and a deep concern for the student's socio-emotional as well as intellectual growth" (Green & Byrd, 2011). Far from focusing exclusively on an ethic of "fair" grading—as though there were a single objective standard through which to grade—maternal pedagogy would operate from a care-based ethic where the student's unique unfolding comes first and foremost. Montessori was one example of an early holistic educator who valued the process of treating children as having unique resources that help them flourish and grow. In contrast, an overanxious effort to control children's behavior leads to a stifling of the gifts that children bring to all life situations, such as being close to nature:

> It would be too soon for us to say: Let the children be free; encourage them; let them run outside when it is raining; let them remove their shoes when they find a puddle of water; and, when the grass of the meadows is damp with dew, let them run on it and trample it with their bare feet. . . . But, instead of this, we anxiously ask ourselves how we can make a child sleep after the sun has risen, or how we can teach him not to take off his shoes or wander over the meadows. (Montessori, 1967, p. 68–69)

One of the key aspects of maternal pedagogy is factoring the full emotional life of both teachers and students in giving feedback and learning in general. Thompson (2017) suggests a wider range of emotions than what is typically associated with competitive classroom dynamics:

> Certainly, feminist scholarship on teaching has helped us understand what nurtures and blocks learning in the classroom and the potential of teaching to foster social justice. Feminist teaching has centered on seeing the classroom as a community of learners (rather than treating faculty as the ultimate and only experts). Learning can be based on cooperation and collaboration, rather than on a star system and competition. Learning doesn't have to be serious all the time. Laughter and ease in our bodies can help us be honest about the reading and own lives. Since many topics that are raised in feminist classrooms directly relate to people's lived experiences in the world, students need to be able to talk about how they relate to the course content. (p. 3)

One of the dark sides to maternal pedagogy, however, is that it might valorize the mother as an all-giving nurturer, which places the teacher in a position of being "never angry or disconnected" (Green & Byrd, 2011) and who represses or suppresses negative thought patterns or emotions as a result of "patriarchal expectations of the self-sacrificing mother and teacher" (p. 60). Here, there is a marked difference between a self-sacrificing, "putting others first" mentality, and the more inclusive factoring of the teacher's whole self "where the needs and complete life of the teacher are as equally acknowledged and valued as the students" (p. 60–61). Notions of the gift might offset this tendency by allowing teachers to see that their work is not just about caring actively but about being receptive to already existing gifts in students.

Gratitude as an Active, Repeated Practice

Many researchers stress that gratitude cannot be performed only once but instead needs to be practiced repeatedly in order for benefits to arise. Emmons and McCullough (2003) divided their research participants into two groups. A "blessings" group was instructed to complete fourteen daily reports about what they felt blessed about on a daily basis, while a "hassles" group was told to write their hassles. The results among the blessings group was an increase in positive mood over the thirteen days of study, in comparison to those who reported hassles.

Educators can also play a pivotal role in facilitating gratitude as a practice among students. Carter et al. (2018) investigated the effects of children keeping a positive events diary, used three times for one week, in which students were asked to write about a "good" event and "why it is good" (causal explanation). A three-month follow-up found that the diary had a long-term impact on sustaining positive feelings in students, particularly for those students who had emotional difficulties. One explanation that the authors give for the success of the intervention is that through writing positive experiences, the "individual develops a more balanced attributional style, reflecting an increase in attributing positive events internally (and externalising negatives)" (p. 115). Other interventions such as writing a gratitude letter to a benefactor and visiting the benefactor to read it to them (Seligman et al., 2005) confirm that positive feelings continue long after the practice itself. However, most studies employing letter writing (Toepfer & Walker, 2009; Toepfer et al., 2012) suggest that numerous letters are required to reinforce the positive effects of gratitude.

Studies in education also illustrate the salutary benefits of gratitude experiences on actively enhancing the quality of student-teacher relationships. In one of the few studies that examines specifically teacher gratitude toward students, Howells (2014) discovered that teachers engage a variety of gratitude practices with their students that promote greater attunement to their student's strengths and intrinsic worth as students. Examples of such gratitude practices include "greeting students, active relationship building, and actions that followed changes of their inner attitude towards their students" (p. 63). Howells notes that acts of gratitude focus on what the teacher receives from the student and lead to an action of wanting to give back in some way. The starting point for these practices, however, rests in the teacher's ability to actively exert the intention of gratitude, even where situations may seem difficult or problematic.

Transpersonal Approaches to Gratitude

Transpersonal approaches often challenge the notion that gratitude needs a giver and a gift. G. K. Chesterton (2013) refers to thankfulness for existence when he notes in his autobiography, "I thanked whatever gods might be, not like Swinburne, because no life lived for ever, but because any life lived at all; not, like Henley for my unconquerable soul (for I have never been so optimistic about my own soul as all that) but for my own soul and my own body, even if they could be conquered." David Steindl-Rast has also suggested that thankfulness stems from a grounded sense of belonging to the cosmos, which taps into spiritual groundedness. He remarks, "It is with gratitude that spirituality begins, with a sense of gratefulness for being alive, gratefulness for the gift of this universe to which we belong. In the give and take of daily living, every action can become a grateful celebration of this belonging" (Capra et al., 1991, p. 17).

Transpersonal gratitude or "cosmic" gratitude (Roberts, 2014) hinges upon the idea of interconnection as a source of gratitude. One of the most significant philosophers who points to this idea is Alfred North Whitehead. Guengerich (2020) suggests a connection between Whitehead's philosophy of interconnection and gratitude, when he describes Whitehead's faith in an underlying order of nature that assures that all beings belong within it, partaking in a harmonious relationship:

> In order for the universe to exist as it does, the many elements have to be connected in one particular way at each particular moment, held together by nuclear, electromagnetic, and gravitational forces. By the next moment, things have changed somewhat, so everything has to be connected in a somewhat different way. But the process is the same. The many elements that constitute the universe become one moment of experience, in which everything is ultimately connected to everything else in one particular way. In so doing, the universe thereby *gains* another moment of experience. In Whitehead's words, "The many become one and are increased by one." (p. 83)

Instead of focusing on specific objects that are given to some people as gifts, Whitehead finds gratitude in a sense of the world *gaining* new connections. Whitehead is especially focused on treating experiences as additional gains that travel through and enrich the universe as a totality.

Contemplative approaches to gratitude stress experiences of "a deep interconnectedness with life" (Miller, 2000, p. 126), letting go (p. 125), and nonjudgmental acceptance through an immersive experience of "relaxed alertness" (p. 124). Contemplative gratitude extends the object of gratitude to a more diffuse thankfulness for life or existence that "does not yet distinguish between giver, gift, and receiver" (Steindl-Rast, 2004, p. 286). Keltner and Haidt (2003) note how contemplative approaches to gratitude can involve states of expanded consciousness of self in relation to the world and others, including feelings of awe and wonder. These states depend less on specific instances of perceived giving and gifts than they do on a nondualistic relationship to the world. Philosopher Martha Nussbaum (2001) in particular has identified wonder as going beyond a typically self-referential eudaemonic approach to emotions. She notes that unlike other emotions, which arise from evaluating situations relative to one's personal framework or goals, wonder "responds to the pull of the object, and one might say that in it the subject is maximally aware of the value of the object, and only minimally aware, if at all, of its relationship to her own plans. That is why it is likely to issue in contemplation, rather than in any sort of action toward the object" (p. 54). Gratitude practices can incorporate a variety of contemplative approaches to enhance a sense of interconnection, such as meditation and mindfulness (Feldman & Kuyken, 2019). Burzyńska (2018) uses a gratitude-based meditation as a way for research participants to contemplate " 'the things for which he/she is grateful for' either once a week or three times a week" (p. 303). In adopting grateful contemplation as a form of meditation, subjects incorporate a contemplative practice to "attend nonjudgmentally to all stimuli in the internal and external world, but not to ruminate on any particular stimulus" (p. 305). Duthely et al. (2017) have studied the effects of a gratitude-based guided visualization as a way to connect youth to a heart-centered meditation on gratitude in which the practitioner "tries to keep the mind quiet, by clearing the mind of as many thoughts as possible" (p. 5). Practices such as fasting (Winner, 2007) are used to encourage a less striving relationship to material success (Kasser, 2002), thereby cultivating a more nuanced appreciation of material and social goods. The key denominator is the importance of *letting go* as a way to receive what is present to experience, rather than trying to *build up* a grateful response through thinking alone. To combat gratitude fatigue (Emmons, 2013a, p. 20), a gratitude-based assessment could combine with a guided relaxation, meditation, or visualization practice to provide a more embodied experience of gratitude, as opposed to relying on reflection and cognitive appraisals alone.

Transpersonal approaches to gratitude tend to stress interrelationships over specific transactions and exchanges. What results is a more complex understanding of emotions that arise during gratitude. Based on semi-structured interviews exploring the lived experience of gratitude Hlava et al. (2014) have developed a tool that expands a standard transactional model of gratitude, which emphasizes benefits received, toward a more reciprocal, relational understanding of gratitude, or what they call shifting from a "reciprocity" to a "mutuality" model toward gratitude, that is, "from the emotional response of tangible benefits" to "an appreciation of the quality of a relationship" (p. 2). They note, "Transpersonal gratitude seems to describe feelings that emerge in response to a transformed view of a benefit and its relationship to the beneficiary. When someone sees himself or herself not as the recipient of a gesture or favor, but as someone participating at the confluence of an intimate relationship with another person or a profound connection with the entire panoply of nature, the benefit is no longer tangible or straightforward" (p. 10). What's significant about this model is that gratitude is not posed as part of an exchange of giving in exchange for receiving, or "an exact, reciprocal balance between extending gratitude and, say, receiving it back, or between giver and receiver." Instead, the emphasis is on the quality of the relationship that develops from acknowledging the gifts that people receive from others. Thus, in contrast to an exchange model of gratitude, the authors emphasize "a transformed view of a benefit and its relationship to a beneficiary" (p. 10).

Another characteristic of transpersonal gratitude is that it does not operate from a narrowed field of emotions that are deemed as positive, such as the joy of receiving a highly esteemed gift or prize. Lambert et al. (2009) suggest the need for studies to extend beyond limited models of gratitude, to embrace less object-based emotions. A sense of awe and mystery are some examples of emotions that these researchers identified in their research. Keltner and Haidt (2003) have similarly noted how contemplative approaches to gratitude can involve emotional states that come from an expanded consciousness of self in relation to the world and others, including a sense of awe and wonder. As an alternative to focusing on the "positive" emotions commonly associated with well-being, such as resilience and joy, gratitude might focus on emotional experiences of celebration. Roberts (2014) has suggested that gratitude could be extended to a sense of belonging in the universe that does not entail a specific giver or receiver. He notes, "In feeling cosmic gratefulness, we 'celebrate' our inclusion in being. It is as though the universe welcomes us into a state of mutual belonging" (p. 72). Contrary to situated approaches to gratitude, transpersonal approaches do not rely on a specific benefactor or beneficiary. Instead, feelings of belonging and inclusion help teachers to cultivate a feeling of belonging with their students, participating in an interdependent circle of feedback through the process of assessment itself.

Finally, whereas intentional gratitude relates to cognitive reframing of difficult or challenging situations, transpersonal models of gratitude incorporate more contemplative approaches to cultivating gratitude. Gratitude practices can incorporate a variety of contemplative approaches to enhance a sense of interconnection, including guided visualization, meditation, mindfulness, and other practices that encourage stopping the continuous flow of thoughts to appreciate what is. Practices such as fasting (Emmons, 2013a, p. 81) have also been used to encourage a less striving relationship to the material world, in addition to cultivating a more nuanced appreciation of material and social goods.

Characteristics of Transpersonal Gratitude Practices

Transpersonal gratitude operates from several approaches that relate to contemplative educational approaches in general. The list below includes some of the characteristics of practices that lean toward transpersonal gratitude:

1. *Embodied*: Gratitude incorporates bodily practices that bring people to direct experience with a grateful emotion, rather than an intellectual comprehension.

2. *Contemplative*: Instead of focusing on words or narratives to reframe situations, transpersonal approaches to gratitude emphasize a direct relationship with the world that stresses nonduality, unconditional acceptance and surrender, slowing down (Emmons, 2013a, p. 92), silence, and solitude, which can "spur a greater awareness of the giftedness of life" (p. 83).

3. *Non-Striving*: In a study of life satisfaction among those who strive for wealth as opposed to those who don't, psychologist Tim Kasser (Emmons, 2013a) found that "aspiring toward greater wealth and more material possessions undermines the ability to be content" (p. 88); Kasser theorizes a simpler yet more nuanced relationship to material things. For Kasser, being present and having "appreciation for what one already has" (p. 90) is more conducive to happiness than an attitude of striving. This orientation goes against the common approach of saying "more is better" (p. 89).

4. *Interrelational*: Rather than privileging gifts and givers or the ability to extend gratitude, transpersonal gratitude arises from

a sense of relatedness that comes from feeling "gifted" by things around us. That is, one contemplates interdependence, not privileging the giver or gift over the receiver. Emmons (2013a) notes, "We are not grateful for the object itself. Rather, we are grateful for the role the object plays within the complex dynamic of everyday experience" (p. 92). This quote notably stresses interrelationship and how things work together or interact (relationships), rather than being grateful for *isolated* situations.

Summary and Discussion

While this chapter has outlined the potentials of gratitude practices to enhance classroom experiences, it also suggests unique challenges. First, even though gratitude relies on the authenticity of the giver and the ability to actively cultivate thankfulness for others' contributions, there is something paradoxically unpredictable and even asymmetrical about gratitude. Since a genuine sense of gratitude relies on an insight into the interdependence and contributions of other beings, it is not always easy for a teacher practitioner to sustain gratitude all the time, particularly in a bustling classroom where students and teachers are bound by the pressure of tight deadlines. Sustaining gratitude requires teachers to be mindful of a careful balance of give-and-take in the classroom, knowing that neither they nor their students can sustain the same emotional energy simply through an autonomous act of choice.

While many forms of gratitude practice focus on sustained attention to pleasurable or enjoyable gifts one has received, this is but one of several orientations to gratitude that have been explored in gratitude research. If teachers limit their gratitude practice to only perceiving highly esteemed qualities in their students, their gratitude becomes conditionally predicated on whether the student satisfies the curriculum requirements or pleases the teacher. However, in addition to the deliberate cultivation of a receptive attitude toward students, teachers also need to practice reframing challenging situations in new ways that allow them to be seen as worthy of gratitude, such as when a student does not submit work that fits required standards or behaves in a challenging way. Finally, as the section on transpersonal gratitude suggests, cognitive reframing of difficulties may not be sufficient for teachers to feel genuine gratitude, as teachers may still not feel emotionally attuned to gratitude even when they cognitively reframe their classrooms or students as the basis for gratitude. Chapters 7 and 10 will explore the use of metaphor and visualization as holistic approaches that teachers can use to more intuitively and emotionally connect with gratitude as a felt experience.

Questions for Discussion

1. Of the different approaches to gratitude mentioned in this chapter, is there one that you feel you can apply to your classroom the most?

2. What are you most grateful for as a teacher? What aspects of being in your classroom can arouse gratitude?

3. Are there aspects of your career as a teacher that you have taken for granted? Consider all the gifts that you bring to your classroom, including the gifts of presence, care, attentiveness, and concern for your students. Take a moment to honor and feel grateful for your own contributions.

Questions for Reflection

1. Think about a time when you experienced gratitude from a student or in a classroom. Describe the situation in as much detail as you can. Then reflect:

    a. What or who was the gratitude directed at?

    b. What kinds of qualities does this gratitude bring up, given the four characteristics of gratitude outlined in this chapter?

    c. Overall, how would you describe the source of gratitude? Was it based on the qualities in the gift itself, what you attributed to the gift, or a more transpersonal gratitude that relies on neither gift, giver, or receiver?

2. Think about an action you could perform as a teacher that might increase a sense of gratitude within the classroom. Then write a class plan showing how you might implement the

gratitude. This can take the form of a lesson on gratitude, for instance, or a gesture that you want to extend to your students, or some idea that you would like your students to try.

3. After writing a class plan of gratitude, feel free to implement it. Write down your expected results in one column, while documenting the actual results in a second column. Did the expectations meet the results? Why or why not?

Chapter 6

The Tragic Side of Gratitude

In chapter 2, I briefly mentioned a potential challenge with using Colin Wilson's St. Neot's margin as a prototype of a surprise experience—namely, that Wilson's experiences with getting a ride happened to turn out for the best for both him and the lorry driver. In other words, some could argue that only *pleasant* surprises count as fostering moments of gratitude and giftedness. But what if the lorry did not get to the desired destination? Wilson would likely not have felt the same sense of relief that he did when the crisis turned out to be averted. Does this mean that gifts and gratitude are dependent on whether a surprise is a pleasant one? If this were the case, then very difficult crises, such as *staying lost* for a prolonged period, might be a source of tremendous alarm and mounting stress.

Chapter 3 also explored the key elements of a surprise experience, such as receptivity, empathy, discovery, and trust. While these characteristics of surprise experience entail an ability to suspend one's judgments to allow an experience to unfold, it remains to be known whether this principle equally applies to situations where surprises are unpleasant. In fact, to the contrary, could an unexpectedly unpleasant surprise lead teachers to become less trustful, more emotionally withdrawn, and altogether less receptive of the surprises of classrooms? In this chapter, I will make an argument for the importance of cognitive reframing and reappraisal as means through which teachers can turn tragedy, loss, and other negative aspects of a surprise experience into gifts.

To address these ideas, I will explore the relationship between gratitude and tragedy, particularly turning to key conceptual framings that may help sustain a sense of giftedness and gratitude in the midst of periods of loss, being lost, transition, or suffering. Afterward, I will discuss how embracing the tragic can be one way of cultivating a deeper sense of gratitude that embraces not only the pleasant but the unpleasant as well. Finally, to tie this chapter to curriculum, I argue that both teachers and students can use tragic stories as a way to reflect on the cyclic nature of life, contemplate the preciousness of what is given, and recognize that gifts are temporarily granted. This can foster many key qualities in the classroom, including humility, contentedness, thankfulness, cooperation, and compassion.

Gratitude and the Tragic Sense of Life

Many exercises in gratitude, including gratitude journaling, encourage writing down all positive experiences, or potentially reframing negative ones as potentially positive (Lambert et al., 2012; Van Beveren et al., 2018). However, some studies suggest that gratitude is more often the result of reflecting on negative things that *could have happened*, which in turn becomes a source of relief. Teigen (1997) reports on a study in which participants were asked to articulate differences between "lucky" and "good" situations. The study found that people were more inclined to feel gratitude when they compare a positive experience they encountered to a more negative one; conversely, feelings of envy arise when the participants compared their situation to what they perceived as more fortunate circumstances in others. This study suggests that feelings of gratitude, like envy, are based on a reflective contrast between one situation and another, or what Teigen refers to as "counterfactual thoughts" (p. 313). By focusing on the gratitude expressions implied in attributing experiences to luck, the study also suggests that gratitude is related to the interchangeability of self and others. We often hear the expression "It could have been me" to describe situations where we find ourselves easily exchanging our own situation for that of others. As an alternative to attributing our success and failure to innate dispositions that are fixed within us, gratitude is often expressed as the experience of being saved, whether by accident or through grace, from a more difficult or problematic situation (Emmons, 2013b).

How, then, does gratitude relate to tragedy? Tragedy and gratitude often seem to be polar opposites, particularly when gratitude is so often linked to the "positive emotions" such as joy. One might even begin to wonder: How can gratitude be cultivated alongside the sense that everything one cherishes is likely to be impermanent anyway? Tragedies traditionally depict a character who, through their own actions and choices, falls from grace to a lower or more compromised realm. While some have described tragic characters as bound by forces of necessity and fate (Cavell, 1979), others emphasize how tragedy hints at the choice between greater or lesser evils (Spronk et al., 2017). The fact that tragic protagonists could have chosen differently makes their sense of loss more twinged with regret and, thus, more poignant. With tragedy comes the fragility of choice as well as the possibility of regret for misguided choices that spell the end of stability or success. In fact, tragedy may also be considered as hinging on the balance between fate and choice (Young, 2013), in the sense that tragic characters are both culpable for their actions and, paradoxically, thrown into situations involving forces beyond their control. However, in this section I will suggest that cultivating a tragic sense of life can also be an invitation to widen a sense of gratitude for both the good and the bad, the highs and the lows of life. In this vein, I will explore the relationship between tragedy and gratitude and how these can be cultivated simultaneously.

Gratitude often depends on the sense of a redemptive turn, which Robert Emmons (2013b) has described as a kind of reversal that leads to gratitude and thus enhances it. Describing situations in which we recollect difficult experiences as a way of cultivating gratitude, Emmons notes,

> This process of remembering how difficult life used to be and how far we have come sets up an explicit contrast that is fertile ground for gratefulness. Our minds think in terms of counterfactuals—mental comparisons we make between the way things are and how things might have been different. Contrasting the present with negative times in the past can make us feel happier (or at least less unhappy) and enhance our overall sense of well-being. This opens the door to coping gratefully. (Emmons, 2013b, para. 10)

For Emmons, gratitude experiences are not just about recollecting the good. In fact, they often heavily rely on a comparison between current benefits and previous deficits or losses. Many of us have likely had experiences in which reflecting on what "could have been worse" can allow us to lighten our sense of regret about present circumstances, thereby paving the way to cultivating the view that everything can be seen as a gift.

A "gift" universe is characterized as a source of abundance, wherein each gift is supported by many others in a wide network of shared relationships. Richard Wagamese (2019) has explored ways in which cultivating gratitude reminds people of their continuity with other beings as well as the ways in which we are granted life through our connections to families, communities, and the earth as whole. He has described a ritual that focuses on gratitude as a widening circle of gifts, suggesting an expanding awareness of self in connection with others:

> Begin with those things that come easily to you. Offer tobacco ties of thanks for your health, family, home, work, school, friends and possessions. Then breathe deeper and try to feel what other things in your world and experience you are grateful for. You will find lots when you are properly centered. Maybe you're thankful for having ten fingers and ten toes, to be able to hear, to see. Maybe there's a skill or an art you carry. Perhaps you're thankful for teachers in your life. The more you focus on the energy of thankfulness, the more things will come to you, and as each does, put a small pinch of tobacco in a small square of cloth and tie it with the string. Keep the string unbroken so that you create a long line of gratitude ties. Think of the tobacco as a sign of regeneration, of continuation. Keep going until you can't think of anything more. When you start to struggle with it, stop. (p. 99)

Wagamese wisely refers his readers to cultivating thankfulness toward things that come easily, and thus characterizes gratitude as the growing circle of inclusion of various gifts, both internal and external. However, it should perhaps be noted that there is a tragic aspect of gifts as well. Just as gifts are given, so they are also carried away in the cycle of life. Alternately, just as beauty is a part of nature that we often consider a gift, so too death and decay also play a necessary role in ensuring that the elements of life can be reborn and used in different ways to sustain new life. There are many applications of this bittersweet truth in curriculum, including the ability to show students how gifts in life are part of a cycle that includes death. Anderson et al. (2017) thus note,

> Nature's complexity also encompasses moral and aesthetic dimensions. Not all of nature is beautiful or easily pleasing

to the senses—along with the blue lakes and leafy forests, we encounter rot and stench and poison ivy. There are stinging creatures and slimy ones. There are life-threatening situations. There are predators and bloody prey, and scavengers feeding by the side of the road. In one Grade 2 classroom, children's excitement as the class pet gave birth turned to fascinated horror as the mother proceeded to eat her babies. Being in nature gives children access to a world behind the sanitized and carefully managed environments of many schools and homes. Inevitable confrontations with such cyclical and elemental forces as birth, death, and sex enable children to explore and raise questions about more difficult or emotionally laden concepts in manageable contexts at their own level of understanding. (p. 68)

The important point here is that when contextualized as a part of the cycle of beauty and life, unpleasant situations that trigger loss and pain can equally be viewed as an integral part of the gifting cycle. This meshes with a view held by ancient civilizations that characterizes the natural world as part of a circle of which human beings occupy one space, or "great chain of being" (Lovejoy, 2017), a sacred, integral approach that sees "the individual tied to wider cosmic ideas in theological discourse" (O'Sullivan, 1999, p. 88). The tragic sense of life is to know that humans are only one part of the whole; conversely, trying to overstep their relationship to the whole leads to what the ancient Greeks referred to as *hubris* or pride.

Why should teachers and students be particularly attentive to the sense of the tragic? One reason is that both teacher and students need to at some point embrace the inevitability of loss and change. Going to university, for example, means that one may need to move to a different city and cope with numerous transitions such as having to deal with time management (Garett et al., 2017). Separation from fellow peers is an inevitable part of this transition and can be accompanied with stages of loss or denial. Even teachers can suffer the loss of their valued students as they move on in other directions (Coy, 2016). Can teachers and learners continue to feel a sense of gratitude in the face of this kind of loss?

Tragedy also offers an opportunity for both teachers and students alike to reflect on the fluidity and relativity of social roles. *Hamlet* is one example of a Shakespearean tragedy in which the protagonist begins to question his social role as his family becomes uprooted by the murder of his father and the questionable ascension of his uncle Claudius. Hamlet spends much of the play in doubt as to how and when to confirm his uncle's role in his father's death. Furthermore, Hamlet's journey to self-knowledge reveals the limits of social identity as he starts to see through the role of king and realize that all are alike in their march toward death. While many tragic protagonists, such as Lear, Othello, and Macbeth, may be said to have created their own fate through faulty choices or personal weaknesses, Hamlet reflects on the limits of his own choice and actions, which also sheds light on the limits of self-knowledge in general.

Rebecca Bushnell (2008) has coined the term "tragedy of knowledge" (p. 68) to refer to how tragic characters such as Hamlet and Orestes undergo a painful state of reversal in fortune (*peripeteia*) that later precipitates a recognition (*anagnorisis*) of who they are and their role in relation to their reversal of fortune. While such tragic characters attempt to bring the state of crisis or reversal back to an original state of justice, Bushnell notes how the resulting knowledge is accompanied with an inability to act, a failure of courage, or a crippling sense of fate or necessity that causes the protagonist to be doomed to fulfill the wiles of a callous or indifferent world. No matter how responsible or accountable the characters feel for their behavior, the question of ultimate responsibility is never clear, as the actions of the main characters intermesh with other characters and even a mysterious divine order. Furthermore, greater knowledge and experience is often not accompanied with a greater ability to act or influence the circumstances. Hence Bushnell (2008) remarks, "The revenge tragedy may initiate an exploration of the mystery of human desire, but the revenger rarely understands himself or his world, until it is too late. But such plays remind us that at the heart of tragedy we find a crisis of knowledge" (p. 68). What is the crisis of knowledge that Bushnell refers to? Oedipus is perhaps the epitome of the tragic figure who, in marrying his mother and killing his father in a fit of youthful anger, discovers his own part in precipitating a plague when it's much too late to avert disaster and downfall. More broadly, however, the tragedy of knowledge alludes to how greater self-knowledge does not necessarily translate into a clear-cut plan of action that can right all wrongs. In fact, greater self-knowledge can induce people into contemplating the complexity of their agency in the world, suggesting that there is neither a singular sense of identity nor clear-cut motivation behind our social engagements. Terry Eagleton (2020) suggests that tragedy allows people to safely explore conflicting paradigms such as the traditional classical view of humans in the cosmos among gods, as opposed to the "modernist" view of humans as the deciders of their own fates. In discussing Oedipus's process of painful self-discovery, Eagleton remarks,

> To be a human body is to be an agent; but it is also to be passive and vulnerable, an object of history as well as a subject of it. The Sphinx is a devourer of raw flesh who tears off its victims' heads and, though Oedipus uses his own head to outsmart it, it too, is metaphorically speaking severed, divorced by his cleverness from the wisdom of the body (a body which is itself a legacy from one's forebears), as well as from the network of pieties and obligations in which all human flesh is caught up. Since the Nature to which the body belongs is older than consciousness, the human animal is an inherently transitional creature, caught on the hop between flesh and spirit. Without reason we perish, as Pelasgus remarks in Aeschylus's *The Suppliants*; but reason does not go all the way down, and it is this lesson that the rationalism of an enlightened age must take to heart. (p. 65)

How does this tragic sense of life relate to gratitude? One potential way is that it allows the human psyche to sense its interconnection with other beings. Sometimes a tragedy or a sense of loss is needed to see beyond human conditioning, in order to realize the limits of one's sense of identity. The life of Buddha is one example of a prince who witnesses suffering and illness around him, which then leads him to question his life and look for a different sense of identity that is more rooted in non-self. Seeing a family member or other loved one fall ill when we are young can also lead us to question the limits of human life and power, which can send us on a journey away from certain presumed realities about ourselves. More specifically, spiritual traditions such as Buddhism link the sense of the precious to something that is evanescent and based on causes and conditions. Traleg Kyabgon (2018), a Tibetan teacher, thus notes, "Recognizing that things are not enduring and that there is an insubstantial quality to life, should give us motivation to enjoy and participate and be fully connected with our loved ones, experiences, and the world" (p. 41). Such a view focuses on how our relationships are precious precisely because they are impermanent, which counteracts a nihilistic perspective that focuses only on "the fact that things do not last" (p. 41). Again, this goes back to the principle of not clinging to a fixed view of self and the world.

Teachers, in a similar fashion, might be led to question the certainty of their own taken-for-granted identities as teachers, which can lead to a more multilayered view of their presence in the classroom, as well as a greater awareness that their very identity is sustained by a fragile grace that hangs over the classroom. Studying tragedy might lead teachers to inquire *with* their students about certain ideas that are often considered unquestionable. Are teachers the absolute arbiters of knowledge and authority? If so, where does that knowledge come from? And are students certain about their own future? Does education lead to a certain fixed outcome—certainty of one's future career and role in life, certainty of expertise, certainty of a fulfilled path to knowledge? Or is the road to knowledge—both of self and others—a messy one that requires a lot of experience and trial and errors? Through a safe exploration of tragic elements, teachers and students might be led to interesting Socratic discussions that render the process of identity formation complex and multilayered.

Related to the tragedy of knowledge is what Bushnell describes as the "tragedy of desire" (*agon*) or "an intense dialogue or confrontation between two characters that defines a tragic conflict of values, wills, or desires" (Bushnell, 2008, p. 73–74). Bushnell mentions the work of Michael Lloyd (1992) who suggests that ancient Greek politics often consisted of intense citizen debates that revealed the ambivalence and contradictions inherent in starkly different views of the world, values, and how people should be governed, even among those of the same class and milieu. The tragedy of desire, for Bushnell, lies in the irreconcilability of values that tragic stories represent, including the conflict between state and family values as embodied in Sophocles's *Antigone*. Although this play focuses on the conflict between the views of Antigone and Creon, it perhaps presages modern literature that focuses on how even a single individual can harbor conflicting and ultimately irreconcilable passions. Bushnell suggests that one of the more penultimate struggles of early tragic stories was the awareness that reason could not always control or manage emotions—a struggle that is often played out in the form of a conflict between personal and political life. Hence, she remarks, "Tragedy continually stages the disastrous consequences of the power of the irrational—both love and hate—in the face of the demands and norms of city, state, and community. Overall Greek tragedy itself demonstrates the inability of reason to control the force of passion, whether it is understood to be 'demonic,' like a virus injected by a vengeful god, or part of a protagonist's *ethos*" (pp. 75–76). Studying tragic works can help both teachers and students better appreciate the unsolvable conflicts of personal life and community, without giving into despair or a desire to "perfect" existence through the fulfillment of all desires.

Even when choices are clear-cut, gratitude is often the flipside of a difficult or dreadful experience that an individual has narrowly avoided, which Teigen (1997) has discerned as a counterfactual what-if scenario: What if this were me? What if this were worse? Without an unfavorable or unpleasant experience to compare to one's present experience, gratitude may seem unfeasible or too abstract. Some thinkers have even suggested that human beings are simply not capable of sustaining feelings of joy long after the joyful experience has subsided. While sad experiences are easily magnified and even remembered for all of a lifetime, happy chances or experiences are often quickly forgotten. The nineteenth-century philosopher Arthur Schopenhauer (2010) maintains that joy is simply not a natural state of being. Comparing experience to the flow of a river in his essay "On the Suffering of the World," he remarks,

> Just as a stream flows smoothly on as long as it encounters no obstruction, so the nature of man and animal is such that we never really notice or become conscious of what is agreeable to our will; if we are to notice something, our will has to have been thwarted, has to have experienced a shock of some kind. On the other hand, all that opposes, frustrates and resists our will, that is to say all that is unpleasant and painful, impresses itself upon us instantly, directly and with great clarity. (p. 41)

Here, Schopenhauer contends that everyday pleasure and comfort are often overlooked or otherwise simply ignored, unless something that is highly desirable (i.e., agreeable to the will) takes exception to these average and everyday experiences. Furthermore, Schopenhauer suggests that it is the *thwarting* of a desired state that captures people's attention, giving them a shock that might awaken them from routine experience. Notably, Schopenhauer asserts that for an experience to induce clarity, it needs to oppose the will. This passage suggests that frustrating experiences or thwarted desires are necessary for people to take notice of their everyday situations and to even be thankful for them.

Schopenhauer's observations dovetail with Colin Wilson's experience of St. Neot's margin (chapter 2), which both suggest that people tend to achieve more clarity when a challenging and life-obstructing situation is presented to them. Conversely, dwelling on minor, distracting stresses and anxieties results in a mechanical, repetitive, and bored state of mind that is too focused on the trivial details of everyday survival and is thus unable to sustain a broader vision of life that might inspire gratitude. Wilson has noted that, lacking a specific focus of concern, the mind will often drift into idle thoughts that are taken out of proportion to their relative importance in an individual's life. Although Schopenhauer does not specifically address gratitude in the above passage, he suggests that the sense of being gifted requires that an experience creates an exception within the mind, or something that "opposes, frustrates and thwarts" the will. Something, in other words, needs to reveal itself as a gift; it needs to make an impression on the mind that shocks people out of the dull or distracting states of everyday habit, ennui, and anxiety. Yet, paradoxically, gratitude is not a desiring or, conversely, frustrating experience. In fact, the function of gratitude serves to reappraise what we already have in a favorable light that lifts it above the routine or ordinary. Perhaps the sense of the tragic accentuates the joys of life, which further leads to a more grateful mindset.

One of the most significant advantages of relating gratitude to *shared suffering* is that it allows people to loosen and relax perfectionistic or idealistic standards of personal achievement in life, under the recognition that no life can ever be perfectly controlled or orchestrated. The unavoidability of suffering forms the basis for renunciation, which, as psychologist Timothy Miller notes, is not necessarily a negative or sacrificial experience if seen in the light of shared humanity:

> A little thought reveals that the idea of renunciation is not quite so depressing as it first appears. Knowing that no one avoids sorrow, humiliation, pain, or death creates a foundation for universal, unconditional compassion. If we know that these things cannot be avoided, then we might try to compete, wish, hope, and fear a little less frantically, which could make life more fun. In other words, when we really get it that life will be painful at times, we become more inclined to "stop and smell the roses." (Miller, 1995, p. 43)

Using a metaphor drawn from computing, modern evolutionary psychology tends to suggest that people are hardwired to experience suffering and pain more strongly than bliss and happiness because in order to survive, early human beings had to focus on and retain memories of unpleasant or dangerous situations. Just as early humans simply could not afford to forget a dangerous or life-threatening experience, so retaining a joyful or blissful moment at the wrong time might lead to perdition. Miller suggests that contemplating an unavoidable suffering that all human beings share can be a source of compassion and, perhaps more importantly, renunciation from an endless striving for more.

Drive theories in evolutionary psychology tend to suggest that people need to actively reverse millions of years of evolutionary shaping that favors a focus on unpleasant or threatening situations. Gilbert and Choden (2014) have explored how meditation and compassion practices can reverse a tendency to see the world as a place of potential danger or scarcity, both of which lead to reactions of avoiding the unpleasant and desiring what is thought to be a scarce resource. In fact, recent books in positive psychology attempt to reverse the tendency. In his book *Hardwired for Happiness*, Rick Hanson (2013) remarks that people can, with the help of guided exercises, create a habit of recollecting pleasant or joyful experiences when they feel stress, instead of following a habitual pattern of overreacting to stressful or threatening situations. According to positive psychology, people can create a habit of going to happy or calm states of being to reverse a bias toward negative states of being in the face of threatening or stressful situations.

In both Schopenhauer's and Colin Wilson's writings, one finds a belief that too much comfort and routine can induce a sense of boredom. This leads people to remain in a state of wanting what is not present or, conversely, trying to create a sense of excitement or *agōnia* to sustain a sense of will and purpose. Schopenhauer (2010) later maintains that too much joy easily subsides into boredom. In one of his most memorable passages, he notes,

> Work, worry, toil and trouble are indeed the lot of almost all men their whole life long. And yet if every desire were satisfied as soon as it arose how would men occupy their lives, how would they pass the time? Imagine a race transported to Utopia where everything grows on its own accord and turkeys fly around ready-roasted, where lovers find one another without any delay and keep one another without any difficulty: in such a place men would die of boredom and hang themselves, some would fight and kill one another, and thus they would create for themselves more suffering than nature inflicts on them as it is. (p. 43)

How might an experience of the everyday, *taken for granted*, be elevated into the status of a gift? Schopenhauer's essay suggests two possible routes:

comparing one's situation with a less fortunate situation experienced in the past (or seen in others), and the other, hope. While the first often relies on a cognitive reappraisal of the everyday taken for granted, the second relies on cultivating a strong sense of meaning and purpose that extends into the future.

The Link between Gratitude and Tragedy

As mentioned in chapter 2, Colin Wilson describes a link between gratitude and dangerous or risky situations that can put someone in a heightened or positive state of alertness and aliveness. Wilson felt that being momentarily threatened or compromised could raise a person above mundane routines and anxieties, since there arises a heightened awareness of *what truly matters*. It's important to try to break this awareness down into distinct steps. First comes a heightened sense of clarity that arises from being aware of a potential setback, threat, or loss in the external world. Second comes the full engagement of the senses in trying to solve the upcoming crisis situation. Third is the diminishment of the background trivial matters, as the mind mobilizes itself to fully handle the threatening situation. Wilson suggests that exhilaration follows when there is a sense that the problem has been solved.

Greek tragedy seems to utilize several techniques that can similarly bring about a sense of focus and exhilaration in the audience. First, there is a sense of a looming crisis or danger that awaits the main character. Second, the key figures mobilize as the crisis comes to its climatic point. Third, the audience undergoes a transformation that parallels those of tragic characters. Edith Hall (2010) remarks,

> According to a character in a fourth-century comedy by Timocrates, the process was one of identification with suffering, which leads to consolation. If a spectator gives conscious thought to individuals suffering worse cases of their own problems, he can reap benefits. Thus an indigent spectator is comforted by the extreme poverty of Telephus; a sick one by the ravings of Alcmaeon; one with bad eyesight by the blinded sons of Phineus. . . . Even the ancient *sub*conscious seems to have been impressed by the sufferings of individual figures of tragedy and the way they dealt with them. (p. 195)

How does the sense of gratitude link with tragedy? Hall suggests that it is partly that the ability to see our own suffering mirrored in others is a way of connecting others' sufferings to our own that makes us feel less isolated. That is, gifts are, in themselves, mirrors and markers of a person's sense of belonging in the universe. They put us on the map, as it were, and tell us that we do indeed belong in the world, and we are being acknowledged even in the midst of our own sorrow or sense of suffering. In the brief moment that we as the audience witness the tragic unfolding, we are unified with others in a shared identification with the tragic protagonist. Furthermore, there is something simultaneously unified and detached when it comes to "tragic gifts." We are unified by the intention of the giver, but we are also simultaneously able to see our own suffering in context, that is, to situate ourselves not within an isolated body but as a part of the universe and ecosystem around us. A tragic gift serves to recontextualize our being by reminding us of our inherent connection with other beings. To be "gifted" is to be indeed given what is our inherent birthright, but in a way that reenvisions the gift as something that is beyond ourselves.

There is an intimate connection between gratitude and the tragic sense of life that needs more unpacking. Without tragedy and the danger of potential loss, would there be gratitude? But at the same time, in order for gratitude to take effect, there cannot be an overwhelming sense of despair. The possibility of something different arising still needs to be preserved. One of the most tragic scenes in ancient Greek writing is in Homer's *Iliad*, in which Paris has just been shot with an arrow. He goes back to his former wife, Oenone, in the hopes that he can be revived using her magic medicine and potions. But because Paris had already tragically left Oenone and chosen Helen to be his wife, Oenone refuses to treat him with the medicine that could have cured him. Here, the tragedy that readers and audiences are presented with is not simply one of death or perdition. Rather, readers are presented with an alternate reality in which Paris had not chosen to run off with Helen and thus spark an entire war between the Greeks and the Trojans. What was otherwise perhaps an uneventful life is now set in context against the chaos that Paris did choose, at the cost of his own life and marriage.

Now why would this be a potential source of gratitude or giftedness to audiences? Homer presents us with two distinct possibilities that simultaneously play out in our minds: one, the exhilarating adventure of the Trojan war, which ended up being a terrible tragedy for many, and two, a more idyllic existence that Paris once had but lost through a series of missteps and temptations. A Homeric (and perhaps modern) audience would take comfort in the fact that their own existence may be close to what Paris forfeited: something that seems uneventful and static is reenvisioned as a source of sanctuary against a chaotic and overwhelming universe. But at the same time, for this picture of life to be consoling and gifting, the possibility of *contrastive peril* needs to arise in order to make the idyllic existence the more favorable one. A hidden dynamic, or threat of chaos, needs to recontextualize the ordered life as something worth having and preserving. In this sense, there is an intimate relationship between chaos and order that underlies a feeling of gratitude. Perhaps one can describe this as a dialectical tension between feeling that one has to achieve the nearly impossible to actualize oneself (as symbolized by the quest narrative and the choice of Paris) and the realization that one already possesses everything they need to feel at home in the universe (the Odyssean recognition of home). But it seems impossible to have one without beholding the other. This is the reason Colin Wilson notes that people often only feel grateful when something that is presented as a potential loss of order is re-presented to them in the form of something they didn't lose after all, as though one were awakening from a bad dream. For gratitude to be possible, the sense of desired order must coexist with a sense of potential crisis or chaos.

Taoism is also one religious view that beholds the good and bad in a dynamic interplay. Some educational thinkers have even made a connection between Taoism and Montesorri (McTamaney, 2007), citing how the education of a child is not dependent entirely on the yang principle of activity and force but needs to be supplemented by a more subtle ying, which represents darkness and passivity. Experiences flow in a dynamic where sometimes one can be in control and some things are completely out of one's control. Gratitude is not just centered around the things that we *can* control. Instead, it also encompasses what simply can't be controlled, which is an invitation to behold forces that are greater than us. The more that people can be exposed to what's beyond their control, the more they can let go of the ego's insistence on always having its way, as well as learn to trust that forces unfold the way they were meant to unfold. This is quite hard to reconcile with tragedy, where one figure is typically presented as having an irretrievable downfall from a place of fortune. But one effect of tragedy is to recontextualize the unfortunate as part of an ever-changing and impermanent world.

The link between gratitude and tragedy is most poignantly seen when we start to examine the view of life and death, as well as impermanence. In one particularly moving essay on overcoming fear, Norman Fischer (2011) writes about how meditation practice has changed the way he relates to the fear of death and loss:

> When I give myself over, for a period of time, or perhaps on a regular basis, to the contemplation of the realities of my aging and dying, I become used to them. I begin to see them differently. Little by little I come to see that I am living and dying all the time, changing all the time, and that this is what makes life possible and precious. In fact, a life without impermanence is not only impossible, it is entirely undesirable. Everything we prize in living comes from the fact of impermanence. Beauty. Love. My fear of the ending of my life is a future projection that doesn't take into account what my life actually is and has always been. The integration of impermanence into my sense of identity little by little makes me less fearful. (p. 297)

Fischer's words serve as a reminder that loss and gratitude go hand in hand, rendering them inseparable partners in the journey of life.

A Tragic Curriculum: What Tragedy Teaches Us to Value

As I suggested at the start of this chapter, I will briefly summarize the qualities that exploring tragic stories can bring to teachers and students alike. How can a reflection on tragedy increase a sense of giftedness and gratitude in the classroom? I suggest the following values may be heightened through a consideration of the tragic: humility, contentedness, thankfulness, cooperation, and compassion.

1. Humility: The ancient Greek vision of tragedy emphasizes *hamartia*, the "fatal inner flaw" that brings down the tragic hero and leads to their eventual fate. At the same time, as philosophers such as Schiller have noted (Young, 2013), tragedy is not completely fatalistic in nature but straddles the tension between necessity and choice. The worldview

that tragedy offers is one in which beings occupy specific places and can potentially upset the balance and harmony if they step beyond their assigned roles. While this may hardly seem compatible with a modernist view that stresses personal autonomy in the marketplace of bought and sold goods, the tragic worldview can remind students and teachers alike that they inhabit distinct ecologies of interdependency, including the classroom, the greater social and political realms, and a larger cosmos. Actions have consequences that initially arise in a person's thoughts and intentions and can subsequently have deeper repercussions. Teaching tragic stories such as *Macbeth* can caution students about the dangers of pride and ambition, as well as the need to see oneself as part of a greater totality. This stresses the way gifts are parts of larger cycles and rhythms of being that do not place one person above or beyond another by virtue of their talents or wealth.

2. Contentedness: The obverse of ambition and pride may be described as a sense of contentment with *what is*, whether good or bad. In the *Iliad*, Paris chooses a life of being lured by the temptations of the goddesses, which consequently initiates a series of actions eventually culminating in his death. Yet the possibility of staying home and being content with what he has looms over the text, inviting the reader to contemplate whether the good life means chasing endlessly after the unattainable and desirable or being happy with what one has and staying faithful to it. Gratitude hinges on the skill of turning toward and properly appraising (given sufficient time) the things one has, rather than pining over imaginary things. Students and teachers who study tragic texts together could explore the nature of contentment and mutually inquire into whether it is possible to be content with what one already has and yet still pursue one's goals and create transformation within the greater society. Tragedy explores, on a grand and often evocative scale, the unique tensions between expansive ambition and simple contentment that all students may face in the course of making decisions about their future.

3. Thankfulness: Many tragic texts explore the tension between loss and redemption, which can bring about a state of thankfulness for things one would otherwise take for granted. Shakespeare's *King Lear* is an example of a text that begins with a king who feels entitled to receive the highest praise as a sign of love from his three daughters yet is later reduced through his own actions to a person who loses the respect and power he once possessed. This makes him truly thankful for a mere jester companion and allows him to bear even the most difficult things with a certain quality of fortitude. Students who read these texts can start to appreciate how fortune is relative to a person's mental outlook; even inconvenience can be a source of gratitude and thankfulness if contextualized in a broader picture of what truly matters in cultivating a good life.

4. Cooperation: When students and teachers reflect on tragic stories, they may start to appreciate the supports that allow them to be successful. People become the gifts through which we can be supported and collectively find success and worth in our actions. Lear, Macbeth, and other tragic characters tend to overlook their helpers and those who are most loyal to them, as reminders that even their own powers are limited and require the help of other beings. Related to cooperation is *altruism*, the ability to place the needs of a whole community above one's own needs. Studying contrastive characters, such as Lear and Kent in *King Lear* and Horacio and Hamlet in *Hamlet*, for instance, can clue students in to how different qualities could offset and complement each other, as well as the virtuous yet sometimes overlooked qualities of patience with suffering, listening to others in their pain, and staying with difficulty rather than trying to escape into an idealized world or vision of oneself.

5. Compassion: When students and teachers can see that tragic situations are universal and part of what it means to be human, they begin to develop a more unified view of life that stresses interrelatedness and empathy. Teachers could try to relate tragedies to the qualities we read about in leaders

in news stories, to build a bridge between the grandiosity of tragedy and the everyday tragedies of life. By connecting the ambitions of Macbeth to our own obsessions with fame and power, or even the minor disappointments of not getting attention or a promotion, we begin to see that tragedy refers to elements of experience that are universal. Rollo May (1991) has written about the relevance of stories and myths in tapping into a shared collective unconscious that allows people to identify with the mythic elements themselves. As long as teachers tap into the shared elements of tragic stories and daily life, they can bring these stories to the students' unique contexts.

The five qualities of humility, contentedness, thankfulness, cooperation, and compassion outlined as key components of tragedy dovetail with a gift-centered worldview, in a sense that they stress both the precarious and surprising nature of human existence. In contrast to the idea that we can achieve seemingly unlimited amounts of power and prestige given a market currency, a gift-centered approach to education and curriculum stresses the finitude of resources that need to be shared among people and all beings; the power of intentionality in assuring that everyone belongs and can participate in sharing resources and talents; contentment with what we are given as opposed to striving to exceed others in competition for scarce resources; a shared interconnection of giver and receiver that fosters empathy and compassion; and, finally, a broader sense of belonging to a cosmos that is more vast than ourselves and is even beyond human comprehension.

Questions for Discussion

1. How does reframing the tragic as gift change the way people may view the sad or tragic moments of life?

2. Does the idea that tragedy could be a learning gift resonate with you? Why or why not?

3. Reflect on how tragedy could be used as pedagogical examination of our status as fallible knowers. How might tragedy foster a sense of epistemic humility (Potter, 2022) that could enhance the ways students claim to know (or not know) in classroom discussions or debates?

Questions for Reflection

1. Reflect on a time in your life in which you had experienced abundance in your classroom. What did it feel like? What exactly was abundant? Was it the sense of abundant learning, time, or another area of life that felt plentiful? Try to recreate this experience clearly in your mind.

2. Now reflect on a sense of extreme loss in your classroom. Reflect on times when, for example, being a teacher felt like a failure to you or you experienced a profound loss of trust in your students or your ability as a teacher. How did that loss translate into a gain or a gift? What did you learn from that gift? What felt precious to you after that period of loss?

Chapter 7

Four Gratitude-Based Metaphors

The previous chapters suggest that it is not always easy to cultivate gratitude, and that doing so can sometimes require an immersive experience, as opposed to one that is based on writing lists of things to be grateful for. This is quite simply because unless a person practices some sense of presence in the moment or an appropriate attitude or mindset of appreciation, it will not always be easy to experience the novelty, let alone the singular miracle, of something *being* as opposed to *not being*. To experience moments freshly often requires a process of bracketing, or epoche—what Buddhist psychotherapist Caroline Brazier (2009) describes as "letting go of preoccupations and, as far as we are able, being willing to go beyond our habits of thought and view" (p. 25–26). Brazier suggests that epoche requires two actions that are commonly found in meditation practices: first, cultivating "a calm clear mind which is not busy with other matters from our lives" and second, an awareness of how "our expectations and assumptions, our frame of reference, distorts our view of others" (p. 26). To see things with fresh awareness requires the ability to see something familiar in a novel way, by bracketing off the conceptual filters through which we experience the everyday, as when a person reduces an experience to a habitual way of seeing or simply beholds things in terms of their everyday labels or schemas.

What keeps the pedagogical experience between teacher and student novel, or at least fresh enough that it would warrant being noticed as a gift? Being gifted requires a sense that something important is always being given to us, yet awareness of these gifts requires the ability to venture beyond the safety and comfort of concepts. Erich Fromm (1992) attributes the clarity of awareness at least in part to a sense of urgency that leads to independent thinking. That is, "One discovers answers to problems only when one feels that they are burning and that it is a matter of life and death to solve them" (p. 43). For Fromm, possessing a burning desire to know and let go of habitual, conditioned thinking is the only way to avoid a kind of automatic living that is heavily dependent on custom rather than original observation.

While thinkers such as Erich Fromm advocate self-analysis as a way to uncover a freshness of thought that is needed to make novel insights about the everyday, I suggest that qualities such as feeling surprised, gifted, and grateful cannot rely completely on thinking or intellect by themselves. In fact, as the work of Lakoff and Johnson (1980) have suggested, we think in metaphors; that is, metaphorical thinking grounds the mind in concrete, often embodied images that link abstract ideas to everyday actions and feelings. Metaphorical thinking can therefore help us more effectively embody the elements of gratitude, surprise, and giftedness that have been explored throughout this book. By imagining surprise, for instance, in terms of opening an unexpected gift from a close friend or family member, we are often able to render concrete something that otherwise might seem abstract and difficult to comprehend. Recollecting a concrete gift that we can see or tangibly feel can then help us to extend the qualities of gifts to larger conceptual framings, such as community, society, or the classroom. Metaphors provide ways of embodying a concept, using concrete experiences with specific spatial dimensions. Embodying a metaphor relies on structures of experience that "are based on how humans, in human bodies, experience the world" (Johnstone, 2018, p. 47). Whereas the abstract concept to which the metaphor is mapped is referred to as the *target domain*, the domain from which the images are drawn is referred to as the *source domain*, or what has been aptly referred to as an "image donor" (Nordquist, 2020).

Educators Sanders and Sanders (1983) have in addition suggested that metaphors can be used to accelerate learning by helping students organize and remember an abstract concept. They note, "One reason is that the discovery of a metaphor to represent what we already know is an exciting discovery; it therefore responds to our basic need for 'novelty'; another reason is that students are able to associate intellectually the 'big picture' (the concept) with the details to be learned. . . . Emotionally, students are experientially involved; the new knowledge fits into the experiences of their lives, and self-motivation naturally results" (p. 51). Sanders and Sanders here suggest that metaphors not only tap into a student's abilities to creatively innovate but they also create a more engaging relationship to the subject material that emphasizes the direct lived experience of a concept. In fact, re-presenting what is apparently already known by casting it in a new light is one of the many intriguing possibilities posed by metaphorical thinking. Miller (2019) similarly views metaphor as an opportunity for active learning that engages the search for foundational principles: "Metaphor encourages the student not only to make connections but also to see patterns. In comparing revolutions to volcanoes, the student must examine the patterns and principles common to both and then make the connection between the two. The most powerful connections between the components of a metaphor are not similar details but similar principles, as in the example of the kidney and fuel filter. The student must understand the underlying function of each object to see the connection" (p. 105).

By encouraging learners to cognitively stretch the meaning and implications of a concept, metaphors encourage extensional thinking and imaginative applications of concepts to new subject areas or topics. Many educators have used metaphor to help students visualize what it might look or feel like to peer inside the human body, for example, thereby helping students embody a concept. Embodying a concept also helps to keep students more engaged and empathetic toward the subject matter being taught, particularly when the subject matter itself is seemingly remote from everyday life or abstract in nature. Many studies make strong connections between embodiment and seemingly "bodiless" subjects such as history (Egan, 1991). Henshon (2019) suggests that teachers can cultivate empathy to understand how to best connect with their students' unique learning needs, as when one anatomy instructor had allowed a blind woman to hold a preserved brain in order to better understand and appreciate its functioning, thereby allowing the student to "experience the brain directly and to create her own pattern of understanding" (p. 19). While Egan and Henshon respectively focus on how teachers use embodied approaches to engage students, it could equally be argued that teachers *themselves* need creative ways of embodying abstract concepts, particularly through metaphor and visualization, the latter of which will be discussed in more depth in chapter 10.

In this chapter, I suggest that cultivating the feelings of surprise, awe, and wonder associated with seeing the world as gifted can sometimes entail a metaphorical reframing that allows a person to refer to a thematic reference point, while simultaneously allowing new insights into familiar experiences. I will here explore four possible metaphorical framings of the classroom that seem conducive to a notion of gratitude: the tapestry, the jewel net, the holding space, and Kirk Schneider's own metaphor of the fluid center. These will be described in the sections below, followed by a brief reflection under each that teachers can try. By no means are these metaphors exhaustive of how giftedness can be embodied in daily life, and readers are encouraged to use this chapter both to explore the metaphors presented and to craft their own.

The Tapestry

One of the most powerful analogies I have encountered that has generated feelings of gratitude came from my reading of William Somerset Maugham's *Of Human Bondage* (1999). In this semi-autobiographical text, the protagonist, Philip, encounters many people on his journey who allow him to face the ways in which he is bound to fixed ideas, including fame, infatuation, art, morality, and so on. Through his explorations, Philip learns to become a master of himself instead of allowing his obsessions to lead to self-destruction. One of the most powerful metaphors I encountered in this book is the idea that life, when looked at from a certain distance, can be seen as taking on a definite shape, or tapestry, which is symbolized in the book by the Parisian carpet. Through a conversation between Philip and his friend Cronshaw, Maugham articulates a philosophy of life that, inspired by the philosopher Baruch Spinoza, is less about certainties and more about interwoven complexities that can only be directly lived, rather than turned into an abstract principle or rule:

> "D'you remember that Persian carpet you gave me?" asked Philip.
> Cronshaw smiled his old, slow smile of past days. "I told you that it would give you an answer to your question when you asked me what was the meaning of life. Well, have you discovered the answer?" "No," smiled Philip. "Won't you tell it me?"
> "No, no, I can't do that. The answer is meaningless unless you discover it for yourself." (Maugham, 1999, pp. 406–407)

The metaphor of life presented here is a kind of artistic tapestry that upon first appraisal seems chaotic, but when taken as a whole, starts to look like something organized from a distance. Now why would the metaphor of a tapestry be such an apt one that might generate feelings of gratitude? One possible reason is that suffering is rendered part of an unfolding totality that has a meaning only in the context of a whole. This decidedly ecological metaphor positions all moments as meaningful in the context of a potentially undisclosed yet gradually revealed whole, which presents itself as a mystery or unfolding surprise. Conversely, we suffer ingratitude only because what we are looking at in the moment is not seen for all its interconnection with both past and future. We might even judge ourselves according to standards of success and failure that are too exacting and don't take into account the totality of what we could learn from each and every experience.

How does the tapestry metaphor relate to gratitude? It seems that in order to have a grateful mindset, one must have a deep faith and trust in how things fall into place, as well as the potency of things. Kristi Nelson (Nelson, 2020) refers to the potency as "poignancy" or a sense of gravity that things in life truly matter and have importance in the context of one's present experience. Tapestries similarly evoke ordered spaces that contain a certain amount of chaos. In other words, they attempt to strike just the right balance between unity and diversity—allowing the qualities of things to be appreciated for their uniqueness, while also acknowledging their contingency and interdependence in a broader picture of the world. This is somewhat antithetical to a Western worldview that might privilege the individual over the perspectives in which individuals live. Francis Cook, in his classic study of Hua-yen Buddhism, refers to how ancient Chinese paintings were starkly contrasting with Western portraiture. Whereas the latter emphasizes the individual person at the expense of the rest of the landscape, the former often depicts people as small compared to the overall landscape. Cook (1977) remarks, "The viewer is struck by a sense of continuity among the various elements of the scene, in which all are united in an organic whole. The humans in the picture, which are almost always there, have their rightful place in this scene, but only their rightful place, as one part of the whole. Nature here is not a background for man; man and nature are blended together harmoniously" (p. 6). Cook maintains that the smallness of people is even emphasized by the disorderly aspect of some forms of Eastern art, where the natural world is seen as the tension of conflicting yet harmonizing forces that are not entirely symmetrical. But there is a certain beauty and containment in that asymmetry. Similarly, Tibetan mandalas have been described as spaces where conflicting psychic forces can be contained and illuminated without feeling anxious about trying to balance or equalize these forces.

Tapestries also evoke a sense of belonging, as in the belief that everything in creation has a unique and contextualized place in the universe and all moments have a meaning. According to the view espoused by the "great chain of being" (Lovejoy, 2017), there is perfection in plenitude: all beings occupy a specific place, just as all experiences belong within the whole. But what's paradoxical about this model is that diversity implies the perfection of all, even when one thing appears imperfect. Things only appear imperfect because there is some template that we are imposing upon the world from above that is telling us that things have to be a certain way. When this insistence on perfection—on having things a certain prescribed way—is broken, one can become more attuned with the advantages of what is already present. In fact, things in the "now" are no longer seen as imperfect when there is no desire for perfection through the addition of something else.

Tapestries evoke the falling together of different situations in time. They also hint at the relativity of "good" and "bad" as parts of an unfolding and unrevealed drama that relies on mystery and suspension of knowing to sustain a compelling narrative thread. One of the most humorous examples of the tapestry principle comes from the fable of a Chinese farmer whose son breaks his leg while trying to tame a horse. Although the story seems to show instances of someone continually generating bad luck, the farmer sagely notes that what appears to be bad luck ends up working out for the better in the end:

> Later that week, the farmer's son was trying to break one of the horses and she threw him to the ground, breaking his leg. The neighbours cried, "Your son broke his leg, what terrible luck!" The farmer replied, "Maybe so, maybe not." A few weeks later, soldiers from the national army marched through town, recruiting all boys for the army. They did not take the farmer's son, because he had a broken leg. The neighbours shouted, "Your boy is spared, what tremendous luck!" To which the farmer replied, "Maybe so, maybe not. We'll see." (Mavani, 2018, para. 3–4)

This story recursively shows "bad luck" moments unexpectedly turn out well for the farmer, thereby demonstrating how something that is considered a calamity is actually a blessing in disguise. The point of the story is to show that there is no final conclusion or ending when a bad situation happens. In fact, what seems to be a disadvantage may later turn out to contain a hidden advantage.

Tapestries evoke both nuance and contradiction, as when opposite strands of life are woven together to create an integrated whole. Related to the tapestry metaphor is that of weaving, where various threads are indeed unified into a collective whole, yet not without the tensions of opposing perspectives and views. Palmer (2017) succinctly characterizes good teachers as those who "weave the fabric that joins them with students and subjects," where "the heart is the loom on which the threads are tied, the tension is held, the shuttle flies, and the fabric is stretched tight" (p. 11). Because teaching is thus made from discordant threads that are held together by tension, there is always the possibility for the teaching heart to be broken, or at least to suffer the agonies of tension and conflict that happen in classrooms daily. Hunt (2010) has similarly suggested the tapestry to symbolize trust in an unfolding mystery, when he refers to friendship as a revealing "tapestry of trust": "We need a trusting climate to reveal our heart's desires because doing so makes us quite vulnerable. And as our friendship grows, the tapestry of trust becomes stronger and we are more willing to reveal our heart's desires" (p. 160). Similar to Palmer, Hunt's metaphor of the tapestry suggests interconnection as well as the continual sustenance of opposites in a pattern that interlocks and mutually supports the whole.

I have found in my own life that the tapestry metaphor transcends a sense of success and failure by suggesting a more nuanced and organic view of life. According to this view, we needn't approach situations by trying to force them into a kind of straitjacketed perspective but, instead, can see the situation as a mystery that contains elements of good and bad. This doesn't mean that we negate good and bad altogether, since this would entail no need for improvements in life. Instead, it suggests that all situations are enfolded in wholes and therefore need to be seen in the context of a whole to avoid the suffering of attachment, particularly to narrow or constrictive views of success and failure. *Attachment* here suggests a kind of passionate clinging to a tightly held goal or framework—a way of thinking that attempts to isolate results rather than contextualizing these same results into a broader picture that lovingly embraces contradictions while holding opposites in a single totality. Through the capacity to see things in terms of broader wholes, we are able to view people and situations less judgmentally, as there is a much broader base from which to create and honor what is given to us. The vastness evoked through the metaphor of the unfolding tapestry also leads to a sense of awe or belonging to a much grander place than the small self can contain. Ciaramicoli (Ciaramicoli & Ketcham, 2000) refers to this quality as humility when he writes,

> Humility is that place at the core of our being where we can settle into ourselves and find a point of rest. From this vantage point we can see that we are not the center of the universe but

> only one small, insignificant part, and that realization is ultimate freeing. Seeing ourselves within the vast sphere of living things, we understand our relative insignificance. And that realization releases us from the desire to be the best, the brightest, the richest, or the most beautiful, and lets us settle into the humble truth of who we are. (p. 172)

One of the most important aspects of this passage is the way it links genuine humility to a sense of vastness that allows us to see beyond, at least momentarily, a hierarchical way of being that privileges some over others or sets people against each other on a grading curve. By evoking the sense of grandness and mystery, we are able to get our minds out of self-preoccupation and bring the wonder back into learning in the classroom.

Teacher's Reflection on the Tapestry Metaphor

Reflect on the time you first became a teacher, even going so far back as the first day of teaching your very first class. Reflect on what you brought to that classroom: your hopes, previous experiences in education, joys of being a student and later becoming a teacher, mentors encountered along the way. You may even choose to write a loose chronology of all the experiences that have led up to your current teaching practice. Feel free to write whatever comes to your mind that has inspired you to teach and gave you the necessary tools to succeed.

After writing your reflections or chronology, take a look at what you wrote and contemplate the following points:

1. *To what extent could you have predicted how your teaching career was to unfold, prior to embarking on the journey of becoming a teacher? Highlight any specific points or experiences in the chronology that were, in retrospect, unexpected and unplanned.*

2. *Were there specific episodes in your career as a teacher that seemed random or irrelevant to teaching at the time and yet, paradoxically, turned out to have an unexpectedly important and meaningful impact on your journey as a teacher?*

3. *To what extent does looking back on your teaching experiences foster a sense of an overall design, much like the intricate designs of a work of art or a tapestry? You may wish to artistically represent your teaching journey using a drawing that shows the*

subtle ways in which your teaching role developed nuances and richness by making detours into underexplored terrain.

4. *Take a moment to acknowledge the role of surprising or unexpected detours that enriched your teaching journey, and to what extent this connects with the tapestry metaphor explored in this chapter.*

The Jewel Net

The jewel net of Indra is yet another analogy that takes a person deeper into gratitude. According to this metaphor that originates in Hindu and Buddhist traditions, all phenomena relate to each other as reflections, similar to a net of jewels that is spread out infinitely. Instead of being a bounded part of the net, the jewel directly reflects other experiences. Therefore, rather than feeling that each part is only a singular insignificant component, we recognize that we are each inseparable reflections of a greater universe that we inhabit.

Unlike the tapestry metaphor, which refers to the interdependence of all things in an unfolding story, the Indra net metaphor extends this analogy to suggest that even a single object becomes a reflection of the infinite and eternal. Although the concept may seem lofty and unattainable, spiritual practitioners often report situations unfolding in a way that reflects a prevailing harmony or order. In fact, when a person lets go of the idea that anything is out of harmony, they will likely experience a more harmonious vision of the world, in which every being behaves exactly according to the causes and conditions that influence it. Flora Courtois (1971) writes about the experience of all moments harmonizing together in a flowing interconnection:

> The whole world seems to have reversed itself, to have turned outside in. Activity flowed simply and effortlessly and to my amazement, seemingly without thought; nothing seemed to go out of bounds; there was no alternation between "self-control" and "letting go," but rather a rightness and spontaneity to all this flowing activity. This new kind of knowing was so pure and unadorned, so delicate, that nothing in the language of my past could express it. Neither sense nor feeling nor imagination contained it yet all were contained in it. In some indefinable way I knew with absolute certainty the changeless unity and harmony

in the universe and the inseparability of all seeming opposites. A paradoxical quality seemed to permeate all existence. Feeling myself centered as never before, at the same time I knew the whole universe to be centered at every point. (Boban, 2020, p. 19)

What kind of experience did Courtois have, and how was her experience of the world radically changed? One clue is the last point in the passage, in which she describes herself as centered yet feeling that each phenomenon has its own center as well. She concludes from this that "as in the notes of a great symphony, nothing was large or small, nothing of more or less importance to the whole" (Boban, 2020, p. 19). This passage hints that all the universe is contained in everything, which evokes a holographic picture of the universe in which all things are seen as mirroring others (Grof & Bennett, 1992). Furthermore, the patient in this vignette relates how each being starts to mirror the other, and there is an underlying being that unifies them all. This seems to be taking the tapestry metaphor a touch deeper because there are no longer distinct entities that occupy a specific fixed place and are separate. Each entity forms a *mirror* for the others, which creates a deep sense that despite all seeming movement, there is no ultimate movement at all. This also evokes a holographic vision of the universe in which distinct opposites start to lose their sense of duality or struggle. Life is a gift, but there is nothing to give and receive—only reflections that point to one universal whole. Cook (1977) articulates the jewel net analogy from the Buddhist Flower Ornament sutra:

> Far away in the heavenly abode of the great god Indra, there is a wonderful net which has been hung by some cunning artificer in such a manner that it stretches out infinitely in all directions. In accordance with the extravagant tastes of deities, the artificer has hung a single glittering jewel in each "eye" of the net, and since the net itself is infinite in dimension, the jewels are infinite in number. There hang the jewels, glittering like stars of the first magnitude, a wonderful sight to behold. If we now arbitrarily select one of these jewels for inspection and look closely at it, we will discover that in its polished surface there are reflected *all* the other jewels in the net, infinite in number. Not only that, but each of the jewels reflected in this one jewel is also reflecting all the other jewels, so that there is an infinite reflecting process occurring. (p. 2)

One of the most striking features of the jewel net analogy is its lack of opposition: the sense that all phenomena are *reflective* of each other entails less of a distinction between the giver and receiver of gifts. According to this view of nonduality, the gifts of the universe are precisely gifts because they reflect an underlying unity of all creation. When a gift reflects my own being, it reminds me that I am not alone in the universe, and all the elements are simply being reused in different combinations to create new and exciting situations. Giver and receiver, furthermore, occupy equal positions within this perspective.

The jewel net analogy helps us to lessen an anxiety that is often associated with not being able to tackle everything that one wants to do in life. In chapter 1 I described the fear of missing out (FOMO) as a pervasive anxiety that escalates in a technological society where everything is literally at one's fingertips. If there is so much to do and so little time, how can we maximize how we use our time? The jewel net analogy suggests that, in fact, all activities are reflections of the same mind. Whatever we are currently applying our life to is already a reflection of all that is within ourselves. If we take the attitude that each action we take is a deeper expression of who we are, we can see the meaning of even simple tasks like writing an email or beholding a flower. Each thing we do is a cosmic connection that mirrors the true nature of reality, which is always in everything. Even microscopic things contain that very same reflection of the universe. In this way, nothing is insignificant because even the tiniest of things or gestures already contains the whole.

According to this view, "more" is not necessarily better or comprehensive. Instead, a special quality of attentiveness can help people to better see and appreciate the depth and mystery of things as they are. Referencing Simone Weil's unique concept of attentiveness, Zaretsky (2021) remarks,

> Rather than the contracting of our muscles, attention involves the canceling of our desires; by turning toward another, we turn away from our blinding and bulimic self. The suspension of our thought, Weil declares, leaves us "detached, empty, and ready to be penetrated by the object." To attend means not to seek, but to wait; not to concentrate, but instead to dilate our minds. We do not gain insights, Weil claims, by going in search of them, but instead by waiting for them: "In every school exercise there is a special way of waiting upon truth, setting our hearts upon it, yet not allowing ourselves to go out in search of it. . . . There

is a way of waiting, when we are writing, for the right word to come of itself at the end of our pen, while we merely reject all inadequate words." (Zaretsky, 2021, para. 7)

Traditional notions of concentration and attention emphasize a contracting, narrowing experience, as when a teacher tells a student to *concentrate* or *pay attention* to the exclusion of all other distracting elements, including what's happening outside the classroom window. Weil's concept of attention starts not with the desire to concentrate but with the dropping of all desires altogether. It's also notable that rather than using the metaphor of *focusing on* an object—the way a light beam narrows and targets a particular object of attention—Weil is using the passive voice: *readiness to be penetrated by the object*. Waiting involves being passively open to seeing the object for what it truly presents to us, and this requires a special kind of abstaining from categorizing or defining the experience.

In my own experiences at work, I have often found that when I am given a challenging problem that requires complex analysis, I often default to prior techniques or experiences in order to process the new experience. It is almost as though, in my anxiety to understand, I am trying to overlay my previous ideas, conclusions, and experiences in order to *contain* the mystery of the new or novel. Of course, I am also warding off the anxiety that comes from being overwhelmed by too many unknowns or loose threads that a complex problem often offers me. But also, I display an intolerance of *not knowing*, as though uncertainty or even difficulty grasping a situation leads to frantic efforts to grasp at something that covers up my misunderstanding. It is as though I lack patience with my own confusion, which is perhaps coming from a childhood in which not being able to learn was linked with having to stay after class to work on a problem, not having the pleasure that comes from "getting something," or being faced with impatient teachers or tutors.

Waiting is intimately connected with a gift paradigm, in the sense that giftedness is not based on a timely accounting for things. No one can set a deadline on when they receive a gift, since gifts are not based on strict contractual agreements or deadlines. In a similar way, understanding, connecting with, or grasping a situation requires an initial ability to behold something without necessarily knowing how to connect with it. Quite often, the simple ability to behold without judgment or preconceived notions of how to relate to something or someone is the willingness to go along with what something or someone is, which often yields unexpected turns and surprises. But as the jewel net analogy suggests, all gifts are enfolded in an overall sense of being already connected deeply with something. With the faith that all is unified in some way, we can feel less anxious, knowing that eventually we will find connection with anything as long as we have the patience to be present with something without imposing on it.

TEACHER'S REFLECTION ON THE JEWEL NET METAPHOR

Picture your classroom as a network of interconnected, precious jewels. Even the inanimate aspects of the classroom, such as the whiteboard or markers, become integral parts of the classroom experience that contribute, collectively, to some form of learning. Take a moment to appreciate all the ways in which the individual parts of the classroom work together to contribute to a unified teaching and learning experience. Reflect deeply on how each part of the classroom contains the whole within it as well as the surrounding community. A student's journal assignment, for example, is a reflection of not only the student's inner life but more so the complex relationships that shape the student's style and identity in multilayered ways. In addition, reflect on the ways that even a single student's contribution to the presence of the classroom adds meaning to the whole. The way students engage group presentations, for example, could set the tone for others' presentations. Even one student's participation in class could positively or adversely affect the overall group dynamics in the classroom.

Finally, take a moment to explore the ways in which your identity as a teacher is a reflection in itself of the totality of a classroom. Consider, for instance, how your understanding of success and failure colors the experience of students, and how their experiences of success and failure in turn contribute to yours. Then gently acknowledge the sense of shared connection as well as your unique personal connection to the classroom dynamic.

The Holding Space

The holding space is yet another metaphor that entails being able to behold opposites without needing to reject suffering or pain. To "hold" space for someone means to allow a person's experiences, including one's own, to emerge exactly as they are without trying to dam up threatening experiences or disown less desirable ones. Just as a mother holds a child, so we can also calmly hold our experiences close to us in a spirit of gentleness, compassion, and warmth. The idea of the holding space originates in D. W. Winnicott, who suggested that good parenting allows for a proper balance between protecting the child and allowing the child to explore their own world and test their ability to cope and flourish within it. Describing Winnicott's theory of holding space, MacIntyre (1999) notes, "The ordinary good mother provides the child with a setting in which the child is secure enough to test out, *often destructively*, what can be relied upon in its experience and what cannot" (p. 89–90, italics mine). The value of "destructiveness" at this stage is that it teaches the child the boundaries of the external world while giving the child self-awareness of a broader range of emotions that wouldn't normally surface in a totally secure or safety-proof environment.

How is the holding space related to gratitude and gifts? Being able to hold space for emotions that are difficult can allow people to begin to see the hidden gifts that are contained within them. Something that seems to be difficult can always have a hidden gift embedded within it, such as the ability to allow teachers to widen their coping range as well as explore their resourcefulness when facing difficulties. If only we can contain our emotions and feel them without labeling them, judging them, or rejecting them, we have this opportunity to *reframe* situations as ones that we can learn from. This is sometimes referred to as seeing the teacher in all things (Preece, 2006). The holding space can also allow a person to cultivate nuanced insights into the intimate connection between suffering and giftedness. As Schopenhauer and others have intimated in their writings (see chapter 6), suffering is intimately connected with gratitude. Without suffering, there could be no sense that the world presents gifts in the form of grace. In fact, suffering is one way in which we are reminded daily of our interdependence and of the fact that we are not truly separate, self-contained beings.

Many meditation teachers have articulated awareness as a kind of "holding" container for emotions, thoughts, and every other phenomena. Kabat-Zinn (2005) describes it this way:

> If you move into pure awareness in the midst of pain, even for the tiniest moment, your relationship with your pain is going to shift right in that very moment. It is impossible for it not to change because the gesture of holding it, even if not sustained for long, even for a second or two, already reveals its larger dimensionality. And that shift in your relationship with the experience gives you more degrees of freedom in your attitude and in your actions in a given situation, whatever it is . . . even if you don't know what to do. (p. 89)

Holding, in the context of Kabat-Zinn's example, refers to a capacity for awareness to contain all states of being, no matter how painful, without identifying with the pain itself. In fact, awareness itself is what can allow people to inhabit their experiences without reacting to them or trying to act according to known habits or familiar ways of handling situations.

Can someone who irritates or annoys us be a gift? This may seem a bit far-fetched for some people, considering the pain or suffering they may feel in the moment they are slighted or bothered. But perhaps this suffering can be reframed as a hidden gift. Fundamentally, the painful experience shows us how much suffering is created by the sense of a separate self that feels cut off from the universe. According to this view, people will tend to feel that others are either *with* or *against* them. Those who treat us according to how we wish to be treated are seen favorably, whereas those who treat us against how we wish to be treated are seen unfavorably. Now, what would it mean if the people who go against our wishes were to awaken us to something that is beyond "self" and "other"? What exactly is this mind that experiences the self and other? When we feel that there is something more to this mind than what is encompassed by this body, we can then process the experience itself as a gift that allows us to go beyond the suffering that is in self-grasping. To go back to the example of someone irritating us, we must ask the question, Who is it that irritates "me"? Is this person someone separate from me and therefore *in opposition* to the self? Or, more fundamentally, is what I am experiencing an inherently nondualistic experience, in which the self and other are unified? When I investigate this issue deeply, I find that the difference between self and other is purely arbitrary in the sense that what I experience as the "self" of this body does not limit my whole total experience. If it were the case that I am my body, how could I possibly experience the things around me?

When people are irritated or annoyed, they often follow a logic that begins with the belief that others have intentions that are separate from themselves. Unless you bend to *my* will, I will suffer the possibility of being continent to *your* will and wishes. This belief that there is a *me* whose intentions and designs are separate from *you* can even be extended to the belief that the universe itself operates from intention. But the more we probe into this, the more we might begin to wonder: Where does intention begin? What is the prime intent behind any experience or situation? Can we truly say that *this happened* because someone or something intended it to be so? People's anger and annoyance with others often stems from the belief that another person *intended* to thwart *me*—an idea that, again, reinforces the belief that there is a separate I that is at odds with a creator being. But what if there were no unified intentions behind what happens to us, but instead people are simply operating from their own ideas? According to this idea, there is no intention that touches another person: instead, people are motivated by their own distinct ideas or thoughts. In this sense, no intention can really penetrate another person's being. So this idea that people's intentions are interpenetrating or struggling for expression may well be a kind of illusion. But what is the gift we can impute from all of this? I believe that it is the idea that irritation and suffering eventually take us to a place that points beyond it—that is, when viewed a certain way, it inducts us into the realm of mystery, where there could potentially be more than just the self or others.

Teacher's Reflection on the Holding Space

Picture your mind and heart as a still body of water, calm and clear. Then try to imagine all the minor setbacks you experience as a teacher as the pollutants that are filling the water. Drop by drop, see how all the disappointments, setbacks, missed opportunities, "failed" lesson plans, and so on contribute to a polluted water, making the water cloudy, more agitated, and less clear. Honor the fact that this calm and clear body of water can hold all the pollutants with a sense of containment and equanimity. The body of water is so boundless that it can easily contain the poisons without being affected by them. In addition, honor the fact that no matter how dirty this pool gets, the nature of holding these toxic materials remains the same; that is, the space is always still, open, and unmoving.

Then imagine that the body of water is slowly starting to expand outward, thereby becoming a vast ocean that contains an infinite number of experiences—an awareness that stretches out endlessly. In this way, all those pollutants start to become a very small fraction of the very large ocean of experience. To perceive things in this way, you might want to reflect on the ways in which one "bad" day of teaching is quite small compared to the vast amounts of experience, educational or otherwise, you have acquired both as a teacher and as a fellow inhabitant of the planet. Trust that, regardless of the experience you are suffering now, this still ocean has been able to contain a plethora of experiences and still survive each situation, having grown better from it. Acknowledge the fact that holding is a form of allowing and thus healing.

The Fluid Center

Kirk Schneider (2004) uses the term *fluid center* to describe a sense of balance between the stability of a centered being and the movement of change. Describing the fluid center as "structured inclusiveness—the richest possible range of experience within the most suitable parameters of support" (p. 10), Schneider aptly characterizes the balance between being humbled by the vastness of an awe-inspired experience and not succumbing to despair in the face of this vastness. As Schneider later articulates, "The fluid center begins and unfolds through awe, the humility and wonder of living. It is precisely through awe that we come to know how daunting life is, and how readily our presumptions crumble; and yet, conversely, it is precisely through awe that we are awakened to life's majesty, and how dramatically our despair is misplaced. Somewhere in that dynamism is vivacity—the heart, soul, and core of which is both fluid and central" (pp. 10–11). Fluid center is an important feature of gratitude, as I shall argue here, because without a center, the world and appearances can become overwhelming. It's very easy to get lost in thoughts and to lose a sense of focus or inner integrity. On the other hand, having too much stability can also be deadening or static. There needs to be a balance between these twin poles to be able to function in a busy and unpredictable situation such as the classroom.

What is key to Schneider's model of the fluid center is a sense of awe, which Schneider characterizes as a sense of "humility and wonder" or a feeling of being one part of a greater whole that is immense. Schneider thus notes,

> Awe is defined as the capacity for humility, reverence, and wonder: the thrill and anxiety of living. It is further defined as the realization of the delimiting and emboldening sides of living, not as separate poles but together as dialectical "wholes" of experience. In a nutshell, awe comprises *dialectical* sensibility of discovery, adventure, and boldness melded to and in the context of safety, structure and support. Awe mitigates against alienation (polarization)—either in the form of hyper-humility (humiliation) or hyper-boldness (arrogance). (p. 93)

Here, Schneider articulates awe as a dialectical tension between adventure on the one hand and safety on the other. As we will explore in later chapters, a strong centeredness can be a powerful access point to gratitude because we feel deeply connected to our own bodies, and this ties into the sense of belonging. The body is an inseparable part of the whole, and to be in touch with the body as it is now is to be in touch with the cosmos itself. The view of being integrally connected to the world is reinforced in a modern scientific worldview. As Rechtschaffen (2014) beautifully articulates,

> Science, when looked at closely, offers a far more profound explanation of existence than any fiction writer could ever imagine. At one time, arising out of pure emptiness, a big bang occurred, scattering energy into nearly infinite space. The building blocks that now form everything from stones to human brains are made from the same atomic soup. In fields ranging from molecular biology to astrophysics, modern science is continually discovering how miraculously interconnected everything is. From the great gears of the universe turning in tandem to molecules in our bodies swirling in a perfect symbiosis, we have proof everywhere of the underlying interdependence of all things. (p. 66–67)

Science can be a tool through which we can reflect on our deep symbiosis with other beings as well as an *inherent* sense of belonging that is not dependent on one's social standing or appearance. It can certainly be a relief to realize that no matter where we are in life, we are all connected because the very constituents of our bodily being are the constituents of the cosmic whole. Brian Swimme (1996) refers to the cosmos as a place of enchantment, where all elements participate in a dance of matter and energy. What's beautiful about the metaphor of the dance is that there are no wallflowers in the cosmic party—all are invited, and all can play a part in their own special way that is incomparable to the other parts. The universe, according to Swimme, is deeply alive and alluring, in a continual dialogue with itself as it gives rise to infinite permutations and combinations. It's not just human or sentient beings that are animated with such aliveness, but the entire universe is surrounded with life.

One of the most promising elements of the fluid center metaphor is the way it offers a balance between venturing into the unknown and staying centered within one's body. Only with a relaxed mindset that emphasizes letting go can awe be regarded as safe, and individuals can become comfortable as fellow participants in a shared creative unfolding.

TEACHER'S REFLECTION ON THE FLUID CENTER

Consider all the ways in which your classroom is a site of surprise. Take a particular moment of an unpredictable teaching experience that felt chaotic, and gently revisit that chaotic situation by telling yourself: no matter what's happening around me, there is a still and solid center within. As you are imagining the unfolding experience, use your awareness to recognize that you are fundamentally still and in this moment: nothing can take you away from this moment.

The Importance of a Gratitude Mindset

Throughout this chapter, metaphors have been used to articulate an ontology, or a way of being, that emphasizes feeling gifted by the universe. At the very least, these metaphors inspire a sense of awe and wonder by suggesting the infinite plenitude of all unfolding situations in classrooms. Taken individually, these metaphors also suggest that all things equally gift each other, insofar as they are mutually interconnected and are inextricably intertwined through complex relationships that stretch endlessly into the past and future. In contrast to an exchange metaphor, which sees all things as equally exchangeable using a single universal currency, the metaphors presented in this chapter maintain the unique characteristics of each individual being, which thus makes them sacred and irreplaceable gifts. Most of all, truly immersing oneself in any one of these metaphors will evoke a vision of plenitude: the world is already *more than enough* and has enough riches to sustain each one of us.

How might we characterize a mindset based on gratitude? Christophe Andre (2011) perhaps captures it best when he remarks, "I am surrounded by a crowd of human beings who have loved and helped me, smiled at me, and given me things, who continue to do so now, and will do so tomorrow. Gratitude is being aware of their debt, rejoicing in it and experiencing our joy" (p. 262). Some people might envision the process of gratitude as taking stock of what is and what one has, almost like having a collection of things and prizing and cherishing them. But the problem with this notion of gratitude is that all the things we have are subject to impermanence. A gratitude that is based only on a model of acquisition is not sufficiently acknowledging the interdependent nature of the universe. It also feeds into an exchange paradigm that emphasizes ownership ("What's mine is mine, what's yours is yours").

Being grateful is a state of mind; as such, it needs to be continually renewed in each moment. It is done by not reflecting on what one wants to happen in the future, but rather savoring and appreciating what is currently happening in the present. Why? This is because whatever we think will happen hasn't necessarily borne fruit, and in any case, all we really have is in the present moment. In this way, always being in the present, we don't try to seek what hasn't come about yet, nor do we subsequently reject what is already in front of us.

To summarize, some of the elements of a gratitude mindset that have been introduced in this chapter are as follows:

1. Ability to see the present as already inherently perfect.

2. Not thinking there is something "out there" that is beyond one's grasp, but seeing all beings as parts and reflections of the same united creation.

3. Reflecting on the fragility and impermanence of what is here, and how it passes into something else. Being able to appreciate these moments precisely insofar as they are fleeting and transient.

4. Feeling that each moment is a unique and special learning opportunity.

Questions for Reflection

1. Which metaphor in this chapter did you find most impactful in fostering a sense of surprise and gifts in the classroom?

2. Is there a personal metaphor or image that connects you to gratitude and gifts? Reflect on an image, metaphor, idea, or memory that you can use to embody gratitude and evoke it when needed. Describe what that means and its impact on your mind and body. Make a plan to incorporate this metaphor into your classroom thinking.

Part III

Applications in Teaching and the Classroom

Chapter 8

The Grateful Teacher

Exploring a Gifted Orientation in Classrooms

The practice of seeing classroom situations as gifts is not without its challenges, which I will explore in this section. Becoming a teacher who feels gratitude, abundance, and a sense of being gifted by what students bring to their classrooms requires a novel orientation that is based on a practice of beholding the imperfect, as well as a broader, more holistic view of what a classroom is and does. As I described in chapter 6, to be *thankful* for the gifts that we possess can imply both a sense of abundance and a sense of the fragility and impermanence of gifts. What people cherish the most—life, family, loved ones—are all subject to change, and this can at times be a source of grief and loss when it is seen in a classroom that is filled with flux. As Miller (2018) suggests when writing about love, the dark side of love is loss. I believe the dark sides of gratitude for teachers might be characterized as clinging to things that are subject to change and destruction; counting on the things we have as sources of certainty and security; the sense of frailty in relation to identity; and, lastly, the inevitability of loss. In the next sections, I will attempt to articulate a teacher identity that is able to weather the challenges of gratitude, in particular how an orientation of clinging to a role can be transformed into one of awe.

Challenges to Teacher Gratitude

Clinging

Clinging can take on many forms, including clinging to a sense of one's identity as a "knowing" teacher, that which often relies on a sense of a comprehensible relationship between the teacher and the student. As a teacher for both ESL adults and young students, I have often encountered situations in which I have had difficulty understanding a student's meaning and organization of content. While the certainty I feel is that of being in a position to correct the student's writing or verbal communications, it can at times be difficult, if not impossible, for me to correct what I cannot understand, for reasons of inability to interpret a second language learner's ideas. In times like this, I may struggle with the question of who is to *blame* for the faulty communication (me or the student), or whether my skills as a teacher or knower might not be up to the challenge of interpreting the student's full meaning and intent. Clinging, here, takes the form of relying on a role that feels secure for me, as long as I am able to comprehend the student. But in failing to comprehend the student, I may find myself in a failing position with nothing to rely on. Much of this clinging also relies on underlying *transactional* or *transmission-based* models of learning (Miller & Seller, 1990), which sometimes envisions bits of information and skills somehow traveling from the teacher's mind into the students. Successful transmission is thus framed metaphorically as an act of decoding what's in a learner's mind and correcting or refining that meaning according to an institutionally inscribed, respected genre, such as the thematic essay.

Practicing gratitude can, at times, become challenging, particularly if we are used to viewing gifts as tangible or *graspable* objects from which we can derive meaning. One teacher in my doctoral study (Brown, 2022) was initially put off by having to correct grammatical mistakes for her French second language students' oral presentations. When she did the gratitude visualization, however, she was able to better appreciate the underlying efforts of the student to express themselves in a foreign language. That is, the focus of the gratitude shifted away from the *product* of the assignment itself and toward a reimagining, based on her own personal experience, of tangible efforts that the students were making to try to be understood. By shifting the focus away from a foreseeable object or goal and toward a framing of the student's efforts, challenges, and intentions, the teachers were able to see many more gifts in how the students sincerely struggled to make meaning and express themselves. There was also an extended appreciation of what the students were going through and their efforts to communicate an underlying meaning that was uniquely their own.

Without tangible products and goals, can a teacher still see viable connections with their students? Can they still, for that matter, see themselves as functioning educators? Miller (2018) has cited one touching vignette in which a teacher was apprehensive about taking a job for which she had little or no knowledge or experience. She was later told that simply being present with the students was already a value. That is, the teacher may have been used to seeing herself as a disseminator of tangible pieces of knowledge, rather than having gifts to give to her students that are less tangible and more related to her existential being and attention in the classroom. What this requires is a reimagining of gifts as being intangible, process-based, and existential, as opposed to tangible, outcomes-based, and material. The sense of giftedness thus needs to creatively extend to things that are unseen, mysterious, and uncertain, such as the unexpected gifts that come from connections and from interbeing itself.

As articulated in chapter 6, tragic stories in ancient Greece and Rome have often centered around the disastrous results of clinging to unrealistic or unfounded expectations. In Virgil's *Aenead*, we find the titular character forever haunted by a violent past even when he plunges forward to Italy after the defeat of the Trojans. As Jennifer Wallace (2020) reflects, "Shadows and echoes of the traumatic violence experienced by the destruction of Troy reoccur as reiterated events and uncanny flashbacks throughout the epic and especially in the various battles and victories in Italy" (p. 44). In one vignette, we learn of the character Dido as someone who wants to keep Aeneas as her lover on Carthage, only to later find that his allegiance to her is not as strong as his longing to found a new home for the Trojans. Dido's love for Aenead goes sour and, in a rage, Dido burns the island and ends up killing herself in sorrow. Teachers too have expectations that they carry from past ideals, even those lost or buried in the unconscious. This story analogously might turn upon how teachers react to their students when students simply don't reciprocate their passion as expected. Like Dido, we may find ourselves attaching to our students' apparent indifference and comparing their apathy with our passion, which can lead to resentment and not feeling appreciated by students. What the teachers are clinging to is the unconscious belief that their hard work in sustaining the classroom should be reciprocated in a form that is somehow equivalent to their efforts. This sets up the teacher for a spiral of disappointment, which students can readily detect and take advantage of.

Quite simply, clinging to the expected outcomes of a situation or relationship dovetails more with an exchange model than a gift model, since it hinges upon a sense of equivalence and predictability. As Visser (2008) has pointed out, true giftedness relies on an asymmetrical relationship between the giver and receiver, which entails that gifts do not rely on equal transactions. In fact, one of the many paradoxes of the gift is that it transcends the transactional or the expected. Giftedness is bestowed by grace. Thus, to receive a gift—and to be open to the unexpected of the gift—requires a certain yielding attitude of surrender to the unknown. We can never know exactly when or where we will receive a gift, yet we must practice openness and confidence in the abundance of gifts in order to be available for them.

Does absence of clinging entail total detachment from the classroom? Going back to chapter 1, if teachers are not to be stressed by their students or classrooms, are they to become robots who shelve their feelings as opposed to fully feeling and expressing them? Throughout this book, I have emphasized that the valuable surprises and gifts teachers can encounter with their students and classrooms need not be accompanied by a strong sense of attachment. To the contrary, giftedness implies abundance, which means that teachers do not feel a need to cling to or grasp anything, whether positive or negative, about the classroom experience. In fact, as Hanson (2013) relates, enjoyment of the gifts one experiences in the classroom need not entail clinging or grasping whatsoever. Thus, he suggests, "When you notice something good in your experience, gently encourage it to last without trying to hold on to it" (p. 88). Attempting to achieve this balance will thus help undo the habit of wanting to possess or cling to a source of joy.

Overreliance

Overreliance can take the form of trying to uphold a sense of authority or institutionally sanctioned set of rules and discourses. Teachers in my doctoral study (Brown, 2022) often reported relying extensively on a rubric to be able to decide how to grade a student. Even when the rubric could never precisely pinpoint how much a student *deserves* for a piece of writing or work, the teachers still insisted on relying on the rubric to help organize their thinking prior to and during assessment. Past routines or ways of assessing students tend to creep into a teacher's yearly repertoire and establish themselves as habits, even when the circumstances in which students learn may have changed or the assignment no longer holds true or relevant to students. While rules and guidelines may give teachers a sense of thankfulness and inner security, teachers may need to discern when rules are getting in the way of an authentic interaction with students.

Overreliance might also take the form of depending on a student to validate the teacher's beliefs about the value and importance of subject matter. When I was teaching online classes to junior students about Homer's *The Odyssey*, I would often interpret silence as incomprehension or perhaps even boredom! Later, when the students were asked to discuss a writing topic related to the theme, I could see them starting to relate the story to themes such as justice, personal identity, death, family, and so on. I learned throughout this process that the meaning of the story itself cannot always be gauged from students' initial reactions. Instead, there are many ways of explaining or presenting the text, and sometimes many kinds of discussions may need to be attempted before one can see how the students respond to it. To rely on students' immediate response is to show both a lack of trust in the material and a lack of faith in the unique conditions and temporal unfolding of the class itself.

Ultimately, relying on a few sources of thankfulness can often lead to disillusionment, as those sources of gratitude change or transform into something else. Stephen Murphy-Shigematsu (2018) articulates this view in the Japanese culture as *mono no aware*, which "expresses compassion and sadness in our awareness of the transience of all things, which in turn deepens our appreciation of their truth or beauty and elicits a gentle sadness at their passing. The love of the glorious yet fleeting beauty of cherry blossoms is characterized by *mono no aware*" (p. 51). Watts (1985) further characterizes the Japanese meaning of *aware* as "when the moment evokes a more intense, nostalgic sadness, connected with autumn and the vanishing away of the world" (p. 181). Murphy-Shigematsu (2018) articulates the idea that gratitude and feeling gifted are accompanied with the bittersweet appreciation of the intransience of all things. This requires a very delicate balance—neither completely trying to possess an object of gratitude and appreciation nor completely withdrawing from the beholding and enjoyment of the beautiful and fleeting. Opening up to the beauty and perfections of one's life always leaves an open door for more painful emotions such as jealousy, particularly for adolescents who are just beginning to explore their amorous emotions through romantic relationships. Jealousy, as philosopher Sissa Giulia (2018) points out, "humbles us. It utterly annihilates us. Jerome Neu, one of the finest phenomenologists of the emotions, argues that a genuine sense of disintegration explains the quality and the strength of this particular form of suffering. Those who admit to such a forbidden emotion can testify to this. It will pass, of course, and we will be over it. But the shock is there" (p. 56). Giulia suggests that far from suppressing or rejecting jealousy, one can contemplate jealousy as evidence of interdependence: our core states of being are intimately tied to our loves and threaten to be torn asunder when our ties with others seem threatened or tenuous. While jealousy can give rise to an unhealthy form of inner disintegration, another route is to learn the art of *contemplating* what we love—seeing the loved for who they are as opposed to expecting reciprocation or feeling entitled to owning the loved. Miller (2018) has described how teaching Cervantes's *Don Juan* in the classroom might allow students to conceptualize love without a sense of possessiveness. Citing Alan Bloom's notion of the erotic ideal, Miller notes, "Marcella is a beautiful woman who, because of her beauty and her lack of response to her many suitors' overtures, is despised by men. When Don Quixote meets her and inquires about her behavior, she states that nature made her beautiful while making all her suitors less attractive. She suggests that they should be satisfied with contemplating her beauty rather than possessing her" (p. 22). Contemplation is precisely one way of beholding the elements of something without involving the self or wanting to possess what one desires. On the other hand, Mark Epstein (2005) notes how many people try to repress their love of beauty for fear that they will face the potential grief of having to mourn beauty's inevitable passing. Noting Freud's theories on melancholy, Epstein describes how people might hold back from contemplating the full beauty of flowers because they subconsciously know that they will eventually wither away. Here, I believe an attitude of non-striving contemplation can allow people to become more vulnerable to beauty around them while not denying their emotions or trying to suppress them.

Many Japanese cultural concepts embody the paradox of accepting an emotion that seems initially to be lacking or imperfect. One such example, as Murphy-Shigematsu (2018) articulates, is the Japanese word *sabishii*, roughly translated as loneliness. At one point he describes how his grandmother articulated how she "likes loneliness," in response to his concern that she would be lonely when he left her to attend school in Tokyo:

> We were using the word *sabishii*, which I understand to mean "lonely," but which to my grandmother seemed to have a deeper meaning. Perhaps to her it was the human condition to be lonely, so that being mindful in those moments connected her to others, because we all experience a sadness that is part of life. Hers was a mature acceptance of loneliness, of the fleeting nature of human experience, the suffering in existence—a mellow and peaceful feeling. Loneliness reminds us that we know love. I felt that there was dignity in sacrifice and service in my grandmother's way of doing her part, freeing me to pursue my path. (p. 50)

Murphy-Shigematsu opens up the possibility of befriending what are initially considered unhealthy emotions that express *lack*, such as loneliness. Loneliness, according to the author, needn't be experienced as a mere negation of some other desirable state; instead, it can be appreciated and turned to as an object of contemplation, or even appreciation. The author's grandmother is able to see loneliness not as an isolated emotion within herself but as a sign of something that is universal to all human experience. Loneliness is not something to be cured but is a window into the human condition as well as the nature of impermanence and the fleeting. This also opens the door to seeing loneliness not as a curse but as a blessing that gifts a person with a potentially more stable and grounded form of joy arising from a wise perspective on suffering.

Shifting the Teacher's Mindset: Abundance, Impermanence, and Awe

From Scarcity to Abundance

In previous chapters, I discussed how the view of the teacher as the sole "giver" in the classroom has many inherent flaws. One is that it views the giver as the sole caretaker of children or students, which can lead to a sense of being disconnected and excessively responsible for how situations unfold in the classroom, without recognizing hidden gifts in even the most mundane or happenstance occurrence. This is a linear view that sees the teacher as positioned hierarchically above the students, or what Palmer (2017) refers to as an "objectivist myth of knowing" (p. 103). According to this view, teachers are positioned as "experts, people trained to know these objects [of knowledge] in their pristine form without allowing their own subjectivity to slop over into the purity of the objects themselves" (p. 103). One entailment of this rather tenuous stance is that teachers are constrained to teach according to the confines of their lesson plan and area of expertise. When teachers buy into the view that they are solely accountable for how learning unfolds in classrooms, they lack a sense of connection that would allow a more relaxed and mutual encounter to happen, or what Palmer refers to as a "community of truth." A second entailment is that teachers become the *guardians* of a high form of knowledge for which they are "a secular priest, a safe bearer of the pure objects of knowledge" (p. 103). This view of knowledge privileges specific subject areas over the messy interrelatedness that can lead to novel ways of looking at things. According to an objectivist framework, knowledge and ways of knowing are inherently *scarce* and, furthermore, can only be obtained through a strenuous qualification process that ends in the conferring of a status as knower. This view, as Palmer puts it, separates the amateur from the expert by creating invisible barriers that prevent the amateur's (presumably inferior) subjectivity from creeping into the more "pure" or pristine objectivity of the expert. Both students and teachers internalize this view when they imagine that knowledge can only be conferred through an arduous process of transmission from expert to student and only in a linear format such as the ubiquitous undergraduate lecture course (Sperber, 2005). By characterizing knowledge as something pure, difficult to obtain, and only transmittable by qualified experts, an objectivist view of education tends to position knowledge as scarce and obtainable only to a select elite.

An attitude of scarcity does not just relate to how teachers are positioned to know the world. In fact, scarcity can also characterize the way teachers relate to one another in their profession. As mentioned in chapter 1, teachers nowadays feel disconnected even from fellow teachers (Ostovar-Nameghi & Sheikhahmadi, 2016), since they are often expected to take sole responsibility for their classrooms, without the assistance of other teachers or administrators. The teacher as sole caregiver can often create an impoverished sense of self that introduces precarity and potential identity "spillovers" that put strain on the teacher's inner life. As Hill (2018) remarks, "The notion of the martyr teacher often suggests that great teachers must live a life of imbalance, poverty, and continual self-sacrifice. In 'Freedom Writers,' Gruwell's character's singular dedication to her students puts stress on her marriage, and she gets divorced. The teachers in 'Stand and Deliver' and 'The Ron Clark Story' are both hospitalized due to overwork" (Hill, 2018, para. 2). Such an idea makes teachers seem omnipotent, all-sacrificing, and at times even all-knowing dispensers of knowledge and care. Andrea O'Reilly (2006) compares this role of teacher to that of the idealized mother-as-caregiver when she notes how patriarchal expectations of mothers often overlook the genuine feelings that mothers can have for children. She distinguishes between the term *motherhood*, which refers to "the patriarchal institution of motherhood which is male-defined and controlled and is deeply oppressive of women" (p. 35), and the term *mothering*, which "refers to women's experiences of mothering which are female-defined and centered and potentially empowering to women" (p. 35). The patriarchal notion of motherhood often characterizes the mother as needing to behave and feel a certain way toward her children, which then suppresses spontaneous feelings she might have in the moment.

Similarly, a "conduit" metaphor (Gozzi, 1998) often pervades narratives about teaching and learning, thereby shaping the way that knowledge is thought to be transmitted from teacher to child. Here, transactions are said to take place via conduits between teacher and student, rather than factoring the natural state of interbeing between teacher and student. This tends to reduce the teacher-student relationship to a transactional analysis rather than as having a flow, meaning, and energy that is already present in experience itself. Such a model furthermore places the teacher in a position of not being able to behold what is already present in experiences themselves, waiting to be revealed through a patient sense of presence and beholding. Instead, with emphasis on performativity as a master narrative of the teaching experience, teachers are seen as actors who take the stage and whose performance depends on socially accepted and reinforced cues. The teacher is subsequently evaluated based on their ability to live up to performance measures.

In what ways is this portrait of teaching reflective of a potentially impoverished ontology—one that denies the multidirectional ways in which living beings sustain each other and are thus mutually essential for each other's survival? The sometimes *dyadic* portrayal of caregiving tends to sidestep a sense of being embedded in the natural world or in the cosmos. When pedagogy focuses exclusively on teacher-student relationships, it overlooks the role that a cosmic philosophy might play in defining how all beings, both living and nonliving, occupy a unique place in the universe and yet are made to mutually interact in harmony. This kind of cosmic vision of the universe does not position teacher as sole giver or student as sole receiver. Instead, a transcendental given forms the basis upon which all interactions arise and perish. This backdrop is sadly missing in many *contractual* perspectives of teaching and learning, many of which are based on transactional models of learning. In lieu of considering teaching as one of many forms of expression within an ordered cosmos, teaching is seen as one of many roles that are initiated by teachers and received by students. This puts the teacher in a position of having to control environments and learning so that they are able to successfully play their part. Variables that are beyond the teacher's control—including interactions or interests that extend beyond the rubric—tend to be suppressed or discouraged in classroom situations. This is because these variables are seen as distractions to an already existing performance and transaction that foregrounds the teacher-student relationship. This betrays a lack of trust in an unfolding moment, which allows for elements of surprise or new learning that was unplanned or not accounted for. "Surprise" simply does not fit with the standard notion of what teaching should be.

What happened for teachers to come to this point? What is it about the role of teacher that might pattern learning as form of control? In this chapter, I explore mechanistic models and contrast these with a cosmic model of teaching that can be grounded in contemplative views of the world. But first, I will look at Maslow's (1999) theory of deficiency vs. being modalities. I suggest that a society that is deficiency-based pervades the view of teacher as a controller of learning. As long as teachers perceive deficiencies in their students, for example, they will view their classroom situation as the continual struggle to keep a classroom "on track" and prevent students from sidelining the main content to be taught. Both time and resources available to the teachers are thus seen as scarce commodities that are easily "frittered away" by students' claims for time and attention.

From "Deficiency" to "Sufficiency": When Being Is Enough

Deficiency models of education suggest that students are motivated to seek specific aims that relate to their well-being in an overarching hierarchy of needs. Examples of educational goals commonly touted in today's neoliberal models include training for a career, becoming marketable, acquiring social acceptability, and having social status. All of these needs are translated into a grading system that favors some students over others; that is, some students are simply more marketable by virtue of high grades or academic achievement. What is also implicit in a deficiency model is the view that education needs to keep pace with an outside economy. This positions education as potentially out of touch with economic trends and "realities" unless it keeps up with the changing economic patterns and trends. What's rife in the deficiency model is that it ramps up the student's sense of separation from a totality. A student is positioned as an isolated being who must struggle up a ladder of grades to achieve a career that is uncertain, alongside fellow students who are also competing for grades and standing. Some might even suggest that what motivates this system is the fear of missing out on something that is just around the corner. Tara Brach (2019) defines this fear of missing out (FOMO) as "the shorthand for how so many of us live—haunted by the sense that there's never enough time, that we'll die without living fully.

Whether we're chasing after the next sensational experience, another person's love, or a drink to soften our fears, in those moments we are missing out on presence. We have left the only place—here and now—where we can realize the truth of who we are, connect caringly with others, and listen to the wind in the trees" (p. 116). Could the desire to master a specific subject, pass grades in school, and gain scholarships also translate to this notion that a person is trying to achieve something that is always just around the corner and therefore makes a person incomplete? Furthermore, could the sense of existential incompleteness be the motivation for this view of education? Both views, that the teacher is a *dispenser* of knowledge and that the student is the *container* of knowledge, assume that students are in need of filling or completion through the administration of knowledge. These ideas dovetail with a deficiency or scarcity model (Macy, 2007), which suggests that human beings must compete or preserve scarce resources in order to survive. Even ecological movements can sometimes smuggle in a deficiency or scarcity mindset by making scarcity their primary motivation. The view that the earth itself is a scarce resource can dovetail with the view that humans must compete and struggle to preserve scarcity against either nature or other humans. And this is also a cause for conflict, even among those who consider themselves ecologically minded.

What is an alternative view of the situation? Part of the problem lies with spiritualities that position the spirit above matter or nature, which may translate to a pedagogy where the teacher stands "above" students rather than working and being in their midst. Armstrong (2022) suggests that a monotheistic emphasis on a single creator standing over creation can sometimes obscure the ways in which humans are embedded in the natural world and are inseparable from it. Mirroring this view is the notion that teachers must influence the minds of their students and thus maintain a certain dominance over the class structure and timeframes. An alternate way of reengaging the world is to be able to see the part as embedded within the whole, instead of striving toward wholeness through one's own efforts alone. People are thus defined neither as complete, self-contained entities nor as striving to become *more whole* through the pursuit of an education. Instead, the process of learning is the unfolding and revealing of what is an already inherent giftedness. Hanh (2015) articulates the natural sense of giftedness that exists beyond grasping and ambition when he remarks,

> If you're like most people, you probably have a notion that there's some as yet unrealized condition that has to be attained before

> you can be happy. Maybe it's a diploma, a job promotion, an income level, or a relationship status. But that notion may be the very thing that prevents you from being happy. To release that notion and make space for true happiness to manifest, you first have to experience the truth that entertaining your current idea is making you suffer. You may have encountered that idea for ten or twenty years without having understood that it was interfering with your natural capacity to be happy. (p. 71)

Here, Hanh presents the view that happiness is not something that comes from having or acquiring but is embedded in the mind that is still and does not fluctuate according to desire and attainment. Such a state of being is naturally grateful because the sense of giftedness is part of being and is not based on acquiring. Fromm (2013) similarly articulates two modes of existence—having and being—and suggests that too much emphasis on having can distort the way of being into something driven by insecurity, greed, and the need to constantly consume in order to feel alive. Fromm notes, "To consume is one form of having, and perhaps the most important one for today's affluent industrial societies. Consuming has ambiguous qualities: It relieves anxiety, because what one has cannot be taken away; but it also requires one to consume ever more, because previous consumption soon loses its satisfactory character. Modern consumers may identify themselves by the formula: I am = what I have and what I consume" (p. 27). Consumption can give rise to all kinds of worrisome states, as Fromm suggests, including the anxiety of never having enough, a constant cycle of consumption as a way to soothe anxieties and cravings and jealousy or envy of some imagined state possessed by others. This feeds into a view of the world as having scarce resources.

But to even view the universe as possessing gifts entails a belief that there are goods in the universe that are inherently benevolent in nature. To be gifted means to behold something that is surprising (in the sense of being discovered), additive, and beneficent. It is to trust and have *faith* that what is given is a gift prior to its full disclosure to understanding. But this also dovetails with the notion that education does not need to produce gifts, but that gifts already exist deeply ingrained in students. Maslow (1999) writes, "A teacher or a culture doesn't create a human being. It doesn't implant within him the ability to love, to be curious or to philosophize, or to symbolize, or to be creative. Rather it permits or fosters, or encourages or helps what exists in an embryo to become real and actual" (p. 176). In contrast to a deficiency model of the student, Maslow's ideas encourage the fostering of an abundance mindset. That is to say, a student already brings infinite gifts and possibilities into the classroom before the teacher even begins to teach. Montessori (1970) articulates this abundance within the learner as the principle through which teachers can be charitable in the amount of space they allow for a child to grow into their full potential, a point that is made from a Christian perspective but could equally apply to other spiritual practices and teachings: "Teaching charity, Christ said, 'Do not put out a smoking candle'—that is, 'Do not bother putting out a candle that is already extinguishing itself.' We can borrow this principle of charity and apply it to education: 'Do not erase the designs the child makes in the soft wax of his inner life.' This is the greatest responsibility for the adult who educates the child who is in the process of constructing himself" (p. 57). This view of charity seems paradoxical because we might normally think of charity as involving exertion of one's own energies to actively shaping the child. But Montessori suggests otherwise—charity begins with allowing the child to develop according to their own inner process of growth and learning. This view is accompanied with the trust that children come from a shared cosmic source that shapes who they are and defines their unique capabilities in the world. The world is thus characterized as abundant.

Does the view of the learner amount to a pollyannaish faith that all will go well in the world for the learner, come what may? To propagate such a view would do a disservice to learners, not to mention leaving them unprepared for what they will face after school. As mentioned in chapters 5 and 6, a gift mindset does not entail that what we, as teachers, receive from our students will always be positive contributions that enhance either our pleasure or our sense of joy in teaching. More so, a gift mindset allows us to accept the possibility that our interdependence with others makes us more vulnerable to pain and circumstances that are simply not within our control. In the next section, I suggest that woven into a cosmology of the gift is the possibility of the tragic.

From Impermanence to Cherishing: The Tragic Side of Teacher Care

When teachers let go of the notion of authority and an objectivist way of knowing, something miraculous and yet simultaneously tragic happens: the teacher's status as a knower can potentially be displaced, thereby giving rise to a sense of contingency or even potential "thrownness." Teachers could expand awareness of the ways in which their students and classrooms are uniquely unfolding, yet without the sense of predictability or control that an object-centered way of knowing entails. Here, Palmer (2017) notes,

> When we make the subject the center of our attention, we give it the respect and authority that we normally give only to human beings. We give it ontological significance, the significance that Barbara McClintock gave to an ear of corn, and acknowledging its unique identity and integrity. In the community of truth, the connective core of all our relationships is the significant subject itself—not intimacy, not civility, not accountability, not the experts, but the power of the living subject. (pp. 105–106)

What happens when teachers let go of the guarantees that expertise will create good teaching and learning? One consequence is that teachers are faced with a diminished sense of autonomy or even the safety or security of a fixed role with their students. With a genuine appreciation of what a student truly offers in the classroom, including the gifts of unique identity and integrity, comes the risk of feelings of loss, as teachers grapple with the finitude of fully knowing their students. In addition, a gift-centered notion of students opens up the possibility of deeper and more complex feelings of admiration, envy, or enmeshment, as teachers start to behold the unique and irreplaceable gifts that only their students can offer individually within the brief time and space of the classroom. No matter how much of a gift is truly *given* from one to the other, a certain part of the gift is not fully owned by the receiver through some abstract concept such as fairness or deservingness. In fact, gifts can at times be said to be granted by an act of grace, not by a kind of automatic privileging by virtue of effort or status. In being freely granted to someone else, gifts paradoxically lack the sense of predictability that might come with a fixed salary, a tenured position, or any other "guaranteed" element of teaching. As mentioned in chapter 3, to receive a gift requires a certain degree of receptivity or waiting, which also means that teachers do not control the outcome of the nature, the wherefore, or the timing of the gifts they receive in the form of their students' talents, interests, and expressions.

Impermanence is one of many elements that make the teaching experience rife with fragility and even a sense of the tragic. Impermanence here refers to a sense that relationships are always shifting and cyclic in nature. With this sense of impermanence comes the accompanying instability of power and influence that often accompanies tragic stories. Writing from the perspective of teaching religious studies, Kieran Scott (2017) describes how tragedy could be an apt metaphor for teaching because it straddles an ambivalent line between being able to impart valuable knowledge and the inevitable disappointments that come with the uncertain transfer of knowledge to students. By "tragic," Scott does not refer exclusively to a terrible downfall or an agonizing state of suffering, but more so to a state of unease that arises from continual dialectical tensions and uncertainties, as pitted against the dominant stereotype of teacher as a sole arbiter of success and failure in classrooms. Scott notes, "The tragic requires interdependent elements that are in conflict with each other: chaos and order, ideal and actual, success and failure. The tragic sense of teaching requires an acute awareness of and a creative navigating between both perspectives" (p. 276). One consequence of a tragic view is that teachers are seen as having influence over students but also being driven by necessity and even the contingencies of the moment, which leads teachers to develop humility, what Scott refers to as "teaching with hope without illusions" (p. 276).

Scott goes on to describe many situational tensions that emerge from an impermanent view of the classroom—in particular the notion that education itself is not a straightforward transition of ideas from one generation to the next, or from teacher to student. More so, it centers around balancing the tension between a paradigmatic knowledge or tradition in a given field of study and the real needs of the learning situation as it plays out in the students' lived experiences:

> Teaching is showing students how to live by the best lights of the tradition. However, the student's past and present experience is a distinctive content in and of itself. A healthy critical and creative tension ought to ensue between the content of the tradition and the content of the student's life. Good teaching directs this conversation to the mutual benefit of each. A living tradition offers students the promise of new life. The tradition, in turn, can be renewed by the novelty and challenge of the neophyte. Students have their own life narrative with their own unique archeology (past) and teleology (future). Attention must be paid to their unfolding life story. However, their individual life story (or text) is immersed in a tradition, a societal story (or text). Good teaching is rhythmically meshing of both unfolding stories. (Scott, 2017, p. 282)

What are the implications of a more impermanent, tenuous, or "tension-grappling" model of teaching? One implication is that teachers shift away from an idealized notion of what they give to their student in terms of their time and subject matter and toward beholding the uniqueness of both teacher and student contexts. Impermanence entails that teachers and students alike are vulnerable to the contingency of the gifts in classrooms. Not only can the gift of the student remain unmeditated and unique, but it can remain couched in an encounter that is neither calculated nor predetermined in any way. This kind of an encounter is not graspable and cannot be replicated from one classroom to the next, creating a tragic sense that the relation between teacher and student is always unknowable and never fully realizable, with no clear foreseeable outcome of learning itself. Yet it also suggests that a teacher is connected to a larger vision of life, in which gifts are constantly signaling the cosmic give-and-take that is forever enhancing our lives. To prevent harboring a sense of nihilism, teachers need to accept that both they and their students are sources of inexhaustible giving, which need not and simply *cannot* be planned into curriculum. Sometimes this acceptance can take the form of gently acknowledging that each moment contains many gifts that are only waiting to be received and discovered by a trusting mind and heart.

From "Closedness" to Awe

Paul Pearsall (2007) has written a book about awe where he characterizes this state as one of going beyond a rational, fixed logic to embrace an often terrifying sense of vastness. While some kinds of awe can come from simply marveling at the way the universe is comprised of many complex processes unknowable to the human mind, Pearsall also suggests that everyday awe can come from an experience of illness, a setback, or another reminder of our own lack of total control over our lives. In such moments, even something as seemingly ordinary as having a working body can start to look extraordinary, if not miraculous. Pearsall relates how his own journey into illness allowed him to experience both surprise and awe when a routine checkup turned out to show normal results instead of expected catastrophic ones:

> As the doctor sat thumbing intently through the pages of my lab results in search of a negative finding, he finally looked up and said, "Well, I don't see anything remarkable here." Those

words were hardly out of my physician's mouth before I felt the stirrings of the awe response . . . I was mystified by the miracle that continued in my life and felt a chill go down my spine as something I don't understand made me grab immediately at my right hip, the original site of my cancer. The rational dread of what could have gone wrong subsided, as did the irrational terror that any slight sign could mean cancer's return. Yet I felt awe's unique nonrational fear of the magnitude of what life can hold in store for us, how being so close to death brought me so much closer to life. (pp. 169–170)

Two elements, the rational and irrational, are notable in the awe experience. While the dread of illness seems rational in the sense that it encourages a person to seek treatment for their illnesses, the "nonrational" fear that Pearsall refers to is more deeply tied to an overall lack of predictability. When beheld in its totality, the whole of life is filled with strange and unexpected twists. If we were ever to know in advance how our life would unfold and how much unexpected suffering or anguish we might experience in it, would we want to live it, or would we recoil from life in fear? What stops that fear from becoming overwhelming is the sense of wonder that life can behold so many contradictory emotions, and yet the mind and heart can still witness the whole experience with calm equanimity. Pearsall suggests, based on his own research into awe experiences, that repeated exposure to experiences of wonder, magnitude, and dread can paradoxically lead to serenity, what he refers to as "a sense of being in a state of energetic peace with and reflection about the world," which can lead to being "energized by that 'peace through reflection' during both good and bad times" (p. 185). Repeated exposure to fearful experiences can often erode an illusory sense of comfort and control, giving rise to a sense of respect and curiosity for all the states of being that we are all going to experience in some form or another.

Pearsall is not the only thinker to relate awe to what are considered negative emotions such as dread, fear, or vulnerability to the unknown. Matthew Fox (2006) has developed an educational theory of awe that curiously includes cosmology, compassion, and chaos, which he claims embraces the shadow nature of learning such as knowledge of death. Cultivating a healthy pedagogy that acknowledges the whole life cycle is much needed, particularly in urban centers, where teachers and students may not be able to see the cycles of life very closely. More importantly, Fox wants to reintroduce wisdom into the classroom, by which he means a natural longing of the heart for knowledge, which connects us in profound ways (pp. 83–84). Whereas knowledge is about something outside of me, wisdom includes the deepest part of me, the part that dreams, that longs for something without quite knowing or pinning down what that is. Wisdom follows the heart's uneasiness and uncertainty even if no answers are guaranteed, and the teacher has to admit, they are also not in the know about it. This goes against popular cynicism that insists that everything has already been explored (p. 40).

What allows teachers to open up to awe in their classrooms without becoming overwhelmed by the vastness of its interactions? Pearsall suggests that one key factor is the way awe allows us to focus on the sources of stress without becoming too intently attached to them, knowing that they fit within a bigger context or tapestry of experience (see chapter 7 of this book). Hence, Pearsall remarks that the practice of awe has allowed him to "focus intensely on my pain and put it into a larger context" (p. 157). Maslow (1993) similarly describes "states tending toward holism, i.e., the whole cosmos, all of reality, seen in a unitary way; insofar as everything is everything else as well, insofar as anything is related to everything; insofar as all of reality is a single thing we perceive from various angles" (p. 124). This suggests that individuals could cultivate confidence that all experiences, whether pleasant or unpleasant, are parts of a unified whole and are reflections of each other.

Summary

As this chapter has explored, teachers may feel challenged by practicing gratitude in their classrooms as a result of beliefs or fixed views about the teaching process. Clinging to a sense of authority and routine can sometimes prevent teachers from opening up to the gifts that are continually unfolding in the present moment within their classroom, which can take the form of a spontaneous discovery of novel connections students make based on their unique contexts and subjectivities. Teachers may also feel hemmed in by educational policies that stress quantifiable results over and above the process of learning itself, as well as the pressure to help students succeed in a competitive marketplace. A transmission-based model of education suggests that teachers are conduits to relay the traditional knowledge of a subject—a position that does not allow teachers to see their students as abundant sources of learning and inspiration. A more cosmological vision of the universe (Fox, 2006) suggests awe and wonder can remedy this by seeing both the teacher and student as interconnected.

Questions for Discussion

1. Which of the challenges outlined in this chapter do you feel would most impact your ability to experience gratitude and gifts in the classroom?
2. Describe some strategies that you would use to manage or mitigate the challenges of practicing gratitude.

Chapter 9

Six "Gift Aporias"

Core Conundrums in the Practice of Gratitude and the Gift in the Classroom

As suggested in chapter 8, the practice of gratitude and gifts in the classroom is not without its problems and dilemmas. Teachers in my doctoral thesis study (Brown, 2022) had to navigate complex and unexpected tensions between how they assessed student writing prior to visualizing it as a gift and how they later came to adopt the gift visualization of seeing student writing as a gift. Furthermore, as I hinted in chapter 5 on current gratitude studies, the repeated practice of directing gratitude outward toward many situations in the classroom can pose its own unique set of challenges. Gratitude fatigue is one potential challenge that comes when teachers try to extend gratitude toward all situations. Although repeated practice of gratitude through, for instance, gratitude writing is bound to strengthen the ability to feel gratitude over time (Wong et al., 2018), teachers may sometimes find the practice of journaling and listing particularly tedious or mechanical after a while.

In this chapter, I will explore some of the reasons why gratitude and the gift economy may not always be easily sustained in classrooms and might even raise unique unsolved questions or dilemmas that often result in paradox or unsolved riddles. I theorize along the lines of twentieth-century European philosophers such as Heidegger and Derrida (Derrida & Kamuf, 1992) that there is something inherently paradoxical about the nature of gifts themselves that can give rise to a variety of contradictions, particularly as teachers attempt to implement gratitude in the classroom. I refer to these contradictory tensions as *aporias*—questions for which there is no easy answer and through which teachers may learn to sit with the unresolved tensions that are part and parcel of the nature of gratitude and gifts. In the foregoing sections, I will explore these unique tensions by exploring each subsection as a kind of question that teachers may need to struggle with.

Throughout this chapter, I will use the concept of *aporia* to describe the paradoxical beholding of opposites that takes the form of an unsolvable question or dilemma. Takhar (2021) has characterized this as a state consisting of doubt, uncertainty, and temporal disjunction. Although aporias present themselves as extremely difficult or sticky questions that involve no easy resolution, framing a question as an aporia puts less emphasis on the solution and more emphasis on the process of growth that comes from exploring and beholding the tension of opposites. Skillfully sitting with a complex problem is one way of allowing us to bring ease to the contemplation of complexity, without having to unilaterally solve an issue, take decisive action, or eradicate tensions between conflicting sides or narratives. As I will suggest throughout this chapter, a gift orientation can allow teachers to behold opposites and explore them in unique and challenging ways that can involve play and discovery. Kirk Schneider (2004) echoes the dialectical nature of wisdom itself when he notes, "We need to discover . . . that beliefs, assurances, and perceptions contain their own contraries, and that wisdom derives from sorting out these contraries, filtering them through, and risking a decision in spite (and in light) of them" (p. 60). Instead of trying to resolve contradictions and polarities such as "limitation and freedom, form and vitality, order and disorder, individuality and collectivity, diversity and unity, degeneration and regeneration, humor and sacredness, and earthiness and spirituality" (p. 64), teachers could do well to behold the opposites as a way of broadening and deepening their ability to sit with the often contradictory nature of gifts and how they depart from a traditional model of the classroom.

Aporia No. 1: Are Classroom Gifts "Free"?

Teachers in Kerry Howells' study of gratitude (Howells, 2012) reported experiencing the practice of gratitude as a burden or an obligation—one of many activities on their to do list that needed to be checked off. I suspect that the sense of gratitude and gifting being moral obligations is not entirely a new one, considering that thinkers such as Marcel Mauss (1990) have theorized about a spirit called *hau* that impels gift givers in Indigenous cultures to reciprocate gifts given, thereby returning the spirit of the gift back to the donor. Mauss speculates that the power and reciprocity of gifts stems from a strong belief that spirits *within* the gift long for the return to their original owner, which in turn sparks a compulsion for the receiver to return the gift. Yet Mauss is not the first to have explored this idea. Ralph Waldo Emerson had also, albeit in a slightly different form, explored the nature of obligation in receiving gifts. Emerson notes,

> It is not the office of a man to receive gifts. How dare you give them? We wish to be self-sustained. We do not quite forgive a giver. The hand that feeds us is in some danger of being bitten. We can receive anything from love, for that is a way of receiving it from ourselves; but not from any one who assumes to bestow. We sometimes hate the meat which we eat, because there seems something of degrading dependence in living by it. (Schrift, 1997, p. 26)

For Emerson, the receiver of a gift may feel resentment because of the sense of dependency that a gift might hint at, as well as a sense of indebtedness to the giver. Some cultures maintain encoded rules about gifts that suggest receivers should not be given anything that is beyond their means to give back. If this rule is not followed, resentment is bound to arise, as well as a sense of the burdensome aspect of gifts. For both Mauss and Emerson, gifts are not as *free* as we might initially think them to be, since the receiver is bound to feel obligated to reciprocate the gift.

Many prominent gratitude scholars, including Robert Emmons (2013a), have identified gratitude more with a sense of indebtedness than a sense of enjoying the free graces of the world. As identified in chapter 5, gratitude has the double-edged distinction of being either a freely given grace (such as feeling grateful for one's existential being or an unlimited resource) or, conversely, a reminder of one's utter dependence and debt to other beings. This latter interpretation aligns gifts and gift giving to a patriarchal narrative of transactional justice, in which gifts are meant to be returned as a form of exchange. Engels (2018) has noted a tendency for Western models of gratitude to emphasize the sense of indebtedness that people have for benefactors, which can give rise to a sense of resentment toward gratitude practices altogether. While Engels traces the idea of gratitude as indebtedness to thinkers such as Aristotle, Cicero, and Seneca, he suggests that the current neoliberalist strand benefits from positioning gratitude as the acceptance of debt resulting from a consumerist mindset. Engels (2018) poignantly notes his own experiences in reading gratitude self-help books as a dismal and discomforting one: "The contemporary gratitude literature normalizes indebtedness. Reading one self-help book after another, I've come to believe that a central purpose of gratitude literature is to make Americans more comfortable living lives in debt. Intentionally or not, the work of contemporary gratitude authors serves to mollify the American citizenry, so that as we count our blessings and take stock of our many interpersonal, social, and political debts we are less likely to speak out about social and economic injustice" (p. 4). In contrast to an indebtedness narrative of gratitude, Engels suggests a shift in the rhetoric of gratitude toward a more democratized version of gratefulness that aligns with an existential joy of living—an experience more drawn out through contemplative and meditative practices than through a rote listing of those to whom we are indebted. Engels contrasts a gratitude that emphasizes a rule-based "paying back" form of gratitude—debt as something to be overcome yet simultaneously tolerated in a consumer-based neoliberal society—with a more existential gratefulness that focuses on the birthrights that make us alive, including the body and breath. Through a process of contemplation, *indebtedness* transforms into *belonging*, as the grateful person learns to meditate on how dependence is a part and parcel of being embedded in the world. Rather than commodifying life as something to be paid for, this form of gratitude aligns with Heidegger's view of being in the world of other beings (Horrigan-Kelly et al., 2016) and thus inseparable from others who are *equally dependent* on a common whole.

Classroom dynamics might hold similar situations when teachers and students practice gratitude together. Teachers in my study (Brown, 2022) often felt resentful when they attempted to practice feeling grateful or gifted for a gift that, at times, frankly did not seem to involve much effort on the student's part. Although the teacher was actively encouraged, through the visualization itself, to "see the gifted" in the writing they were about to receive and evaluate, this injunction did not always work with underachieving students and sometimes backfired altogether. This was particularly true when teachers perceived themselves as *putting in more effort* than the students and somehow expecting a similar amount or intensity of indebtedness from the student. Here, belief in the relative parity between giver and receiver efforts tends to overshadow the value of the student's gifts, as teachers struggle to feel gifted when their own efforts outweighed that of their students. One potential reason for this is the feeling that being gifted by the student's work might have appeared to be a form of emotional labor (Hochschild, 2003), particularly when the teacher failed to be impressed yet felt called upon by the gift visualization practice to see gifts in all students' work. When faced with the dilemma of wanting to feel grateful for work that didn't feel like a gift, the teachers were bound to feel either self-blaming for lacking sufficient grateful feelings or resentful that they were forced to assume feelings of gratitude that did not come naturally to them.

In education, one often sees the tension between gifts as free and as obligation played out in the tricky balance between allowing students to choose their own assignments and negotiate grades and providing guidance on assignment requirements and grading. On the one hand, students are often told they claim exclusive accountability and responsibility for their own learning. Learner-centered target setting and co-created rubrics between teacher and student (Fraile et al., 2017; Reddy & Andrade, 2010) are two examples where the student is given free range over the topics or skills they would like to master during a semester, as well as power to evaluate their own learning throughout the semester. This way of managing performance appraisals is thought to freely empower students to chart their own learning instead of being obligated to comply with a fixed rubric. Teachers, in turn, learn alongside their students as they develop their projects, thus being positioned as receivers of the students' gifts. Noddings (2015) has also noted the vital importance that choice plays in allowing students to be accountable for their decisions, which subsequently extends to their roles outside the school:

> Student choice is, or should be, a fundamental component in education. Teachers are officially in control of what goes on in their classrooms, but good teachers recognize student choice as part of collegiality in the best education and also as a basic element in evaluation. We learn a lot about student progress by observing students' choices and how they act on them. Further, education for life in a participatory democracy must necessarily aim at producing people who will make well-considered choices. (p. 150)

Noddings rightly points to the reciprocal nature of evaluation, as teachers learn more about their students when they are actively engaged in the decision process. On the other hand, the process of choosing a topic to learn needs to be guided by the teacher's felt sense of what constitutes learning—much of which hasn't been worked out for students at younger ages. Noddings later recommends that students and teachers together negotiate the assignment structure: "Student choices interact intelligently with teacher choices. If the teacher has suggested a set of topics for projects, students may choose one from the set. Before the set is finalized, the teacher may invite students to make suggestions, and he or she may rightly accept or reject suggestions on the grounds of the teacher's own expertise" (p. 151). Noddings suggests sensibly balancing student choices with teacher guidance and content. Without a sense of structure, can a student know what kinds of projects are worthy of contribution to the class itself? More importantly, considering the nature of grading, are students really free to choose their own grades? If so, what prevents students from overinflating their own sense of what they have learned from a class activity?

These topics touch upon the question of whether learning itself is to be mandated through extrinsic rewards or punishments, or, conversely, whether a school can exist without any extrinsic rewards. Summerhill is one example of an experimental school in which all grading and formalities were abolished in favor of student-directed learning. Can too much freedom for students to choose whatever topics they wish to learn mean a lack of boundaries or guidance from teachers? Stronach and Piper (2009) reflect on this precarious balance:

> When "being yourself" and "having your life" proves problematic, the Meeting not only makes laws but is there to advise and adjudicate. Disputes or complaints may be dealt with informally, or by Ombudsmen, who are older students of either gender appointed to be a first point of assistance. Unresolved or serious complaints may lead an individual to "bring up" whoever has offended them at the Meeting. Any child or adult, in any combination, may do so. An 11-year-old girl explains: "The point about the meeting is to make . . . *me* feel [our stress] that it was totally wrong, this is a strong warning. But if you do it again, we will fine you. If you make contact [violence] you won't get a strong warning, they will probably fine you some odd random things like 'Bully's List,' no television, no screens, no social games." (p. 53)

This passage suggests that the idea of having one's own authentic gifts needs to be mediated by a community that approves these gifts and situates them within the harmony of the classroom. While discipline is needed to ensure that a child is not disrupting the classroom dynamic, the ability to be *moved* is also a factor in improving the receptiveness of students. Kirk Schneider (2004) defines the capacity to be moved as "the maximal capacity to be impacted by experiences—to pause and to feel and to ponder" (p. 147), which he contrasts to "amplification of children's capacity to feel" (p. 149) that is often imposed by marketing ploys targeted at children and other forms of media. When children are only taught how to be *assertive* instead of being *affected by* things, they may forget the gifts that are latent in those around them, thereby privileging their own sense of giftedness over the gifts found in surrounding communities.

Given the above observations, it's expected that a rubric with too much structure and uniformity of assignments is bound to position the student's efforts as standardized and obligatory: not as freely given gifts, but as debts that are owed to the teacher in exchange for a grade. Teachers who spend time marking the same assignment and looking at the same answers to a single question are likely more inclined to compare the same answers when grading, rather than taking the assignment at face value. In my own study (Brown, 2022), teachers who occupied higher grade levels, particularly at the doctoral level, were more inclined to see students' writing as gifts simply by virtue of the fact that the students were creating and initiating their own assignment topics rather than being assigned a topic by the teacher. This seems to be attributed to the fact that the students' efforts are simply perceived more as *their own* when they are given free range to choose their own topics, in much the same way that a gift donor is considered more authentic when they are choosing a gift from their own thought, effort, interests, and initiative. Emerson echoes this observation when he notes the importance of gifts to paradoxically reflect the choices, personality, and efforts of the giver, as opposed to simply the requests and needs of the receiver:

> The only gift is a portion of thyself. Thou must bleed for me. Therefore, the poet brings his poem; the shepherd, his lamb; the farmer, corn; the miner, a gem; the sailor, coral and shells; the painter, his picture; the girl, a handkerchief of her own sewing. This is right and pleasing, for it restores society in so far to its primary basis, when a man's biography is conveyed in his gift, and every man's wealth is an index of his merit. But it is a cold, lifeless business when you go to the shops to buy me something, which does not represent your life and talent, but a goldsmith's. (Emerson, 1991, p. 306)

Emerson attributes the need for gifts to reflect givers because it signals the sacrifice of the giver when their occupation and interests are symbolically inscribed within the gift itself. On the other hand, purchasing a gift that was made by someone else smacks too much of "a kind of symbolical sin-offering, or payment of black-mail" (p. 306), since it starts to seem more like a routine monetary exchange than a genuine sacrifice that comes from a person's inner talents and skills. Emerson even hints that the enjoyment of gifting comes from the giver's felt sense of their own imprint in the gift itself, which enhances their feeling of creatively crafting a gift. This also bears out in studies that show that gift givers who select gifts not part of a preassigned registry signal to the receivers their own "insider" relational knowledge of the receiver's unique tastes (Ward & Broniarczyk, 2016). Quite simply, the sense of *being gifted* often requires teachers to frame their students as not only making a minimal effort but also putting their own authentic personality, choice, and angle into the gift itself. These qualities sought in the gift tend to signal that the giver put thought and effort into making the gift special and personal, instead of acting from a sense of obligation or fulfilling a minimal course requirement to get a passing grade.

To summarize, What exactly constitutes a gift in the classroom, and what distinguishes it from a merge obligation to submit work in exchange for grades or certification? Perhaps not surprisingly, teachers feel most gifted when they are able to frame their students as putting their own personality into their work, which shows evidence of thoughtfulness and intention rather than obligation or routine or ritual offerings. Parallel to Emerson's observation that gifts feel more authentic when they reflect the occupations and talents of the givers, teachers too are inclined to see gifts in the students when the latter are given latitude to choose their own topics or shape a topic according to their own interests. This goes beyond the paradigm of thinking of gratitude as a mere payment of debts and allows the definition of gratitude to expand to attributing creativity and individual effort into a gift.

Aporia No. 2: The Asymmetry of the Gift

Even though gifts have been frequently seen to entail indebtedness, one potential difference between a gift and an exchange is the asymmetry of giving and giving back in turn. In other words, the moment a person receives a gift, they need to be open to "just receiving" rather than in a position to pay it back immediately, as a money transaction would entail. Although the teachers in my study (Brown, 2022) were tasked with visualizing their students' writing as a gift, they were not in any way obligated to return on the imagined gifts. Nonetheless, teachers found themselves giving more generous feedback after they framed their students' writing as a gift. With that being said, did the increased tendency for teachers to give feedback entail that they felt more indebted to express gratitude toward the qualities they discovered in their students' writing?

The Maori concept of *hau* (Mauss, 1990) certainly entails that even when gifts are asymmetrical, there is still a necessary onus for the spirit of the gift to return. But asymmetry also implies that gifts do not always have a clear reciprocation. This is problematic because a teacher who gifts a student does not necessarily receive an immediate result and may even be a sole giver without any expectation of return. After all, the traditional view of the teacher is that they possess some kind of knowledge or position that they are able to give to someone who is less empowered. Writing on the philosophy of Iris Marion Young and the gift, Simone Galea (2006) notes,

> Learning and teaching necessitate an asymmetry between people. This is what we take for granted in thinking of relationships between teachers and pupils. The act of teaching is seen as founded on inequalities of experiences and knowledge between the teacher and the student. The teacher gives something which she has and which she is, which the student does not have. In this respect many teachers think of teaching as a vocation; giving without taking back; giving without expecting anything in return. (p. 86)

The term *vocation* literally refers to a calling (Manen, 1991; Palmer, 2017) or something that brings a teacher forth into the world in response to the "call" of the learner. In this regard, the gift of teaching is positioned as somewhat unequal to that of the student, in that the teacher simply has more to give in the classroom relationship in the form of content knowledge. On the other hand, if teachers' roles were simply to deliver content, then the relationship becomes one of simple transmission, which wouldn't necessarily qualify as a gifting one because for the gifting relationship to be viable, there must be *unequal* exchanges. Returning a gift with the same gift would be considered questionable. Hence, Galea (2006) notes, "Teachers should expect to be given something different from that which they have given. Students' responses that are exactly similar to what the teacher has delivered cannot be considered to be gifts that nourish the relationship between the teacher and the student. Young gives the example of having someone saying back the same thing that the other person has told her. To be given different gifts, teachers need to go beyond the usual acts of delivering" (p. 89). This point is a poignant reminder that the gifts of students should not be routinized into simply fulfilling a rubric or answering prescribed, formulated questions according to the teacher's expectations and requirements. But this also raises the intriguing question: If, in fact, framing gifts in the classroom entails a *loosening* of the symmetrically between teacher and student effort, could this also entail a slippage of standards? Would it mean that students could submit substandard work and pass it off as a kind of gift because it's coming from the student's sincerity and effort? When seen as a metaphor in education, giftedness straddles a fine line between exceptionality and being so out of the ordinary that it does not serve a wider purpose in the classroom or community of learning. Giftedness, according to many scholars, needs to be something that is received and recognized as valuable, rather than being simply an exceptional score or number on a test. As Sternberg et al. (2011) note, "There is good reason to think about productivity, or at the very least, potential productivity, as a criterion for giftedness. Simply receiving high scores on an IQ test trivializes what it means to be gifted" (p. 5). However, gifts do not necessarily need to be tangible ones; sometimes it is the absence of a predictable or timed gift that allows spaces for students and teachers alike to be reflective and creative. Too much gifting may be considered either controlling and manipulating the classroom with rewards or spoon-feeding the student. Galea poignantly remarks, "When the teacher gives nothing, she can give her students and herself time to think about their interactions and the space to make themselves differently in the light of their interactions. These moments of not giving give time and space for teachers and students to become different from each other and from what they have been" (p. 91). Galea suggests the need to make room between moments of gifting and receiving, allowing both teachers and students to grow and evolve over time.

Also related to asymmetry is the idea that classrooms must allow spaces for the unexpected—that is, for teachers and students to see learning as a journey that begins in one place and ends in an unexpected or mysterious place. This is where a sense of wonder is so crucial to the experience of feeling gifted. If students knew exactly where a lesson is taking them, what would be the value of learning or attending class? This sense of wonder could equally apply to teachers, who are not simply feeding minds with pre-programmed material but are guiding individuals on a journey that is unique to each learner and can therefore inspire rich dialogue and interpretation. Galea describes the sense of wonder as crucial to Iris Marion Young's vision of the gift in education:

> The student wonders what lesson the teacher will give today or she may wonder if she knows the solution to that problem. This sense of wonder at not knowing is what instigates listening to the teacher. The teacher develops her lessons through a sense of wonder, an expectancy of how her lesson will be accepted. Lessons are developed after wondering what the needs and interests of the student are. Again the teacher has to listen to travel towards her students. (Galea, 2006, p. 90)

Young's vision of education suggests that teachers need to balance between a sense of structure and the ability to yield to students' unique and creative interpretations of an assignment. If teachers control the assignment requirements too strictly, students may submit assignments that are identical with each other, which takes away the sense of wonder that Galea hints at. Furthermore, Young's philosophy of the gift suggests that students' needs are not already known prior to creating the assessment itself but come from a sense of wonder within the teacher: What do these students need to learn, and how will they best learn? What will engage them the most? A teacher must always be open to questioning whether their assignments fit with the students' needs or needs to be adapted or changed. The asymmetricality of gifts in the classroom hinges on the way that assignments and assessments need to stay open to spontaneity, adaptability, and change, in much the same way that gifting relationships surrender to wonder, mystery, and receptiveness. Not only is there no "one gift fits all" in classrooms, but even the choice of *what* to gift students, and what students gift to teachers in return, is continually being reframed and negotiated at every moment in the learning process.

Aporia No. 3: How to Sustain Novelty in Gifts

Giftedness is often characterized by a sense of novelty, and this book has continually attempted to connect gifts with the experience of surprise. In fact, as Vandevelde (2000) remarks, "The external point of view on the gift, which highlights the matter of reciprocity, is so deceptive. True enough, one can calculate the equivalences and the interest rates between exchanged gifts a posteriori. One may even be capable of predicting the next move in the gift game, but from an internal point of view this game requires indetermination, risk and uncertainty, surprise and wonder" (p. 3). One of the interesting implications of novelty is that one might begin to wonder how to sustain it over time. Can newness become too familiar to students and teachers? Some have suggested that too much gratitude can seem rote, meaning that it becomes repetitive and predictable, which undermines the original dynamic of receiving a gift. Wood et al. (2010) have noted that the pressure to keep up with daily gratitude lists can position it more as a chore or a hassle rather than as a genuine process of discovery. This tendency to *routinize* gratitude can come from writing down lists of separate instances of objects that one is grateful for rather than feeling gratitude in the midst of a varied and multilayered personal experience. It's thus important that teachers not reduce gratitude to concrete gift objects that represent tangible results but are instead always open to new ways of being thankful for what they have, even through the reframing of things that do not seem to be gifts. Thus, a certain amount of skillfulness is required to keep the practice of gratitude fresh without it devolving into a routine list.

One route through which gratitude can stay fresh is through a nonjudgmental grounding in the present moment, or what Timothy Miller (1995), among others, refers to as "attention." Far from being simply a command to concentrate on a specific topic or subject, paying attention, for Miller, entails a capacity for an unfiltered experience of immersion in the present. Miller notes, "Practicing Attention means doing one thing at a time whenever possible. Practicing Attention means performing every action as if that action is very important, treating every sensation as if that sensation is unique and precious, talking with every person as if that person were president of the United States. Practicing Attention means that no experience is considered common, ordinary, or trivial. Practicing Attention means that you avoid deliberately distracting yourself from your own feelings, experiences, and circumstances" (p. 138).

Several key components of attention dovetail with a view of giftedness in the classroom. The first is the attitude of *seeing the unique* in every moment or circumstance. This is not always an easy thing for teachers to do unless they are able to slow down and fully experience a moment in a nonjudgmental, open way. What if, indeed, teachers were to treat each of their students as having an important destiny to fulfill in life, such as becoming the president? Yet this tendency to see all as exceptional goes against the view of education that stresses the bell curve and trying to separate the "exceptional" from the "average."

Gifts are predicated on an authentic sense of interconnectedness. Bauer and Shanahan (2019) describe authentic gratitude as the result of the felt enactment of one's values over decades of lived experience, as well as "how those values and ideals actually pan out in the varied contexts and vicissitudes of everyday life—a life with other individuals, groups, institutions, and perhaps cultures and a sense of history" (p. 237). The authors note how, particularly in midlife, "one's understanding of interdependence moves beyond the interpersonal to become dynamic, systemic and organismic" (p. 237) as opposed to simply being a static, adolescent ideal. These remarks suggest a much more spontaneous and lived experience of gratitude that comes with integrating and testing out one's ideals against a richly contextualized, interdependent life history.

Teachers may need to attend to balancing the sheer volume of inputs and information from their classrooms with the ability to behold the uniqueness in each of these tasks, particularly given time and energy constraints. This may be a struggle, especially when teachers are more hard-pressed to deal with large volumes of marking in short periods of time. Can a sense of surprise be sustained in the midst of the daily rush and grind of teaching? My doctoral thesis study (Brown, 2022) suggests that although teachers may struggle to incorporate a gratitude practice into their daily assessments of students, they can certainly cultivate an attitude of taking small moments to slow down and savor their students' work. This needn't be a mechanical process that applies uniformly to every student's effort or work, but it can be a general attitude that can be practiced with time.

The sense of novelty is thus not only a function of the kinds of assignments given in classrooms, but it can also come from an attitude of wonder, discovery, and attentiveness. As my study has shown, teachers who develop the capacity to *expect* surprises are more likely to find them, as long as the sense of expectancy is not bound to a fixed result or preconceived view of what constitutes a "suitable" gift within the students. At the same time, however, the process of gifting requires a sense of ritual or routine that prepares individuals to both give and receive gifts. Teachers in my study (Brown, 2022) expressed how the simple act of listening to a guided meditation on gratitude helped to ground them in the present, as well as view even the act of *being* a teacher as a gift. The sense of grounding in the body prior to assessing the student writing allowed the teachers to slow down, become more relaxed, and center their awareness, which thus prepared them to behold their students' writing with a sense of tranquility and equanimity. I would suggest that the novelty of gifts also has to be accompanied with a routine that allows the mind to be centered, grounded, and relaxed.

Aporia No. 4: Gifts and Partiality

In classrooms, teachers are often considered to be the arbiters of "fairness" (Rasooli et al., 2023), who administer a wide variety of assessments that range from fair marking to imposing standards of practice that equally apply to all students. Common to these notions of fairness is the idea that objective criteria can in fact determine what is fair and not fair. Teachers are often lulled into the belief that emotions are opposite to fairness and may tend to suppress their emotions in order to promote a sense of neutrality in the interests of not favoring students. Yet, as many researchers can attest (Dunbar & Baker, 2014; Hargreaves, 1998), the act of teaching is a deeply emotional one. Emotions do play a significant part in the way teachers assess and interpret the quality of a student's work. Partiality can thus become a source of anxiety for teachers, as they navigate being emotionally invested in their students' work while also simultaneously trying to be as fair as possible. But at the same time, some would suggest that in order to consider a gift, one must also cultivate partiality, both in the way a gift is specifically chosen for a receiver and how the person enjoys the gift. A gift that is not well chosen or thoughtlessly chosen can sometimes be much worse than not receiving a gift at all. Similarly, for teachers to feel gifted in their classrooms, they must experience a felt sense that the student put something of themselves into the gift that they have provided, without putting so much of themselves that it loses the spirit of what the teacher wants to receive. This careful balance between a giver's genuine identity and the receiver's genuine need is what characterizes partiality in the gift.

To understand this aporia, one could set up an imaginary situation in which students strive for high marks simply for the sake of advancing into prestigious institutions, winning top honors, or being the "teacher's pet." In these scenarios, students may become quite adept at being able to detect what the teacher is looking for in an assignment, based on the teacher's criteria and emotional responses to certain kinds of student work. Even if the teachers are given assignments that meet the course requirements, teachers would not necessarily feel gifted, much less consider the assignments to be gifts, should they begin to recognize the self-serving or opportunistic motives behind the gifts. This is similar to what Simon Keller (2013), in his discussion of partiality, refers to as treating relationships as *projects* in themselves rather than seeing the intrinsic value of the persons with whom we relate:

> A person who characteristically thinks of her relationships when she acts well toward others is not someone you would want as a friend or a loved one. A friend who is always thinking of improving your relationship, a colleague whose main concern is with the value of collegiality, a parent who thinks mainly of how important it is to have a good relationship with his child—all of these characters are annoying to have around, and all of them seem to be missing what really matters in their relationships. (Keller, 2013, p. 63)

Where Keller takes issue with these cases of concern with projects is that the caregivers in a relationship seem more concerned with an abstract principle of excelling in an endeavor than the actual persons themselves. Conversely, the receivers of gifts in these relationships might sometimes feel the giver as lacking in care for them as individuals. In a classroom dynamic, this might play out in the form of students investing a lot of concern for excelling in school yet missing the interactive moments that constitute genuine learning. For these students, achieving grades becomes a game of pleasing the teacher rather than learning to invest in the subject with a sense of real love and participation.

Teachers in my doctoral thesis study (Brown, 2022) had sometimes worried that by becoming more empathic and attuned with their students' work and efforts, they would start to lose the whole value and purpose of marking. The teachers experienced themselves as becoming, at times, so invested and merged with the feelings and experiences of their students in their writing that they worried that they would lose the spirit of marking itself. This reflects a feeling of being gifted by the student's self-disclosure—the sense that the student sincerely used their assignments as an expression of their true selves. In exchange, the teachers felt somewhat more open to step beyond the role of simply assessing students' writing in favor of connecting with their students. Paradoxically, this also caused the teachers to feel more interested in their students and to grade even higher than they normally would, since it allowed them to see truly new and novel connections with their students.

Perhaps the greatest struggle the teachers in my study had to wrestle with was recognizing that empathy enhances the assessment process by allowing teachers to discover qualities in their students that they would otherwise overlook by simply following a rubric. This expands the notion of what it means to be impartial by suggesting that emotions and interconnection can play a key role in holistically assessing a students' learning and results—a point that perhaps problematizes the notion of impartiality by suggesting a broader range of emotions and states of mind that might factor into the fair grading of a test or an assignment. This takes teachers beyond the staid notion of impartiality as a simple process of divesting reason of all emotions.

Aporia No. 5: Is There Such a Thing as Too Generous?

The teachers in my study (Brown, 2022) often struggled with questions of whether they became too generous as a result of feeling or generating gratitude. These attitudes sometimes dovetail with notions of fairness, but more often they entail a sense of equal exchange between teacher and students. The teachers in particular reported that their marking had become much more empathic as a result of the gratitude visualization, as they tended to become more generous in commenting to students about what they liked the most in their writing and work. But at the same time, teachers raised the commonplace question: Does being too generous toward students inadvertently lower the standard of quality in terms of what students submit as assignments? Is there such a thing as being "too generous" when it comes to grading, and can an overgenerous classroom sometimes make students less motivated to perform quality work?

The fear of being too generous parallels a commonplace conception of education as needing to be tough, demanding, and competitive in order for students to be motivated to succeed. As Becky Thompson (2017) suggests in her work on tenderness in pedagogy, learning can include elements of playfulness and joy, which figure heavily into the learning experience. Thompson uses rituals to debunk the notion that students come into the classroom as "separate" bodies, suggesting instead a pedagogy of mutual accountability in which all are instrumental in the success of others:

> Starting with the naming ritual is a step toward recognizing each other's humanity by understanding that names matter—they hold stories to people's heritage, to what they know and don't know

> about their ancestors, to family relations, to gender. It is a start in seeing each other. . . . It also helps us get grounded in the classroom together, to bring our bodies to the session, to sit close, see each other's faces. It also helps us notice, collectively, who is not here—as we decide who might reach out to the missing person. At the end of the class session, I ask everyone to stand (or sit) in a circle, find each other's eyes, and then hold the connection for at least a few seconds, with the silent commitment that we all leave the class together at the end of the semester with an A. Your A is my A is our A. I ask that we hold each other's eyes, knowing that not everyone may get to come back next week. All manner of the unexpected can dislodge, dishevel, dismember a class. What can we do with our eyes to pull each other back together the following week? What can we do to know that my A means little without yours? (p. 42)

For Thompson, the shift from "I" to "we" helps to frame the classroom cooperatively, thereby necessitating a pedagogy that turns upon generosity.

Another key aporia to explore is how teachers can practice generosity without rendering their students too passive. When teachers intend to "give" students all the answers without student effort and initiative, they may mislead students into believing that knowledge is gained without the messiness and trial-and-error that often precedes true discovery. Teachers may need to decide the balance to strike between supporting their students' learning and allowing them to discover what's important to them. This ties back to the notion that gifts cannot be predicted in advance of the act of giving, and each gift depends on both the spirit of the giver and the readiness of the receiver to appreciate the gift and thereby make it a part of themselves.

Aporia No. 6: Do Gifts Require A "Giver"?

It would seem perhaps a truism that gratitude requires a sense of giver, gift, and receiver, particularly if we accept the definition of gratitude as indebtedness to a giver (Emmons, 2013a). Defining gratitude as "a response to another's goodness," Roberts and Telech (2019) note,

> Gratitude represents the benefactor as more than a supplier of benefits. It is a response not simply to beneficence but also to

bene*volence*—goodwill. Natural events and malicious persons both may cause some end of mine to be fulfilled, and I may be glad *that* the beneficial state of affairs came to be, but such good fortune doesn't usually dispose me to feel grateful *to anyone*. This is plausibly because I do not take these benefits to be expressions of benevolence or goodwill . . . gratitude is thus an interpersonal or social emotion. (p. 1)

Most of the examples in this book have pointed to gratitude as an interpersonal dynamic in classroom situations. Teachers cannot be grateful for students' work unless they are able to see the student as capable of beneficent efforts, intentions, and thoughts. An extreme example of failure to feel gratitude in response to student work would be the rising incidence of electronic plagiarism, as documented in the study by Harwood and Asal (2007) of online learning in K–12 schools. For these authors, what constitutes effort is now being challenged, as students leverage widely available AI and translation software to craft essays, in addition to heavily appropriating others' texts into their own assignments. While the technologies seem new, the copying of existing texts from other sources is certainly not; as Harwood and Asal (2007) note, an indelible part of creation involves taking up and innovating other cultures' materials. However, the rise of online plagiarism raises an interesting question: Are teachers to feel gifted by a student's ability to plagiarize, even when the plagiarism is skillfully applied and innovated upon? To what extent does the originality of the student determine a teacher's sense of gratitude for their work? What, exactly, constitutes "originality" to begin with? And, more to the point, given the fact that there is no "pure originality" without the inspiration of other creators, just how much originality must be present for teachers to feel gifted by a student's efforts? These questions touch upon the extent to which a gift requires a unique, thinking and individual giver, or whether simply the feeling of being benefited by something is enough to constitute grateful appreciation. With the rise of students using artificial intelligence to help write term papers, questions emerge as to how educators are to gauge the effort, originality, and ownership of a student's text.

Do gifts, conversely, require thanks from a willing or grateful receiver? Are teachers bound to reciprocate their students' efforts? Not every source of gratitude necessitates a repayment. Callard (2019) maintains that debts of gratitude suggest "the existence of norms governing the reception of benefits" (p. 83), and furthermore that the feeling of indebtedness is more related to the *giver* than the gift itself. Donating a kidney, to use Callard's example, entails a sacrifice on the part of the giver that seems to necessitate an inherent sense of indebtedness to the giver. On the other hand, *appreciating* something and expressing gratitude for it tends to be directed more to the gift itself than the giver. Callard uses the following example:

> Suppose my best friend gets me, for my birthday, the quirky dress only she could have known I'd love. I am delighted; I feel grateful; I thank her—or perhaps the look on my face is thanks enough. I do not feel myself to be under any sort of standing normative burden. The demands of gratitude are exhausted by what I feel and express in reaction to the dress. She'll be happy that I'm happy, and that will be all. In this case, there is no debt of gratitude, no discomfort. My gratitude is a purely positive emotion, akin to joy, admiration, and pride. (p. 83)

Although in this example there is certainly a sense of gratitude to the intention of the giver (and her apparent knowledge of the receiver's unique tastes), there is no *debt* incurred for the gift itself. Instead, the feeling of being gifted seems to focus mainly on the nature of the gift itself. Teachers and students who keep gratitude journals are often appreciative of the gift objects they have received in the past, without necessarily feeling indebted to the giver. As Callard puts it, "Gift gratitude doesn't put someone under a standing normative burden; it doesn't leave a remainder" (p. 89). *Perfect* gifts, then, are ones that are so uniquely suited to the receiver that there is no sense that the receiver owes anything by way of equivalence to the giver. The gift itself is experienced as precisely fitting to the receiver. Similarly, when teachers seek to feel gifted by their students, they are not necessarily looking for how they are personally indebted to the students or vice versa. Rather, they look for ways in which the students provide unique and unusual opportunities for the teachers to connect with the students and their writing, as well as meet the student at the level and experiences they are most familiar with. This perhaps explains why the teachers in my study often referenced the *sincere effort* of the students as well as the way they personalized assignment questions to make them uniquely their own. The teacher felt gifted when the student attempted to answer a preassigned question in an authentic way that relates their true interests and passions with the teachers'. This appreciation does not require reciprocating on a specific gift, but only a feel for the unique way that the student approached the gift itself.

Not all giftedness in the classroom need come from students. Teachers can often feel appreciative simply for the ability to teach, as I learned from my study, as well as the ability to use their bodies to help others. Having a classroom cycle of teaching and learning was yet another ability that the teachers appreciated from their students. Cosmic gratitude is simply gratitude to have moments of self-love and self-care that the teachers highly appreciated when they slowed down and took a moment to be *in the moment* of assessing their students' writing. This suggests that appreciation and giftedness need not be limited to a teacher's appraisal of a student's writing but could extend to simply being a teacher in the classroom. This meshes with Callard's observations, as well as Steindl-Rast's (2004) ideas, about *thankfulness* as something that does not depend on a specific person or benefactor but can extend to the simple acknowledgment of being in the world and being granted the chance to live.

Discussion: Living the Core Paradoxes of Surprise, Gratitude, and Giftedness

Although some might be inclined to think that gratitude and feeling gifted are always welcomed emotions, second wave positive psychology (Ivtzan et al., 2015) suggests that positive emotions dialectically interweave with negative ones to generate nuanced experiences. The paradox of the gift is that too many gifts may actually lead to a sense of taking for granted the individuality of each gift. Similarly, a teacher who develops too much gratitude for the seemingly inconsequential may end up losing the uniqueness of achievements and effort. There may even be a leveling off of the significance of being gifted by student effort if the teacher is too focused on practicing gratitude simply for its own sake, rather than evaluating the merits of the student work itself. If student work does not warrant the merit accrued to gifts, should teachers continue to bestow a sense of giftedness upon it?

One way of exploring this core paradox is to examine Irving Singer's (2009) distinction between bestowal and appraisal-based views of love. Singer suggests that with the rise of the Christian notion of *agape*—the unconditional love that God bestows upon human beings—the notion of love shifted from one of appraising the value of the other to bestowing love on the other regardless of their relative merits. Too much agape can lead to an unconditional and indiscriminate embrace of a student's efforts, even if none of them are based on genuine efforts. This might be considered the downside of practicing excessive gratitude without regard for the relative merits of the students' achievements. Parker Palmer (2017) similarly describes how classrooms need to preserve the tension between boundedness and openness. He remarks,

> The boundaries around a teaching and learning space are created by using a question, a text, or a body of data that keep us focused on the subject at hand. Within those boundaries, students are free to speak, but their speaking is always guided toward the topic, not only by the teacher but also by the materials at hand. Those materials must be so clear and compelling that students will find it hard to wander from the subject-even when it confuses or frightens them and they would prefer to evade its demands. Space without boundaries is not space, it is a chaotic void, and in such a space no learning is likely to occur. (p. 77)

It's possible to identify parallels between Palmer's paradox of bounded-and-open with that of *eros* (appraisal) and *agape* (bestowal). Whereas the former refers to a clearly defined path toward learning core subject matter through assignment completion, the latter refers to the creative allowances that teachers and students bring to the crafting and appraisal of assignments, whereby process is valued over content and teachers learn to bestow value on their students' unique subjectivities and interpretations of assignments. While this book has certainly advocated for more of the latter, I suggest that true gratitude and surprise needs to be contextualized within a structure that equally honors content and subject matter. Considering *every* student contribution, whether relevant or irrelevant to the core subject area, as a gift may do a disservice to students and teachers alike. Similarly, teachers who use gratitude practices to bypass the challenges of setting high standards for student work are not necessarily benefiting their students, let alone themselves.

Questions for Discussion

1. What tensions do you feel when attempting to practice gratitude or a surprise mindset into your classroom? Write a reflection exploring the key tensions and how you might address them through the practices discussed in this book.

2. Why might the metaphor of the gift be inherently fraught with contradictions? Are these contradictions inevitable, or are there ways we can lessen the contradictory thoughts or feelings we might have around seeing students' contributions as gifts?

Chapter 10

Gift-Based Visualizations

The last part of this book consists of guided visualizations that are designed specifically for teachers, to instill a sense of surprise and giftedness in the classroom. These visualizations can be used to inspire teachers to cultivate attitudes of surprise and giftedness. It is hoped that you can find a visualization that suits you and stay with it over a period of time, or adapt one or more of these visualizations to suit your needs.

Visualization has formed a significant component of my thinking as a holistic researcher. Ever since I first embarked on my doctoral thesis journey, I have been using both guided meditations and visualization as ways of embodying the concept of gratitude, particularly as it relates to a metaphor that evokes giftedness or a progression of images that link giftedness to a specific situation in a teacher's life. My doctoral thesis (Brown, 2022) involved having individual teachers listen to a guided visualization that I prepared based on the notion of seeing student writing as a gift, prior to assessing the students' writing. The metaphor of beholding a gift started as a simple visualization of a gift that a teacher held as important in the past, which then branched out into other ways that the teacher felt gifted by the communities and societies they have inhabited as well as the world as a whole. Metaphors (Lakoff & Johnson, 1980) have often been used as part of the visualization process to render concrete an otherwise abstract topic or idea, such as love or gratitude. By couching assessment as the metaphor of revealing a students' gifts, I was encouraging teachers to potentially reframe their familiar ways of doing assessment using a completely new metaphorical framing, which, however unfamiliar, later became a part of the teacher's overall ways of relating to their students' writing.

Visualization has been used in many spiritual traditions to evoke integration, wholeness, and healing. One key premise of the guided imagery process is that images are more deeply connected to wisdom because they aren't tied to habitual thinking. Davenport (2009), for instance, defines guided imagery as "a process that focuses our attention inward to receive the impressions, pictures, and dream figures arising from our true nature. These images are the natural expression of our intuition, unconscious mind, and deepest self. They hold the key to living a life of greater ease and fulfillment. Guided imagery gives us a way to receive our heart's wise advice, unmediated by the habitual thinking and limiting beliefs that drive the vast majority of our day-to-day experience" (p. 1). Here, Davenport privileges imagery as potently revealing parts of our makeup that may not always surface through everyday habitual thinking. However, it's important to note that objects of visualization *in themselves* don't hold that much power, nor need they be detailed or complete to be effective. Rather, it's the mind itself that endows objects with the energies to heal or introduce a more wholesome view of the world. In his book *Boundless Healing*, Tibetan Buddhist teacher Tulku Thondup maintains that the objects of visualization are intended to invoke the natural healing and harmonizing powers of the mind. Like mental anchors, positive images can be used to draw out the mind's capabilities by giving the mind something specific, concrete, and habitual to focus on. Tulku Thondup (2000) thus remarks,

> The true power of healing does not come from someone or something else, nor is it something that arises out of the blue. The peaceful mind is the true source of healing. . . . However, it is very hard for most of us to focus directly on the true qualities of our minds, so we get in the habit of relying on other people and other things. The common teachings advise us to take advantage of this habitual reliance by focusing on positive mental objects as a way to rouse the inner strengths of our minds. (p. 51)

Visualization can be a tool to bring out the natural spaciousness and non-grasping nature of the mind, as long as the object itself does not become a source of clinging. Thondup suggests that "even if our meditation uses positive images, words, feeling, and beliefs, we can be too forceful in how we apply these qualities of the mind" (p. 37), which can result in a craving and grasping mindset that elicits tension in the body. It's therefore essential that guided visualizations, like meditation, be approached using an exploratory mindset, while dropping expectations of specific outcomes or results. The visualization itself needs to be seen as a source of continued discovery and surprise, rather than as a formula designed to "manufacture" these qualities using willpower or exertion.

While some may not believe that they can easily visualize a situation or muster the necessary concentration to do so, it's important to consider that the visualization need not be complete, detailed, or thorough to be useful or effective. Notes psychologist Paul Gilbert (2009),

> It is important to recognize that when we "imagine things" we usually don't see detailed pictures in our minds. Generally, images are fleeting and we get fragments and glimpses of things. For example, if I ask you to imagine your favourite meal, or the house you might like to live in, or what you will be doing tomorrow, you probably will not get a clear picture in your mind; more like fleeting impressions and feelings. When we talk about imagery we are really trying to create "a sense of" as opposed to "a clear picture of." It is about how we direct our attention, the focus of our minds. (p. 145)

In the sections that follow, I will introduce different kinds of visualizations that bring to light an aspect of a teacher's presence in the classroom that evokes surprise, wonder, and giftedness. Taken together, these visualizations differ from the previous chapters' reflections and visualizations in the sense that they follow an expansive approach that starts with appreciation for one's own embodied being (visualization 1) and widens into an appreciation of the classroom as a body and classroom interactions as a totality. The concentrically growing nature of the visualizations allows for a gradually immersive as well as expansive, broadening experience of gratitude.

It's recommended, however, that teachers encounter these visualizations using a curious and gentle approach, somewhat akin to an experiment in contemplative self-care (Desmond, 2016). Some guidelines that might prove helpful in adopting these practices include the following:

1. While the visualization can be simply read aloud, it is recommended that the reader record the visualizations, in their own voice, preferably while in a calm state. This way, the visualization can be played anytime and anywhere or as part

of a regular routine. Using one's own voice can personalize the imagery and make it more memorable. Read *slowly* to get the best effect from the practice itself, as the slowness can encourage a more gradual and mindful approach to taking in the images.

2. It's important to follow the relaxation instructions from the beginning of each visualization, rather than trying to rush to the metaphor or main theme of the visualization itself. A calm state can allow the images to percolate into one's subconscious mind, and the relaxation evoked by the opening phrases of the visualization can allow for a more open mind-state that becomes more receptive to unexpected surprises.

3. If one of the visualizations doesn't "work," simply move on to the visualizations that do. Although the visualizations that follow are designed to be read in a specific sequence—starting from meditations on the body and expanding to visualizations related to whole classrooms and communities—it's important that you adopt the visualizations that are more meaningful and resonant with you rather than forcing yourself to follow a fixed sequence or progression.

4. Once you find one or two visualizations that resonate with you, try to make it a daily habit to follow the visualization, preferably just before entering a classroom situation. The more established a daily practice of visualization becomes, the more the attitudes and mindsets generated from the visualizations can have a transformative effect and become habitual.

I hope you will enjoy the visualizations that follow, as well as the thematic explanations that precede each visualization.

Visualization No. 1: The Gift of Embodiment

Before doing this visualization, it's important to reflect on what it means to be embodied or have a bodily presence. The following paragraphs will help to warm us up prior to the visualization on embodiment: appreciating our sense of the body and its ability to sustain us.

We sometimes hear the idea that all we need to do is "just show up"—that is, to be authentically engaged with our students requires a sense of simply being present, rather than coming to a classroom loaded with expectations about one's own performance. Describing the importance of presence in education, Miller (2000) notes the importance of treating presence as a discipline and a regular practice: "Working on being an authentic presence to students is probably the most important means of nourishing soul. If students feel heard and affirmed in our presence this will support the development of their souls immeasurably. Being present in the way I am talking about requires effort and discipline. Eventually this discipline brings more of an effortless presence but effort is required in the beginning. Energy is required because our minds are pulled in so many different directions" (p. 141). Now does this mean that a teacher can get by on *no* subject knowledge whatsoever? This is hardly the case, as teachers still need to be subject matter experts. But the idea of "just show up" helps teachers realize the importance of an embodied presence in the classroom. Being able to feel one's body not only provides good information about crucial interactions in the classroom but also allows teachers to ground themselves in the present. *Just show up* is indeed a powerful exhortation and a good reminder of the importance of embodiment.

Many psychologists have pointed out that in spite of the occasional pains that we might experience around our bodies, the body itself can be a simple source of joyful emotion and pleasure. Rick Hanson (2013) notes, "Take the insula, which is continually 'listening' to your body as it tells the brain how it's doing. The central functions of your body are usually doing just fine, even if there are some aches or a wonky digestion. Repeatedly tuning into a mild but pleasant state of physical well-being, such as experiencing that there is plenty of air to breathe, could sensitize your insula to a viscerally important positive experience that is available with each breath" (p. 43). Hanson's passage reminds us that the body is a source of physical well-being that can help teachers slow down and increase their sensitivity to body changes and signals. Quite often, teachers may rush into the lesson plan of a class without taking moments to pause and check in with their bodies. But having a good sense of the body can help teachers to better gauge how their students are absorbing the material that they are presenting, thus altering the pace of a class so that students are in tune with the work and curriculum.

Reflecting on the gift of *embodiment* is twofold. Firstly, through body scan, we come to appreciate the intricacies of the body and how each body part supports each other in mutual harmony. If you have ever examined the internal workings of the human body, you will find that there is a splendid harmonization that happens even when we are performing a relatively simple process like raising our arm. Reflecting on the body is a surefire way not only to feel gratitude for having a body that supports us day-to-day in its functioning but also to sense the interconnectedness of all things, from the minute detail to the most intricate of body designs. Marveling at the complexity of the body also dovetails with the work of Matthew Fox, who asks his readers to reflect deeply on how the body sustains us and has developed over millions of years of evolution into what it is today. Fox (2016) describes seemingly miraculous body processes that sustain us daily, such as the way the skin protects the body from illness or the eyes register immense bits of visual data, in addition to the many chemical reactions that sustain physical and mental health, such as endorphin production. He himself has experienced the marvels of the body when he describes,

> When I went to bed after writing about the muscles and the eyesight and the skin, I lay there before falling asleep thinking how wonderful my body is and how much blessing it has offered me and offered the world—and how wise it is, how little brainpower it requires of me to operate so efficiently and well. It just goes about its job, like so much else in nature. Surely this is the meaning of grace, of unconditional love. I slept more peacefully that night, having ended the day with praise and gratitude. (p. 104)

This visualization can also help us appreciate that the body is not subject to my sole agency, let alone to a single overriding self. When one sincerely contemplates the body as the harmonization of so many interconnected parts, can we even begin to know where the body starts and where it ends? At what point can we really say that the body has an overriding ego or a "driver" who controls all the functions? And here is where we start to realize that there is no overriding sense of self that is holding the whole process together, much less controlling it. It's important, therefore, to become more aware of the body as interconnection of many discrete parts, as a way of counterbalancing the tendency to think of selves as prepackaged "wholes" with clearly defined roles and boundaries.

Perhaps most importantly, meditating on the body's shifting processes can be useful in showing us our commonality with other creatures. I once read a statistic that noted that 99% of human DNA is found in a chimpanzee (Crow, 2002)—meaning that, except for a few minor alterations, our specific genetic arrangements are shared with other species and in fact could be thought of as an iteration of those species' experiences. This reflection on the commonality of all beings can help us to reduce ego-clinging because we are not insisting that we are one special or unique being who is above and beyond others. Instead, all we are in this world is one iteration or *reflection* of all that always was and forever will be. We are not the "ultimate" and nor are we "the evolutionary trash bin." In fact, everything we do is just a reflection of an unfolding process that infinitely mirrors itself in other forms. The value of looking at biology in this way is that it can open us up to a more spiritual way of looking at the body—one that sees the body as not just a mere "thing" but as a very complicated arrangement or design.

To intimately know the body, one must somehow tap into it, but how? One way is through a guided body scan, in which the teacher can be directed to examine all the parts of the body using a relaxed mind and attitude. The guided body scan serves several main functions, foremost of which is to allow greater precision of bodily awareness as well as to improve mindfulness and attention through "systematically sweeping through the body with the mind, bringing an affectionate, openhearted, interested attention to its various regions" (Kabat-Zinn, 2005, p. 250). In the same vein, Kabat-Zinn suggests that the body scan can allow people to "tune in to some of the remarkable anatomical structures, biological functions, and more poetic, metaphorical, and emotional dimensions of the various regions of the body and each region's particular individual history and potential" (p. 251). Another aspect is that it allows the body to truly relax, through an attitude of not indulging scattered thoughts as well as by simply allowing the sensations to arise *as they are* without trying to control or force them to relax. A third aspect is slowing down the awareness to appreciate each part of the body and how it functions. This requires a radical change of perspective, since we are normally pushing our bodies to respond to different situations without realizing the kinds of stresses to which the body is normally subjected. What if all we needed to do, to the contrary, was to tend to the body as it is now, in this moment, without judgment or reservation? In this moment, we don't judge the experience of the body in terms of existing body tropes or discourses that are inscribed within a given culture. Instead, the practice is one of purely experiencing the body. At some point in the process of performing a body scan, one might even start to experience the body as a single, undivided sensation that is not subject to differentiation of parts.

Although direct contemplation might be a positive outcome of practicing the body scan, it's essential that teachers start to develop some specific undiscovered vocabulary of the body, which thus allows them to differentiate between bodily states. Rechtschaffen (2014) refers to learning the "language of the body" as akin to that of learning the language of a foreign country: "Often when I ask students and adults, 'What are you noticing right now in your bodies?' they don't exactly know how to answer. With these embodiment lessons we and our students will learn to identify our physical sensations. We can experience pleasant, unpleasant, and neutral sensations, all of which we can learn to approach with a sense of calm inquiry" (p. 156). Rechtschaffen has developed a guided visualization for students in which he has them "going to take a journey of awareness in the country of our bodies" (p. 158), where "to get around, we need to learn the language of sensations and feelings" (p. 158). By envisioning the body as a foreign country, Rechtscahfen prepares his students to suspend any habitual thoughts or memories they would carry into the experience, including ideas they have about what "works" or "doesn't work" about their bodies. This allows a much less premediated space in which to view the body.

I further suggest with this visualization that meditating on the body can generate gratitude if we are aware of how the body supports us day-to-day. One way of tapping into gratitude is by looking more deeply at how the body cooperates to bring about one's survival. What kind of work does the body need to do to survive? Isaac Asimov's (1992) delightful book on the human body is one thorough examination of how body parts work together to keep people alive. Although the book delves considerably into the common *ailments* that afflict the body, Asimov is quick to point out how his descriptions paint a picture of a resilient structure that is surprisingly immune to the common stresses of life. Comparing the body to an automobile, he notes, "The automobile, the largest and most intricate machine most of us deal with directly on a regular basis, is considered ancient if it lasts ten years, despite the manufacturers' claims that new technology has made it more efficient and dependable. Compare it to the human body that is far more fragile, less amenable to repair, and subject to infinitely greater and more considerable difficulties and yet can last 100 years or more" (pp. 309–310). One way of framing this in terms of gratitude is to marvel at the way the body itself is working hard to keep human beings alive, whether waking or sleeping. In spite of its fragility and resistance to easy repair, human bodies are capable of sustaining a great deal of input and activities. But there is a different kind of gratitude that emerges when we start to recognize that the body is not a permanent entity. Despite its resilience and the many years of evolution that made it what it is today, human bodies are subject to decay and impermanence, which make them even more precious to behold during the time in which we are able to sustain our health. Sheng Yen (2008) suggests that the body can be a great tool through which people can contemplate the impermanence of all being: "The body is constantly going through changes, so when you experience physical discomfort or pleasure, there is no fixed nature to that feeling. After some time it will pass. The physical body also feeds hunger, thirst, and other sensations. All of these are also transient and they too will change along with the body" (p. 8). Sheng Yen further suggests that "becoming keenly aware of the body's changeable nature and inevitable decay will help us be less attached to it. We can free ourselves from its limitations or restraints; we can become more detached from its workings, motions, and sensations" (p. 9). Sheng Yen suggests that bodily impermanence is one way of becoming less attached to cherishing the body or perceiving it to have a fixed and permanent nature.

Are these two ways of beholding the body—appreciating its resilience and contemplating its inevitable decay—incompatible with each other? I believe that, as suggested in this book, gratitude rests in the tension between cherishing something as a gift and letting it pass to something else, which is the cycle of receiving and gifting that undergirds the gift economy. To appreciate the gift is to be aware of its strengths while contextualizing it as subject to the forces of the natural world that lead it to pass into other hands and paths. Just as the body can be appreciated for how it can function in a stressful world, so it must also be appreciated in the context of inevitable disease to which it is privy. Without this sense of impermanence, the body would be considered something static and eternal.

Visualization on the Body as a Gift

Sit in a comfortable position. Make sure your spine is straight and your feet are fully planted. Take a moment to scan your body, starting with the top of your head. Feel the muscles in the temples and forehead. Feel the muscles in your eyes. There is no need to push yourself to relax. Just be aware of each sensation and tell yourself that it's ok to feel the sensations just as they are, without giving any judgment to these sensations. Allow yourself to marvel at and appreciate all the nuanced muscles and tissues that are working together to create the sensations you are feeling.

Continue to scan the body, from the facial muscles, cheeks, and jaw. Allow your jaw to hang down a little without opening your mouth. Feel where the head connects to the neck, and where the neck gently borders into the shoulders.

If the shoulders feel too arched, you can gently roll the shoulders. Continue down to the chest. Notice how the chest is feeling before proceeding to the stomach, then the abdomen. Feel the spine from where it meets the neck all the way down to the base where it meets the pelvis. Visualize all the muscles in the chain of the spine, supporting the spine and ensuring that your upper body is erect. Appreciate the work that the muscles in the vertebrae are doing to keep the upper body as straight as possible.

Continue to scan the lower parts of the body, starting from the waist, the thighs, the knees. Notice how these parts of the body feel. Feel the energy of the body sinking down into the lower extremities, along with the sinking sense of gravity. Feel the calf muscles, ankles, and feet. Appreciate how the lower parts of the body have been able to support your whole body throughout your life.

Consider all the ways your body provides you what you need to teach and connect with your students.

Take a moment to consider the breath and how the lungs are able to take in the oxygen needed to keep the body and brain functioning and alive. Stay there for a moment and appreciate it.

Consider the circulation of the blood, and how the heart pumps blood throughout the body. Consider how your digestive system naturally functions to convert the food you eat into the energy needed to teach your students.

Consider the kidneys and how they work hard every moment to deliver waste away from the body and thereby prevent toxins from entering the bloodstream.

Consider the nervous system and how it carries signals to and from the brain to deliver vital information and execute various vital functions.

Consider the body as a totality. The body is operating 24 hours a day, performing many complex functions independently of a controlling self or a will. Feel a natural sense of gratitude for all these functions of the body and what they do to enable us to effectively teach. Even if one or more of these parts of the body are not functioning optimally or functioning at all, consider the ways in which most of the body still continues to function the way it needs to.

Think of this body as a temporary gift. Consider that the processes of the body are subject to change over time, and this body will function only in the span in which we live. Be thankful for the journey this body of yours has made from birth until the present moment, without our having to force it to work or choose it to work. This body, like a close friend, has been with us since the very beginning, yet we sometimes forget the body in our moments of stress, worry, overthinking, or work. Take a moment to thank your body and simply use your awareness to receive the body's signals as a totality in this present moment.

Now consider your bodily presence in the classroom. Appreciate the way the body enters the classroom—how simply being embodied in itself allows us to be physically present with our students, available for their questions, available for their learning. Consider how your body serves the complex functions of teaching, demonstrating, coaching, and mentoring. Consider the ways the nervous system responds to multilayered, complex inputs from the environment and allows for deliberation and interaction. What would teaching be like without a body? Would teaching be possible? What happens when we are not "with" our body or fail to appreciate the body when teaching?

Now consider all your students in the classroom, whether in person or online. We often refer to the classroom colloquially as the student body, *but have we ever considered the individual bodies of our students? Contemplate how each student comes to the classroom with their own unique embodiments, feeling states, moods, and sensations. Consider the efforts that their bodies are making to arrive at the classroom. Consider the miracle of the body—how it allows both student and teacher to interact with each other, to be fully present in the same space, to inhabit the world, to draw from the resources of the world and create new things from it. Consider the body as the container through which our thoughts and creations interface with one another, albeit for a brief period. Consider all the bodies in your classroom, including yours, as a unique and special gift.*

Visualization No. 2: The Classroom as a Gift Body

As mentioned in the previous visualization, the classroom itself has often been conceptualized as a kind of body—one that, like the human body, consists of many interrelated connections. Christopher Bache (2008) has envisioned the "living classroom" as a kind of energy that students attend to continuously. This is one way of seeing the classroom as a dynamic and flowing process in which gifts are exchanged across different identities, relationships, and communities. When we start to envision the class as a collective whole, individuals are no longer striving against each other but are actively contributing to the entirety. This also suggests the metaphor of the classroom as an ecosystem.

It's perhaps not a surprise that the body becomes an apt metaphor for how teachers interact and coexist with their students in the classroom. Describing the indispensable role of the embodied teacher in the classroom,

Selwyn (2019) remarks, "The bodies of human teachers are an invaluable resource when engaging learners in abstract thought. Teachers use their bodies to energize, orchestrate, and order the performance of teaching. Many subtleties of teaching take place through movement, such as pacing around a room, pointing and gesturing. Teachers make use of this 'expressive body'—lowering their voice, raising an eyebrow or directing their gaze" (p. 114). According to Selwyn, the teacher's embodiment becomes indispensable for the communication of important ideas and concepts in the classroom. Classrooms truly embody concepts not only through their physical presence and gestures but also through the kinds of values and beliefs they are actively exuding. As Schumacher (1973) reminds his readers, it's vital that ideas and values invite participation rather than estrangement: "When a thing is intelligible you have a sense of participation; when a thing is unintelligible you have a sense of estrangement. 'Well, I don't know,' you hear people say, as an impotent protest against the unintelligibility of the world as they meet it. If the mind cannot bring to the world a set—or, shall we way, a toolbox—of powerful ideas, the world must appear to it as a chaos, a mass of unrelated phenomena, of meaningless events" (p. 89). This is one way of suggesting that without a sense of active participation in some shared way of being, the facts that are acquired in education are quite abstract or even meaningless. But it also suggests that classrooms are not arranged from a top-down model. Instead, they are immersive experiences that require the active participation of many students with their diverse needs and energies. No single teacher or student can embody the "perfect" pedagogical situation, since learning is a going affair that involves a constant interaction of unexpected and even mysterious forces that cannot be completely controlled or predicted.

Related to the classroom body metaphor are musical metaphors, which compare classrooms to musical compositions or arrangements involving multiple participants. Educator Patricia Jennings (2015) uses the metaphor of *orchestration* to describe how she manages classroom dynamics, especially when relations between teacher and students are often not in accordance with a preexisting plan:

> Each of these [classroom] elements has dynamics. My speech can be soft or loud, calm or harsh. I can move slowly or quickly. I can stand up, or I can sit down on a chair or the floor. The classroom can be bright or dark. I can arrange the furniture in ways that feel cramped or spacious . . . I like to imagine that the

art of arranging these elements is like musical orchestration. A composer skillfully combines sound elements and their dynamic qualities to create the beautiful sounds we call music. When we are mindful of the elements of the classroom that we can control, we can, like a composer, orchestrate these elements to create the optimal conditions for learning. (p. 139)

Jennings makes several interesting connections in this passage. One is the idea that teachers are not totally *in control* of the classroom but can nonetheless influence individual components, in much the same way that a conductor orchestrates music. The second is the care in which teachers can invest in the arrangement of the classroom without necessarily anticipating a fixed outcome. *Arranging* a classroom is thus framed as a holistic art that involves the orchestration of many details, essentially composing the experience of a classroom. At the same time, the orchestration does not entail that the students must behave in a certain way or reciprocate on the care provided. Teachers can put great care and intentionality into the design of the classroom yet still remain aware that the outcome is never going to be exactly as planned. Jennings points to the intriguing possibility of what a gifting mentality can contribute to the classroom, especially when there is no fixed expectation of an exchange or a set arrangement that must be dogmatically followed. This is similar to the ways in which we invest care in our health but are not necessarily in control of whether we remain healthy or not. The body is subject to many variables that need to be accounted for, but with a spirit of moderation.

Many meditation practices position the body as naturally extending to the environment. There is often a noted tendency to treat the body as something that is separate from the outside world. However, with more subtle stages of meditation, we can come to see the body and environment as inseparable. One example of a meditation approach found in Chan Buddhism is silent illumination, which proceeds in stages, starting with awareness of the body and extending outward to see the body and environment as one. In the first stage of silent illumination, "one simply maintains an awareness of the whole body sitting there. Eventually, body and mind become one—your awareness is of the total body rather than its separate parts" (Sheng Yen, 2008, p. 17). However, as the practice deepens and the mind becomes clearer, "the body, mind and environment become one—internal and external are united" (p. 17). What does this entail? According to Sheng Yen, the boundary between the body and environment naturally dissolves because the environment is perceived as "your great body," which "no longer disturbs you or stirs up wandering thoughts" (p. 17). The "silent" aspect of this practice consists in the ability for the mind to remain unperturbed by the environment and body, while the "illumination" refers to the ability to maintain clarity regarding all the surroundings. The crispness of awareness that results comes from a still and calm mind, as well as the ability to see things as part of a larger totality without being overly attached to them.

Visualization of the Classroom as a Body

Sit in a comfortable position. Relax from head to toe just as in the previous visualization. Make sure your body is completely at ease and is as comfortable as possible.

Consider the fact that as you enter the classroom, you are deeply connecting to a shared body of wisdom, knowledge, community, and love. Also reflect that there are many things within the classroom that truly lie within your influence. Consider the minute details that can add quality and value to the teaching experience, including the lighting, temperature, room setup, space, and other related factors. Reflect on how these elements can create a safe place where students can be comfortable while learning. The detail and planning put into the classroom is truly an act of intention and care that involves the subtle orchestration of small steps. Even the plants in the classroom can add to an atmosphere and tone that can contribute to the unfolding experience of teaching and learning. Like the food, exercise, clothing, and sleep that we use to take care of our bodies, consider the ways in which we actively nurture the classroom with elements of mindfulness, compassion, and care.

Think about what happens when the body becomes ill or there are imbalances in the body. What do we do to take care of ourselves and ensure the recovery of our health? Are we harsh toward our bodies, or do we make small changes to ensure that the body can readjust and heal? How does the body become healthy again? Then reflect: Are there elements of the classroom that can sometimes seem disharmonious, out of balance, and contrastive? Consider that, like the living human body, the classroom is subject to moments of disharmony and chaos, and many different experiences make up that classroom experience.

Begin to regard the classroom as a body that needs continual maintenance and care—one that is naturally subject to unpredictability and turmoil. Yet, at the same time, also reflect on how resilient this classroom body is. Reflect on the gifts that all students bring to the classroom, big or small, that contribute to the health of the classroom body.

Consider the classroom body as not limited to a single semester but as continuing over time. All the shared wisdom and love of the classroom does not go away, but instead lingers in the spaces and walls of the classroom, permeating every nook and cranny. Consider how, like the body, the classroom preserves memories and lives on in the form of new awakenings and growth.

The classroom body, like your body, is a miraculous orchestration of many parts. Consider the caring ways that you protect the classroom through even the simplest gestures or preparations.

Visualization No. 3: Embracing Challenge, Difficulty, and the Tragic as Gifts

In many situations, people tend to think of gifts as positive or joyful in nature. Who would, after all, give a gift that is painful or evokes tragedy and loss? If taken literally, the gift metaphor might tend to restrict people to only focus on positive or pleasurable things as gifts, rather than embracing every moment as a potential or actual gift. Along these lines, people rarely consider illness or pain to be "true gifts." Instead, they seek uplifting experiences and refer to these as gifts. Yet, as Tulku Thondup (2000) suggests, objects and situations can become gifts exactly insofar as we invest in them with new ways of thinking, as well as endow positive energy into them. In describing the healing benefits of visualization meditations, he notes,

> Mental objects help us to heal, not because of the power of the images and words themselves but because of our minds' power to see those images and words as positive. It can be very healing to understand the truth of this. When we realize that true healing power lies in our own minds, that realization can bring us strong confidence. By knowing that we all have buddha nature, we become more confident about our inner resources. We gain the ability to be more peaceful in our minds. (p. 51)

While Thondup refers specifically to the notion of buddha nature as expounded in Buddhism, other spiritual practices have similarly adopted the notion of an intrinsic peacefulness and sense of worth that is not tied to the outside world and circumstances. Through a fundamental faith in the inherent goodness of things, which is often symbolized through the metaphor of ocean and waves, Thondup articulates how "we should remember that all things are perfect in their nature and that turmoil is like stormy waves on a deep blue ocean" (p. 49).

Can teachers embrace difficulties, or even difficult students, as gifts? Thondup suggests that when people are not bound or dependent on external things, they are able to see gifts in the very fact of being, which spills over to objects themselves. In one vignette, he describes how one of his friends was able to reframe a debilitating illness as an opportunity or a challenge. In one sense, seeing the inherent goodness in all things, regardless of their stature or their place in the universe, is one way to frame all things as gifts. But, in the absence of this ability, we can also see that all situations, no matter how dire or dark, can hold opportunities for growth and improvement. At the very least, difficult situations can end up teaching us the values of patience and resilience, provided that we are able to approach these situations as opportunities for spiritual practice rather than as obstacles or impediments.

When it comes to classrooms, how might challenges be seen in a positive light? One way is to frame experience in terms of an ecological system of balances, in which all experiences, emotional states, and phenomena have their own unique value in the "ecology" of the mind. If a teacher can see the different states of their mind in the classroom as having equal validity, they will experience a deeper inner harmony, in which all emotional states occupy a natural place without upsetting the other states. In this way, even when the teacher is upset about a student's behavior, they become less conflicted about this mood state and can value it equally alongside other emotional states and thoughts. One consequence of this view is that each student is accorded a special place in the ecology of the classroom, and therefore there is no such thing as a valueless contribution. Indigenous scholar Arlo Starr (2020) describes the impact of an Indigenous worldview in which all beings have a sacred and irreplaceable role to play in the scheme of all things: "In Indigenous thought, everyone and everything is of value already, on its own it doesn't need a dollar amount attached to it to be worth something. . . . What does this do to a child's self-esteem to understand that from the very beginning everyone is valuable, has a place in things, and plays a vital role in keeping balance?" (p. 147). Cultivating an ecological view of both situations and emotions is one way of allowing for the celebration of diverse thoughts and feelings, none of which really and truly conflict with one another because they are fundamentally allowed to coexist within the same mind and heart. At heart, such a view allows for the possibility of coexisting energies that may vie for our attention but can in fact exist within the same mind. Timothy Miller (1995) refers to the ability to allow for differences of priorities to be the foundation for compassion when he writes, "Compassion is the intention to think and act as if you are no more entitled to get what you want than anyone else is. This intention is based on the conscious understanding that everyone wants about the same things for about the same reasons. Almost all human desires arise from similar instinctive sources" (p. 98).

What are the implications of this view? One of the radical implications is that teachers and students have equally viable goals in the classroom. Even when teachers are leading a classroom, they do so with the understanding that their students are coming into the classroom with their own identities and their own desire for happiness. Miller further writes that when one sees compassion in this way, "The assertion that another person is bad, wrong, weak, lazy, ugly, or stupid is just a disguised assertion that you are more entitled to get what you want than he is" (p. 99). This comment suggests that judgments are based on a misguided belief that one is more entitled than the other to success and happiness.

Equipped with the idea that *all* students have equally valid goals and ideals, how might teachers shape their classrooms and responses to students? For one, teachers can let go of the notion that the only goal is what is set up in the classroom rubric. Teachers can start to recognize their students as unique individuals whose goals are unique and may, as such, create challenges through conflicting goals or viewpoints. Nonetheless, acknowledging the validity of these goals is one way to make space for them and see them as an important part of the teacher's journey.

GUIDED VISUALIZATION: SEEING THE UNCHANGING JOYFULNESS IN ALL

Sit in a comfortable position. Relax from head to toe just as in the previous visualization. Make sure your body is completely at ease and is as comfortable as possible. Contemplate a particular aspect of the classroom, or the student body, that seems challenging or problematic. Visualize what that challenge is. What does this challenge feel like in the body? Does it feel still, dull, sharp? Try to get a sense of what sensations arise and from where. Start to become aware of the sensations in the body as you are experiencing this problematic situation. Rather than trying to resist that situation or mentally fix it, try to lean into the challenge by allowing yourself to feel the difficulty nonjudgmentally. Know that experiencing the pain of the situation won't harm you. You are allowed to let that response reside within you without having to do anything about it, much less judge yourself for having it.

Now consider: by resting into your response to the situation or problem instead of acting on it immediately, how do you feel? When you are not separated from the emotion, perhaps you will begin to befriend the emotion itself, knowing that it is continually changing and even coexists alongside other emotions. The student who doesn't do their work isn't always a troublemaker; the one who comes late for class is not always a nuisance. In fact, the troubling energy can be a way to keep the classroom on its toes, and invites creativity or newness. Your own relationship with that student is not necessarily bad. In fact, it can be a way of helping you to innovate your teaching to become more inclusive of that student, as well as develop patience and a simple trust that the class will not be broken as a result of the conflicts you are experiencing. In this way, you can recognize the complexity of both your emotions and your students'. In addition, take a moment to honor the fact that your understanding and experience of another cannot be reduced to a single emotion, no matter how intensely it happens to feel in the moment.

Consider this problem as a gift in the sense that you are learning to negotiate the feelings of separation that might have arisen from your previous responses and reactions to it. By pushing a difficult problem aside, you may have created an expansive divide between yourself and that problem that presumably resides "out there." But does that problem really exist as a separate entity from yourself?

Now consider: these challenges are inseparable from my unfolding being. They are there to help me grow and are not meant to be antagonistic to my being. When I stop dualistically separating my individual self from the challenges I face in my classroom, I can embrace these challenges as literally an inseparable part of the journey. I can accept these challenges and have a basic trust that they are gifts for my growth as a teacher.

Visualization No. 4: Presence as a "Present"

What if presence were the *only* prerequisite for good teaching? Although this seems counterintuitive, it certainly challenges the anxiety that teachers sometimes feel when faced with an unpredictable and variable classroom situation. How much of the teaching relationship is indeed *planned*, per se, and which parts truly require the intervention of a teaching outline?

One of the reasons presence is an important component in a teacher's sense of self-worth is that it reminds teachers of the many resources at their fingertips, including the very body itself that they use to teach. At the very least, being present constitutes what Vanessa Rodriguez refers to as "spinal cord teaching" or a kind of teaching where "teachers activate their sensing limbs to gather information that will advise their response." Here, "teachers respond directly to the observed learner's behavior or respond based on their own teacher-driven goal" (Rodriguez & Fitzpatrick, 2014, p. 86). What these passages suggest is that certain forms of basic teaching require very little planning and may only require the sense of interaction that is basic to even animals. However rudimentary this form of teaching happens to be, it contains hardwired elements of establishing rapport that don't require extensive thought or reflection. It is so basic to being that it sometimes only requires the opportunity for interaction itself. This interaction is already an inherent part of the teaching relationship, and thus defines all being.

Sometimes, when I am about to teach my primary school students, I am struck by the dilemma of knowing that not everything I teach can cater to the immediate learning needs of the students. The lesson plan constantly needs to be modified and adapted, particularly as young minds tend to waver or change in their interest levels and learning patterns. "Teaching," in these instances, must first involve establishing a caring and authentic presence with the students, for instance, by starting with an ice-breaking question that relates somewhat to the topic at hand. Here I am not so much interested in the quality of answers I receive from the students as I am by the sense of genuinely wanting to engage the students where they are. But this also requires that I bring my own curiosity to the table. During my lesson on Roald Dahl's *George's Marvelous Medicine*, which humorously describes how George makes a medicine to deal with his belligerent grandmother, I began by asking the students whether they have tried experiments at home, what their parents said about these experiments, and whether the outcome of the experiment matched with what the students were expecting from it. Now, while these questions do relate somewhat to the theme and situations of the book, the point is not to test the students' reading comprehension or even to explore themes of the book. The intention is more to draw out students' already existing knowledge and experience that is based on elements of experimentation and play—all key features of a students' experience that are not necessarily planned. This then allows students to feel that they indeed know a great deal about the subject matter even before accessing the details of the book, in addition to engaging the students in what they know.

Presence is of course not the only prerequisite to being a teacher. However, the ability to acknowledge the value of being present, even when one doesn't always know what will happen in the classroom, is an important characteristic and quality of feeling that one has many gifts to share in the classroom.

Visualization on Presence as a "Present"

Picture yourself as fully present in your classroom. Get rid of all distractions and discover how your presence is a gift. Imagine your body standing in front of the classroom. Imagine your whole demeanor and how positive it can be to simply acknowledge the unique moment in which you are standing here in this world, in this moment and not in any other moment. Honor the fact that you inhabit this world from the unique vantage point of your own experiences, past, and history. Your present is the culmination of many rich and complex experiences that only you can fully see, hear, feel, touch, and be aware of.

Imagine that even when you are scared, apprehensive, unable to see how to manage the classroom situation, that all this is contained within your body. Your body is an expansive, singular whole that can house a plethora of different emotions, often conflicting or contradictory to one another yet all contained in one whole. Imagine that your body is an endless vista of space. No matter what emotions flow in and out of it, that space remains what it is, and there is no affecting of one emotion or the other. The body and mind can both infinitely contain all the emotions without any conflict or contradiction.

Tell yourself that you are all you need in this moment. All you have is embodied within you, and you are able to face the class fully equipped and prepared to be with your students. Remind yourself that no matter how dire or negative a situation may seem, you have experienced many situations in the past that have prepared you for this moment. Take a moment to appreciate all the ways in which your present moment is the culmination of a long and rich journey and process. Realize the gifts you have that allow you to handle the difficulties no matter what they happen to be.

Visualization No. 5: Seeing Plenitude in All

The idea of plenitude dates back to philosophies that invoke abundance in all things. Early Christian writers such as Aquinas and Augustine imagined a chain of being that a creator being has populated with all number of beings in the universe. The principle of plenitude, as stated in Lovejoy's *Great Chain of Being*, suggests an idea popular in the Middle Ages, that a creator being was made as perfectly good and beneficent. However, to truly be beneficent, this creator had to create a gradation of beings that, even when they suffer *privation* of the good, complement each other in creating an overall picture of the good. Several points come out of this powerful analogy. The first is that of abundance and being able to accommodate many disparate elements in one unified whole—a point that many philosophers have wrestled with throughout history (Huxley, 1931). The confidence suggested in this metaphor of multiplicity is that all experiences, no matter how diverse and fecund, lead up to the same eternal principle of the good, no matter how disparate those elements happen to be. It could be argued that the creator according to this metaphor is the stillness that lies within creation, since this creator being is thought to be so self-sufficient that it doesn't even need its creations to "complete it." On the other hand, it can also be said that the creations are pointing to the creator because they are imminently *part of* (though not *identical to*) the creator. Again, what does this vision of life attempt to do? I believe it attempts to resolve one of the deepest existential questions, which is, Why are there so many things in the world? Would the world not have been self-sufficient with just one being? The tension between one and many is what Aldous Huxley, in his essay "One and Many" (1931), refers to as a major philosophical problem that many throughout the ages have wrestled with in some form or another: "Every man tries to pretend that he is consistently one kind of person, and does his best consistently to worship one kind of God. And this despite the fact that he experiences diversity and actually feels himself in contact with a variety of divinities (or at any rate with extremely dissimilar aspects of the same Unknown God who may be presumed to lie beneath them all)" (p. 2). Huxley suggests that rather than trying to reduce the world to a single principle, it's best to cultivate a perspective that continually includes and accommodates diversity in its many forms. This allows many phenomena or mental states to exist simultaneously within the same self instead of being repressed or pushed into the background. As Huxley later suggests, the tension between "one" and "many" within the same being needs to be reconciled.

> If I were wholly diverse—a mere succession in time of unconnected states—I should obviously inhabit a wholly diverse universe, in which instant succeeded discrete instant, event followed causeless and resultless event, incoherently. If, on the contrary, I were a simple perfected unity, my world would be as simply perfect as the universe inhabited by a stone. That is to say, it would be non-existent, since I myself would have no consciousness either of my own or of any other existence. (Huxley, 1931, p. 12)

Now, how might this be a consoling vision of life? Why would people gravitate to this? In fact, it suggests that plenitude actually is a constant reminder of stillness. It addresses the existential anxiety that people feel: living in a world of so many different beings, how can anything or anyone be in harmony? Living in a fast-paced, accelerated world, one starts to believe that they are trying to grasp at things that are constantly floating away. But the principle of plenitude suggests that, contrary to being chaotic, the world does in fact possess a hidden or latent order and harmony, when looked at from a certain distance without getting drawn into the details of experience. From this perspective, all emotions, people, situations, and so on can harmonize. This is where the still center complements the principle of plenitude, by calmly (and non-enviously) *allowing* all things to emerge and thus form their own self-justified place in the universe.

One of the comforting insights about the principle of plenitude is the idea that the world and our place in it is deeply completed and all beings belong within it. Two ideas that form pillars of this concept are that the creator cherishes and allows for all levels of existence, which implies the mutual coexistence of all levels and layers of being, and that all possible beings have an equal value and right to exist, which reverberates with Indigenous philosophies of education and the natural universe. In Buddhism, the notion of *sunyata*, or emptiness, is rife with a plentiful harmony, in which all thoughts are mutually harmonious because they are not in direct contact with each other; nor do they, by implication, become enmeshed with each other. In other words, there is a natural harmony that arises when the mind does not confuse or conflate different phenomena, or forms of being in the world. A good example of this is the ecosystem, in which species must rely on each other for their own existence. Because humans cling to the notion of their own species and the resources required to be comfortable and fulfill their desires, they may tend to neglect the right for other species to exist as well. The notion of sunyata suggests that all beings depend on other beings, which suggests the value of interconnection. Notes Thich Nhat Hanh (2017),

> We can observe emptiness and interbeing everywhere in our daily life. If we look at a child, it's easy to see the child's mother and father, grandmother and grandfather, in her. The way she looks, the way she acts, the things she says. Even her skills and talents are the same as her parents'. If at times we cannot understand why the child is acting in a certain way, it is helpful to remember that she is not a separate self-entity. She is a *continuation*. Her

parents and ancestors are inside her. When she walks and talks, they walk and talk as well. (pp. 13–14)

Contrary to some understandings of the word "emptiness," this concept does not entail an absence or negation. Instead, it refers to the infinite potentiality and mutual enfolding of all things, precisely because all are interacting in a cosmic dance with no beginning or end.

Plenitude is not an easy quality to cultivate if one is attached to fixed ways of being or to rigid notions of value and worth. In schools, the pressures that pre-service teachers may face in trying to meet excessively high demands can sometimes encourage teachers to limit their identities to fixed roles. This limits people to cultivating relationships that are based on results and controlling others or influencing others to fulfill an underlying desire for order. Neuroscientist Judson Brewer (2017) distinguishes between the grasping mindset that is often associated with addictive behavior with a softer and more playful openness to interaction that is relaxed and expansive in nature:

> The mode of subjective experience that lined up with PCC [posterior cingulate cortex] activity—not perception of an object but how we relate to it. In a sense, if we try to control a situation (or our lives), we have to work hard at *doing* something to get the results we want. In contrast, we can relax into an attitude that is more like a dance with the object, simply *being* with it as the situation unfolds, no striving, or struggling necessary, as we get out of our own way and rest in an awareness of what is happening moment to moment. (p. 111)

Brewer points to the possibility that plenitude might involve loosening the grasp that we have on objects that we crave or wish to avoid, in favor of a more diffuse experience of the totality that is in all things. If there is a single theme that has reverberated throughout this book, it's that a sense of plenitude can result in a more relaxed universalism, rather than using spiritual practices to overcome what we think of as bad or destructive tendencies. Gratitude can only authentically arise when people recognize that they are one *among others*, and these others extend infinitely both within and outside. This vision of life, if taken to heart, can mitigate a sense of loneliness, despair, or alienation that comes from the view that only select few are deserving of respect and love in the universe.

Guided Visualization: Seeing Plenitude in All

Take a moment to close your eyes and scan the body, from head to toe. You may want to focus on the sensations of one part of the body or the diffuse body as a whole. Pay attention to the changing sensations of the body. If there is a particular part of the body that is tense or uncomfortable, observe whether that tension changes in the body or stays the same over time. Observe how the sensations of the body are in a state of flux. Even something that seems stubbornly persistent is actually an agglomeration of different kinds of sensations, feelings, thoughts, and so on. Something that seems to be really solid and enduring, such as the pain in the back or legs, may then turn out to be immaterial and transient or fleeting. Be aware of the changing flow of the body and the ideas that are solidified around that flow.

When you are fully aware of the body's changing sensations, start to marvel at the complexity of the body itself. The body is not, after all, a single thing that stays the same over time. In fact, many kinds of sensations and emotions run through the body at any given time: sad, happy, angry, anxious, and so on. Marvel at the ability for the body to harbor such an acute sensitivity that has allowed it to survive and even evolve over time, as feelings solidify into body memories. The body itself is a site of plenitude; feelings, memories, sensations, and processes are all happening without one's conscious control. Take a moment to appreciate the impermanence of this flux. Recognize that even when certain sensations and thoughts have solidified into habits, this does not mean that there is a self or an identity abiding in those thoughts and energy habits. These feelings and thoughts are continually changing.

Now visualize the classroom that you are about to enter. See the students and come to appreciate how they are together. Are all the students working in unison, or do they function in different ways? Do they always harmonize, or is there room for discord? Consider the classroom as a wide space in which a vast plenitude of thoughts, feelings, phenomena, and so on are coalescing and disappearing again, to form still newer thoughts at a later time. Know that none of these things are "you" nor are they permanent. Why take one of these as the definitive classroom experience, when in fact, there is a whole plurality of different perspectives or experiences to choose from?

Recognize that change itself is a gift. Without change, there could be no learning, no challenge, and, ultimately, no real growth. While change entails inevitable losses of what we most cherish, change can also challenge teachers not to cling to tried-and-true, fixed ways of doing things. It can make teachers more open to innovative and untried ways of teaching as well as explore the spaces where new things can be tried. In the midst of change, there are endless possibilities that come through in the way students respond to assignments. No two students handle an assignment or even interpret the meaning and purpose of an assignment in the same way. Yet rather than seeing this as a form of discord, perhaps we can envision plenitude as a sign of the creativity of the classroom.

Visualization No. 6: The Gift of Endless Learning

As teachers, we might want to ask ourselves, Is learning considered a gift? Or are we more focused on the results than on the process of learning? Are we able to enjoy the simple process of teaching and learning as real dynamics, full of change and uncertainty, or are we more content to focus only on test results?

Learning is often a very difficult task with no guarantees. Sometimes, a teacher can be teaching one book that seems engaging to students, only to find that in one particular classroom, the same book fails to inspire the students. Teachers may find themselves wondering what makes the difference between one classroom being successful and another classroom finding no success at all. Do some theories of learning sometimes collude with the idea that learning should always be an *uphill curve*, both for students and teachers alike? The idea that learning is an uphill curve (or what we sometimes call the "learning curve") certainly dovetails with a technical perspective of learning that focuses on isolating variables that impede learning and reinforcing those variables that facilitate learning. However, what is left out here is the value that seeming failure or non-doing can play in the actual learning process. I will explore the notions of failure and non-doing in the next sections.

Failure as Endless Learning

The word "failure" is perhaps one of the most emotionally charged ones in education, most certainly because we are conditioned from a very early age to associate failure with negative reinforcements, such as the threat of punishment if we don't achieve a certain passing mark. "Pass" or "fail," in fact, are synonymous with a dualistic notion where some students are said to pass muster and others fall below the bar—both of which evoke metaphors of upward and downward mobility. Failure is considered not only undesirable but even morally reprehensible, as when teachers and parents attribute failure to a lack of effort or interest in subjects that are thought to matter in a student's life and success. So, is it any wonder that adults might find themselves in the position of trying to ward off the fear of failure? Avoiding failure—or, in the case of teachers, having to fail a student—might consist of deliberately *lowering the bar* so that students don't need to face excessive challenges to achieving a passing grade. Conversely, it might involve a "cram" mentality of forcing students to study strenuously so that they are able to meet high stakes testing standards. In both cases, an obsession with failure can lead to blaming the student or even attributing instances of failure to low intelligence or personal incompetencies. There is a whole psychoanalysis that could be written simply about the sense of failure and what people do to avoid it. Implicit to the wish to avoid failure is the inherent belief that failure is always unequivocally bad. But is failing to prepare for an exam sufficiently really an absolute failure, or is it a learning experience that can teach us how to better prepare in the future? In science, seemingly failed experiments could be reframed as opportunities to revisit a scientist's inherent assumptions about the efficacy of certain procedures. In fact, without a tolerance for failure, scientists may simply play it safe and form no hypothesis that risks being proven incorrect or based on faulty presumptions. I would argue that it is only through the testing of assumptions in real-world situations that one can even expose its potential shortcomings of faults. Without a wide-open space through which to experiment, it's impossible to truly discern which of our assumptions are failures and which are successful, at least for the moment.

Could failure be seen as an endless opportunity rather than as a burden—in fact, more so as a *gift* rather than as a punishment? If we take a moment to think about failures and gifts, we might notice that there are many striking parallels. For one, both gifts and failures are unexpected and often seem to come from factors beyond a student's control or influence. While failures may not seem as "well thought out" as a thoughtful gift, people may be surprised to find that failures are often the result of a diligent and thoughtful application of an idea or principle, only one that simply lacks coherence with the way situations actually unfold. A failure, like a gift, can be predicated on effort and thoughtfulness, even if the result in both cases is not to the recipient's liking (in this case, a teacher evaluating a student's performance, or a *receiver* of gifts). I think in these cases, teachers need to take the lead in redefining what failure might constitute by showing students that it's perfectly natural for them to operate from their own assumptions—that in fact assumptions are a key part of navigating life's battles, and having assumptions that prove faulty is not a crime or a terrible thing. This can also entail not "calling out" a student who is operating from an assumption (as though assuming is wrong), but more so encouraging students to explore their assumptions using a Socratic approach that is based on curiosity.

NON-DOING AS ENDLESS LEARNING

Learning is often characterized as result-oriented and, therefore, measured by doing. This is problematic. After all, are there not periods in which we learn without necessarily being able to see instant results? As long as students are only rewarded for their test scores, learning will continue to be associated with observable behaviors, which overlooks the role of reflection in deep learning. In addition, there are sometimes incubation periods that presage real learning (Gilhooly, 2016). Many studies are currently even suggesting that periods of non-doing and even boredom are absolutely essential to doing creative work. Boredom allows the mind to refresh rather than constantly trying to stimulate itself in order to receive instant gratification.

VISUALIZATION ON ENDLESS LEARNING

Visualization 1

Reflect on a time when you felt challenged or didn't think your students were learning according to the class plan or the way that you would expect them to learn. Think about times when students came to you confused, or they misunderstood the intention of an assignment.
    Take a moment to relate to the confusion or lack of coherence and clarity, both on your part and on the students'. You might want to try to locate that sense of confusion somewhere in the body such as through knitted brows or tension in the forehead. Then reflect on how the confusion was clarified. Was it a conversation with the student that helped clarify the confusion? Was it perhaps an email correspondence that led to the resolution of the confusion? Reflect deeply on how the confusion yielded to a deeper understanding or perhaps a changed view about how the assignment or instructions could have been communicated. Breathe in gratitude for the opportunity to change the lesson plan in accordance with new feedback or information provided by the student. Reflect on how each misunderstanding actually added depth or nuance by revealing a new side of the assignment itself. Realize how even mistakes or failures end up being stepping stones on the way to deepened assignment design.

Visualization 2

Imagine a student with whom you have experienced difficulty over the years. Was there a particular student who seemed so challenging to you that they almost led you to give up teaching altogether? Reflect on what this felt like. Try to locate the feeling as a specific sensation of the body, such as a heaviness or tension.

Then reflect on how, if at all, you were able to resolve the difficulty with this student. Did the student help you become more determined as a teacher? Did they help you resolve feelings of inner failure or inadequacy? How did this experience help you realize that you could survive a difficult student and still maintain the ability to teach, from one semester to the next? Think of all the subtle ways in which difficult students may have gifted you to learn and transform in entirely new ways.

Visualization No. 7: Carrying Forward the Gift

Gifts are not just things that we reciprocate, they are also things that go forward into the future. In *The Art of Living*, Thich Nhat Hanh (2017) uses the poignant example of how his own teachings have lived on in many kinds of people, carrying forward the spiritual teachings. It's a precious opportunity for all to realize that their gifts are not just limited to one single transaction but can literally carry forward into other classrooms in the future.

The notion of carrying gifts forward involves both honoring the past and protecting precious resources for our descendants. From an ecological perspective, David Suzuki (2022) has described seeing the earth as a precious resource that cannot be replicated anywhere else. Rather than using an analogy of ownership of the planet, Suzuki uses the metaphor of stewardship to explain what he sees as a more realistic view of how humans relate to the earth. That is, while human beings have a certain power over technology, this power also comes with responsibilities, among which are the duty to protect the planet's resources for future generations as well as to not upset the balance of nature. According to this view, the earth is neither a permanent resource nor one that solely belongs to humankind. Shifting away from an anthropocentric view helps to see the earth as a gift. Contrary to the idea that humans can somehow artificially synthesize everything given the right kinds of technologies, these ecological views suggest that nothing can arise without nature as the basis for all creation. This also hints at the dangers of excessive greed without a sense of future generations.

How can the ecological view of earth as a gifting resource be applied to educational contexts? Christopher Bache (2008) has compellingly written about the living classroom, which he sees as a kind of collective force that spreads out across different classroom cohorts. This view challenges the notion that a classroom begins and ends in a specific timeframe or semester, suggesting instead that the classroom forms a collective consciousness that spreads over time and even accumulates. While this view might seem mystical, it may not come as a surprise, considering that teachers are constantly refining their knowledge of how to teach a classroom so the classroom evolves over time. Rodriguez (2014) notes, "Though professional teachers may be given direct support through mentoring, professional development programs, or curriculum skills, the most prevalent support is the learner" (p. 135).

Visualization: Carrying Forward the Gift

Take a moment to relax your body. Feel the muscles relaxing from head to toe. Take a moment to appreciate the elements that make the classroom whole: the quality of the classroom design, layout, lighting. Feel how much care you have put into making the classroom a safe, clean, and organized space to learn. Appreciate the staff who work together to ensure that the classroom is a safe and welcoming space. Then think of your students.

Recall times in which the students took initiative to nurture care and compassion for their peers. Recall how students collaborate and are able to become part of the classroom collective. Reflect on how, simply through the effort to be present, students are adding a unique and irreplaceable element to the classroom. How have your students contributed to the shaping and evolution of your classroom? How have they, even in the midst of their difficulties, allowed you to be a better planner of future classes? Reflect on how the cycle of teaching and learning has allowed you to shape future classrooms into their current incarnation.

Imagine your classroom as a gift that is received, nurtured, and passed down to the next semester, the semester after, and so on. This gift is a vehicle through which students can cultivate their learning, but, like any vehicle, it needs to evolve according to the needs of each new cohort. In doing so, reflect deeply on how a classroom has no real beginning and ending. Classrooms are not just physical spaces but also shared energies that live on through the ways in which students are inspired by the classroom dynamic.

Breathe in the joy of all that you have received from your classroom, both in the opportunity to teach and to learn. As you breathe out, imagine that you are carrying all the benefits forward into another cohort of students. See how nothing in learning is wasted. Even if a particular lesson didn't go as well as you expected, imagine that the effort and learning that resulted allowed you to shape your lessons into their current incarnation.

Finally, visualize the learning of both you and your students fanning outward into their own personal spaces, as they take all the accumulated learning and make it their own.

Questions for Discussion

1. Comment on the overall process of visualization and what worked or didn't work for you. Did you find the process easy or difficult? What challenges did you experience when attempting any of the visualizations found in this chapter?

2. Try practicing one (or more) of the visualizations daily, particularly one that resonates with you or has a powerful effect. Write a journal and share some of your findings of the visualization, especially noting the impact that the visualization may have had on your classroom experience or interactions with students.

References

Adyashanti. (2011). *Falling into grace: Insights on the end of suffering*. Sounds True.

Albertson, B. P. (2020). Promoting Japanese university students' participation in English classroom discussions: Towards a culturally-informed bottom-up approach. *Journal of Pan-Pacific Association of Applied Linguistics, 24*(1), 45–66.

Algoe, S. B., & Haidt, J. (2009). Witnessing excellence in action: The "other-praising" emotions of elevation, gratitude, and admiration. *The Journal of Positive Psychology, 4*(2), 105–127. https://doi.org/10.1080/17439760802650519

Ali, M. S., & Jalal, H. (2018). Higher education as a predictor of employment: The world of work perspective. *Bulletin of Education and Research, 40*(2), 79–90.

AnAlayo, B. (2019). In the seen just the seen: Mindfulness and the construction of experience. *Mindfulness, 10*(1), 179–184. https://doi.org/10.1007/s12671-018-1042-9

Anderson, D., Comay, J., & Chiarotto, L. (2017). *Natural curiosity: A resource for educators* (2nd ed.). The Laboratory School, Eric Jackman Institute of Child Study, Ontario Institute for Studies in Education, University of Toronto.

Andre, C. (2011). *Looking at mindfulness: Twenty-five ways to live in the moment through art*. Blue Rider Press.

Antony, J. W., Van Dam, J., Massey, J. R., Barnett, A. J., & Bennion, K. A. (2023). Long-term, multi-event surprise correlates with enhanced autobiographical memory. *Nature Human Behaviour, 7*(12), 2152–2168. https://doi.org/10.1038/s41562-023-01631-8

Apple, M. (2018). *Ideology and curriculum* (4th ed.). Routledge.

Armstrong, K. (2022). *Sacred nature: Restoring our ancient bond with the natural world*. Alfred A. Knopf.

Asimov, I. (1992). *The human body: Its structure and operation* (rev. ed.). Penguin.

Asli, O., & Flaten, M. A. (2012, February 16). In the blink of an eye: Investigating the role of awareness in fear responding by measuring the latency of startle potentiation. *Brain Science, 2*(1), 61–84. https://doi.org/10.3390/brainsci2010061

Atleo, C., & Boron, J. (2022). Land is life: Indigenous relationships to territory and navigating settler colonial property regimes in Canada. *Land, 11*(5), 609. https://doi.org/10.3390/land11050609

Bache, C. (2008). *The living classroom: Teaching and collective consciousness.* State University of New York Press.

Baltzell, A. (Ed.). (2016). *Mindfulness and performance.* Cambridge University Press.

Bauer, J. J., & Shanahan, C. (2019). Gratitude, authenticity and self-authorship. In R. Roberts & D. Telech (Eds.), *The moral psychology of gratitude* (pp. 217–242). Rowman & Littlefield International.

Bausell, S. B., & Glazier, J. A. (2018). New teacher socialization and the testing apparatus. *Harvard Educational Review, 88*(3), 308–333. https://doi.org/10.17763/1943-5045-88.3.308

Beatty, J. E. (2004). Grades as money and the role of the market metaphor in management education. *Academy of Management Learning & Education, 3*(2), 187–196. https://doi.org/10.5465/AMLE.2004.13500516

Beck, A. T. (1999). *Prisoners of hate: The cognitive basis of anger, hostility, and violence.* (1st ed.). HarperCollins.

Belk, R. W., & Coon, G. S. (1993). Gift giving as Agapic love: An alternative to the exchange paradigm based on dating experiences. *Journal of Consumer Research, 20*(3), 393–417. http://www.jstor.org/stable/2489355

Bellugi, D. (2010). Creating the conditions for creativity: Looking at assessment in fine art studio practice. In C. Nygaard, N. Courtney, & C. Holtham (Eds.), *Teaching creativity-creativity in teaching* (pp. 47–64). Libri Publishing.

Benson, J., & Dresdow, S. (2003). Discovery mindset: A decision-making model for discovery and collaboration. *Management Decision, 41*(10), 997–1005. https://doi.org/10.1108/00251740310509526

Bevan-Brown, J. M. (2009). Identifying and providing for gifted and talented Māori students. *APEX, 15*(4), 6–20.

Billingham, C. (2015). Parental choice, neighbourhood schools, and the market metaphor in urban education reform. *Urban Studies (Edinburgh, Scotland), 52*(4), 685–701. https://doi.org/10.1177/0042098014528399

Binfet, J.-T. (2022). *Cultivating kindness: An educator's guide.* University of Toronto Press.

Blackmore, S. (1990). Mental models and mystical experience. In J. Crook & D. Fontana (Eds.), *Space in mind: East-West psychology & contemporary Buddhism* (chap. 5). Element Books.

Blanco Ramirez, G. (2013). Studying quality beyond technical rationality: Political and symbolic perspectives. *Quality in Higher Education, 19*(2), 126–141. https://doi.org/10.1080/13538322.2013.774804

Blount, H. P. (1997). The keepers of numbers: Teachers' perspectives on grades. *The Educational Forum, 61*(4), 329–334. https://doi.org/10.1080/00131729709335278

Blundell, R., Dearden, L., Meghir, C., & Sianesi, B. (1999). Human capital investment: The Returns from education and training to the individual, the firm and the economy. *Fiscal Studies, 20*(1), 1–23. https://doi.org/10.1111/j.1475-5890.1999.tb00001.x

Boban, J. (2020). *Zen and psychotherapy: Partners in liberation*. Wisdom Publications.

Bocking, P. (2020). *Public education, neoliberalism, and teachers: New York, Mexico City, Toronto*. University of Toronto Press.

Bohm, D. (1994). *Thought as a system*. Routledge.

Bolen, J. S. (2021). *Close to the bone: Life-threatening illness as a soul journey*. Conari Press.

Bornstein, M., Lichtenberg, J. D., & Silver, D. (2014). *Empathy*. Routledge.

Boud, D. (2016). Standards-based assessment for an era of increasing transparency. In D. Carless, S. M. Bridges, C. K. Y, Chan, R. Glofcheski (Eds.), *Scaling up Assessment for Learning in Higher Education* (pp. 19–31). Springer Singapore. https://doi.org/10.1007/978-981-10-3045-1_2

Bounds, G. (2018). Heidegger, the given, and the second nature of entities. *Open Philosophy 1*, 256–276.

Bowlby, J. (1973). *Attachment and loss*. Hogarth Press.

Brach, T. (2019). *Radical compassion: Learning to love yourself and your world with the practice of RAIN*. Viking Life.

Brady, A. L. (2008). *Effects of standardized testing on teachers' emotions, pedagogy and professional interactions with others*. ProQuest Dissertations Publishing.

Brazier, C. (2009). *Other-centered therapy: Buddhist psychology in action*. O Books.

Brewer, J. (2017). *The craving mind: From cigarettes to smartphones to love—why we get hooked and how we can break bad habits*. Yale University Press.

Brooks, P. (2022). *Seduced by story: The use and abuse of narrative*. New York Review Books.

Brown, G. T. L., Gebril, A., Michaelides, M. P., & Remesal, A. (2018). Assessment as an emotional practice: Emotional challenges faced by L2 teachers within assessment. In J. de D. M. Agudo (Ed.), *Emotions in second language teaching* (pp. 205–222). Springer International Publishing. https://doi.org/10.1007/978-3-319-75438-3_12

Brown, H. (2019). *Grace and philosophy: Understanding a gratuitous world*. McGill-Queen's University Press.

Brown, K. (2022). A Phenomenological Study of Gratitude-Based Educational Assessment. [Doctoral dissertation, University of Toronto]. ProQuest Dissertations Publishing.

Buck, R. (2004). The gratitude of exchange and the gratitude of caring: A developmental-interactionist perspective of moral emotion. In R. A. Emmons & M. E. McCullough (Eds.), *The psychology of gratitude* (pp. 100–121). Oxford University Press https://doi.org/10.1093/acprof:oso/9780195150100.003.0006

Budd, R. (2017). Undergraduate orientations towards higher education in Germany and England: Problematizing the notion of "student as customer." *Higher Education, 73*(1), 23–37. https://doi.org/10.1007/s10734-015-9977-4

Bunce, L., Baird, A., & Jones, S. E. (2017). The student-as-consumer approach in higher education and its effects on academic performance. *Studies in Higher Education, 42*(11), 1958–1978. https://doi.org/10.1080/03075079.2015.1127908

Burzyńska, B. (2018). Gratitude contemplation as a method to improve human well-being and physical functioning: Theoretical review of existing research. *Journal of Education, Health and Sport, 8*(3), 298–311. https://doi.org/10.5281/zenodo.1198828

Bushnell, R. (2008). *Tragedy: A short introduction.* Blackwell Publishing.

Cajete, G. A. (2015). Indigenous education and the development of Indigenous community leaders. *Leadership, 12*(3), 364–376. https://doi.org/10.1177/1742715015610412

Callard, A. (2019). Debts of gratitude. In R. Roberts & D. Telech (Eds.), *The moral psychology of gratitude* (pp. 83–95). Rowman & Littlefield International.

Camara, W. J., & Schmidt, E. (1999). Group differences in standardized testing and social stratification. *College Entrance Examination Board, New York.* https://files.ericca.ed.gov/fulltext/ED562656.pdf

Capra, F. (2010). *The Tao of physics: An exploration of the parallels between modern physics and Eastern mysticism.* Shambhala.

Capra, F., & Luisi, P. L. (2014). *The systems view of life: A unifying vision.* Cambridge University Press.

Capra, F., Steindl-Rast, D., & Matus, T. (1991). *Belonging to the universe: Explorations on the frontiers of science and spirituality.* Harper.

Carter, P. J., Hore, B., McGarrigle, L., Edwards, M., Doeg, G., Oakes, R., Campion, A., Carey, G., Vickers, K., & Parkinson, J. A. (2018). Happy thoughts: Enhancing well-being in the classroom with a positive events diary. *The Journal of Positive Psychology, 13*(2), 110–121. https://doi.org/10.1080/17439760.2016.1245770

Cavell, S. (1979). *The claim of reason: Wittgenstein, skepticism, morality and tragedy.* Oxford University Press.

Cervone, B. T., & Kushman, K. (2017). *Belonging and becoming: The power of social and emotional learning in high schools.* Harvard Education Press.

Charteris, J., & Smardon, D. (2019). The politics of student voice: Unravelling the multiple discourses articulated in schools. *Cambridge Journal of Education, 49*(1), 93–110. https://doi.org/10.1080/0305764X.2018.1444144

Cheal, D. J. (2016). *The gift economy.* Routledge. https://doi.org/10.4324/9781315681825

Cherry, K. (2020, August 3). *Peak experiences.* Verywell Mind. https://www.verywellmind.com/what-are-peak-experiences-2795268

Chesterton, G. K. (2013). *Autobiography*. Gutenberg Press Australia. https://gutenberg.net.au/ebooks13/1301201h.html

Chetty, R. (2010). Connecting creative capital and pedagogy in postgraduate programmes. In C. Nygaard, N. Courtney, & C. Holtham (Eds.), *Teaching creativity-creativity in teaching* (pp. 139–154). Libri Publishing.

Ciaramicoli, A., & Ketcham, K. (2000). *The power of empathy: A practical guide to creating intimacy, self-understanding, and lasting love*. Dutton.

Cirio, J. (2019). Meeting the promise of negotiation: Situating negotiated rubrics with students' prior experiences. *Writing Program Administration 42*(2), 100–118.

Cochran-Smith, M., Carney, M. C., Keefe, E. S., Sanchez, J. G., Miller, A. F., Baker, M., Fernandez, M. B., Burton, S., & Wen-Chia Chang. (2018). *Reclaiming accountability in teacher education*. Teachers College Press.

Conroy, J. C. (2004). *Betwixt and between: The liminal imagination, education and democracy*. Peter Lang.

Cook, F. (1977). *Hua-yen Buddhism: The jewel net of Indra*. Pennsylvania State University Press.

Cooperrider, D. L., & Whitney, D. (2010). *Appreciative inquiry: A positive revolution in change*. Berrett-Koehler Publishers.

Costa, P. T. Jr., & McCrae, R. (1991). Trait psychology comes of age. *Faculty Publications, Department of Psychology*, 363.

Courtois, F. (1971). *An American woman's experience of enlightenment*. Los Angeles Zen Center.

Covey, S. R. (2013). *The 7 habits of highly effective people: Powerful lessons in personal change* (25th anniv. ed.). Simon & Schuster.

Coy, C. (2016, June 6). *Times teachers actually feel sad about students leaving*. Caleb Coy (blog). https://calebcoy.blog/2016/06/06/times-teachers-actually-feel-sad-about-students-leaving/

Crow, J. F. (2002). Unequal by nature: A geneticist's perspective on human differences. *Daedalus* (Cambridge, MA), *131*(1), 81–88.

Csikszentmihalyi, M. (1996). *Creativity: Flow and the psychology of discovery and invention* (1st ed.). HarperCollinsPublishers.

Csikszentmihalyi, M. (1998). Implications of a systems perspective for the study of creativity. In R. Sternberg (Ed.), *Handbook of creativity* (pp. 313–336). Cambridge University Press. https://doi.org/10.1017/CBO9780511807916.018

Csikszentmihalyi, M. (2008). *Flow: The psychology of optimal experience* (1st Harper Perennial Modern Classics ed.). Harper Perennial.

Csikszentmihalyi, M., & Robinson, R. E. (1986). *The art of seeing: An interpretation of the aesthetic experience*. J. Paul Getty Museum.

Damasio, A. (1999). *The feeling of what happens: Body and emotion in the making of consciousness*. Harcourt.

Daniels, L. M., Pelletier, G., Radil, A. I., Goegan, L. D. (2020). Motivating assessment: How to leverage summative assessments for the good of intrinsic motivation. In S. Nichols, & D. Varier (Eds.), *Theory to practice: Educational psychology for teachers and teaching*. Information Age Publishing.

Dastur, F. (2000). Phenomenology of the event: Waiting and surprise. *Hypatia, 15*(4), 178–189. https://doi.org/10.1111/j.1527-2001.2000.tb00360.x

Davenport, L. (2009). *Healing and transformation through self-guided imagery*. Celestial Arts.

Davies, G., Whelan, S., Foley, A., & Walsh, M. (2010). Gifts and gifting. *International Journal of Management Reviews, 12*(4), 413–434. https://doi.org/10.1111/j.1468-2370.2009.00271.x

Davis, D. S., & Willson, A. (2015). Practices and commitments of test-centric literacy instruction: Lessons from a testing transition. *Reading Research Quarterly, 50*(3), 357–379. https://doi-org.ezproxy.gvsu.edu/10.1002/rrq.103

Derrida, J., & Kamuf, P. (1992). *Given time*. University of Chicago Press.

Desmond, T. (2016). *Self-compassion in psychotherapy: Mindfulness-based practices or healing and transformation*. W. W. Norton & Co.

DeSteno, D., Li, Y., Dickens, L., & Lerner, J. (2014). Gratitude: A tool for reducing economic impatience. *Psychological Science, 25*(6), 1262–1267. https://doi.org/10.1177/0956797614529979

Didion, J. (2005). *The year of magical thinking*. Knopf.

Donald, D. (2019). Homo economicus and forgetful curriculum. In H. Tomlins-Janhke (Ed.), *Indigenous education: New directions in theory and practice*. University of Alberta Press.

Dorovolomo, J., Phan, H. P., & Maebuta, J. (2010). Quality lesson planning and quality delivery: Do they relate? *The International Journal of Learning Annual Review 17*(3), 447–456.

Drummond, C., Mellers, B., Bigony, M., & Fincher, K. (2013). Surprise: A belief or an emotion? *Decision Making : Neural and Behavioural Approaches*, 3–19. https://doi.org/10.1016/B978-0-444-62604-2.00001-0

Dunbar, M., & Baker, W. D. (2014). Teaching as emotional labor: Preparing to interact with all students. *Language Arts Journal of Michigan 30*(1), Article 8.

Dunn, J. R., & Schweitzer, M. E. (2005). Feeling and believing: The influence of emotion on trust. *Journal of Personality and Social Psychology, 88*(5), 736–748. https://doi. org/10.1037/0022-3514.88.5.736

Duthely, L. M., Nunn, S. G., & Avella, J. T. (2017). A novel heart-centered, gratitude-meditation intervention to increase well-being among adolescents. *Education Research International*, 1–12. https://doi.org/10.1155/2017/4891892

Dzigar Kongtrul Rinpoche. (2009). *Uncommon happiness: The path of the compassionate warrior*. Rangjung Yeshe Publications.

Eagleton, T. (2020). *Tragedy*. Yale University Press.

Egan, K. (1991). *The educated mind: How cognitive tools shape our understanding*. University of Chicago Press.

Emerson, R. W. (1991). *Essays: First and second series*. Library of America Paperback Classics.
Emmons, R. A. (2013a). *Gratitude works! A 12-day program for creating emotional prosperity*. Jossey-Bass.
Emmons, R. (2013b, May 13). How gratitude can help you through hard times. *Greater Good Magazine*. https://greatergood.berkeley.edu/article/item/how_gratitude_can_help_you_through_hard_times
Emmons, R. A., & McCullough, M. E. (2003). Counting blessings versus burdens: An experimental investigation of gratitude and subjective well-being in daily life. *Journal of Personality and Social Psychology, 84*(2), 377–389. https://doi.org/10.1037/0022-3514.84.2.377
Engelland, C. (2020). *Phenomenology*. MIT Press.
Engels, J. D. (2018). *The art of gratitude*. State University of New York Press.
Epstein, M. (2005). *Open to desire: Embracing a lust for life using insights from Buddhism & psychotherapy*. Gotham Books.
Eva, A. (2022). *Surviving teacher burnout: A weekly guide to build resilience, deal with emotional exhaustion, & stay inspired in the classroom*. New Harbinger Publications.
Fagley, N. S. (2018). Appreciation (including gratitude) and affective well-being: Appreciation predicts positive and negative affect above the big five personality factors and demographics. *SAGE Open, 8*(4). https://doi.org/10.1177/2158244018818621
Feldman, C., & Kuyken, W. (2019). *Mindfulness: Ancient wisdom meets modern psychology*. Guilford Press.
Fischer, N. (2021). *When you greet me I bow: Notes and reflections from a life in Zen*. Shambhala.
Flynn, C. P., & Greyson, B. (1984). *The near-death experience: problems, prospects, perspectives*. C. C. Thomas.
Foster, M. I., & Keane, M. T. (2019). The role of surprise in learning: Different surprising outcomes affect memorability differentially. *Topics in Cognitive Science, 11*(1), 75–87. https://doi.org/10.1111/tops.12392
Fox, M. (1994). *The reinvention of work: A new vision of livelihood for our time*. Harper Collins.
Fox, M. (2003). *Religion, spirituality, and the near-death experience*. Routledge.
Fox, M. (2006). *The A. W. E. project: Reinventing education, reinventing the human*. CopperHouse.
Fox, M. (2016). *Sins of the spirit, blessings of the flesh: Transforming evil in soul and society*. North Atlantic Books.
Fox, W. (1990). *Toward transpersonal ecology*. Shambhala.
Fraile, J., Panadero, E., & Pardo, R. (2017). Co-creating rubrics: The effects on self-regulated learning, self-efficacy and performance of establishing assessment

criteria with students. *Studies in Educational Evaluation, 53*, 69–76. https://doi.org/10.1016/j.stueduc.2017.03.003

Frans, N., Post, W. J., Oenema-Mostert, C. B., & Minnaert, A. E. M. G. (2020). Preschool/Kindergarten teachers' conceptions of standardised testing. *Assessment in Education: Principles, Policy & Practice, 27*(1), 87–108. https://doi.org/10.1080/0969594X.2019.1688763

Frederick, S., & Loewenstein, G. (1999). Hedonic adaptation. In D. Kahneman, E. Diener, & N. Schwarz (Eds.), *Well-being: The foundations of hedonic psychology* (pp. 302–329). Russell Sage Foundation.

Fredrickson, B. (2004). Gratitude, like other positive emotions, broadens and builds. In R. Emmons & M. McCulloch (Eds.), *The psychology of gratitude* (pp. 145–166). Oxford University Press. https://doi.org/10.1093/acprof:oso/9780195150100.003.0008

Fredrickson, B. (2013). *Love 2.0: How our supreme emotion affects everything we feel, think, do, and become.* Hudson Street Press.

French, M. (1998). *A season in hell: A memoir.* Knopf.

Fromm, E. (1992). *The art of being.* Continuum.

Fromm, E. (2013). *To have or to be?* Bloomsbury.

Fuchsman, D., Sass, T. R., & Zamarro, G. (2022). Testing, teacher turnover, and the distribution of teachers across grades and schools. *Education Finance and Policy*, 1–22. https://doi.org/10.1162/edfp_a_00376

Galea, S. (2006). Iris Marion Young's imaginations of gift giving: Some implications for the teacher and the student. *Educational Philosophy and Theory, 38*(1), 83–92. https://doi.org/10.1111/j.1469-5812.2006.00176.x

Gallagher, S. (2012). *Phenomenology.* Palgrave Macmillan.

Garett, R., Liu, S., & Young, S. D. (2017). A longitudinal analysis of stress among incoming college freshmen. *Journal of American College Health, 65*(5), 331–338. https://doi.org/10.1080/07448481.2017.1312413

Gawain, S. (1982). *Creative visualization.* Bantam.

Gehry Nelson, D. (2022). *Cultivating curiosity: Teaching and learning reimagined.* Jossey-Bass.

Gendolla, G. E., & Koller, M. (2001). Surprise and motivation of causal search: How are they affected by outcome valence and importance? *Motivation and Emotion, 25*(4), 327–349. https://doi.org/10.1023/A: 1014867700547

Ghadiali, A,. (2021). *Intuition: Access your inner wisdom. Trust your instincts. Find your path.* DK.

Giesler, M. (2006). Consumer gift systems. *The Journal of Consumer Research, 33*(2), 283–290. https://doi.org/10.1086/506309

Gilbert, P. (2009). *Overcoming depression: A self-help guide using cognitive and behavioural techniques* (3rd ed.). Robinson.

Gilbert, P., & Choden. (2014). *Mindful compassion: How the science of compassion can help you understand your emotions, live in the present, and connect deeply with others.* New Harbinger Publications.

Gilhooly, K. (2016). Incubation and intuition in creative problem solving. *Frontiers in psychology*, 7, 1076–1076. https://doi.org/10.3389/fpsyg.2016.01076

Giroux, H. (2014). *Neoliberalism's war on higher education*. Haymarket Books.

Giroux, H. (2020). *On critical pedagogy* (2nd ed.). Bloomsbury Academic.

Giulia, S. (2018). *Jealousy: A forbidden passion*. Polity Press.

Gozzi, R. Jr. (1998). The conduit metaphor in the rhetoric of education reform: A critique of hidden assumptions. *New Jersey Journal of Communication*, 6(1), 81–89. https://doi.org/10.1080/15456879809367336

Granziera, H., Collie, R. J., & Martin, A. J. (2019). Adaptability: An important capacity to cultivate among pre-service teachers in teacher education programmes. *Psychology Teaching Review*, 25(1), 60–66. https://doi.org/10.53841/bpsptr.2019.25.1.60

Graves, D. (1983). *Writing: Teachers & children at work*. Heinemann Educational Books.

Green, M. (2004). Transportation into narrative worlds: The role of prior knowledge and perceived realism. *Discourse Processes*, 38(2), 247–266. https://doi.org/10.1207/s15326950dp3802_5

Green, F. J., & Byrd, D. L. (2011). *Maternal pedagogies: In and outside the classroom*. Demeter Press.

Griffin, D. R. (1988). *Spirituality and society: Postmodern visions*. State University of New York Press.

Griffith, O. M. (2016). *Gratitude: A way of teaching* (Repr. ed.). Rowman & Littlefield.

Grimes-Maguire, R., & Keane, M. T. (2005). *Expecting a surprise? The effect of expectations on perceived surprise in stories*. Proceedings of the Annual Meeting of the Cognitive Science Society, 833–838. ISSN 1069-7977.

Grodsky, E., Warren, J. R., & Felts, E. (2008). Testing and social stratification in American education. *Annual Review of Sociology*, 34(1), 385–404. https://doi.org/10.1146/annurev.soc.34.040507.134711

Grof, S., & Bennett, H. Z. (1992). *The holotropic mind: The three levels of human consciousness and how they shape our lives* (1st ed.). HarperSanFrancisco.

Gross, M. A., & Hogler, R. (2005). What the shadow knows: Exploring the hidden dimensions of the consumer metaphor in management education. *Journal of Management Education*, 29(1), 3–16. https://doi.org/10.1177/1052562903260034

Guengerich, G. (2020). *The way of gratitude: A new spirituality for today*. Random House.

Halbesleben, J. R. B., & Wheeler, A. R. (2009). Student identification with business education models: Measurement and relationship to educational outcomes. *Journal of Management Education*, 33(2), 166–195. https://doi.org/10.1177/1052562908320658

Hall, E. (2010). *Greek tragedy: Suffering under the sun*. Oxford University Press.

Hanh, T. H. (2015). *Silence: The power of quiet in a world full of noise*. HarperOne.

Hanh, T. H. (2017). *The art of living*. HarperOne.

Hanks, J. (2019). From research-as-practice to exploratory practice-as-research in language teaching and beyond. *Language Teaching*, *52*(2), 143–187. https://doi.org/10.1017/S0261444819000016

Hanson, J. H. (2015). The anthropology of giving: Toward a cultural logic of charity. *Journal of Cultural Economy*, *8*(4), 501–520. https://doi.org/10.1080/17530350.2014.949284

Hanson, R. (2013). *Hardwiring happiness: The new brain science of contentment, calm, and confidence*. Harmony.

Hargreaves, A. (1998). The emotional practice of teaching. *Teaching and Teacher Education*, *14*(8), 835–854. https://doi.org/10.1016/S0742-051X(98)00025-0

Harwood, P. G., & Asal, V. (2007). *Educating the first digital generation*. Praeger.

Harwood, H. B., Hall, M., Edwards, K. J., & Hill, P. C. (2022) Tangible experiences of grace: A qualitative investigation of divine grace in Roman Catholics. *Pastoral Psychology*, *71*(3), 359–376. https://doi.org/10.1007/s11089-021-00983-0

Hendricks, C. (2013). *Problems with grading rubrics for complex assignments*. You're the Teacher (ubc.ca blog). https://blogs.ubc.ca/chendricks/2013/01/23/problems-with-grading-rubrics-for-complex-assignments/

Hénaff, M. (2019). Derrida: The gift, the impossible, and the exclusion of reciprocity. In J.-L. Morhange (Ed.), *The philosophers' gift: reexamining reciprocity*. https://doi.org/10.5422/fordham/9780823286478.003.0002

Henig, J. R. (1995). *Rethinking school choice*. Princeton University Press.

Henriksen, D., Richardson, C., & Shack, K. (2020). Mindfulness and creativity: Implications for thinking and learning. *Thinking Skills and Creativity*, *37*, 100689–100689. https://doi.org/10.1016/j.tsc.2020.100689

Henshon, S. E. (2019). *Teaching empathy: Strategies for building emotional intelligence in today's students*. Routledge.

Herman, J. L., Abedi, J., & Golan, S. (1994). Assessing the effects of standardized testing on schools. *Educational and Psychological Measurement*, *54*(2), 471–482. https://doi.org/10.1177/0013164494054002022.

Hesse, H. (1990). *The glass bead game*. Henry Holt & Co.

Hill, N. (2018, July 25). *Teachers, we don't have to be martyrs*. EducationWeek. https://www.edweek.org/teaching-learning/opinion-teachers-we-dont-have-to-be-martyrs/2018/07#:~:text=The%20notion%20of%20the%20martyr,marriage%2C%20and%20she%20gets%20divorced

Hillman, J. (1996). *The soul's code*. Random House.

Himelfarb, I. (2019). A primer on standardized testing: History, measurement, classical test theory, item response theory, and equating. *The Journal of Chiropractic Education*, *33*(2), 151–163. https://doi.org/10.7899/JCE-18-22

Hlava, P., Elfers, J., & Offringa, R. (2014). A transcendent view of gratitude: The transpersonal gratitude scale. *International Journal of Transpersonal Studies*, *33*(1), 1–14. http://dx.doi.org/10.24972/ijts.2014.33.1.1

Hochschild, A. R. (2003). *The managed heart: Commercialization of human feeling; with a new afterword*. University of California Press.

Holecek, A. (2013). *Preparing to die: Practical advice and spiritual wisdom from the Tibetan Buddhist tradition*. Shambhala.

Horkheimer, M. (1974). *Eclipse of reason*. Oxford University Press.

Hornof, M. (2008). Reading Tests as a Genre Study. *The Reading Teacher, 62*(1), 69–73. https://doi.org/10.1598/RT.62.1.8

Horrigan-Kelly, M., Millar, M., & Dowling, M. (2016). Understanding the key tenets of Heidegger's philosophy for interpretive phenomenological research. *International Journal of Qualitative Methods, 15*(1), 160940691668063–. https://doi.org/10.1177/1609406916680634.

Howells, K. (2012). *Gratitude in education: A radical view*. Sense.

Howells, K. (2014). An exploration of the role of gratitude in enhancing teacher–student relationships. *Teaching and Teacher Education, 42*(Complete), 58–67. https://doi.org/10.1016/j.tate.2014.04.004

Hsu, M., Bhatt, M., Adolphs, R., Tranel, D., & Camerer, C. F. (2005). Neural systems responding to degrees of uncertainty in human decision-making. *Science (American Association for the Advancement of Science), 310*(5754), 1680–1683. https://doi.org/10.1126/science.1115327

Hughes, J. C. (2006). *Teacher stress, teacher efficacy, and standardized testing: A study of New York City public school teachers*. [Doctoral dissertation, Fordham University] ProQuest Dissertations Publishing.

Hunt, D. E. (2010). *To be a friend: The key to friendship in our lives*. Dundurn Press.

Huntington, P. J. (2009). *Loneliness & lament: A journey to receptivity*. Indiana University Press.

Huot, B. (2002). *(Re)articulating writing assessment for teaching and learning*. Utah State University Press.

Huron, D. (2006). *Sweet anticipation: Music and the psychology of expectation*. MIT Press.

Huxley, A. (1931). *Do what you will*. Chatto and Windus.

Hycner, R. H. (1985). Some guidelines for the phenomenological analysis of interview data. *Human Studies, 8*(3), 279–303. https://doi.org/10.1007/bf00142995

Hylen, M. G. (2022). *Cultivating emotional intelligence: The 5 habits of the emotions coach*. Rowman & Littlefield.

Ivtzan, I., Lomas, T., Hefferon, K., & Worth, P. (2015). *Second wave positive psychology: Embracing the dark side of life* (1st ed.). Routledge.

Jacobs, J. (2014). Beyond the factory model: Oakland teachers learn how to blend. *Education Next, 14*(4), 35–41.

James, D. (2014). Investigating the curriculum through assessment practice in higher education: The value of a "learning cultures" approach. *Higher Education, 67*(2), 155–169. https://doi.org/10.1007/s10734-013-9652-6

Jennings, P. A. (2015). *Mindfulness for teachers: Simple skills for peace and productivity in the classroom*. W. W. Norton & Co.

Jensen, H., & Rørbæk, L. L. (2022). Smoothing the path to practice: Playful learning raises study happiness and confidence in future roles among student teachers and student ECE teachers. *Studies in Educational Evaluation, 74*, 101156–. https://doi.org/10.1016/j.stueduc.2022.101156.

Johnsen, I., & Tømmeraas, A. M. (2022). Attachment and grief in young adults after the loss of a close friend: A qualitative study. *BMC Psychology, 10*(1), 10–10. https://doi.org/10.1186/s40359-022-00717-8

Johnstone, B. (2018). *Discourse analysis (introducing linguistics)* (3rd ed.). Wiley-Blackwell.

Joughin, G. (2008). Transforming holistic assessment and grading into a vehicle for complex learning. In G. Joughin (Ed.), *Assessment, learning and judgement in higher education* (pp. 1–19). Springer Netherlands. https://doi.org/10.1007/978-1-4020-8905-3_4

Kabat-Zinn, J. (2005). *Coming to our senses*. Hachette.

Kabat-Zinn, J. (2013). *Full catastrophe living*. Bantam Books.

Kabat-Zinn, J. (2020). *The mindful attitude of beginners mind*. Mindfulness Training. https://mbsrtraining.com/attitudes-of-mindfulness-by-jon-kabat-zinn/mindful-attitude-of-beginners-mind-jon-kabat-zinn/

Kagan, J. (2002). *Surprise, uncertainty, and mental structures*. Harvard University Press.

Kailo, K. (2002). *The gift economy: A feminist perspective on patriarchal capitalism*. Paper presented at session, the gift economy: A feminist perspective on patriarchal capitalism. World Congress on Women, Kampala, Uganda, July 2002.

Kasser, T. (2002). *The high price of materialism*. MIT Press.

Kauppinen, I. (2014). Different meanings of "knowledge as commodity" in the context of higher education. *Critical Sociology, 40*(3), 393–409. https://doi.org/10.1177/0896920512471218

Keats, J., & Rollins, H. E. (1958). *The letters of John Keats*. Harvard University Press.

Keller, S. (2013). *Partiality*. Princeton University Press.

Keltner, D., & Haidt, J. (2003). Approaching awe, a moral, spiritual, and aesthetic emotion. *Cognition and Emotion, 17*(2), 297–314.

Kim, D., Lim, J. H., & An, J. (2022). The quality and effectiveness of Social-Emotional Learning (SEL) intervention studies in Korea: A meta-analysis. *PloS One, 17*(6), e0269996–e0269996. https://doi.org/10.1371/journal.pone.0269996

Kinsella, E. A. (2007). Technical rationality in Schön's reflective practice: Dichotomous or non-dualistic epistemological position. *Nursing Philosophy, 8*(2), 102–113. https://doi.org/10.1111/j.1466-769X.2007.00304.x

Kirp, D. L. (2005). This little student went to market. In R. H. Hersh & J. Merrow (Eds.), *Declining by degrees: Higher education at risk*. Palgrave Macmillan.

Knepp, K. A., & Knepp, M. M. (2022). Academic entitlement decreases engagement in and out of the classroom and increases classroom incivility attitudes. *Social Psychology of Education*, 25(5), 1113–1134. https://doi.org/10.1007/s11218-022-09716-4

Kohn, A. (1999). *Punished by rewards: The trouble with gold stars, incentive plans, A's, praise, and other bribes.* Houghton Mifflin.

Kohn, A. (2005). *Unconditional parenting: Moving from rewards and punishments to love and reason.* Atria.

Kong, D. T., & Belkin, L. Y. (2019). Because I want to share, not because I should: Prosocial implications of gratitude expression in repeated zero-sum resource allocation exchanges. *Motivation and Emotion*, 43, 824. https://doi-org.myaccess.library.utoronto.ca/10.1007/s11031-019-09764-y

Krentler, K. A., Hampton, D. R., & Martin, A. B. (1994). Building critical thinking skills: Can standardized testing accomplish it? *Marketing Education Review*, 4(1), 16–21. https://doi.org/10.1080/10528008.1994.11488435

Kyabgon, T. (2018). *Integral Buddhism: Developing all aspects of one's personhood.* Shogham Publications.

Lakoff, G., & Johnson, M. (1980). *Metaphors we live by* (1st ed.). University of Chicago Press.

Lalla, A., & Sheldon, S. (2021). The effects of emotional valence and perceived life stress on recalling personal experiences and envisioning future events. *Emotion*, 21(7), 1392–1401. https://doi.org/10.1037/emo0001050

Lambert, N. M., Graham, S. M., & Fincham, D. (2009). A prototype analysis of gratitude: Varieties of gratitude experiences. *Personality & Social Psychology Bulletin*, 35(9), 1193–1207. https://doi.org//10.1177/0146167209338071

Lambert, N. M., Fincham, F. D., & Stillman, T. F. (2012). Gratitude and depressive symptoms: The role of positive reframing and positive emotion. *Cognition and Emotion*, 26(4), 615–633. https://doi.org/10.1080/02699931.2011.595393

Lanoue, G. (2023). Gift giving, reciprocity and community survival among Central Alaskan Indigenous peoples. *Humans*, 3, 47–59. https://doi.org/10.3390/humans3010006

Levy, D. (2016). *Mindful tech: How to bring balance to our digital lives.* Yale University Press.

Lewis, R. (1999). *Work as a spiritual practice.* Harmony.

Liaw, S., & Goh, K. (2003). Evidence and control of biases in student evaluations of teaching. *International Journal of Educational Management* 17(1), 37–43.

Litman, J. A. (2008). Interest and deprivation factors of epistemic curiosity. *Personality and Individual Differences*, 44(7), 1585–1595. https://doi.org/10.1016/j.paid.2008.01.014

Llewellyn, K. R. (2012). *Democracy's angels: The work of women teachers.* Queen's University Press.

Lloyd, M. A. (1992). *The agon in Euripides*. Clarendon Press.
Lommel, P. van. (2010). *Consciousness beyond life: The science of the near-death experience* (1st ed.). HarperOne.
Lorini, E., & Castelfranchi, C. (2007). The cognitive structure of surprise: Looking for basic principles. *Topoi, 26*(1), 133–149. https://doi.org/10.1007/s11245-006-9000-x
Lovejoy, A. (2017). *The great chain of being: A study of the history of an idea* (1st ed.). Taylor & Francis.
Loy, D. (2019). *Nonduality: In Buddhism and beyond*. Wisdom Publications.
Luna, T., & Renninger, L. (2015). *Surprise: Embrace the unpredictable and engineer the unexpected*. TarcherPerigee.
MacIntyre, A. (1999). *Dependent rational animals: Why human beings need the virtues*. Open Court.
Macy, J. (2007). *World as lover, world as self : Courage for global justice and ecological renewal*. Parallax Press.
Mageo, J. M., & Quinn, N. (Eds.). (2013). *Attachment reconsidered: Cultural perspectives on a Western theory*. Palgrave Macmillan.
Maguire, R., Maguire, P., & Keane, M. T. (2011). Making sense of surprise: An investigation of the factors influencing surprise judgments. *Journal of Experimental Psychology, Learning, Memory, and Cognition, 37*(1), 176–186. https://doi.org/10.1037/a0021609
Malo, A. (2012). The limits of Marion's and Derrida's philosophy of the gift. *International Philosophical Quarterly, 52*(206), 149–168.
Manen, M. van. (1991). *The tact of teaching: The meaning of pedagogical thoughtfulness*. Althouse Press.
Manen, M. van. (2015). *Pedagogical tact: Knowing what to do when you don't know what to do*. Left Coast Press.
Marcel, G. (1962). *Man against mass society*. Gateway.
Marion, J.-L. (2020). *Being given: Toward a phenomenology of givenness*. Stanford University Press. https://doi.org/10.1515/9780804785723
Marut, L. (2014). *Be nobody*. Beyond Words.
Maslow, A. H. (1993). *The farther reaches of human nature*. Penguin.
Maslow, A. H. (1999). *Toward a psychology of being*. J. Wiley & Sons.
Maugham, W. S. (1999). *Of human bondage*. Modern Library.
Mauss, M. (1990). *The gift*. Routledge.
Mavani, J. (2018, September 8). *Maybe so, maybe not. We'll see*. Medium. https://jaymavs.medium.com/maybe-so-maybe-not-well-see-c35f53da68e1
Matravers, D. (2017). *Empathy*. Polity Press.
May, R. (1991). *The cry for myth* (1st ed.). Norton.
Mayer, R. C., Davis, J. H., & Schoorman, F. D. (1995). An integrative model of organizational trust. *Academy of Management Review, 20*, 709–734.

Mayer, J. D., & Salovey, P. (1997). What is emotional intelligence? In P. Salovey & D. J. Sluyter (Eds.), *Emotional development and emotional intelligence: Educational implications* (pp. 3–34). Basic Books.

Mayhall, C. W. (2003). *On logical positivism*. Wadsworth/Thomson Learning.

McKown, C. (2019). *Assessing students' social and emotional learning: A guide to meaningful measurement*. W. W. Norton & Co.

McCullough, M. E., Kilpatrick, S. D., Emmons, R. A., & Larson, D. B. (2001). Is gratitude a moral affect? *Psychological Bulletin*, *127*(2), 249–266. https://doi.org/10.1037/0033-2909.127.2.249

McLeod, K. (2001). *Wake up to your life: Discovering the Buddhist path of attention*. Harper.

McNeil, L. (2000). *Contradictions of school reform: Educational costs of standardized testing*. Routledge.

McTamaney, C. (2007). *The Tao of Montessori: Reflections on compassionate teaching*. iUniverse.

Mellers, B., & McGraw, A. P. (2004). Self-serving beliefs and the pleasure of outcomes. In I. Brocas & J. D. Carrillo (Eds.), *The psychology of economic decisions: Reasons and choices*. Oxford University Press.

Metzinger, T. (2013). The myth of cognitive agency: Subpersonal thinking as a cyclically recurring loss of mental autonomy. *Frontiers in Psychology*, *4*, 931–931. https://doi.org/10.3389/fpsyg.2013.00931

Meyer, W. U., Reisenzein, R., & Schützwohl, A. (1997). Towards a process analysis of emotions: The case of surprise. *Motivation and Emotion*, *21*(3), 251–274.

Midal, F. (2017). *The pure joy of being: An illustrated introduction to the story of Buddha and the practice of meditation*. Shambhala.

Miller, J. P. (2000). *Education and the soul: Toward a spiritual curriculum*. State University of New York Press.

Miller, J. P. (2006). *Educating for wisdom and compassion: Creating conditions for timeless learning*. Corwin Press.

Miller, J. P. (2018). *Love and compassion: Exploring their role in education*. University of Toronto Press.

Miller, J. P. (2019). *The holistic curriculum* (3rd ed.). University of Toronto Press.

Miller, J. P., & Seller, W. (1990). *Curriculum: Perspectives and practice*. Copp Clark Pitman.

Miller, T. (1995). *How to want what you have: Discovering the magic and grandeur of ordinary existence*. Henry Holt & Co.

Minkel, J. (2014, December 30). *The promise and peril of turning student learning into a number*. EdW. https://www.edweek.org/teaching-learning/opinion-the-promise-and-peril-of-turning-student-learning-into-a-number/2014/12

Montessori, M. (1967). *The discovery of the child*. Ballantine.

Montessori, M. (1970). *The child in the family*. Discus.

Moore, T. (1996). *The re-enchantment of everyday life*. HarperCollins.

Moustakas, C. (1994). *Phenomenological research methods*. Sage.

Munnich, E. L., Foster, M. I., & Keane, M. T. (2019). An appraisal of surprise: Tracing the threads that stitch it together. *Topics in Cognitive Science, 11*(1), 37–49. https://doi.org/10.1111/tops.12402

Murphy-Shigematsu, S. (2018). *From mindfulness to heartfulness: Transforming self and society with compassion*. Berrett-Koehler Publishers.

Nairn, R., Choden, & Regan-Addis, H. (2019). *From mindfulness to insight: Meditations to release your habitual thinking and activate your inherent wisdom*. Shambhala.

Naparstek, B. (1994). *Staying well with guided imagery*. Warner Books.

Nelson, K. (2020). *Wake up grateful: The transformative practice of taking nothing for granted*. Storey Publishing.

Nichols, M. P. (2009). *The lost art of listening: How learning to listen can improve relationships*. Guilford Press.

Noddings, N. (1986). *Caring: A relational approach to ethics and moral education*. University of California Press.

Noddings, N. (2010). *The maternal factor: Two paths to morality*. University of California Press.

Noddings, N. (2012). *Peace education: How we come to love and hate war*. Cambridge University Press.

Noddings, N. (2015). *A richer, brighter vision for American high schools*. Cambridge University Press.

Noordewier, M. K., Scheepers, D. T., Stins, J. F., & Hagenaars, M. A. (2021). On the physiology of interruption after unexpectedness. *Biological Psychology, 165*, 108174–108174. https://doi.org/10.1016/j.biopsycho.2021.108174

Nordquist, R. (2020, February 12). *Source domain in conceptual metaphor*. ThoughtCo. https://www.thoughtco.com/source-domain-conceptual-metaphors-1692115

Nouwen, H. (2020, August 18). *Receiving the gifts of others*. Henri Nouwen Society. https://henrinouwen.org/meditation/receiving-the-gifts-of-others/

Nussbaum, M. C. (2001). *Upheavals of thought: The intelligence of emotions*. Cambridge University Press.

Nygaard, C., Courtney, N., & Holtham, C. (Eds). (2010). *Teaching creativity: Creativity in teaching*. Libri Publishing.

O'Reilly, A. (2006). *Rocking the cradle: Thoughts on motherhood, feminism, and the possibility of empowered mothering*. Demeter Press.

O'Sullivan, E. (1999). *Transformative learning: Educational vision for the 21st century*. Zed Books.

Orr, D. (1991). *What is education for? Six myths about the foundations of modern education, and six new principles to replace them*. The Learning Revolution. https://www.context.org/iclib/ic27/

Ortony, A., Clore, G. L., & Collins, A. (1988). *The cognitive structure of emotions*. Cambridge University Press.

Osho. (2017). *Trust: Living spontaneously and embracing life*. St. Martin's Press.
Osteen, M. (2010). Jazzing the gift: Improvisation, reciprocity, excess. *Rethinking Marxism*, *22*(4), 569–580. https://doi.org/10.1080/08935696.2010.510303
Ostovar-Nameghi, S. A., & Sheikhahmadi, M. (2016). From teacher isolation to teacher collaboration: Theoretical perspectives and empirical findings. *English Language Teaching* (Toronto), *9*(5), 197–205. https://doi.org/10.5539/elt.v9n5p197
Otto, J., Sanford, D. A., & Ross, D. N. (2008). Does ratemyprofessor.com really rate my professor? *Assessment and Evaluation in Higher Education*, *33*(4), 355–368. https://doi.org/10.1080/02602930701293405
Palmer, P. (2017). *The courage to teach: Exploring the inner landscape of a teacher's life*. Josey-Bass.
Panksepp, J., & Biven, L. (2012). *The archaeology of mind: Neuroevolutionary origins of human emotions*. Norton.
Paricio, J. (2017). Students as customers: A paradigm shift in higher education. Debats. *Journal on Culture, Power and Society*, *131*(3), 137–149. http://dx.doi.org/10.28939/iam.debats-en.2017-11
Patel, P., Hancock, J., Rogers, M., & Pollard, S. R. (2022). Improving uncertainty tolerance in medical students: A scoping review. *Medical Education*, *56*(12), 1163–1173. https://doi.org/10.1111/medu.14873
Pearsall, P. (2007). *Awe: The delights and dangers of our eleventh emotion*. HCI.
Pereira, A. G., Woods, M., Olson, A. P., van den Hoogenhof, S., Duffy, B. L., & Englander, R. (2018). Criterion-based assessment in a norm-based world: How can we move past grades? *Academic Medicine*, *93*(4), 560–564. https://doi.org/10.1097/ACM.0000000000001939
Peterson, S. (2008). *Writing across the curriculum: All teachers teach writing*. Portage & Main Press.
Phillipson, S. N., & McCann, M. (2007). When geniuses fail: Na-Dene' (Navajo) conception of giftedness in the eyes of the holy deities. In R. J. Sternberg (Ed.), *Conceptions of giftedness*. Taylor & Francis.
Popham, W. J. (2001). *The truth about testing: An educator's call to action*. Association for Supervision and Curriculum Development.
Posner, D. (2004). What's wrong with teaching to the test? *Phi Delta Kappan*, *85*(10), 749–751. https://doi.org/10.1177/003172170408501009
Potter, N. N. (2022). The virtue of epistemic humility. *Philosophy, Psychiatry & Psychology*, *29*(2), 121–123. https://doi.org/10.1353/ppp.2022.0022
Powell, W. R., & Kusuma-Powell, O. (2010). *Becoming an emotionally intelligent teacher*. Corwin.
Preece, R. (2006). *The wisdom of imperfection: The challenge of individuation in Buddhist life*. Snow Lion.
Privette, G. (2001). Defining moments of self-actualization: Peak performance and peak experience. In K. J. Schneider, J. F. T. Bugental, & J. F. Pierson (Eds.), *The Handbook of humanistic psychology* (pp. 161–180). Sage Publications.

Quigley, C. F., & Hall, A. H. (2016). Taking care: Understanding the roles of caregiver and being cared for in a kindergarten classroom. *Journal of Early Childhood Research: ECR, 14*(2), 181–195. https://doi.org/10.1177/1476718X14548783

Rasooli, A., Rasegh, A., Zandi, H., & Firoozi, T. (2023). Teachers' conceptions of fairness in classroom assessment: An empirical study. *Journal of Teacher Education, 74*(3), 260–273. https://doi.org/10.1177/00224871221130742

Rechtschaffen, D. (2014). *The way of mindful education: Cultivating well-being in teachers and students*. W. W. Norton & Co.

Reisenzein, R. (1994). Pleasure-arousal theory and the intensity of emotions. *Journal of Personality and Social Psychology, 67*(3), 525–539. https://doi.org/10.1037/0022-3514.67.3.525

Reddy, Y. M., & Andrade, H. (2010). A review of rubric use in higher education. *Assessment & Evaluation in Higher Education, 35*(4), 435–448. http://doi.org/10.1080/02602930902862859

Reynolds, A. (2022). "Where does my £9000 go?" Student identities in a marketised British higher education sector. *SN Social Sciences, 2*(8), 125–125. https://doi.org/10.1007/s43545-022-00432-6

Rimm-Kaufman, S. (2020). *SEL from the start: Building skills in K-5*. New York: W. W. Norton & Co.

Rimm-Kaufman, S., Strambler, M. J., & Schonert-Reichl, K. A. (2023). *Social and emotional learning in action: Creating systemic change in schools*. Guilford Press.

Roberts, R. (1989). *Serendipity: Accidental discoveries in science*. Wiley.

Roberts, R. C. (2014). Cosmic gratitude. *European Journal for Philosophy of Religion, 6*(3), 65–83. https://doi.org/10.24204/ejpr.v6i3.163

Roberts, R., & Telech, D. (2019). *The moral psychology of gratitude*. Rowman & Littlefield International.

Rodriguez, V., & Fitzpatrick, M. (2014). *The teaching brain: An evolutionary trait at the heart of education*. New Press.

Rogers, C. (2004). *On becoming a person: A therapist's view of psychotherapy*. Constable.

Romanelli, F., Bird, E., & Ryan, M. (2009). Learning styles: A review of theory, application, and best practices. *American Journal of Pharmaceutical Education, 73*(1), 9–9. https://doi.org/10.5688/aj730109

Ruddick, S. (1995). *Maternal thinking: Toward a politics of peace*. Beacon Press.

Rust, V. D., & Kim, S. (2021). Globalisation and global university rankings. In *Third international handbook of globalisation, education and policy research* (pp. 241–255). Springer International Publishing. https://doi.org/10.1007/978-3-030-66003-1_13

Ryan, M. J. (2018). *Radical generosity: Unlock the transformative power of giving*. Conari Press.

Ryan, von der Embse, N. P., Pendergast, L. L., Saeki, E., Segool, N., & Schwing, S. (2017). Leaving the teaching profession: The role of teacher stress and educational accountability policies on turnover intent. *Teaching and Teacher Education, 66*, 1–11. https://doi.org/10.1016/j.tate.2017.03.016

Sadler, D. R. (2005). Interpretations of criteria-based assessment and grading in higher education. *Assessment and Evaluation in Higher Education, 30*(2), 175–194. https://doi.org/10.1080/0260293042000264262

Samuels, B. (2013). *Being present*. Inside Higher Ed. https://www.insidehighered.com/views/2013/01/24/essay-flaws-distance-education#ixzz2IujdcaLm

Samuels, M. (2013). *Healing with the mind's eye*. Trade Paper Press.

Sanders, D., & Sanders, J. A. (1983). *Teaching through metaphor: An integrated brain approach*. Longman.

Santman, D. (2002). Teaching to the test?: Test preparation in the reading workshop. *Language Arts, 79*(3), 203–211.

Schein, E. H. (2021). *Humble inquiry: The gentle art of asking instead of telling*. Berrett-Koehler Publishers.

Schon, D. (1984). *The reflective practitioner: How professionals think in action*. Basic Books.

Schopenhauer, A. (2010). *Essays and aphorisms*. Penguin.

Schneider, C. (2005). Liberal education. In R. H. Hersh & J. Merrow (Eds.), *Declining by degrees: Higher education at risk*. Palgrave Macmillan.

Schneider, K. (2004). *Rediscovery of awe: Splendor, mystery, and the fluid center of life*. Paragon House.

Schrift, A. D. (1997). *The logic of the gift: Toward an ethic of generosity* (1st ed.). Routledge.

Schumacher, E. F. (1973). *Small is beautiful: Economics as if people mattered*. Harper.

Schwartzman, R. (2017). Unma(s)king education in the image of business: A vivisection of educational consumerism. *Cultural Studies ↔ Critical Methodologies, 17*(4), 333–346. https://doi.org/10.1177/1532708617706126

Scott, K. (2017) The tragic aspect of teaching: Hope in face of uncertainty. *Religious Education, 112*(3), 275–286. https://doi.org/10.1080/00344087.2017.1303301

Seligman, M. E. P., Steen, T. A., Park, N., & Peterson, C. (2005). Positive psychology progress: Empirical validation of interventions. *American Psychologist, 60*(5), 410–421. https://doi.org/org/10.1037/0003-066x.60.5.410

Selwyn, N. (2011). *Education and technology: Key issues and debates*. Continuum International Pub.

Selwyn, N. (2019). *Should robots replace teachers?* Polity Press.

Shadmi, E. (Ed.). (2021). *The legacy of mothers: Matriarchies and the gift economy as post-capitalist alternatives*. Inanna Publications & Education.

Shay, S. (2005). The assessment of complex tasks: A double reading. *Studies in Higher Education, 30*(6), 663–679. https://doi.org/10.1080/03075070500339988

Sheldrake, R. (2009). *Morphic resonance: The nature of formative causation*. Park Street Press.

Sheng Yen. (2008). *The method of no method: The Chan practice of silent illumination*. Shambala.

Sheng Yen. (2009). *108 adages of wisdom*. Dharma Drum Publications.

Sheng Yen. (2013). *Tea words volume II*. Dharma Drum Publications.

Sherry, J. F. (1983). Gift giving in anthropological perspective. *The Journal of Consumer Research*, *10*(2), 157–168. https://doi.org/10.1086/208956

Shindler, J. (2009). *Transformative classroom management: Positive strategies to engage all students and promote a psychology of success*. John Wiley & Sons.

Siebert, D. C., Mutran, E. J., & Reitzes, D. C. (1999). Friendship and social support: The importance of role identity to aging adults. *Social Work* (New York), *44*(6), 522–533.

Singer, I. (2009). *The nature of love: Plato to Luther* (rev. ed., vol. 1). Irving Singer Library. MIT Press.

Singh, A., & Manjaly, J. A. (2022). Using curiosity to improve learning outcomes in schools. *SAGE Open*, *12*(1). https://doi.org/10.1177/21582440211069392

Slote, M. (2013). *From enlightenment to receptivity: Rethinking our values*. Oxford University Press.

Smith, T. W., & Colby, S. A. (2007). Teaching for deep learning. *The Clearing House*, *80*(5), 205–210. https://doi.org/10.3200/TCHS.80.5.205-210

Spady, W. G. (1994). *Outcome-based education: Critical issues and answers*. American Association of School Administrators.

Sperber, M. (2005). How undergraduate education became college lite—and a personal apology. In R. H. Hersh & J. Merrow (Eds.), *Declining by degrees: Higher education at risk*. Palgrave Macmillan.

Spronk, B., Stolper, M., & Widdershoven, G. (2017). Tragedy in moral case deliberation. *Medical Health Care Philosophy*, *20*(3), 321–333. https://doi.org/10.1007/s11019-016-9749-7

Stahl, A., & Feigenson, L. (2015). Observing the unexpected enhances infants' learning and exploration. *Science*, *348*, 91–94. https://doi.org/10.1126/science.aaa3799

Starkey, L. (2012). *Teaching and learning in the digital age*. Routledge.

Starko, A. J. (2010). *Creativity in the classroom: Schools of curious delight*. Routledge.

Starr, A. (2020). Economics of generosity and ghost dance of Indigenous education. In G. A. Cajete (Ed.), *Native minds rising: Exploring transformative Indigenous education*. J. Charlton Publishing.

Stauss, B. (2023). *Psychology of gift-giving* (1st ed.). Springer Berlin / Heidelberg. https://doi.org/10.1007/978-3-662-66393-6

Steffen, L. (2009). Finding abundance in a world of scarcity. *Creative Nursing*, *15*(2), 66–69. https://doi.org/10.1891/1078-4535.15.2.66

Steindl-Rast, D. (2004). Gratitude as thankfulness and as gratefulness. In R. A. Emmons & M. McCulloch (Eds.), *The psychology of gratitude*. Oxford University Press. https://doi.org/10.1093/acprof:oso/9780195150100.003.0014

Sternberg, R. J., Jarvin, L., & Grigorenko, E. L. (2011). *Explorations in giftedness*. Cambridge University Press.

Stone, M. (2003, March 18). EC professors fare (somewhat) well on ratemyprofessors. com. The Leader. http://www.elmhurst.edu/~leader/archive/2003/cultue_03_18/ratemyproffessor.htm

Stotsky, S. (2016). Testing limits. *Academic Questions, 29*(3), 285–298. https://doiorg.ezproxy.gvsu.edu/10.1007/s12129-016-9578-4

Stronach, I., & Piper, H. (2009). The touching example of Summerhill school. In P. A. Woods & G. J. Woods (Eds.), *Alternative education for the 21st century: Philosophies, approaches, visions* (pp. 49–64). Palgrave Macmillan. https://doi.org/10.1057/9780230618367_4

Suzuki, D. (2022). *The sacred balance: Rediscovering our place in nature.* David Suzuki Institute.

Suzuki, S. (1994). *Zen mind, beginner's mind: Informal talks on Zen meditation and practice.* Weatherill.

Swimme, B. (1996). *The hidden heart of the cosmos: Humanity and the new story.* Orbis Books.

Takhar, J. (2021). Aporia. *Journal of Marketing Management, 37*(1–2), 21–22. https://doi.org/10.1080/0267257X.2020.1769709

Taras, M., & Wong, H. M. (2023). *Student self-assessment: An essential guide for teaching, learning and reflection at school and university.* Routledge.

Tassone, B. G. (2019). Existentialism and ecstasy: Colin Wilson's phenomenological account of peak experiences. *PhaenEx, 13*(1), 46–85. https://doi.org/10.22329/p.v13i1.4909

Taylor, C. (1991). *The malaise of modernity.* House of Anansi.

Teigen, K. H. (1997). Luck, envy and gratitude: It could have been different. *Scandinavian Journal of Psychology, 38*(4), 313–323. https://doi.org/10.1111/1467-9450.00041

Teigen, K. H., & Keren, G. (2003). Surprises: Low probabilities or high contrasts? *Cognition, 87,* 55–71.

Thera, N. (2008). The power of mindfulness: An inquiry into the scope of bare attention and the principal sources of its strength. In N. Thera (Ed.), *Pathways of Buddhist thought.* Taylor & Francis.

Thompson, B. (2017). *Teaching with tenderness: Toward an embodied practice.* University of Illinois Press.

Thondup, T. (2000). *Boundless healing: Meditation exercises to enlighten the mind and heal the body.* Shambhala.

Tiedens, L. Z., & Linton, S. (2001). Judgment under emotional certainty and uncertainty: The effects of specific emotions on information processing. *Journal of Personality and Social Psychology, 81*(6), 973–988. https://doi.org/10.1037/0022-3514.81.6.973

Todd, S. (2014). Between body and spirit: The liminality of pedagogical relationships. *Journal of Philosophy of Education, 48*(2), 231–245. https://doi.org/10.1111/1467-9752.12065

Toepfer, S. M., Cichy, K., & Peters, P. (2011). Letters of gratitude: Further evidence for author benefits. *Journal of Happiness Studies, 13*(1), 187–201. https://doi.org/10.1007/s10902-011-9257-7

Toepfer, S., & Walker, K. (2009). Letters of gratitude: Improving well-being through expressive writing. *Journal of Writing Research*, *1*(3), 181–198. https://doi.org/10.17239/jowr-2009.01.03.1

Trautmann, S. T., Vieider, F. M., & Wakker, P. P. (2008). Causes of ambiguity aversion: Known versus unknown preferences. *Journal of Risk and Uncertainty*, *36*(3), 225–243. https://doi.org/10.1007/s11166-008-9038-9

Turkle, S. (2011). *Alone together: Why we expect more from technology and less from each other*. Basic Books.

Underwood, J. D. M. (2015). *Learning and the e-generation*. John Wiley & Sons.

Valdesolo, P., Shtulman, A., & Baron, A. S. (2017). Science is awe-some: The emotional antecedents of science learning. *Emotion Review*, *9*(3), 215–221. https://doi.org/10.1177/1754073916673212

Van Beveren, M.-L., Harding, K., Beyers, W., & Braet, C. (2018). Don't worry, be happy: The role of positive emotionality and adaptive emotion regulation strategies for youth depressive symptoms. *British Journal of Clinical Psychology*, *57*(1), 18–41. https://doi.org/10.1111/bjc.12151

Vandevelde, A. (Ed.). (2000). *Gifts and interests*. Peeters

Vanhamme, J., Lindgreen, A., & Beverland, M. (2021). The paradox of surprise: Empirical evidence about surprising gifts received and given by close relations. *European Journal of Marketing*, *55*(2), 618–646. https://doi.org/10.1108/EJM-03-2019-0277

Vanslyke-Briggs, K. (2010). *The nurturing teacher: Managing the stress of caring*. Rowman & Littlefield.

Vaughan, G., & Estola, E. (2007). The gift paradigm in early childhood education. *Educational Philosophy and Theory*, *39*(3), 246–263. https://doi.org/10.1111/j.1469-5812.2007.00326.x

Vaughan, G. (2013). Mother sense and the image schema of the gift. *Semiotica*, *196*, 57–77. https://doi.org/10.1515/sem-2013-0047

Vincent, D. (2020). *A history of solitude*. Polity Press.

Visser, M. (2008). *The gift of thanks: The roots and rituals of gratitude* (1st ed.). Harper Collins.

Wagamese, R. (2019). *One drum: Stories and ceremonies for a planet*. Douglas and McIntyre.

Wallace, J. (2020). *Tragedy since 9/11: Reading a world out of joint*. Bloomsbury Academic.

Wang, R. (2012). *Yinyang: The way of heaven and earth in Chinese thought and culture*. Cambridge University Press.

Ward, M. K., & Broniarczyk, S. M. (2016). Ask and you shall (not) receive: Close friends prioritize relational signaling over recipient preferences in their gift choices. *Journal of Marketing Research*, *53*(6), 1001–1018. https://doi.org/10.1509/jmr.13.0537

Watts, A. (1972). *Essential Lectures 07: Work and Play—Alan Watts (organism.earth)*. The Library of Consciousness. https://www.organism.earth/library/document/essential-lectures-7

Watts, A. (1985). *The way of Zen*. Vintage.

Watters, A. (2021). *Teaching machines: The history of personalized learning*. MIT Press.

Weil, S. (2001). *Waiting for God*. G. P Putnam & Sons.

Weiskrantz, L. (2009). *Blindsight: A case study spanning 35 years and new developments* (rev. ed.). Oxford University Press.

White, P. (1999). Gratitude, citizenship and education. *Studies in Philosophy and Education, 18*(1–2), 43–52. https://doi.org/10.1023/A:1005183220317

Whitehead, M., Lilley, R., Howell, R., Jones, R., & Pykett, J. (2016). (Re)Inhabiting awareness: Geography and mindfulness. *Social & Cultural Geography, 17*(4), 553–573. https://doi.org/10.1080/14649365.2015.1089590

Wilde, O. (1976). *De profundis and other writings*. Penguin.

Williams, R. (1991). *The trusting heart: Great news about type a behavior*. Crown.

Wilson, C. (1985). *The essential Colin Wilson*. Harrap.

Wilson, C. (2016). *The outsider*. TarcherPerigee.

Wilson, J. T. (2016). Brightening the mind: The impact of practicing gratitude on focus and resilience in learning. *The Journal of Scholarship of Teaching and Learning, 16*(4), 1–13. https://doi.org/10.14434/josotl.v16i4.19998

Wilson, T. D., & Gilbert, D. T. (2008). Explaining away a model of affective adaptation. *Perspectives on Psychological Science 3*(5), 370–386.

Winner, L. F. (2007). *Mudhouse Sabbath: An invitation to a life of spiritual discipline*. Pocket Classics.

Wolfstone, I. F. (2019). Sharing economies and Indigenous matricultures in the land now called Canada. *Canadian Woman Studies, 34*(1–2), 15.

Wong, Y. J., Owen, J., Gabana, N. T., Brown, J. W., McInnis, S., Toth, P., & Gilman, L. (2018). Does gratitude writing improve the mental health of psychotherapy clients? Evidence from a randomized controlled trial. *Psychotherapy Research, 28*(2), 192–202. https://doi.org/10.1080/10503307.2016.1169332

Wood, A. M., Froh, J. J., & Geraghty, A. W. (2010). Gratitude and well-being: A review and theoretical integration. *Clinical Psychology Review, 30*(7), 890–905. https://doi.org/.2010.03.005

Wright, M. J., Sanguinetti, J. L., Young, S., & Sacchet, M. D. (2023). Uniting Contemplative Theory and Scientific Investigation: Toward a Comprehensive Model of the Mind. *Mindfulness, 14*(5), 1088–1101. https://doi.org/10.1007/s12671-023-02101-y

Yeo, M., Manarin, K., & Miller-Young, J. (2018). Phenomenology of surprise in a SoTL scholars' program. *Teaching & Learning Inquiry: The ISSOTL Journal, 6*(2), 16–28. https://doi.org/10.20343/teachlearninqu.6.2.3

Young, J. (2013). *The philosophy of tragedy: From Plato to Žižek*. Cambridge University Press.

Zaretsky, R. (2021, March 9). *Simone Weil's radical conception of attention*. Literary Hub. https://lithub.com/simone-weils-radical-conception-of-attention/

Zhou, Y., & Dong, C. (2023). Nourishing social solidarity in exchanging gifts: A study on social exchange in Shanghai communities during COVID-19 lockdown. *Humanities & Social Sciences Communications, 10*(1), 627–11. https://doi.org/10.1057/s41599-023-02152-5

Index

abundance
  classrooms, experienced in, 187
  cooperative ethics and, 6
  creativity and, 6
  education, in context of, 5
  gift-centered view of, 172
  mindset of, 5–6, 211, 214, 217–220, 223
  scarcity, vs., 5–6, 150–151
  visualization of, 272–275
Adyashanti, 104, 108
Aenead, The (Virgil), 213
Apple, Michael, 21, 117–118
aporia, 15, 231–252
  classroom instances of, 232–250
  definition of, 231–232
  tension and conflict, expressions of, 232
Armstrong, Karen, 150, 221
assessment
  bell curves and, 135
  communities of practice and, 156
  formative vs. summative, 47, 135
  gift metaphor and, 253
  gratitude-based, 162–163
  holistic view of, 26, 246, 262
  outcome-based, 24–25
  partiality and, 244–246
  reciprocal nature of, 97, 235
  student-driven, 136–137
  unpredictability and, 241
  value centered, 23
attachment (mental state), 195, 214
attachment theory (psychology), 35, 102, 107
attention, 25, 62, 71, 77, 82, 86, 89, 120, 199–200, 242
  technology's impact on, 35–36, 71
  See also attentiveness
attentiveness, 126, 153, 199–200
awe, 14, 163
  definition of, 205
  empathy, relation to, 96
  encounter-based, 84
  fluid center (Schneider) and, 205
  humility, relation to, 195–196
  illness and, 226–227
  nature-based, 150
  peak experience and, 61
  rational vs irrational, 227
  science, as a way of cultivating, 206
  self-reference, lacking in, 162
  shadow aspects of, 227
  surprise, related to, 61
  transpersonal gratitude and, 163

Bache, Christopher, 137, 263, 281
bare awareness, 2, 71
beginner's mind, 7, 104. *See also* mindfulness

behaviorism, 13, 126
bell curve, 3, 135, 141, 243
belonging (sense of), 150, 161, 163
body scan, 257, 259–260
Brach, Tara, 220–221
Brazier, Caroline, 189
Brooks, Peter, 58–59
Brown, Hunter, 60, 67, 117
Buddhism, 12
    Buddha, life of, 175
    causes and conditions, perspectives on, 104
    emptiness (sunyata), concept of, 274
    generosity (dana), view of, 152
    Hua-yen school of, 193
    imperfection, views on, 90–91
    impermanence, concept of, 175
    nature, views of, 150
    silent illumination, practice of, 265
    spiritual awakening, found in, 2
    visualization practices in, 254
    wants vs needs, views on, 72
    workplace, ideas of, 46–48

care
    ecologically-minded, 280
    ethics of, 90, 158
    feminist views of, 159
    fostering growth and learning, 10
    one caring vs. one cared for (Noddings), 128
    pedagogical theories of, 32, 128–131
caregiving
    gift economy and, 131
    media stereotypes and, 129
    patriarchal notions of, 129–130
    See also care; teacher identity
ceremony, 82–83
choice, 37
    consumerist view of, in schools, 4
    gift giving, and, 154, 237–238
    gratitude and, 182
    infinite illusion of, 35, 37
    reflective aspect of, 27–28
    student-driven, 46, 235–236
    vocational (*vocare*), 49
    tragedies and, 171, 174
    writing process and, 44–45
classroom
    living energy, as (Bache), 137
    temporality of, 50, 51
clinging, 85, 87, 102, 211–214
    attachment theory and, 103
    control-based, 70
    ego-based, 48
    visualization and, 254
    See also attachment
cognitive dissonance, 16
Collaborative for Academic, Social, and Emotional Learning (CASEL), 9. *See also* social-emotional learning (SEL)
contemplation
    confusion and, 232
    desire, as an approach to, 216
    direct form of, 82, 260
    gratitude, approach to, 161–162, 234
    objects of, 71, 217
Cook, Francis, 193, 198
counterfactual thinking, 170–171, 177
Courtois, Flora, 197–198
creativity
    deep learning, relationship to, 44
    incubation period, 44–45
    mindfulness and, 2
    risk, relation to, 73
    scarcity, as inhibiting, 6
    surprise, and, 44
curiosity
    extrinsic motivation as inhibiting, 34
    learning, relation to, 45–46
    love, as a form of, 46
    open-ended inquiry, form of, 45, 73

deep learning, 27, 120, 279
  definition of, 44
  expressive writing, in, 44
Derrida, Jacques, 6, 231
desire
  achievement-based, 32–33
  competition, relation to, 32–33, 35
  curriculum, in 40–41
  ecological sustainability of, 33, 36
  exceptionality and, 38
  gratitude, relation to, 177
  identity, and, 34
  insatiability of, 39–40
  subject-oriented vs object-oriented, 39–40
  technology, connection to, 35–36
  tragic views of, 176
desire-based curriculum, 31–41. *See also* desire
discovery, 72–24, 97–101
  accidents, stemming from, 97
  constructivism, and, 100
  fostering thinking, 99–100
  inquiry, form of, 99
  mindset of, 97–98
  phenomenology of, 98

embodiment
  gratitude and, 162, 164
  learning, connection to, 191
  meditation on, 256–263
  metaphor and, 190
  teaching, element of, 53
Emerson, Ralph Waldo, 89, 233, 237–238
emotional contagion, 9
  empathy, and, 93
emotional intelligence (EQ), 8–11, 94
  definition of, 11
emotional labour, 157, 234
emotional valence, 57
empathy, 92–97

care-based ethics, and, 128
  connection to awe, 95–96
  cultivation of, 191
  definitions of, 80, 93, 109
  emailing and, 94
  forms of (cognitive, emotional, compassionate), 94
  fostering gratitude, way of, 125
  hierarchical classroom, challenges, 92
  impartiality and, 245
  mirroring, as form of, 93–95
  self-compassion and, 94–95
  social-emotional learning (SEL) and, 9
  transportation theory, and, 73, 95
Engels, Jeremy, 233–234
epoche, 64, 189. *See also* phenomenology
Epstein, Mark, 33–34, 39–40, 216
exchange economy
  anthropocentric notion of, 133
  autonomy, emphasis on, 135–136
  bell curves and, 135
  consumerism and, 119–120, 134
  contractual theories of, 148–149
  devaluing domestic work and, 131–132
  economic cycle of, 6
  education and, 134
  extrinsic rewards and, 133
  gift economy, compared to, 131–132
  logic of, 7
  monetization of work, 131
  patriarchy and, 131–132
  outcome-based, 6
existential gratitude, 234
  characteristics of, 68–69
  definition of, 67
  See also gratitude
expressive writing, 44–45

factory model (in education), 28, 117–118
failure, perspectives on, 46–47, 73, 277–278
fear of missing out (FOMO), 35, 199, 220–221
fluid center, metaphor of (Schneider), 14, 191, 205–207
Fox, Matthew, 48, 83, 227–228, 258
Fromm, Erich, 24, 32, 88, 189–190, 222

Galea, Simone, 157, 239–241
gender pronouns (as used in this text), 16
gift economy, 69, 131–137
   definition of, 132
   ecosystemic framing of, 133–134
   education, role in, 134–137
   feminist theories of, 131–134
   non-hierarchical, 137
   See also gifts
giftedness (in education), 137–140
   Indigenous models of, 38
   individual vs collective, 140
   qualities of, 138
   pentagonal model (Sternberg et al.), 137–138
   social constructivist view of, 139
gifts
   asymmetrical, 116, 238–241
   challenging the autonomous self, 116
   cosmological view of, 127
   cyclic nature of, 172
   improvisational (Osteen), 116
   indebtedness, 116, 233
   Indigenous views of, 38, 123, 132
   logic of (Derrida), 6
   mystery, and, 7
   poverty of (Marion), 7
   reciprocity of, 121, 132
   relational view of, 132–133
   seed/embryo metaphor in, 125–126
   surprise, and 115–116
   sustaining novelty of, 241–244
   uncalculated, 6
   unconditional, 122
   See also gift economy; giftedness
Giroux, Henri, 4, 38
Glass Bead Game, The (Hesse), 49
grace, 66–69, 76, 143, 170
   gifts, relation to, 117, 224
   gratuity, and, 224
   indebtedness, vs. 233
   suffering, relation to, 202
   surrender to the unknown, and, 214
   tragedy and, 176
gratitude, 147–166
   asymmetry of, 157–158
   characteristics of, 147–148
   childhood impressions of, 147
   contrastive peril and, 182
   emotional labour, as form of, 157
   existential, 67–68
   indebtedness, form of, 147, 234
   loss, relation to, 3
   nature, connection to, 150
   practices of, 159–160
   prosocial aspects of, 155–156
   receiving qualities of, 152–154
   reciprocation, 155–157
   resacralization, form of, 52
   self-directed, 53
   tragedy, relationship to, 169–187
   transpersonal, 159–165
   wholeheartedness, and, 154–155
gratitude fatigue, 154, 162, 231
gratitude journaling, 151, 170, 231
Great Chain of Being (Lovejoy), 173, 193, 272
guided imagery
   definition of, 254
   healing, role in, 71–72
   See also visualization

Hamlet (Shakespeare), 173–174, 185
Hanson, Rick, 68, 87, 94–95, 156, 179, 214, 257
Heidegger, Martin, 85, 124–125, 231, 234
hidden curriculum (Apple), 117–118
holding space (Winnicott), 201–204
holistic education, 12, 44
Horkheimer, Max, 123–124
Howells, Kerry, 154–157, 160, 232
humble inquiry (Schein), 88. *See also* receptivity
humility
  awe-based, 205
  empathy and, 195–196
  epistemic form of, 143, 186
  giftedness, form of, 140
  tragic view of life and, 170, 183, 225
  trust, relation to, 103
Hunt, David, 81–82, 195
Hylen, Michael, 8–9, 22

Iliad, The (Homer), 181–182, 184
illness
  awe, relation to, 226–227
  gratitude, source of, 267
  reprioritizing behaviors, and, 69–70
impermanence, 183, 207–208, 211
  meditation on, 261
  teaching and, 224–226
inclusive teaching, 10

jealousy, 215–216, 222
Jennings, Patricia, 91, 264–265
Jewel Net of Indra, the 197–201

Kabat-Zinn, Jon, 7, 69, 87, 202–203, 259
knowledge
  acquisitive view of, 24, 32–33
  constructivist view of, 99–100

logos vs *techne* (Plato), 29
  objectivist myth of (Palmer), 217
  participatory view of, 124–125, 143
  subject mastery of, 38–39, 84–85
  See also learning
Kohn, Alfie, 33–34, 134

learning
  acquisitive model of, 24, 27
  complex forms of, 43
  cyclic nature of, 11, 22–23, 39
  failure, as part of, 46–47, 277
  intrinsic vs. extrinsic, 33 44, 121, 134
  process based, 277
  timeless, 44
  transformative, 44, 60–61
  transmission model of, 53, 212
  uncertainty as vital part of, 27
Lewis, Richmond, 46–48
listening, active, 9
Llewellyn, Kristina, 129–131
logical positivism, 13, 28
loneliness, 216–217, 275

MacIntyre, Alisdair, 153–154, 202
Marcel, Gabriel, 122–123, 148–149
Marion, Jean-Luc, 6–7
Marut, Lama, 32, 38
Maslow, Abraham, 13, 52, 55, 61, 63–64, 81, 84, 97, 108–109, 220, 222–223, 228
Maugham, William Somerset, 192
Mauss, Marcel, 132–133, 137, 149, 232–233, 239
meditation
  abundance, as fostering, 179
  acceptance, cultivation of, 105–106
  benefits of, 12
  gratitude-based, 162
  group practice of, 53
  guided visualization, used in, 253–256, 267

meditation *(continued)*
  holding space, as, 202–203
  loss, process of, 183
  non-striving, form of, 104–105
  pain management, and, 71–72
  perfectionism, as letting go of, 90–91
  silent illumination, form of, 265–266
  teachers' practice of, 82
metaphor, 190–192
  classroom as ecosystem, 263
  conduit metaphor (of learning/teaching), 219
  consumerist (in education), 13, 27, 118, 120
  embodied aspects of, 191
  embryo/seed metaphor, 125–127
  gift as metaphor, 144, 253
  gratitude-based, 191–192
  learning tool, as, 59, 190–191
  market-based, 27, 46, 118, 135
  musical metaphor, 264–265
  tapestry as metaphor, 192–197
  target vs source domain, 190
  tragedy as educational metaphor, 225
  TV screen metaphor, 87
  visualization, used in, 253–256
metaphorical thinking, 190. *See also* metaphor
Miller, John P. (Jack), 12, 35–36, 44, 46, 59, 71, 73, 93, 105, 161, 191, 211–213, 216, 257
Miller, Timothy, 34–35, 178–179, 242, 268–269
mindfulness
  attitude of, 7
  body scan, link to, 259
  email writing and, 94
  gratitude and, 162–164
  present moment, and, 65–66
  receptivity, and, 91
  See also meditation
Montessori, Maria, 126–127, 142, 158, 223
Moustakas, Clark, 66, 89
mothering, 129, 158, 218–219. *See also* parenting
mystery (sense of), 11, 26, 45–46, 60–61, 71–73, 84, 109, 126, 141–143, 163, 193–196, 200, 204, 241

narrative (in literature) 44, 58–60, 95
negative capability (Keats), 43
neoliberalism, 4, 33, 118, 125, 134–135, 220, 233–234
Noddings, Nel, 128–129, 133, 152–153, 156–157, 235–236
nurturance stress, 31–32. *See also* teacher burnout

online learning, 35–36, 215, 248
  intimacy, substitute for, 36
  isolation, and, 35
  plagiarism and, 248
  socialization, effects on, 35–36
  teacher rating tools, 119
over-reliance (on teacher authority), 214–215

Palmer, Parker, 1, 86–87, 105, 195, 217–218, 224, 239, 251
parenting
  anxieties projected on children, 33
  attachment styles and, 102–103, 107
  attentiveness to child's growth, 126
  attitudes toward children's success/failure, 33–34, 277–278
  calling (*vocere*) and, 49
  holding space and, 202
  interrelation to children, 136, 245, 274–275

nurturing children's gifts, 126, 139, 140
   See also mothering
partiality, 244–246
peak experience (Maslow), 13, 55, 61, 63–65, 72, 77
Pearsall, Paul, 96, 226–228
pedagogical tact (Manen), 5
perfectionism, in teaching, 53, 90–91
phenomenology, 84
   attitude and stance of, 89
   bracketing, and, 189
   defined, 84
   surprise and, 61–76
Plato, 29
plenitude, 6, 193, 207, 272–277. *See also* abundance
positive psychology, 179, 250
presence, 35, 53, 71, 80, 107, 126, 176, 219, 221, 255–257, 264, 270–272

Qu'ran, 150

reason, 29–30, 60, 153, 175–176
   instrumental view of, 34, 123–124
receptivity, 81–92
   artistic temperament (Wilde) and, 89–90
   attention, form of, 82
   caring, relationship to, 90–91
   definition of, 81
   friendship and, 82
   giving vs. receiving, 82
   hearing sounds as a form of, 87–88
   social value of, 82–83
   teaching as a form of, 82
   TV screen metaphor of, 87
   undervalued in classrooms, 81
   waiting, as a form of, 89
Rechtschaffen, Daniel, 206, 260
resacralizing (Maslow), 52

Rogers, Carl, 92, 102–103
reflection, 28–29
rubric, 49, 98, 101, 106, 134–135, 214, 219, 235, 237, 240, 246, 269. *See also* assessment
Ruddick, Sara, 158

scarcity mindset, 5–6, 179, 218, 221. *See also* abundance
Schneider, Kirk, 191, 205, 232, 237
Schon, Donald, 28–29
Schopenhauer, Arthur, 177–179, 202
Schumacher, E. F., 47–48, 264
Scott, Kieran, 225
Sheng Yen, 72, 150, 261, 265
Slote, Michael, 33, 37–38, 81, 90
social emotional learning (SEL), 2, 8–11
   components of, 9
   definition of, 7
   EQ, relationship to, 8–9
   self-regulation and, 2
   surprise, and, 9–11
soul, theory of (Miller), 105
soul's code (Hillman), 126
St. Neot's margin (Wilson), 13, 61–76, 93, 169, 177
Starr, Arlo, 268
standardized testing, 3, 21
   competition based, 21
   depersonalization and, 23
   disadvantages of, 21–22
   efficiency-based, 24
   genre, as, 22
   measurable outcomes of, 21
   objective view of, 26
   one size fits all approach, 21
   overlooking complex problems, 26–27
   socio-emotional growth, effects on, 22–23
   student creativity, effects on, 22

standardized testing *(continued)*
  teacher accountability for, 21, 25
  teacher autonomy and, 26
  teacher-student relationships, impacts on, 23, 24, 31
  time constraints presented by, 23
student identity, 134–136
success
  attachment to, 195
  gratitude and, 148
  employment at graduation, based on, 123
  individual vs. collective, 38
  teacher accountability for, 130
  workplace definition of, 46–47
surprise
  actively fostered, 8
  benefits, for teachers, 10–11
  characteristics of, 54–55, 79
  cognitive appraisal, role in, 56–58
  definition of, 40–41
  Four Pillars of, 80–111
  gifts, relation to, 5
  habituation, effects on, 56
  learning benefits of, 5, 55
  liminality of, 43
  memory retention, and, 5, 55, 57, 59
  metaphor as form of, 59
  narrative-based, 57
  negative reactions to, 79
  perspective taking and, 58
  phenomenology of, 61–76
  planned forms of, 57, 98–99
  primary vs secondary emotion, 56
  scientific research on, 55–61
  teachable moments, and, 60, 86, 105
  temporality, relation to, 51–52, 55
  transactional notion of, 59, 219
  transformative model of, 60–61
Suzuki, Shunryu, 104

Taoism, 105, 108, 182
Taylor, Charles, 34, 82, 124, 136, 142
Taylor, Frederick Winslow, 28
teachable moment, 60, 86, 105
teacher burnout, 25, 141
  attrition rates, and, 25
  causes of, 25–26, 31
  emotional labour, and, 157, 234
  standardized tests leading to, 141
  stress, relationship to, 25
teacher identity
  accountability and, 21
  caregiver, as, 31
  maternal pedagogies and, 157–159
  objectivist myth of, 27, 31
  patriarchy, influence of, 129–130
  self-sacrificing/martyrdom, 129
technical rationality, 27–31
  behaviorism, influence of, 28
  defined, 27–28
  logical positivism, influence of, 28
  Newtonian model, and, 30
tragedy, 169–187
  characteristics of, 171
  classroom benefits of, 173, 183–186
  death and impermanence, link to, 183
  desire-based *(agon)*, 176
  envy, compared to, 170
  fate vs. choice, balance of 171
  gratitude, relation to, 170–171
  knowledge, and, 174
  metaphor for teaching, 225
  redemptive turns, and, 171
transportation theory (literature), 73, 95
trust, 101–107
  accepting change, and, 106
  classroom, in, 105–106
  complexity theory, and, 106
  contemplative framing of, 104
  definitions of, 101

early childhood development, and, 102–103
health benefits of, 101
self-acceptance, as form of, 103
tolerance for ambiguity, and, 102
teachable moments, 105
transcending self-image, 105
Turkle, Sherry, 35–36

Vaughan, Genevieve, 132, 158
visualization, 253–282
gift based, 105, 162, 231, 235
guided, 11, 253–282
metaphor, as part of, 253
techniques of, 253–356

waiting, 89, 200

Weil, Simone, 89, 199–200
Wilde, Oscar, 89–90
Wilson, Colin, 61–76, 79, 93, 169, 177–180, 182
Winnicott, D. W., 153, 201–202. *See also* holding space
workplace (spirituality of), 46–48
cosmic participation, and, 48
ego diminishment, form of, 48
failure, coping with, 46–47
sense of community, and, 48
spirituality of, 47–48
vocere (vocation), as, 48–49
writing assessment, 11. *See also* assessment

Young, Iris Marion, 239–241

www.ingramcontent.com/pod-product-compliance
Lightning Source LLC
Chambersburg PA
CBHW030117240426
43673CB00041B/1315